Troubled Experiment

EARLY AMERICAN STUDIES
Daniel K. Richter and Kathleen M. Brown, Series Editors

Exploring neglected aspects of our colonial, revolutionary, and early
national history and culture, Early American Studies reinterprets
familiar themes and events in fresh ways. Interdisciplinary in character,
and with a special emphasis on the period from about 1600 to 1850, the
series is published in partnership with the McNeil Center for Early
American Studies.

A complete list of books in the series is available from the publisher.

Troubled Experiment

Crime and Justice in Pennsylvania, 1682–1800

JACK D. MARIETTA AND
G. S. ROWE

PENN

University of Pennsylvania Press

Philadelphia

Published by
University of Pennsylvania Press
Philadelphia, Pennsylvania 19104-4112
Library of Congress Cataloging-in-Publication Data

Marietta, Jack D.
  Troubled experiment : crime and justice in Pennsylvania, 1682–1800 / Jack D. Marietta
and G. S. Rowe
    p.   cm. — (Early American studies)
  ISBN-13: 978-0-8122-3955-3 (alk. paper)
  ISBN-10: 0-8122-3955-5 (alk. paper)
  Includes bibliographical references and index.
    I. Crime—Pennsylvania—History—17th century.   2. Crime—Pennsylvania—History—
18th century.   3. Violence—Pennsylvania—History—17th century.   4. Violence—
Pennsylvania—History—18th century.   5. Law enforcement—Pennsylvania—History—
17th century.   6. Law enforcement—Pennsylvania—History—18th century.   7. Criminal
law—Pennsylvania—History—17th century.   8 Criminal law—Pennsylvania—History—
18th century.   9. Pennsylvania—History—Colonial period, ca. 1600–1775.   I. Series   II.
Rowe, G. S. (Gail Stuart), 1936–
HV6793.P4 M37   2006
364.974809/03—dc22   2006042161

For Kay and Mary

Contents

Tables and Figures

Figures

Introduction

All things in common nature should produce
Without sweat or endeavor: treason, felony,
Sword, pick, knife, gun, or need of any engine,
Would I not have, but nature should bring forth,
Of its own kinds, all foison, all abundance,
To feed my innocent people.

—*Shakespeare*, The Tempest

This is a history of crime in a place where there should have been no significant crime and a history of laws and law enforcement where there should have been little need for them.[1] The place, after all, was Pennsylvania, the "Holy Experiment," "the golden age . . . which has apparently never existed except in Pennsylvania," the "best poor man's country on earth," a land with "peace and happiness reigning with justice and liberty among this people of brothers."[2] It was "a worldly success," "an ideal colony," "a hopeful torch in a world of semidarkness."[3] If any place enjoyed the prospect of liberating men and women from the conditions that presumably engender crime—poverty, oppression, and war among them—Pennsylvania was it. And yet, in this same place, a husband killed and mutilated his wife, and then crushed the skulls of his two children and a neighbor's child. An eight-year-old girl was raped in her Chester County home while her parents were out of the house. A cordwainer who sat at his front door in Philadelphia, smoking his pipe, died when an unknown person drove a knife through his heart. Can crimes as repulsive as these have occurred in a society that received the effusive praise that Pennsylvania did? Did Pennsylvania, and does Pennsylvania, deserve the praise? How many murders and rapes could Pennsylvania have sustained before it forfeited its nonpareil reputation? The three cases above, although each had its distinctive twist, were not oddities. Violence and crime abounded in Pennsylvania, and the six innocent victims mentioned here were merely a small handful of the total.

The grimmer side of life in Pennsylvania suggested by these cases did not go unnoticed even while the good reputation of the province escaped intact. While eighteenth-century admirers sang the praises of the province, there were dissenters. From grousing to shrieking about it, in every decade some Pennsylvanians remarked about crime. Among the earliest, William Penn conceded the presence of "Lewdness and all manner of Wickedness" in the province. "Sabbath breaking, drunkenness, idleness, Unlawful gaming and all manner of prophanesse" raised complaints in 1693; a year later observers bewailed that "publick peace & administration of Justice was broken and violated" daily. In 1700 the Provincial Council admitted that "some laws [were] simply ignored by all." And thereafter, punctuating the passing decades, came laments about "the growth of vice," "frequent riots," "disorderly Practices," "barbarous Transactions," "numerous robberies and burglaries," "audacious Encroachments onto Indian lands," "murders," "horse thefts," "Licentiousness," the "Increase of Vagrants and Idle Persons," and "the jails . . . full." And at the close of the century, Moreau de St. Méry observed that Pennsylvanians outside Philadelphia "have neither justice nor public security."[4]

Remarks of this sort comprise part of this history of crime in Pennsylvania. We, the authors, surveyed the narrative record of crime from newspapers, broadsides, pamphlets, correspondence, court papers, and other sources, looking for people's thoughts about crime and justice. But we also undertook to count every crime recorded in the extant justice records and other public sources. This aggregation of data confirms the critics' complaints: crime troubled the province and state of Pennsylvania, making it no luminous exception to the timeless cruel and selfish behavior of men and women that historians more freely acknowledge in places other than Pennsylvania.

The reputation for liberty, tolerance, and affluence that Pennsylvania gained despite its acknowledged problems can be explained in the case of both its past and its present admirers. In the success of Pennsylvania, the savants of the Enlightenment invested their hopes for a vastly improved world. As for that part of the good reputation constructed by modern Americans and historians, we honor our liberal ancestor. Our statue in New York harbor bears the title "Liberty Enlightening the World," and we Americans believe we have been doing it at least since William Penn arrived on the Delaware. Among the philosophes of the Enlightenment—Voltaire, Montesquieu, Abbé Raynal, Chevalier de Jaucourt, the Encyclopedists—Pennsylvania became a byword; it proved the wisdom of their liberal critique of the ancien régime and of their prescriptions to change it or replace it. It became an article in the liberal credo, a secular gospel: "People could be happy without masters and without priests." In the *Encyclopedie* and Raynal's *History of the Indies* they broadcast the success of Pennsylvania until it became general knowledge among literate, hopeful men and women.[5]

After independence in 1776, attention to America swelled along with hope for change in Europe. While an independent United States inspired European liberals as Pennsylvania earlier had, it was still the image and model of Pennsylvania that served Europeans' need. Even in the new republic, New England (outside Rhode Island) had to live down its intolerant past; Massachusetts preserved its religious establishment even into the 1830s. South of Pennsylvania, slavery and the racial caste system prevented these states from gaining the homage of progressive Europeans. The last, best hope of man lay north of Maryland. Only neighboring New York and New Jersey rivaled Pennsylvania's progress. As William Bradford told James Madison in 1774, Pennsylvania was to America what America was to the rest of the world—a peculiar "land of freedom."[6] Nevertheless, in the 1780s, even as an independent United States convinced more and more hopeful men in the West of the practicality of turning a welcome corner in the history of human relationships, exemplary Pennsylvania sentenced to death more felons in ten years than illiberal, retrograde Massachusetts condemned in fifty.

So far as they went, Enlightenment philosophes did not misrepresent Pennsylvania to the world. Pennsylvania fulfilled the prescriptions of the Enlightenment and classical liberalism. Neither imperial or provincial government, organized religion, social hierarchy and ascribed status, nor economic privilege thwarted Pennsylvanians in pursuing their happiness or cultivating their individual identities. More than any other society in America, or anywhere, Pennsylvania liberated men and women from tradition and encouraged them to pursue their personal happiness and separate wills.

The exceptional and liberal character of Pennsylvania and its good reputation began with its openness, the quintessence of the "Holy Experiment." Penn created a refuge for all peoples; Pennsylvania took anyone who came. But troublesome people as well as unobtrusive ones arrived. When the troublesome ones exasperated Penn, however, neither he nor his successors erected mechanisms for casting out these irregular people, the way New England conspicuously did. The tolerance and the incapacity to exclude, which were so progressive and admired, created unmistakable problems for the peace of the province.

Colonial Pennsylvanians enjoyed a very generous amount of autonomy within the British Empire—more than almost all other colonists in America. They came "as close as was practically possible to building a republican colony within a monarchical empire," historian Alan Tully summarizes.[7] Superlative leaders like Thomas and David Lloyd, John Kinsey, Isaac Norris II, and Benjamin Franklin piloted provincial govern-

ment along the Whiggish mainstream of American political development so deftly that the Pennsylvania House of Representatives "claimed
and exercised greater privileges than any other legislative body in the
[British] empire."[8] This responsive government secured for Pennsylvanians what they wanted from government: religious liberty, low taxation,
no obligation to serve in the military, eased access to land, free markets,
and naturalization for immigrants. In turn, Pennsylvanians commonly
treated their government with indifference, but it was "the indifference
of the satisfied."[9] Another historian, Stephanie Wolf, writes that the
goals of the Holy Experiment were negative: to leave the obligations to
others, enjoy the benefits, and be left alone.[10] In behaving so, Pennsylvanians anticipated modern Americans.

Penn's Frames of Government, 1682–1701, established religious liberty for every Pennsylvanian. Anyone could worship and proselytize as
he or she pleased, or ignore religion entirely, neither subscribing to any
faith nor having to support anyone else's faith and practice. The state
was really indifferent to one's convictions, as long as practicing one's
religion did not violate the public peace. Additionally, in everyday public life there were no election-day sermons, no fast or feast days, no public Christmas or Easter observance, and no public religious invocations
or prayers (except for silence). While taverns were closed on Sunday,
they were open on Christmas and all other traditional observances in
the Christian calendar. Publicly sanctioned religious observances which
bedevil civil libertarians and jurists in modern America had little equivalent in early Pennsylvania and caused no problem.[11]

Clerics exercised little influence in public life. Quakers, the founders
of the province, had no ordained, paid clergy. Clergymen who were
accustomed to influencing public life elsewhere—especially the Anglicans, but also various Presbyterians, Reformed, and Lutheran ministers—were astonished at being relegated to the sidelines.[12] Even within
the enclaves of their parishes or congregations, clergy complained of
their impotence and the congregants' impertinence.[13] Pennsylvania, it
was said, was heaven for farmers but hell for government officials and
ministers—a leading remark for investigators into crime and its causes.[14]

The allure of Pennsylvania for the hundreds of thousands who
migrated there was above all else the prospect of personal economic
growth. It was reputedly the best poor man's country on earth. "The soil
is good," in Pennsylvania, said evangelist George Whitefield, "the land
exceedingly fruitful." Gottlieb Mittelberger, who tried to dissuade Germans from coming to Pennsylvania, nevertheless observed: "The people
live well, especially on all sorts of grain, which thrives very well, because
the soil is wild and fat. They have good cattle, fast horses, and many bees.
. . . Even in the humblest and poorest houses in this country there is no

meal without meat, and no one eats bread without the butter or cheese, although the bread is as good as with us." Historian James Lemon confirms these observations: "Early Pennsylvania farmers and their families, with few exceptions, ate heartily, were well-clothed, and sold a surplus of goods. They were able to live comfortably even though they only scratched the surface of the soil."[15] "A direct relationship" exists, James Henretta has written, "between the material environment, on the one hand, and the consciousness and activity of the population on the other."[16] Because the land and the markets for their produce returned benefits beyond what they experienced in Europe and what they could obtain elsewhere in America, Pennsylvanians came to view their world with the eyes of entrepreneurs. When Adam Smith in 1776 argued on behalf of free markets, Pennsylvanians had worked within that milieu of freedom and hope for decades and were only too ready to affirm Smith's truths.[17]

individuals reigns

In sum, freed of lords, landlords, priests, and colonels, Pennsylvanians were as much their own men and women as the Enlightenment liberals could have hoped for in that day. That being so, one would expect to find contented and grateful people in Pennsylvania and not men and women committing crimes at rates that distinguished them from their American neighbors and from Englishmen. With as few overbearing institutions as they had—the fewest in the known world—they should have escaped the frustrations and moral degradation of the Old World. But in fact, they did not conduct themselves as though they had escaped. Their crimes beg for an explanation that cannot be found within the conceits of the Enlightenment and newborn liberalism.

This history begins, in Chapter 1, with the criminal laws and courts of Pennsylvania between 1682 and 1718—a renowned, critical feature of the liberalism of the colony and the high esteem it enjoyed. Chapter 2 treats crime, magistrates, and the administration of justice during this same period. Chapter 3 marks a change that was as significant as any that occurred before 1800—the emergence of crime as a permanent problem. It analyzes the men and women who were the perpetrators and victims of crime and treats the causes of crime, with an emphasis on immigration. Chapter 3 also describes the province's retreat after 1718 from liberal jurisprudence in reaction to crime. Chapter 4 advances the story of homicide and assault through the rest of the century. Chapter 5 doubles back chronologically and covers Pennsylvania's attempts to secure justice in a society whose growth outstripped that of any colony in America—growth that ironically brought calamity to an indispensable feature of the Holy Experiment, justice for Native Americans. Chapter 6 moves to the American Revolution, the crime associated with political overturning, the attempt at republican reform of civil society, and the resolution of Native Americans' enjoyment of justice in Penn's experiment. Chapter 7 treats the concluding two decades of the eighteenth century and their distinguishing features: liberal criminal-justice reforms, novel crimes and public disorder, and dissatisfaction with the criminal justice in the commonwealth. The Epilogue examines the conditions and causes of crime in Pennsylvania and makes a case that that crime and its causes in the United States recapitulate the experience of Pennsylvania.

In Pennsylvania, all clocks did not strike at once. In a history with many clocks—clocks marking changes in crime itself, changes in the criminal laws and their enforcement, changes in attitudes toward crime, immigration, and more—a few clocks struck closely enough to suggest that the 118-year history of crime and justice divides roughly into three periods. The first period, almost forty years, is the best defined of the three because it clearly experienced the least crime and exhibited the greatest effort to advance liberal criminal justice. The next five decades showed increased crime, a retreat from idealism, and the use of sanguinary solutions to crime. The final period began with the Revolution and renewed aspiration to liberalism. But other clocks did not strike the change of an hour: crime persisted as it had for decades and in the end denied the founders of Pennsylvania the achievement they sought.

Crime was high in Philadelphia + PA. Higher than anywhere else. Three periods of crime history:

1) 1682 - 1720 : least crime, most liberal justice

2) 1720 - 1770 : ↑ crime, less idealism and the use of "sanguinary" solutions to crime

3) American Revolution ~ 1800 : renewed aspirations towards liberalism

Chapter 1

Criminal Laws and Courts

Good government is a constitution of just laws.
—*William Penn*

The history of the criminal law in Pennsylvania between 1682 and 1800
consists of two periods of intense questioning and reassessment separated by nearly fifty years of stability. The first period, of nearly forty
years, witnessed an attempt to create a legal system which ran counter
to traditional western societies in its abhorrence of capital punishment
and its commitment to rehabilitation. In its initial form it was as progressive and as enlightened as any conceived prior to the late eighteenth
century. In the end it fell victim to instability, uncertainty, political jeal-
ousy, and imperial pressure. Its sequel, beginning in 1718, repudiated
much of the colony's earlier commitment to reform. A reactionary,
anglicized criminal code, it had the clear advantage of bringing to Pennsylvania's laws stability and certainty that the colony had not experienced in the earlier enlightenment. Finally, by 1800 the criminal law
had oscillated back to its earlier liberalism. Idealism impelled the return
to liberalism—not the religious idealism of the Quaker founders of
Pennsylvania, but the secular ideals of the American Revolution. There
were differences of substance and spirit between the first and the final
periods, but for all the differences, at the close of the eighteenth century, Pennsylvania returned to an emphasis on rehabilitation and the
rejection of capital punishment. This chapter treats the first of the three
periods.

The earliest criminal laws of the colony were more renowned than any
in its history and contributed mightily to the unstinting praise heaped
upon Pennsylvania by European admirers. Their paeans to these laws
and their conception of a civic utopia on the Delaware far outlived that
earliest law code. These laws originated in the psyche and experience of
William Penn. When Charles II granted to Penn the Charter of Pennsylvania in March 1681, among the powers he conveyed to the new proprie-

tor was that of initiating and promulgating laws to govern moral and civic conduct in the new colony.[1] Both parties anticipated that Pennsylvania would adopt English law. To what degree that law could be modified to fit Penn's vision of a novel, enlightened society in the New World was for the moment left unexplored. His suffering at the hands of the English government impelled him to attempt something new. Having been confined in the Tower of London for publishing a pamphlet offensive to the authorities, and having been twice incarcerated in Newgate Prison for violations of laws touching preaching, he resolved that his colony would offer to its people greater freedom and toleration. He hoped that peoples of diverse languages, customs, religions, and national origins would live in peace and harmony in Pennsylvania, participating meaningfully in their government, and worshiping as they saw fit. "Good government," he wrote in the summer of 1681, "is a constitution of just laws." The society Penn anticipated in Pennsylvania would require novel and truly just criminal laws. He was prepared to supply them.[2]

Penn understood that he would have to offer laws deviating from English practice. At the beginning of his enterprise, he could hardly appreciate the trouble he would incur in attempting that deviation. Experimenting within the British Empire won Penn centuries of good repute, but many foes in his lifetime. Until his death, men who envied Penn's privilege as proprietor of a colony and his ability to experiment with laws, courts, and civil society vexed him. Like no other colony in America, Pennsylvania would find its laws overturned and its bench reproached. He anticipated a happier course than the rough treatment that ensued.

Rough treatment at the hands of the government led Penn to this enterprise. As a student of the law, as a defendant, as a convict, and as an observer of the criminal trials of Quaker associates, Penn discovered the faults of English law. His unhappiness centered on the way the law criminalized conduct Penn viewed as non-criminal, and on its acceptance of unwritten rules of behavior (*lex non scripta*). To penalize individuals for their religious convictions made little sense to Penn; to bludgeon people with the law into accepting the church of the State must surely fail, he concluded. As he told authorities when he himself was arrested for preaching doctrines anathema to the State, "Force may make hypocrites, but it can make no converts."[3]

The practice of relying upon common law forms to punish dissenters like himself also appeared to Penn patently unfair and unwise. He believed it inequitable and despotic to harass citizens with laws they did not comprehend and could not read. His own indictment in 1670, resting as it did on the common law, he believed too vague, too little understood by citizens to be just. Unwritten law was no law at all, he maintained. "When there is no law," he argued, "there is no transgression."[4]

Penn's and other Quakers' denunciations of English law were not isolated protests. Dissatisfaction with English law and English legal practices surfaced among a variety of Englishmen as early as the reign of James I, when Parliament strove to improve the execution of justice and to lower its cost. Subsequently, religious radicals, even apart from Quakers, protested that English law should conform more closely to Scripture. Political radicals like the Levellers demanded the strengthening of local courts over central tribunals, simplified legal procedures, and the elimination of lawyers. Even after the outbursts of radicalism of the Revolution and Interregnum, critics of the law pressed on with attempts at reform. In the 1660s and 1670s, Francis Bacon and Matthew Hale were at the forefront of the effort. As late as 1677, Thomas Sheridan's *A Discourse of Parliament, of Laws* urged a simpler and more equitable law as well as a simplification of judicial forms and procedures. Sheridan also pushed to eliminate what he viewed as the crushing severity of English criminal sanctions.[5]

Quakers also sought to reduce the number of capital sentences or eliminate the death penalty completely. They preferred to rehabilitate rather than to execute or to corporally punish criminal offenders. Penn drew upon this tradition of legal and penal reform.[6] In his *The Great Case of Liberty of Conscience* (1670) and *England's Great Interest in the Choice of This New Parliament* (1677) he expanded upon it by advocating the decriminalization of religious crimes. Later, in America, he expanded it further by publicly tolerating diversity and dissent.

Penn and other Englishmen who sought a more enlightened law and more just legal sanctions stirred opposition and suffered for their efforts. In 1676, England felt that its colonies threatened its supremacy in several ways—social, economic, and political. The crown moved to put an end to all such threats and establish—or reestablish—its influence and authority over its plantations. Given that determination, any colonial law, practice, or scheme that even appeared to undermine the authority of England raised suspicion or alarm in Whitehall. Penn's creation on the Delaware must be understood in this context. If Penn were prepared to erect this novel plantation and populate it with forward-looking men and women, he must know that contrary-minded Englishmen were equally prepared to resist him. Their envy did not augur well for a people, the Quakers, said to "Despise all Dominion & dignity that is not in themselves."[7]

Even with the laws and courts he desired, unobstructed by envious Englishmen, Penn did not believe that he alone could guarantee a just

Penn believes people who come will (margin note)

society. He also had to attract men and women of good will and enlightened principles. "I know some say, let us have good laws, and no matter for the men that execute them," he wrote in the preface of the Frame of Government, "But let them consider, that though good laws do well, good men do better, for good laws may want good men, and be abolished or evaded by ill men; but good men will never want good laws nor suffer ill ones."[8]

For all his conviction that he could recruit desirable settlers for Pennsylvania, Penn was not willing to rely exclusively on the good will of the inhabitants of Pennsylvania, nor on his own success in attracting such individuals. History had taught him that "Law . . . was added because of transgression. . . . the law was not made for the righteous man; but for the disobedient and ungodly, for sinners, for unholy and prophane, for murderers, for whoremongers, for them that defile themselves with mankind, and for men stealers, for liars, for perjured persons, &c." One end of government, according to the Charter, was "to terrify evildoers." In part to that end Penn submitted for consideration the forty "fundamental laws."[9]

The first criminal laws of Pennsylvania were forty "fundamental laws" (called "Laws agreed upon in England") that Penn attached to the First Frame of Government—the colony's first constitution,[10] However, insofar as the "Laws agreed upon in England" represented a penal code, it was a curious criminal code, indeed. No list of specific crimes or punishments was included, although sections 17, 30, and 37 made clear that offenses such as bribery, extortion, and defamation and felonies such as murder, rape, arson, incest, sodomy, sedition, and burglary "shall be respectively discouraged, and severely punished."[11] The forty laws were, in the estimation of historian Charles M. Andrews, little more than "a compendium of moral precepts and convictions."[12] Both their tone and their substance made clear that though the laws would seek to "terrify evildoers," Pennsylvania was not to be locked into a Mosaic code, or into the English system with its harsh punishments and its lengthy list of capital crimes.[13]

laws wouldn't be tough (margin note)

William Penn sailed into Delaware Bay on October 24, 1682, debarking in Philadelphia five days later. The struggle to get settlers to accept his governmental proposals and his criminal code began almost immediately. His acquisition of the Lower Counties from the Duke of York in August of that year compounded his difficulties. The addition of the Lower Counties forced Penn to embrace an area governed since 1676 by the Duke of York's Laws, which offered a harsher view of criminal law than that entertained by Penn and his followers. The Duke of York's Laws (generally called simply the Duke's Laws) provided capital punishment for the denial of God, murder, bestiality, sodomy, kidnapping, bearing false witness to take a life, rebellion, invasion, and striking one's mother or father. For servants assaulting their masters or mistresses, the penalty was corporal punishment at the discretion of the court short of "life and member." Convictions of burglary or highway robbery brought branding on the forehead for the first offense, death for the third. To be found guilty of stealing hogs or canoes was punishable by having one's ears cut off.[14]

The addition of the Lower Counties also brought under Penn's governance substantial numbers of non-English and non-Quakers, aborigines, Finns, Dutch, and Swedes with different values, assumptions, priorities, and institutions. They often spoke little or no English.[15] Absorbing the Lower Counties, along with the early arrival of Germans and Welsh in the Pennsylvania counties, compelled Penn to broaden his vision still further to consider non-English speakers, their history, and their needs. As early as 1643 Swedish courts were punishing crime in the area. Dutch tribunals were active after 1655. These courts continued to mete out justice even after the arrival of the English in 1664, adjusting to and absorbing the Duke's Laws as best they could.[16]

The heterogeneity arising from the acquisition of the Lower Counties, and persistent complaints by Maryland's Lord Baltimore that the duke's title to the area was uncertain and, thus, Penn's claim was too, spelled trouble for Penn's desire to achieve a quick consensus on government and a criminal code. Even though the Duke's Laws had been enforced haphazardly and only for a brief period in the region, culture, religion, and politics there underlay long-range opposition to Penn and his laws.[17]

Like their colonial neighbors, Pennsylvanians were determined to codify their laws. The first criminal statutes enacted in Pennsylvania under Penn's proprietorship came during an assembly in Chester. Forty-two men from six counties, New Castle, Kent, Sussex, Philadelphia, Bucks, and Chester, summoned by Penn in December 1682, were asked to ratify fifty laws in addition to the forty fundamental laws that accompanied the Frame of Government.[18] The only real limits to the formation of a criminal code, other than the imagination and intelligence of those who formulated the laws and those asked to ratify them, were the Charter provisions that Pennsylvania laws "bee consonant to reason and not repugnant or contrarie to the Lawes of England," and that they be submitted within five years to the Lords of Trade for review.[19] After considerable wrangling, the Chester assembly approved sixty-one statutes, "Laws as shall best preserve true Christian and Civil Liberty, in opposition to all unChristian, Licentious, and unjust practices." Known as the "Great Law," they formed the basis for Pennsylvania's legal code for the next two decades. Twenty-six of the statutes focused on criminal offenses.[20]

12   Chapter One

These criminal laws, mirroring the social views of the predominantly Quaker assembly that gave birth to them, seriously modified portions of the Duke's Laws while abolishing others. The result was the mildest criminal code of any continental English colony and one much milder than England's.[21] Murder alone was made a capital offense, although because no provision was made for treason, that offense continued to be capital under the English common law. Forfeitures, corporal punishment, and imprisonment were substituted for capital sanctions for such offenses as rape, sodomy, bigamy, and incest. A second conviction for these offenses carried with it life imprisonment. Attacks upon property, including thefts, arson, forgery, and counterfeiting, were punished by having defendants pay some multiple of the lost property. Few crimes brought lengthy incarceration. Swearing, profanity, playing cards or dice, promoting or engaging in unlicensed lotteries, and drunkenness, for instance, earned five-day sentences. Assaulting a magistrate brought one month's confinement. Challenging a person to a fight could lead to three months' incarceration if the convicted could not pay a five-pound fine. Only a conviction for incest could bring as much as one year at hard labor.[22]

Despite its apparent mildness, the Great Law held some potential for harshness. Its provisions for the punishment of criminal offenses were often unduly vague or discretionary, permitting unscrupulous or hard-minded judges to exact severe penalties.[23] For instance, at the discretion of two justices of the peace, servants assaulting their masters or mistresses were to be punished "suitable to the Nature and Circumstances of the fact." The same sentence held for general assaults and sedition. Children physically attacking their mother or father could be confined "during the pleasure" of the parents. Defamation was to be "severely Punished."[24] The assembly which met in New Castle in March 1684 took steps to curtail some of the discretion exercised by judges when it ratified a law establishing that if a statute called for whipping but failed to designate the specific number of stripes to be laid on, punishment should not exceed twenty-one lashes.[25] Still, considerable magisterial discretion remained.

Important safeguards were incorporated to ensure that justice would prevail. Except in the case of very minor infractions, jury trials were guaranteed for persons accused of criminal offenses. Witnesses in criminal trials were charged with "promising to speak the truth, the whole truth, and nothing but the truth" under penalty of perjury. All criminal offenses except capital cases were made bailable. Statutes ultimately provided that there must be at least eight days between verdicts in the Provincial Court and the execution of those verdicts. The law also provided that individuals unjustly imprisoned could receive double damages. In addition, for many offenses fines could be paid in lieu of corporal punishment or confinement.[26]

Events surrounding the first official session of the Assembly in Philadelphia in March 1683 suggest that most Pennsylvanians were content with the mild criminal code written at Chester in December 1682. Although that 1683 body put its stamp of approval on eighty-one laws, only eight were new criminal statutes. Those eight statutes manifested the same spirit and worldview as had previous penal laws. Thus, the criminal code that emerged from the December and March assemblies embodied Quaker enthusiasm for justice that was mutual, fair, and proportionate to the crime. It also reflected Quaker abhorrence of the death penalty. Capital punishment was anathema to most, if not all, of those present.[27]

Provisions accepted by the March 1683 Assembly for informally arbitrating many disputes combined with often unqualified judicial personnel and inefficient courts to mitigate further any severity in the criminal law. Three "Common peacemakers" whose "Arbitration may be as Valid as the judgments of the Courts of Justice" were to be named in each county. Arbitration was available in other forums as well. When a dispute arose between Andrew Johnson and Hance Peterson in the spring of 1684, the governor and Council told them to forego formal court proceedings and "to shake hands and to forgive One Another." They then ordered, "the Records . . . concerning [this] Business should be burnt."[28] These mechanisms functioned in criminal as well as civil cases. Moreover, the use of peace bonds that bound potential troublemakers to good behavior under penalty of financial loss short-circuited many criminal proceedings that might otherwise have ended up in court with formal penalties.[29] Quaker meetings also dealt with personal altercations and disputes that in other colonies found their way into the criminal courts. The result was a remarkably humane and mild criminal justice system.[30]

The most oppressive facet of the Pennsylvania legal system was its acceptance of the English practice of assessing participants a series of fees for writs and services. Justices and clerks were paid to issue legal writs and to prepare and carry out legal proceedings. The most onerous aspect of this tradition thrust upon defendants, even those acquitted of criminal charges, the cost of confinement and trial.[31] Thus, even though fifteen-year-old James White of Kent County was exonerated of buggery charges in October 1704, he was assessed fees totaling £24, an amount more than twice that paid to the king's attorney for the year. Unable to pay those fees, young White was sold into servitude for four years to work off his debt.[32]

Early Pennsylvania law differed markedly from others in colonial

America. Compared to the Duke's Laws and to the Massachusetts Book
of Laws, it was both the briefest and the most forbearing. The Massachusetts Book of Laws of 1660 embraced one hundred twenty-three categories of crimes, twice as many as did Pennsylvania's Great Law. The
Duke's Laws contained one-third more crimes than did Pennsylvania's
code. And further, as Christopher K. Seglem has shown, the body of laws
in Pennsylvania was also briefer, simpler, and more merciful than the
law described in Michael Dalton's *Countrey Justice*, a guide for justices of
the peace that circulated widely in Anglo-America.[33] A comparison of
the Pennsylvania criminal code with that of colonial Connecticut, in
terms both of the punishment meted out to offenders and of the number of capital felonies, also makes clear the greater toleration and
leniency of the former. The many religious-based crimes in Connecticut,
for instance, were nowhere to be found in the laws of Pennsylvania. If
Pennsylvania's collection of laws appears benign and enlightened to the
modern reader, to officials in Whitehall in that day it appeared problematic at best and very likely deserved to be quickly dispatched.[34]

By permitting liberty of conscience Penn made possible the reduction
of the many religious offenses and punishments so characteristic of the
law in Massachusetts and Connecticut. Penn believed that religious toleration won for a government its subjects' gratitude and loyalty and
thereby actually strengthened the government's hold over its subjects
rather than weakened it. Disgruntled subjects would seek to escape its
clutches and combine against it. "What if I differ from some religious
apprehensions publiquely Impos'ed," he asked then Secretary of State,
Lord Arlington, upon his arrest for expressing publicly his Quaker
beliefs, "Am I therefore Incompatible with the well-being of humain
Societys?" He was determined that his colony should provide the sanctuary for religious experimentation that England did not, and that no
criminal liability would be attached to such activity.[35]

Yet the Pennsylvania criminal code had its detractors, who recounted
various crimes that had occurred in order to support their depiction of
a troubled colony. As early as 1684 the acerbic and Quaker-baiting Dr.
Nicholas More, a surprise choice to be the Chief Justice of the Provincial
Court, asserted that the criminal law was too lenient to deter crime in
the province. He groused that there was "Mutch robrey in City and
Countrey, Breaking of houses, and stealing of Hoggs. . . . Vices creepe
in like the old Serpent and are now almost too strong for them."[36] In
the first decade, there were in fact cases of crime and contempt of the
courts to support a case anyone wished to make against Penn or Pennsylvania. When Bucks County's Thomas Tunneclif was brought to court
accused of mistreating Hannah Overton and her children, and placed
under security for his future good behavior, he "abused the bench &

Said I Care not A pin for none of you."[37] On occasion court personnel
suffered more than verbal disrespect. When bailiffs in Philadelphia
sought to arrest a debtor of James Claypoole, they found the debtor
armed, belligerent, and attended by men with swords, and the bailiffs
"were afraid for their lives."[38] In 1687 a terrified Jane Coverdale in
Bucks County sought protection from the law against Philip Conway
who, she maintained, "came to her bed side & did Say he has sworn he
wold fuck her either by night or by day & about A month after that he
Came to the house & sd he had Sworn about 4 yeares he wold fuck her &
she Said she was so afraid less hee Should lay violent hands on her." One
night in 1684 Philadelphia County's John Rambo slipped through a hole
in the roof of the Peter Cock home and dropped into the room where
Bridgett Cock and her two sisters slept. According to deponents, Rambo
"did then & there forciblie, disquietlie, & mutinouslie & impudentlie
frighten and disturbe manie of the said Peter Cock's familie, and att that
time aforesaid, keepe[,] force and compell Bridgett . . . to stay in bed
with [him], and did then & there promise and firmlie contract [him]self
to marrie the said Bridgett." Rambo subsequently was convicted of a
breach of contract because he "defloured & dishonoured" Bridgett,
then reneged on his promise to marry her and to support the child born
of their union.[39]

And even if one agreed that there was a crime problem to be
addressed, debate erupted over who should properly address it. As early
as 1684 questions over the establishment of a Provincial Court triggered
assertions from the Assembly that its members should have the power of
annual review over all criminal laws. The Assembly also asked whether it
could not disallow current criminal laws that proved ineffective.[40] By
1693 confusion over the criminal law was endemic. Penn had temporarily lost control over the colony, permitting the Crown to appoint as governor Benjamin Fletcher, current governor of New York. Nothing that
Penn and Pennsylvanians had done antagonized the Crown more than
Pennsylvania's indifference toward assisting in the war against France;
King William III utterly disagreed with the Quaker pacifist doctrine. Similarly, Governor Fletcher had no greater concern than getting the
Assembly to appropriate money for the defense of New York. The issues
of the criminal law of Pennsylvania and the refusal of Quakers to swear
and administer solemn oaths were appended to the rancorous difference over defense.[41] The anger generated by any one of the issues
infected deliberations over all of them.

In the case of the criminal laws, when pressed to confirm the criminal
laws already in effect, Fletcher announced that he could not approve
them. "In your former Law books," Fletcher told Pennsylvania officials,
"I find sundry Laws that are altogether repugnant to the Laws of

England, and seem to supersede them. . . . You must not expect that I will pass those Laws into acts." Fletcher's demand for a look at the complete rolls of laws produced considerable embarrassment on the part of Pennsylvania authorities. Few of them could in good conscience refute Fletcher's assessment that because of laxity in maintaining the rolls, a careless use of the seal, and failure routinely to submit statutes for review, by 1693 it was not clear which laws were in force and which had no legal standing. Despite numerous instructions that the laws be compiled, printed, and made available to the public, little had been done.[42] The Council, embarrassed by the condition of its own records, and those of the Assembly, replied rather lamely that "wee have manie reasons to believe that our Laws are of force manie years we have exercised the government by these Lawes, and we know & can prove that William Penn carried the greatest bodie of them to England & conceive that they were deliver'd to the King."[43]

Even before Fletcher forced the issue, trouble had been brewing in respect to the law rolls. When Penn appointed John Blackwell his deputy governor in 1689, the Proprietor favored permitting all previous statutes to lapse, to be replaced by a new body of laws. Such a move, he maintained, would restore some much-needed law and order in his colony. Late in 1688 and early in 1689 David Lloyd who, among his many offices, exercised the powers of Clerk of the Records and was responsible for seeing the seal affixed to new laws and for maintaining ongoing records of legislation, exacerbated conditions by refusing to make available records desired by the Council and Blackwell.

Lloyd's recalcitrance led some to argue that his actions and attitude "tend[ed] very much to the hurt & Dammage of the People" and, indeed, constituted a misdemeanor. Those less charitable deemed his actions treasonable. When, after considerable wrangling and acrimony on both sides, the Council was able to review the two sets of records, they discovered them to be "not authentic." John Bristow, a member of Council and a justice in Chester County, conceded that "the Laws have been all along uncertaine."[44] The charter granted by William and Mary in 1694 to restore Penn to ownership of his colony proclaimed that Pennsylvania had "fallen into Disorder & Confusion" and that the "publick peace & administration of justice was broken & violated."[45]

The Assembly's petition of right to Fletcher in 1693 asking that he confirm the colony's criminal code, "until their majesties' pleasure shall be further known," and Fletcher's willingness to do so, temporarily clarified the penal code. Greater diligence in passing, enrolling, publishing, and reviewing criminal laws produced both benefits and liabilities. The colony's records improved markedly from that point. On the other hand, more systematic review of Pennsylvania laws in the last decade of

the century and beyond brought a greater number of royal disallowances of those laws.

Pennsylvania authorities vehemently denied allegations that crime
troubled the colony, or that the criminal laws were confused and ineffective. "As to the growth of vice," the Council conceded, "Wee cannot but
owne as this place Hath growne more populous, & the people increast,
Looseness & vice Hath also Creept in." Still, the Council insisted that
all necessary steps had been taken so that "offenders Hav[e] received
deserved & exemplary punishments, according to the Law."[46] Yet Penn,
having been reinstated, regarded the criminal code as insufficiently
clear or effective; in 1696 he urged a reexamination of the code. A year
later he credited bad news from the colony: "The reports," he said, "are
. . . that there is no place more overrun with wickedness, Sinn so very
Scandallous, openly Committed in defiance of Law and Virtue: facts so
foul, I am forbid by Comon modesty to relate them."[47] The preamble to
a 1698 law admitted that "the several punishments mentioned in the
said laws being so easie that they have not answered the good end proposed in the making thereof, for that many dissolute persons, notwith-
standing the said laws, have committed divers thefts and robberies
within this government."[48] As late as 1700 Penn acknowledged, "there
are . . . some Laws obsolete, others hurtful, others imperfect." The
Council conceded that everyone simply ignored some laws.[49]

Ironically, the criminal code which so troubled Penn helped mightily
to secure Penn's and Pennsylvania's fame in Europe. In his *Lettres philo-
sophiques* (1734) Voltaire wrote that "William Penn could boast of having
brought to the World that golden age of which men talk so much and
which probably has never existed anywhere except in Pennsylvania." For
Voltaire, Pennsylvania's Quakers were the embodiment of civic virtue,
and Pennsylvania a "human paradise." Montesquieu described Penn as
the greatest lawgiver since antiquity, "a veritable Lycurgus."[50] But in
reality Pennsylvania had taken on a different character from that of its
enlarged reputation; for at least sixteen years prior to these accolades,
Pennsylvanians had begun to distance themselves from their earliest
vision of law and punishment.

The Assembly (having by 1696 achieved the right to initiate laws) radi-
cally revised the colony's criminal statutes. The result in 1700 was a mea-
surably longer and harsher code.[51] An example of the shift toward
harshness was rape, where the new law called for a punishment of thirty-
nine lashes for persons convicted of a first offense, in addition to a
seven-year prison term and forfeiture of a defendant's entire estate if he
were single, and one-third of his estate if he were married. A second
conviction for rape was to result in castration and branding on the forehead with the letter R. Branding was also designated as punishment for

an initial conviction for theft, with life imprisonment for a second conviction. Conviction for sodomy brought with it a life sentence with a whipping to be administered every three months if the defendant were single, castration if the convicted felon were married. Should a person be found guilty of arson and prove unable to pay the costs of the damage, he or she could now "be sold to the behoof of the injured party." Punishment was made more severe for conviction of both adultery and theft of goods under the value of fifteen shillings. Fines for such crimes as sedition and dueling were increased. Any person "who shall swear in his or her common conversation by the name of God, Christ, or Jesus" for the fourth conviction could be deemed a "common swearer" and receive twenty-one lashes once every three months for seven years, a total of five hundred eighty-eight lashes.[52] To improve the likelihood that courts would be more efficient and punishment more expeditious, laws were enacted for the better attendance of justices at the several courts, and to fine veniremen who refused to serve when summoned.[53]

In comparison with the earlier provincial laws, these were harsh. By comparison with contemporary English laws, they were far less punitive; England prescribed death for rape, sodomy, arson, and felony theft. The Privy Council vetoed the Pennsylvania laws because they were inconsistent with the laws of England—an objection that aggressive American legislators heard regularly from the Council. The penalty for arson (indentured servitude) had to go because "selling a man is not a punishment allowed by the laws of England." The punishment for breaking into houses also contradicted English practice. Castration, the sentence for recidivist rapists, was "a punishment never inflicted by any law in any of Her Majesty's dominions." In addition, the Council rejected the provision relating to bestiality because it punished males more severely than it did females.[54] Had Pennsylvanians instead capitalized rape, sodomy, arson, and felony theft—and respected patriarchal values—their revised statutes would have survived Council scrutiny.

What were the legislators trying to do? First, they were *not* deterring real licentiousness among Pennsylvanians. There was no need. One rape was prosecuted before 1701, no arson, and no sodomy.[55] No significant number of grave crimes populated the court dockets before 1701. As for the recidivists, who were singled out for the worst punishment, they did not exist before 1701—or for the next half century. The legislators, in other words, were not synchronizing the criminal code with actual crime. But maybe the legislators were ignorant of the thin criminal record and thought there was a problem. That is a questionable presumption in a small society like seventeenth-century Pennsylvania, where the legislators were also magistrates or certainly knew the magistrates.[56] There were, admittedly, complaints about crime, and they have been recited above. But the source of these complaints often impugns their veracity: Complainers like Nicholas More, Robert Quary, Edward Randolph, and the vestrymen of Christ Church wished to see the proprietary regime and Quaker power damaged or ended, and it served their ends to paint Pennsylvania as licentious and chaotic to the Board of Trade, the Privy Council, the Bishop of London, and others in England. These critics obliged anxious Penn and Quakers to take seriously the reputation for crime without the existence of crime.[57] The legal revisions of 1700 become, in this context of imperial pressure, an attempt to quiet credulous authorities in England by beefing up deterrence in Pennsylvania. Of course, the attempt failed, because the new laws defied the Privy Council's timeless determination that colonial laws not contradict metropolitan law.

After the laws were passed, but before they were replaced in 1705, their enforcement supports the Assemblymen's intention of solving a political rather than a crime problem. Between 1701 and 1705 no harsh sentences were pronounced such as the laws permitted. Of course, there was little need for such sentences since there were no cases of rape, and only three of attempted rape, one case of "buggery," no arson, and no recidivists.

As a consequence of wholesale disallowances of the 1700 laws, the Assembly, which met in Philadelphia in October 1705, was forced to rewrite much of the criminal code to satisfy the Privy Council. The result was a code, with its elimination of the offending sections of the 1700 edition, that was more severe than the earliest criminal laws, but again, not nearly as severe as England's code or the codes of other American colonies. Murder remained the only capital offense, but punishment was adjusted so that a person convicted forfeited half of his estate. The remaining half went to his wife and children if the felon were married, or to his next of kin if he were single. Burglary was to be punished by whipping, six month's imprisonment at hard labor, and restitution on the part of the defendant. Felony theft was punishable by whipping and the demand for double restitution. Those found guilty also had to wear "a Roman T for six months." Punishment for rape was modified so that individuals convicted were to be given thirty-one lashes on their bare backs, to serve seven years' hard labor, and to forfeit their entire estate if single, one-third if married. A person found guilty of a second offense was to suffer branding on the forehead as well as life imprisonment. Adultery was assigned a punishment of twenty-one lashes and a year's imprisonment or a fifty-pound fine. A second conviction brought a similar whipping and seven years imprisonment or a one- hundred-pound fine. The penalty for fornication was now proclaimed to be twenty-one lashes and a ten-pound fine; for bigamy it was thirty-nine lashes and life

the laws changed to satisfy royal demands

imprisonment. Conviction for sodomy and buggery also meant life imprisonment and corporal punishment (not to exceed thirty-nine lashes) every three months. Life imprisonment was the punishment for arson as well. Finally, riot was more carefully defined and brought into conformity with English law.[58]

The 1705 enactments reaffirmed provisions for separate trials for Negroes—whether slave or free—originally legislated in 1700, and provided that blacks convicted of murder, the rape of a white woman, buggery, or burglary should forfeit their lives. Punishment for blacks attempting rape, theft of goods valued above five pounds, or fraud was a combination of branding, thirty-nine lashes, and exile. Should the value of goods in theft cases fall below five pounds, convicted slaves were to suffer corporal punishment up to thirty-nine lashes and their masters were to make restitution to the victim of the theft. Twenty-one lashes were mandated for cases where "any Negro" was convicted of carrying a gun, sword, club, "or weapons whatsoever" without the express permission of his master.[59] The enlargements of criminal punishments of 1705 were the first to break faith with the benevolent earliest law code of the province by adding capital punishments. The change was a double stroke against enlightenment too, because only one people, blacks, were to suffer more possible executions.

Few substantive additions to the penal code were made following 1705. In October 1710, the Assembly did add a forty-shilling fine for persons organizing or profiting from "riotous Sports, Plays and Games," such as bowling, tennis, horseracing, or cards.[60]

As relentlessly as in the past, the Privy Council, the Board of Trade, and other English officials continued to scrutinize Pennsylvania in the first decade of the new century. The Council disallowed more laws for Pennsylvania than for any other colony, attesting to the aggressive character of Pennsylvania Assemblymen. In 1706, fifty-two of one hundred and five laws submitted to the Privy Council for review were nullified. Because of the long time lapse between the passage of a law in Pennsylvania, its review and possible repeal in England, and the information of repeal reaching Pennsylvania, concerned Pennsylvanians were left uncertain.[61] To relieve the uncertainty, the Assembly increasingly resorted to subterfuge. To circumvent the royal veto the Assembly passed laws with a life span of less than five years. It also reenacted laws that had been annulled, and refused to send laws to England for review, or procrastinated before complying. Also, the Assembly sought to salvage laws it thought essential to the well-being of Pennsylvania citizens, and deliberately to encroach upon powers heretofore reserved to the Proprietor, Council, and crown.[62]

Between the changes in 1705 and 1800, the criminal laws were

changed twice again, and the changes were major ones compared with
the prior adjustments. The first major bout of change came in 1718, and
the second after the American Revolution. The first arose partly because
Quakers refused to take an oath of allegiance when serving as court
officials, witnesses, or jurors. Because of their religious principles, Quakers preferred simply to affirm a belief in Christ and fidelity to the proprietor.[63] The 1682 Chester Assembly determined that such affirmations
were acceptable in lieu of oaths. It also held that Quaker witnesses were
to promise to "speak the truth, the whole truth, and nothing but the
truth."[64]

Complicating matters in Pennsylvania by 1689 was a Parliamentary
statute requiring an oath of fidelity and allegiance to the King. Pennsylvania recognized that statute in 1696, but continued to permit an affirmation to substitute for the oath. The Pennsylvania Assembly formally
reconfirmed the efficacy of affirmations in 1700.[65] Despite this sanction,
disputes over affirmations by Quakers continued to threaten and con-
fuse criminal processes. Anglicans and other non-Quakers protested
that because Quakers took no oaths, proceedings in which they were
involved lacked legality. The affirmations matter was one of the three
best levers that Anglican imperialists could use to dislodge Quakers from
power (the others being military defense and piracy).[66]

William Keith, who became governor in 1717, acted decisively to end
the confusion. Though not a Quaker himself, Keith harbored none of
the animosity toward the Society of Friends that characterized his immediate predecessors, John Evans and Charles Gookin. His own gregarious
personality permitted him to work with diverse factions to reach com-
promises. His timing was fortunate. The most important coincidence for
Keith and for all Quakers was the Hanoverian succession to the English
throne, the fall of Tories and High Churchmen from power, and the
long ascendancy of Sir Robert Walpole in English government. The enemies of Quaker Pennsylvania no longer got a hearing in England, and
they were always too few in Pennsylvania to oust Quakers—as long as
there were no international wars afoot to check Quakers' popularity.[67]
Moreover, by the time he took office Pennsylvanians were beginning to
entertain the idea of changing the criminal code—not just succumbing
to Englishmen imposing changes upon them. An influx of German Pala-
tines and Scots-Irish settlers, beginning in 1717, threatened to create
troubles—crime, as it turned out.[68] Keith understood the growing concern and was prepared to take advantage of this sentiment to strengthen
the courts and the penal code. He had an important ally in this regard,
for David Lloyd, trained in English law, a powerful voice in the Assembly,
and, soon to be Keith's chief justice, also believed in the necessity of
change.[69]

Keith shrewdly packaged several changes which, while completely sat-
isfying no one, satisfied enough men to get the package passed and
escape the royal disallowance. To imperialists he offered to bring the
criminal code of Pennsylvania more closely into compliance with
England's than it had ever been. For that he expected some indulgence
from the English: they should concede the affirmation to the Quakers
and stop impugning the authority of Pennsylvania's courts, judges,
jurors, and decisions. Pennsylvanians and Quakers would finally have to
abandon their progressive, liberal laws as well as their scheming to concede only half a loaf of deterrence to the English, as in their legal revisions of 1700 and 1705. Pennsylvania would have to adopt capital
punishment as never before. But with the advent of troublesome and
criminal immigrants, Quakers would likely be more willing than before
to sacrifice the past. The contestants on both sides of the Atlantic were
prepared to deal.

The quick acquiescence of the Assembly confirms that Keith's compromise struck a responsive chord. Under Lloyd's tutelage, it moved to
legalize affirmation and to adopt "such statutes of England to the province as may be proper to our present circumstances, where our laws are
deficient."[70] As for the English, Sir Robert Walpole silenced the Tories'
and Church's opposition to the affirmation when in 1722 he pushed
through Parliament an act legitimizing the affirmation in England.[71]

Historian Herbert Fitzroy labeled the new law—"An Act for the
advancement of justice and the more certain administration therof"
(1718)—"the most important single act in the criminal legislation of
colonial Pennsylvania."[72] Based on English statutes, the bill identified
twelve capital felonies—treason, misprision of treason, murder, sodomy,
buggery, rape, robbery, burglary, arson, infanticide, malicious mutila-
tion, and witchcraft. It also increased punishment for larceny. Written
largely by Lloyd and reflecting his almost pathological obsession with
detail, the bill carefully and copiously laid out the new penal code. It
observed that "it [was] a settled point that as the common law is the
birthright of English subjects, so it ought to be their rule in British
dominion." It conceded that "acts of parliament have been adjudged
not to extend to these plantations, unless they are particularly named in
such acts," and that "some persons have been encouraged to transgress
certain statutes against capital crimes, and other enormities, because
those statutes have not been hitherto full extended to this province."

The bill made explicit the Acts of Parliament that were to be in force
in Pennsylvania. An example is the bill's treatment of treason. It proclaimed that "all inquests and trials of high treason shall be according
to the due order and course of the common law, observing the direction
of the statute laws of Great Britain, relating to trials, proceedings and

judgments in such cases." It also enacted the 1624 English statute on infanticide, whereby the burden of proof fell on the shoulders of the accused single woman; she must prove her child was born dead. Failure was sufficient to assign the death penalty. Outlawry proceedings, with their denial of trial by jury and their death penalty, also became a part of Pennsylvania law as a result of this bill.[73]

There was little echo of William Penn's penal code in the new legislation. It embraced capital punishment as eagerly as earlier legislation had avoided it. It did mitigate some harshness, providing that in all capital cases, "lawful challenges shall be allowed" and "learned counsel [be] assigned to the prisoners." It also permitted benefit of clergy for those capital crimes in England where benefit was accepted. Women too were to receive benefit of clergy in those prosecutions where it was applicable to men.[74] But these were minor turns from a new course set toward more severe criminal justice. It was symbolically fitting that within two months of the passage of the 1718 Act, William Penn died. His death came at a time when many of his hopes for his Holy Experiment were dead as well.

To administer what he trusted would be a novel criminal code in his colony William Penn was willing to accommodate unconventional judicial arrangements. The Charter that empowered him to enact and promulgate laws for his new colony also placed in his hands the authority to shape the judiciary there. He could determine the number and types of courts that would serve Pennsylvanians, and the place and frequency of their meetings. He could name their personnel. He enjoyed "full power and authority to . . . remit, release, pardon, and absolve (whether before judgment or after) all crimes and offenses whatsoever . . . and to do all and every other thing . . . where unto the complete establishment of justice, unto courts and tribunals, forms of judicature, and manner of proceedings do belong."[75] Penn took seriously the opportunity to fashion a truly progressive judiciary, as the "Laws agreed upon in England" demonstrate.

The "Laws agreed upon in England" did not define conduct so much as characterize judicial institutions and means by which to judge criminal behavior. All courts were to be "open" and justice was not to "be sold, denied, nor delayed." People "of all persuasions" were to be permitted to appear in court "according to their own manner" and to "plead their own cause themselves." If they were unable to plead their own case in these forums, their friends could so do for them. All pleadings, processes, and records were to "be short and in English, and in an ordinary and plain character, that they may be understood and justice speedily administered." Juries "as near may be, peers or equals, and of the neighborhood" were to be guaranteed. Individuals "wrongfully imprisoned or prosecuted" were to receive "double damages against the informer or prosecutor." Prisons (whose grim reality Penn knew first hand) were to "be free, as to fees, food, and lodging." Fines were to be "moderate."[76]

The "Laws agreed upon in England" offered only a very general blueprint for the new colony's judicial structure. Through his Frame of Government Penn permitted others the authority to legislate the specific details of that edifice, in particular his Council. Initially reserving to himself authority to appoint judicial personnel, subsequently Penn empowered the Council to erect "standing courts of justice in such places and number, as they shall judge convenient for the good government" of the colony.[77] Penn's willingness to transfer significant powers from himself as proprietor to the Council (a reasonable act so long as that body remained under his control and manned by his friends, and so long as the Assembly remained subservient to the Council) ultimately meant that it would be individuals other than Penn who shaped the judicial hierarchy of Pennsylvania during most of its colonial experience. Penn's own absences from Pennsylvania also soon placed substantial powers in the hands of a series of lieutenant governors.

The first courts under Penn's authority convened shortly after the arrival of Lieutenant Governor William Markham in August 1681. Markham held a court at Upland in November of that year where several assault and trespass accusations were prosecuted.[78] Upon Penn's arrival in New Castle, on October 27, 1682, among his first acts was to issue commissions to six justices of the peace in that county, and to announce that courts would soon meet. But even before Penn's debarkation at New Castle, justices of the peace in the Lower Counties had exercised functions under the authority of "Pensilvania."[79]

More formal and permanent judicial arrangements were instituted in March 1683. The Assembly in Philadelphia in that year more clearly identified and defined the county courts. County courts of common pleas and courts of quarter sessions were established for Philadelphia, Bucks, and Chester Counties, and modifications were made in those for New Castle, Kent, and Sussex Counties. Courts of common pleas were directed to adjudicate civil suits and the quarter sessions, criminal matters. The criminal courts were now required to impanel twelve-man juries, and to insist upon unanimity among veniremen to carry guilty verdicts rather than to allow a simple majority to do so. They also were to meet quarterly in each county and to exercise criminal jurisdiction in all save the most heinous capital crimes such as treason and murder.

The 1682 Chester Assembly overlooked provisions for the trial of capital causes or for the hearing of appeals. Both issues were rectified somewhat in 1683 when legislation prescribed the form and procedures in

criminal cases, and vested the governor and Council with appellate jurisdiction. Courts of quarter sessions also were empowered in 1684 to be
courts of equity at law.[80]

A Provincial (supreme) Court was founded in the spring of 1684. Con-
sisting of five judges charged with meeting twice a year in Philadelphia
to handle "all causes as well Criminal as Civill, both in Law and Equity,
not determinable by the respective County Courts," and with having two
justices ride circuit twice each year in each county, it was directed to
exercise original powers in cases such as murder and treason. It also was
to act as a court of appeal for cases originating in the county courts.
Difficulties centering on the court's personnel, schedule, and routine
quickly persuaded the Council in 1685 to strip the Provincial Court of
its original jurisdiction in civil matters and to return it to the county tribunals. It also removed the court's oyer and terminer responsibilities,
providing instead for special commissions of oyer and terminer to be
awarded any three judges to try "heinous crimes." The number of its
judges in that year was reduced from five to three.[81]

The Provincial Court was restructured again in May 1690. In that year
the court's bench was increased to five and it was again given responsibility to try oyer and terminer cases and to hold *nisi prius* courts on circuit. In addition, the high court was permitted to review appeals in civil
cases involving more than £10 if the appellant provided sufficient security to prosecute the appeal and to pay costs. The court was given appellate jurisdiction over all matters in equity or law. Though the 1690
changes improved the capacity and reputation of the court, in 1700
members of the Council and the Assembly still were debating ways to
solidify the high court and to make its procedures "more easie & less
expensive."[82]

Although the largely Quaker architects of the early Pennsylvania judiciary rejected much of the form and practice under the Duke's Laws
when constructing their own scheme, important procedures and precedents were retained. The penchant for informal arbitration of conflicts
under the Duke's Laws, the use of coroner inquests, the prohibition of
sheriffs or clerks acting as attorneys, the insistence on the necessity of
two witnesses to convict in capital cases, and the conveying of equity
power upon county courts found their way into the Pennsylvania justice
system. In 1686, "to a Void of to[o] Frequent Clamors and manifest
Inconveniences w[hi]ch usually attend mercenary pleadings," the former prohibition on lawyers practicing for fees was brought forth for
reintroduction.[83] The ritual and ceremony imposed under the Duke's
Laws, English in their origins, was adopted wholesale by Pennsylvania
authorities, as were numerous forms and procedures such as the "Grand
Inquest" or grand jury system.[84]

Legislation in 1683 provided for three "peacemakers" to be appointed in each county and entrusted to handle disputes between and among individuals. Their arbitration was to "be as Valid as the judgments of the Courts of Justice." Despite early enthusiasm for the employment of the peacemakers, the practice of utilizing them in minor criminal matters became less popular by 1692, when the Assembly reassessed procedures relating to them. Still, the Assembly provided that arbitration mechanisms would remain available to citizens, and the practice of relying upon arbitrators continued even into the late nineteenth century.[85]

Agencies in early Pennsylvania other than arbitrators and the formal courts wielded judicial powers in criminal cases. By virtue of his judicial powers the Proprietor, and later a train of lieutenant governors, wielded impressive influence in criminal proceedings. Empowered by charter to remit fines and punishments, to release or pardon those charged with criminal conduct, and to "absolve (whether before judgment or after) all crimes and offenses whatsoever," Penn did not hesitate to participate actively in criminal cases before his first departure in 1684. Executive involvement in criminal prosecutions provoked little adverse public comment until Lieutenant-Governor John Evans summarily aborted proceedings in several cases involving friends and cronies.[86]

From its beginning the Council exercised important judicial functions. Its members worked with the governor to create laws by proclamation and to clarify practices and punishments attached to those laws. In July 1683, for instance, the Council granted masters power to punish their runaway servants and to chastise persons who "shall Inveyle any Servant to goe from his Master." Upon hearing complaints of "tumultuous gatherings of negroes" in Philadelphia in July 1693, the Council ordered constables to gather up the rioters, incarcerate them for twenty-four hours "without meat or drink," and to give them thirty-nine lashes.[87]

Prior to 1684 Council members also were charged with "sitting in judgment upon criminals impeached" and with considering appeals from the county courts. Because until 1684 no court existed to deal with grave crimes, or those not clearly under the jurisdiction of the county courts, members of the Council also were asked to adjudicate them. Rumors that counterfeit money was circulating stirred the Council in the summer of 1683 to issue a warrant for the apprehension of Robert Fulton and Samuel Buckley. It was the Council, too, that heard testimony in the case, then directed the sheriff to summon both a petit and grand jury, and an attorney to draw up an indictment against the two men. Once the grand jury had brought forth a true bill and the petit jury had heard the case, Governor Penn delivered the charge to the jurors. Similar procedures were employed when allegations of being a witch were leveled against Margaret Mattson late in 1683.[88] Maritime matters, including crimes at sea, also came to the Council. Until the creation of a vice-admiralty court in 1698, admiralty jurisdiction fell largely to Councilors. [89]

Council hears cases

The Council's most important judicial functions were anchored in its powers of administration. By 1685, in the absence of Penn, it appointed county justices. The Council also interpreted a 1685 court bill so that the bill invested the Council with power to appoint the Provincial Court. Later, the Council gained this power by statute. The Council routinely determined the times and places of courts, issued commissions for special tribunals, and, by reviewing procedures and verdicts stemming from disputes over the foregoing questions, wielded impressive judicial influence in the young colony. However, its appellate powers were diminished in 1684 when the Provincial Court was formed.

The King (or Queen)-in-Council was also a part of the Pennsylvania judiciary. The King-in-Council represented for Pennsylvania, as for other colonies, a court of last resort, even in criminal matters. The original charter provided that all appeals from the judicial judgments of Pennsylvania were to be lodged in England. As we have seen, however, the Privy Council's greatest impact on Pennsylvania society and on the Pennsylvania judiciary came from its nullification of the province's laws. The Assembly, too, exercised judicial functions, including some associated with criminal prosecutions. Even though no judgments were appealed to the Assembly from the court system in the early years of the colony, during the administration of John Blackwell, the Speaker of the Assembly, John White, and his fellow assemblymen made claims of being "the supreme Judges of this Govern[men]t." Their bold assertion had little basis in fact or history and earned them a quick and severe rebuke from the Council, but the issue did not end. As early as 1684 the Assembly had taken advantage of a discussion on the formation of the Provincial Court to raise questions about its own powers to enact and review laws and to appoint judicial personnel. As the Assembly expanded its powers of appointment and control of the purse, and as its power to initiate legislation grew during the last decade of the seventeenth century, it also increased its capacity to shape the colony's judiciary. Its power to impeach justices and to remove them from office plainly circumscribed the judiciary.[90]

From the beginning, establishing the rules and procedures by which Pennsylvania courts were to be governed was a matter of great moment for the Council and judicial officials. Their nervousness arose partly from the newness of judicial institutions in Pennsylvania and some citizens' tendency to ignore them. Quakers were notorious for bowing to no authority but God. Thomas Tunneclif's 1687 remark to the bench of the Bucks County court that "I Care not A pin for none of you," was far too typical for authorities to rest easy.

Jurists also disagreed over matters of court form and procedures. One such incident occurred in March 1685/6 when Martha Wilkins was brought to court in Philadelphia charged with being pregnant with an illegitimate child. She readily acknowledged her condition and, ignoring the traditional excuse used to gain public sympathy and judicial leniency, confessed "shee was not tempted to it by any promise of marriage." She asked to be tried "By the bench of Justices without a petty jury." The prosecuting attorney would have none of that. Despite her admitted culpability, he insisted that Wilkins face a jury. He argued "that it was contrarie to the law to try the prsoner wtout a pettie jurie, & that her pleading guiltie was but her Conviction & not her trial." He also maintained that "Everie criminal must be found guiltie by two Juries att least"; that is, a grand jury and a trial jury. A heated exchange with his fellow justices ensued, in which he was subsequently overruled. Because of incidents such as this, almost every court session saw the addition of rules of conduct, and every judicial bill became more detailed in describing practices and forms.[91]

However, most of the problems for the courts of Pennsylvania before 1720 orbited around one issue, the use of affirmations in the province. The issue had a long history before Governor Keith largely settled it in 1718. For four decades, Quakers insisted that affirmations could legally be substituted for oaths, while the political rivals of the Quakers harangued that they could not. Could Quaker witnesses, jurors, and justices legally administer justice, the rivals asked again and again? The refusal of Quakers either to tender or to swear oaths brought into question the legitimacy of court proceedings and sanctions. Resourceful defendants could throw their trials into confusion by insisting that their judges, jurors, and witnesses be sworn. So long as these disputes remained unresolved, the legal basis of Pennsylvania courts continued to be challenged.

In addition, the courts frequently were caught up in struggles between proprietary and antiproprietary parties or factions which, in turn, overlay conflicts between Council and Assembly.[92] Because antiproprietary forces found their strength in the counties and the Assembly, proprietary governors and their Council confederates naturally looked to the less populist judiciary. Opponents of Penn were unwilling to concede to governors and councilors equity jurisdiction and the discretionary power inherent in it, preferring their own custody of the county courts or Supreme Court. Finally, the antiproprietary partisans labored to reduce the Council's appellate powers in favor of the Supreme Provincial Court. Proprietary interests conceded neither, and so the acrimony and confusion increased among the courts and justices.[93]

Pressure in the 1690s to reduce piracy and violations of the trade and navigation acts deepened the legal confusion in Pennsylvania. Fearful that a lukewarm effort to punish pirates and smugglers would lead the crown to revoke the colony's charter, proprietary interests clamored for compliance with the Navigation Act of 1696. To that end they advocated a vice-admiralty court for Philadelphia. Penn's opponents, including David Lloyd, were not enthusiastic. Concerned that vice-admiralty courts (which did not employ juries) would not only compromise individual rights, but favor imperial interests over Pennsylvania ones, they urged that maritime cases (including those of a criminal nature) be tried in county courts.[94]

To circumvent vice admiralty power, the Assembly enacted the Pennsylvania Act of Trade. It stipulated that actions against violators of the English trade and navigation laws "shall be tried according to the course of the Common Law, known practice of the Courts of Record within this government by twelve Lawful men of the neighborhood, where the offence is Committed." Imperial officials railed that the Pennsylvania law "utterly destroyed the design & intent" of the Navigation Act of 1696.[95] The King-in-Council moved to repeal the Pennsylvania Act of Trade and urged Penn to dismiss Lieutenant Governor Markham, Lloyd, and other proponents of the bill.[96]

The year 1701 marked a major effort to improve the consistency and effectiveness of Pennsylvania courts with the passage of the "Act for Establishing Courts of Judicature in this Province and Counties Annexed," passed on October 28. Primarily the work of David Lloyd, the act established a judiciary whose major outlines lasted until the Revolution. For the first time in the history of the colony, Pennsylvania courts and their functions were described in copious detail. The act dispelled most of the earlier confusion about court procedures and the various jurisdictions of courts. It systematically identified the types of county courts, the schedule for each, their functions, duties, jurisdiction, and limitations on their powers.[97] It offered examples of various forms of writs for the edification of court officers untrained in the law. Sheriffs and justices struggling to command the form of the law now had at hand the forms of all summons, arrests, and attachments. The act virtually walked a peace officer through his legal duties. Justices were encouraged to emulate "the methods and practices of the Kings court of common pleas in England. . . . always keeping to Brevity, plainness and verity, in all Declarations and pleas and avoiding all Fictions and Colour in pleadings."[98]

The greatest single benefit of the 1701 reform bill stemmed from its careful demarcation of jurisdictions, especially of appellate courts. As we have seen, rivals for judicial power frequently clashed over the jurisdiction of governor, Council, and Provincial Court (which had failed to meet regularly). In his 1701 bill, Lloyd clearly tried to separate original and appellate jurisdictions. Original jurisdiction for the most part was assigned to county courts. The exceptions were criminal prosecutions involving murder, manslaughter, rape, sodomy, treason, burglary, arson, and buggery. Most of these crimes now came under the original powers of the Supreme Provincial Court. All appellate jurisdiction was assigned to the governor and the Supreme Provincial Court.[99]

The act of 1701 included a section authorizing the Governor to grant a number of important writs, including that of habeas corpus, and other "Remediall writts." He could also issue writs of errors, but the law stipulated that such writs must be based on errors of law, not clerical errors or technical errors of pleadings, pleas, or process. Writs of errors could not arise from minor defects in the form of writs, returns, bills, pleadings, or verdicts.[100]

Lloyd's bill also attempted to solve the perennial question of affirmations versus oaths—and the problems that trailed off from that question. The bill prohibited any court from establishing rules which would "Debarr" individuals from holding public offices or from serving in the courts "who for conscience sake, shall scruple" to swear oaths.[101] But the new law hardly caused the detractors of Quakers to lose a step in their assault on the courts and regime.

The 1701 bill, in combination with the charter for Philadelphia of the same year, established a judiciary that Pennsylvanians at the end of the eighteenth century could recognize. The Philadelphia charter created a municipal government wherein the mayor, recorder, and aldermen acted as justices of the peace in the Mayor's Court, handling all civil and noncapital criminal acts in that jurisdiction. The Mayor's Court functioned as a court of quarter sessions within the city limits.[102] Unfortunately for the smooth functioning of the Pennsylvania judiciary in the short term, the Judicial Act of 1701 fell victim to royal disallowance in 1705.[103] Partly because of the disallowance and partly due to political divisions within the colony, the colony made do with a judiciary of dubious legitimacy until 1710. A knot of confrontational Churchmen in Philadelphia and the Lower Counties expected to restore royal government to the province by obstructing all public business, including the courts. They depended upon their demand for an oath to do the work of driving the Quakers to despair and the Crown to overhaul the proprietary. If Quakers continued to refuse to swear solemn oaths, the Churchmen would bring the courts to a standstill. They argued that the Queen-in-Council on January 21, 1702/1703 ordered judges to swear and agree to administer oaths to whoever might wish to swear. Because Quakers could not do either, and because most of the justices in Chester and Bucks Counties were Quakers, courts in those counties presumably would cease to function. The lawyer George Lowther was in the forefront of the effort at paralysis, especially at the higher court where capital cases were tried. When the courts in Philadelphia county stalled, Lieutenant Governor Andrew Hamilton created ad hoc courts composed of Anglican justices, but these too briefly failed when Anglican jurors refused to serve after being persuaded that the courts were illegal. Subsequently, Governor John Evans replaced Quaker judges with Anglicans both in the Supreme Provincial Court and in the county courts of Philadelphia, and once again the courts ground to a halt.[104]

After 1705, the Assembly strove to write a judiciary bill both it and the crown officers could accept, even as governors Evans and Gookin threatened to establish a court system by executive ordinance. Evans and Gookin envisioned a judiciary wherein the governor and Council would wield power much greater than that of the county courts, for instance, through exclusive equity jurisdiction. Lloyd and most assemblymen insisted upon locating equity in the county courts and the Provincial Court. Lloyd also wished to recognize the growing importance of lawyers and to identify methods by which practitioners could join the bar. His draft law stipulated that all lawyers practicing before Pennsylvania courts "shall be learned in the Laws of England."[105]

The Pennsylvania judiciary changed in yet other important ways in 1705. Although prior to 1700 the laws of Pennsylvania did not recognize the existence of slavery in Pennsylvania, separate criminal courts for black offenders, free or slave, were created in the first five years of the new century. Originally established in November 1700 but nullified by the Queen-in-Council, these special courts were reestablished in 1705. They were to be overseen by two justices of the peace and six prominent freeholders, and were to try crimes ranging from petit theft to capital felonies.[106] Confusion surrounded these courts from their inception.[107] William Penn argued that special courts for blacks offered better protection for Negro defendants. But enthusiasm for such courts more likely arose from slaveowners' concern for speedier rather than surer justice for blacks. The owners did not want to lose the services of their accused slaves when the slaves would be detained by protracted, formal sittings of the regular courts. And by providing for six prominent freeholders to assist the two justices of the peace rather than employing a traditional jury, these "Negro Tryals" made it easier for slaveowners to control both verdicts and punishments.[108]

Blacks tried in these courts were denied traditional rights accorded white defendants in mainstream courts, including the right to an attorney, the right to question all accusers, and the right to a jury. These courts offered a summary process, not opportunities to be judged by one's peers. However prejudicial to blacks in Pennsylvania, these courts never applied the inhumane penalties meted out to African Americans in New York and New Jersey, and they discouraged extralegal punishments of suspected blacks. No Negro was lynched in Pennsylvania prior to 1800 and only one—a Sussex County black man—apparently was incinerated in 1690 after killing his master.[109] Pennsylvania blacks accused of criminal behavior faced these specially commissioned courts until they were abolished in March 1780.[110]

During the political impasse between 1705 and 1710 Pennsylvania's courts functioned on the basis of ordinances issued by Governors Evans and Gookin, albeit with brief lapses in 1708 and 1709. Both governors vindicated their proclamations based on the proprietor's rights in the 1682 Charter, rights that the Assembly hotly contested. It was not until 1710, when tempers had cooled sufficiently and both sides recognized the urgency of having an Assembly bill formally reestablishing the courts, that a judiciary bill was successfully enacted and sustained for any period. An "Act For establishing Courts of Judicature in this Province" became law on February 28, 1710.[111]

Comprehensive like the 1701 act, the 1710 statute made few major changes in the previous court structure. It did change the name of the Provincial Court to the "Supream court" and reduced the number of its justices to four. A significant change came in the formation of equity courts, as justices of the "Supream court" were given authority to issue all major writs and to hold a "Court of Equity" in every county. Justices of the county courts also were empowered to hold courts of equity four times a year in each county.[112] These arrangements held sway until February 20, 1713, when on the grounds that they contained provisions that unduly increased the cost of litigation they, too, were struck down.[113]

Nullification of the 1710 judiciary act once again placed the criminal justice system under a cloud. Old quarrels revived, especially over the proper distribution of judicial power. The Assembly was obliged to change strategy. Rather than offer a major bill, the repeal of which would again stagger the entire judiciary, it put together a series of bills, which collectively became the Judiciary Acts of 1715.[114] Still, pouncing on what Pennsylvanians viewed as peripheral or minor flaws in the legislation, the King-in-Council voided the bills in 1719.[115]

Even before the 1715 bills were struck down, the Supreme Court had ground to a halt. The Assembly vehemently refused to accept blame for the closed court. Assemblymen informed Governor Gookin that "there was great Uneasiness among the People, by reason several Criminals lay in the several Gaols of the Province, who were not tried or yet brought to Trial." They demanded that the governor and justices in the Supreme Court explain "the great Delay . . . in the Trial of Criminals."[116] Despite prodding from the Assembly the high court failed to schedule criminal trials for almost twenty-four months.

Stability was substantially achieved with the passage of the "Act for Establishing Courts of Judicature in the Province," enacted on May 22, 1722. The 1722 bill, which held closely to David Lloyd's vision of 1701, survived. It reaffirmed the composition and functions of courts of quarter sessions. Of the "competent number of justices in every of the said counties, nominated and authorized by the Governor," any three could hold general sessions of the peace and gaol delivery to adjudicate criminal matters. Any three also could "hold special and private sessions, when and as often as occasion shall require." In addition, each justice had full power "in or out of sessions" to "take all manner of recognizances" compelling people to appear or to issue sureties to maintain the peace. The courts had to meet for at least three days in Philadelphia county, and for at least two days in the remaining counties.

The Provincial Court, now termed the "Supreme Court of Pennsylvania," was to hold two sessions each year in Philadelphia, in September and April, with three judges (one to be styled the "chief justice") named by the governor. Two judges of the court were required to ride circuit annually in each county. The court was to handle noncapital cases in the county of their origin. Capital cases committed in sparsely settled areas were to be tried in Philadelphia. The Supreme Court was now denied original jurisdiction in civil proceedings, a condition that persisted for more than six decades.[117]

The repeated changes in the criminal laws and uncertain authority of the courts in early Pennsylvania largely ended in the 1720s. In one respect that was a welcome change. In another, it was not, because the change did not come without sacrificing a vital part of Penn's vision of a more humane civil society. Despite all the problems that populated the first four decades and the despair they caused in the founder, this was the time when Pennsylvania most deserved the praise that it later received. However much William Penn despaired, the Crown and Anglicans meddled, and colonists agitated, justice generally prevailed. Criminal suspects were indicted, juries impaneled, decisions rendered, and sentences executed. Better yet, less crime occurred in this period than ever after and when it did occur, the law treated the perpetrators with more patience and care than ever after.

Chapter 2
"While We Lived Not Broken in Upon"

> For rulers are not a terror to good works, but to the evil. . . . if thou
> do that which is evil, be afraid; for he beareth not the sword in vain.
>
> —*Romans 3:14*

To persuade the Crown to curb or end the liberties and exceptions that
it had allowed in Penn's "experiment" on the Delaware, rivals of William Penn and Pennsylvania Quakers maligned the conditions of public
life in the province. But these opponents received unintended help
from the Quakers themselves. By their own behavior in public life,
Quakers amplified the note of discord by falling out among themselves.
They fought with each other over public power, and as a consequence
even caused a schism in the Society of Friends. This sorry historical
record prompts some historians to declare the Holy Experiment an early
failure.[1] But failure is too sweeping a judgment; politics, as sorry as it
was, was not the whole of public life. The record of crime, justice, and
the peace received little or no attention in the verdicts of historians. This
chapter examines the record of the public peace and the justice system
in the first four decades, including the amount and kinds of crime, the
workings of the courts, and the personnel of the system. The record
proves to be quite the opposite of the picture left by Pennsylvania's earliest detractors, and while it does not revise the strictly political history of
the province, it enlarges the history of public life. The enlargement
rings of civility and decency, but also rigor and caution.

The rates of crime in the public record in Pennsylvania from 1682
through 1720 refute the harsh depictions of Pennsylvania society. Any
accurate measurement of the amount and gravity of crime in Pennsylvania begins with murder and manslaughter, since homicides best expose
faults in any society or government and are the mostly accurately
recorded crimes. The first four decades in Pennsylvania show the fewest
occurrences of homicide in any period through 1800—sixteen indict-

TABLE 2.1. HOMICIDE ACCUSATIONS AND INDICTMENTS IN PENNSYLVANIA, 1682–1800

Years	Homicides accused	Homicides indicted
1680s	1	1
1690s	4	4
1700s	2	1
1710s	10	10
1720s	18	18
1730s	16	16
1740s	17	16
1750s	30	29
1760s	64	56
1770s	99	82
1780s	154	82
1790s[1]	98	67
Total	513	382

[1]Figures for the 1790s are too low due to missing dockets in RG-33, Eastern District, Courts of Oyer and Terminer, roll 6. There are only scattered cases after 1794, mostly from Northampton and Philadelphia Counties.

ments from 1682 through 1719. (Table 2.1) Of course, there were fewer Pennsylvanians in those decades than later, and a better estimate of homicide at the time is the rate per 100,000 persons. For the historically significant period of 1682 through 1717 (the years of William Penn's oversight and the near absence of capital laws), the homicide rate as measured by indictments for Pennsylvania was 1.0, the lowest it would ever be and one that rivals low rates in the most admired nonviolent nations today (Tables 2.2 and 2.3).

Between 1682 and 1718—when capital punishment applied only to murder and treason—few death sentences were imposed. Only two individuals, Judith Roe and Derrick Jonson, were executed in this period, both for murder. One African American who murdered his master in the Delaware counties apparently was burned to death. It is not clear, however, if this burning was carried out by the court or by aroused citizens. Two others, Negroes Toney and Quashy, both slaves, were convicted of burglary, but were exiled rather than executed.[2]

Quaker judges reluctantly sentenced individuals to die. They showed no disposition to apply capital punishment in order to deter potential miscreants. Had Pennsylvania been the vulnerable, disordered new society that its detractors and some historians have depicted, judges and prosecutors might have felt some need for deterrence and for capital sentences. But the capital sentences did not exist and presumably neither did the need to deter potential criminals. Prosecutors (the king's attorney or a substitute in capital cases) too did their part to avoid dis-

TABLE 2.2. HOMICIDE ACCUSATION AND INDICTMENT RATES PER 100,000 POPULATION IN PENNSYLVANIA, CHESTER COUNTY, PHILADELPHIA, AND SURREY AND SUSSEX, ENGLAND

Years	Pennsylvania accused	Pennsylvania indictments	Chester County accused	Chester County indictments
1680s	1.5	1.5	0.0	0.0
1690s	2.7	2.7	4.8	4.8
1700s	0.9	0.5	2.8	0.0
1710s	3.6	3.6	7.5	7.5
1720s	4.5	4.5	5.9	5.9
1730s	2.3	2.3	2.9	2.9
1740s	1.6	1.5	1.1	0.6
1750s	1.9	1.9	4.0	4.0
1760s	3.0	2.6	3.1	2.7
1770s	3.4	2.6	4.9	4.5
1780s	4.0	2.1	2.5	1.3
1790s[1]	1.9	1.3	2.6	1.7

Years	Urban Surrey[2] indictments	Sussex indictments
1660–1679	8.1	2.6
1680–1699	5.0	1.9
1700–1719	3.9	1.2
1720–1739	2.8	1.1
1740–1759	2.0	1.9
1760–1779	1.7	0.5
1780–1802	0.9	0.6

Years	Philadelphia accused	Philadelphia indictments
1720s[3]	3.3	3.3
1730s	6.9	6.9
1740s	5.9	5.9
1750s	3.1	3.1
1760s	7.4	7.0
1770s	6.5	6.2
1780s	1.0	0.8
1790s	0.2	0.2

TABLE 2.2. (CONTINUED)

Years	Philadelphia indictments[4]
1839–1845	3.7
1846–1852	3.1
1853–1859	4.0
1860–1866	2.4
1867–1873	3.3
1874–1880	3.7
1881–1887	2.4
1888–1894	2.2
1895–1901	2.7

[1]See note at Table 2.1.
[2]Source for Surrey and Sussex data is J. M. Beattie, *Crime and the Courts in England, 1660–1800* (Princeton, N.J.: Princeton University Press, 1986).
[3]There is only one homicide indictment in Philadelphia before1720, in 1697, and reliable population estimates before 1720 are rare. Therefore the table begins with the 1720s.
[4]Roger Lane, *Violent Death in the City: Suicide, Accident, and Murder in Nineteenth-Century Philadelphia* (Cambridge, Mass.: Harvard University Press, 1979).

TABLE 2.3. HOMICIDE ACCUSATION AND INDICTMENT RATES PER 100,000 POPULATION BY HISTORICAL ERAS IN PENNSYLVANIA, CHESTER COUNTY, AND PHILADELPHIA

	Pennsylvania accused	Pennsylvania indictments	Chester County accused	Chester County indictments
1682–1717	1.1	1.0	1.9	0.9
1718–1732	3.4	3.4	9.0	9.0
1733–1754	2.0	1.9	2.4	2.2
1755–1764	1.0	1.0	1.2	1.2
1765–1775	4.9	4.2	5.3	5.0
1776–1783	1.9	1.5	3.1	2.2
1784–1794	3.8	2.5	2.6	1.5
1795–1800[1]	1.5	1.1	3.2	2.2

	Philadelphia accused	Philadelphia indictments
1718–1732	2.2	2.2
1733–1754	6.0	6.0
1755–1764	1.6	1.6
1765–1775	12.2	11.6
1776–1783	1.0	1.0
1784–1794	0.4	0.2
1795–1800	0.3	0.3

[1]See note, Table 2.1.

comforting the Quaker bench by the ways they chose to prosecute the accused. A more aggressive prosecutor in the Jonson case would have pushed for the execution of Brighta, Jonson's wife, and perhaps also of Eliza, his sister, both of whom were originally indicted along with Jonson.[3] A Bucks County Negro named Jack was responsible for the death of a young white man in 1688, but was not executed. A dozen years later, even though another Bucks County black man was thought guilty of rape, he also escaped execution. Although rape was not a capital offense for white inhabitants in Pennsylvania prior to 1718, blacks were judged by more flexible standards. After 1718, these blacks would have been condemned to die and been executed.[4]

Other than homicide, the two gravest capital crimes in England and in most of America outside Pennsylvania were burglary and robbery. They were especially alarming because the perpetrators threatened the lives and wellbeing of the victims in the act of taking their property, whereas mere thieves took property by stealth and without threat. Neither crime troubled early Pennsylvanians much. In Chester County, the only jurisdiction for which there are complete records, eleven robberies and burglaries occurred in the first thirty-six years. Five are recorded in the incomplete judicial record in Bucks County—Bucks being the second of the three original counties and the only other one with records for that period. As for other forms of violence to persons, assaults of all kinds (physical and verbal) numbered ninety-eight in Chester County. In the decade 1700–1709, for which a rate of offenses per 100,000 can be reliably derived in Chester, the assault rate was seventy-five. Compared to its rates through the rest of the eighteenth century, that figure was unexceptional. Finally, there was one riot in Chester, in 1718. Overall, with respect to that category of crime usually labeled "serious" (violence, threats of violence, or callous disregard for persons and property), Pennsylvania enjoyed a period of grace. Other newborn governments and societies in early America, excluding New England, have no comparable record of social peace or civility. If Native Americans are included in this judgment of civility—and they should be—Pennsylvania had no rival, because only Pennsylvanians planted themselves on the North American continent without conquering the indigenous people. That was so many homicides forgone.

When grave crimes occupied so little of the energy of the justice system before 1720, what were the remaining concerns of the system, if any? There have been few times or places in the long course of American history when people and government have been not been preoccupied with homicide, theft, riot, or some ominous disharmony, and thus able to spend their energy on other regulations of community life.[5] New England has offered the most conspicuous American example of that freedom from concern for damage to person and property that afforded New Englanders the ability to enforce moral rigor and uniformity. What of Quaker Pennsylvania? Did the liberal and humanitarian bent for which it was so often commended lead Quaker founders to dismiss out of hand the idea of policing people's personal lives, demanding uniform behavior of them (while permitting them freedom of conscience and other civil liberties)? As the previous chapter pointed out, from its beginning Pennsylvania prohibited a long list of what are commonly called immoral behaviors: sexual misconduct including fornication, bastardy, incest, sodomy, and bestiality; also, drunkenness and tolerating drunkenness, violating or disrespecting the Sabbath, swearing, profanity, cursing, gambling, card-playing, dicing, the theatre, "riotous" sports, and even scolding and behaving "clamorously."[6] Moreover, the men who wrote the laws and enforced them generally were Quakers, with founder William Penn in the lead.

Quakers unmistakably influenced Pennsylvania government from 1682 until 1756, or even longer. Persons referring to Pennsylvania frequently alluded to Quaker leadership. At home and abroad, Pennsylvania was the Quaker province or "Quaker country." Historians have long explained the significance of the Quaker ascription for Pennsylvania's governmental and religious institutions. But what did it mean for the more common and familiar routines of life that Pennsylvania was run by a religious denomination that was as uncompromisingly moral as any that ever existed in America?[7] Some Quakers insisted that Pennsylvania's magistrates apply morals laws resolutely. Quaker John Churchman, a model public servant and officeholder, explained to the mayor of Philadelphia that "the nature of his office as a magistrate" obliged him "to take care that he bore not the sword in vain, but put the laws into execution against evil doers, such as drunkards, profane swearers, &c, and to be . . . a terror to the wicked."[8] To be a terror to evildoers was the biblical commission that St. Paul had explained in *Romans*, chapter 13—a text which became the mainstay of Christian and Quaker political science. Quakers wished all Pennsylvanians to be sober people like themselves. Quakers were renowned for inviting a variety of peoples to Pennsylvania, but that liberality did not include indifference toward common lasciviousness.[9] And so, does Pennsylvania deserve to be put in the same historical company as those vaunted moralists, the New England Congregationalists?

Prosecutions (charges or presentments to the grand juries) of immorality in Pennsylvania from 1682 through 1800 comprised 8.9 percent of all prosecutions.[10] The varieties of behavior that were prosecuted are listed in Table 2.4. That 8.9 percent is plainly a small proportion of all prosecutions when compared with other American jurisdictions that avowedly enforced morality. In the Massachusetts Court of Assistants, for

example, between 1630 and 1645, drunkenness and illicit sex were the
two greatest preoccupations of the court, while theft and violence, which
typically rank first and second in crime statistics, were almost no problem at all. Much later, in prerevolutionary Massachusetts, the law still
"required of men an uncompromising adherence to truth and an aus-
tere mode of life that left no room for sensuous pleasure." Extramarital
sex, "Singing & Fidling & Dauncing," and strolling on the Sabbath were
some of the crimes punished.[11]

Historian William Nelson found that as late as 1760–1774, 38 percent
of all prosecutions in seven counties in Massachusetts were for various
sexual immoralities. In New Haven, Connecticut, "fornication was by far
the largest category of criminal cases on the county court dockets from
about 1690 until 1770." Astonishingly, in Plymouth County, Massachusetts, 1725–1785, "Fifteen percent of all prosecutions were for breach of
the Sabbath, and another 3 percent were for profane speech." The criminal law was concerned primarily with protecting community religious
and moral values. As in earlier Puritan Massachusetts, the objective of
criminal law in the prerevolutionary period was "to give legal effect to
the community's sense of sin, and to punish those who breached the
community's taboos."[12] New England reputedly declined from some
primitive standard of moral behavior and saw immorality increase—or
by a different characterization, it became secularized and ignored
immorality. And yet, despite all the "Jeremiads" preached about decline, New England remained an exceptional land that expected propriety from its people.

By comparison with New England's, Pennsylvania's effort at enforcing
moral standards was brief and arguably faint. The way to explain Pennsylvania's distinctive history of enforcing morals is by addressing different kinds of morals crimes. Most such crimes have no obvious victims the
way that assault, theft, and other crimes do. Consensual sexual relations,
gambling, and profanity are a few examples of victimless crimes. The
most zealously moralistic communities prohibit these and other victimless behaviors—usually because they believe that the behaviors in question violate divine prohibitions. They offend God, if not all men.

How the Quakers ranked among moralistic communities, how acutely
they prohibited victimless crimes, is addressed in Table 2.4, which displays the whole range of morals behaviors. The data show that in the
decade 1701–1710 the prosecution of many varieties of victimless crime
declined and thereafter disappeared. Drunkenness, swearing, and violating the Sabbath especially were prosecuted only in earliest Pennsylvania.
If one variety of victimless crime, fornication, is removed from the victimless subtotal, 80 of 107 of the prosecutions occurred before 1710,
and 74 before 1700. Details from early cases from Chester County indi-

TABLE 2.4. ACCUSATIONS OF MORALS CRIMES IN PENNSYLVANIA, 1682–1800

	1680s	1690s	1700s	1710s	1720s	1730s	1740s	1750s	1760s	1770s	1780s	1790s	Row total	Row percent
Fornication	3	8	6	8	9	29	47	83	158	141	115	57	664	25.0
Bastardy	10	19	10	20	32	49	119	141	188	213	346	478	1625	61.1
Adultery	4	2	1	3	4	2	19	21	15	15	51	51	188	7.1
Bigamy	0	0	0	0	1	1	0	0	1	4	15	23	45	1.7
Buggery	0	0	1	0	0	2	1	2	2	2	5	8	23	0.9
Sodomy	0	0	0	0	0	0	0	0	0	1	1	1	3	0.1
Incest	0	0	0	0	0	0	1	0	0	0	0	2	3	0.1
Sexual subtotal	17	29	18	31	46	83	187	247	364	376	533	620	2551	96.0
Drunkenness	24	14	1	0	0	0	0	0	0	0	0	2	41	1.5
Tolerating drunkenness	4	0	0	0	0	0	0	0	0	0	0	0	4	0.2
Violating Sabbath	2	7	1	0	0	0	0	0	0	0	0	0	10	0.4
Profane swearing	7	9	3	0	0	0	0	0	0	0	0	0	19	0.7
Blasphemy	0	0	1	0	0	0	0	0	0	0	0	1	2	0.1
Scolding	1	0	0	0	0	0	0	0	2	1	1	1	6	0.2
Practicing magic/ witchcraft	1	3	0	0	0	0	0	0	0	0	0	0	4	0.2
Gambling	0	2	0	0	0	0	0	0	1	6	0	8	17	0.6
Horse racing	0	0	0	0	0	0	0	0	0	0	0	2	2	0.1
Conducting lottery	0	0	0	0	0	0	0	0	0	0	0	2	2	0.1
Nonsexual morals subtotal	39	35	6	0	0	0	0	0	3	7	1	16	107	4.0
Totals	56	64	24	31	46	83	187	247	367	383	534	636	2658	100.0

cate that the violations occurred in a small population and an intimate community where privacy was meager and neighbors reported on each other. The majority of this rural population were Quakers, too, who overlay their commitment to public rectitude with a commitment to religious piety and community standards.

What occurred within the confines of other people's homes was treated as a public concern and probably a religious one, and what one did in public at inappropriate times and places was also more than one's own business, even though ostensibly no one was harmed. John Sunderland, for example, was fined five shillings because he permitted Robert Stephous to get drunk at his house. Albotus Hendrickson attested that he saw Harmon Johnson so drunk at Thomas Boules' house that Johnson "lay and pist himself." After a trial and conviction, the court fined Boules ten shillings for permitting such drunkenness. While drunk, Richard Crosby coaxed some people to fight, and also slandered Swedes. Wildham Collett was found traveling the road with a yoke of oxen on first day (Sunday) in Concord Township. Peter Worral of Marple was "cocking" [making] hay on first day. Jacobus Vanculine raced a horse for a wager on first day. William Curtis and George Chandler abetted a wrestling match. Richard Crosby pretended he could tell fortunes and judge who had stolen goods.[13]

After 1710, almost all the moral rigor Quakers practiced within the Society of Friends disappeared from the law enforcement in the province.[14] Prosecutions of immorality continued thereafter, but they were mostly against bastardy, where the motives for prosecution were ambiguous, not especially religious, and hardly Quaker sectarian.[15] By 1710 at the latest, the Quakers had become a minority of Pennsylvanians. They were barely a majority of Philadelphians at about 1690 and according to James Logan, Quakers outside the city only equaled those within. Two decades later they were an even smaller portion of the province.[16] Even before 1710, the interlude of royal government in the 1690s and the incessant hectoring by disgruntled Anglicans in the province had sensitized Quakers to their own political liability: Quakers stood accused of jeopardizing the whole justice system because of their peculiar refusal to swear and administer solemn oaths.

How hard could they push their other religious preferences upon a hostile, politically potent population of non-Quakers? Even while they were the majority, diversity (part of their own design for Pennsylvania) troubled Quakers. The increasingly diverse people of Pennsylvania diluted any consensus about proper behavior, and fewer people belonged to any association able and willing to supervise its people's behavior. Requisite sobriety among Quakers, as well as Mennonites and other pietists, may have been supercilious niceties for many other Germans and for the Irish and Scots-Irish. While some of the newcomers, like Swiss and German pietists, troubled the Quakers very little, others, like the Anglicans and Scots-Irish, contested the Quakers on many fronts, including ethics and the working of the justice system. Surely affected by their dwindling numbers and the envy of non-Quakers, it was easier, and probably inescapable, that Quaker leaders chose to allow more liberty and personal independence to others and to forego enforcing the public ethical model that New England represented. Especially since the freedoms that Pennsylvanians already enjoyed were in most part due to the politically progressive Quakers additional freedoms was the natural choice. Being Quakers, they forswore for themselves the liberty and privacy they provided for other Pennsylvanians; they were moralists who quit moralizing in the public arena.

The Quaker character of early Pennsylvania justice appeared in more than the crimes committed and prosecuted. Criminal justice procedures also imitated the sectarian methods that Quakers used in resolving conflict among their brethren and in sanctioning miscreants within the Society of Friends.[17] More than at any time before 1800, the provincial courts in the first four decades cultivated arbitration and informal resolution of differences, including differences that were clearly criminal, and not civil torts. The hope thrived that conflicts could be resolved short of formal legal proceedings, through mediated discussions.

The early Council was particularly aggressive in urging people away from resolving their conflicts in the more formal and public setting of a court. Council members believed that in the courts, conflict might deepen and the parties become more disruptive. A 1684 dispute involving Andrew Johnson and Hanse Peterson ended when Councilors advised the disputants to "shake hands, and to forgive One another." To terminate the quarrel symbolically the Council ordered all paperwork involved in the misunderstanding to be burned.[18] Arbitration and informal negotiations were generally pretrial measures capable of eliminating the need to press for a more formal, time-consuming, costly, and public resolution. When Richard Wells complained against one of his neighbors, it was "ordered that he be referred to the Peacemakers, and in case of refusal to the County Court." In another case the parties were "advised to make the business up between themselves; otherwise to have a trial by the County Court."[19] Formal trial procedures followed only if efforts at reconciliation and accommodation failed.

Victims who withstood the pressure to settle their claims outside court often discovered that judges preferred to bypass trial procedures in favor of releasing the accused under bonds for his or her future good behavior. When in 1689 Robert Woodward was presented to the court for his abuse of Justice John Simcock he was released only after being ordered to find two sureties to guarantee his good behavior for the next year. A charge of minor misconduct brought John Cook before a Chester court in 1693, but when "nothing more Appear[ed] against him," he was discharged under the stipulation that he bond himself to maintain the peace.[20] Placing individuals under heavy bond did not always guarantee the desired results. In October 1687, Bucks County's Thomas Tunneclif was required to provide sureties for his good behavior after he badgered Hannah Overton and her children until they feared for their lives. Yet no sooner had Tunneclif been bonded than he went into a rage, shouting, "I Care not a Pin for none of you[;] you have abused & wronged me & [I] bid [you] do [your] worst."[21] Despite such failures, the use of peace bonds persisted.[22]

Even after grand jury indictments and the opening of trial, some judges insisted upon permitting court-appointed referees to search for informal accommodation; indeed, they interrupted proceedings to assign them. Anne Milcone's charges in 1684 against Gilbert and Martha Wheeler were put aside briefly in Bucks County when they "Joyntly desired theire tryall may be deferred until the next Court day to see if it Cann . . . be Ended betwixt them" by informal discussions. Although animosity in July 1685 between James Stamfield and John Hurst led to an assault, "upon their Submission each to [the] other and promising ye Court to live peacefully and quietly," the prosecutor dropped all charges. Individual counties annually designated three "peace makers" to facilitate such proceedings. Procedures as well as the rationale behind such refereed proceedings were clarified in the Arbitration Act of 1705 and in a series of subsequent Supreme Court cases.[23] Even after lawyers multiplied and commonly participated in criminal trials, judges continued to assign cases to referees. Hiring an attorney did not signal the end of arbitration.[24]

Peace bonds rather than fines or corporal punishment were often employed to guarantee the good behavior of citizens only suspected of intemperate or illegal actions. Following George Davis's attack upon the county sheriff in Sussex in May 1687, he was required to provide security for his good behavior for one year and a day. Friends of William Bradford were forced to enter into recognizances of £20 each to guarantee his good behavior for "half a year" after he, in June 1687, "in the hearing of the court" cried, "God Damn it and you all."[25]

Of all the charges in the years 1682–1718, 28.0 percent ended on the docket books unresolved or unknown. Many of them were likely arbitrated outside of court—or handled summarily by clerks or justices.[26] Of the sentences in Chester County cases that ran much of the judicial course, 19.6 percent were ended by negotiating and compromising among the parties. Another 19.2 percent of sentences were of the "other" outcomes category, and were ended by restoring property, posting a bond, removing an obstruction, writing a nuptial agreement, or other settlements. Some defendants escaped punishment altogether. Thus, when Martha Harmson of Sussex County "Caused two Baynes of Matremony" to be posted under an alias promising to marry one Anthony Enlose, and was discovered to be already married, the court simply ordered the notices removed and forbade Mrs. Harmson to marry Enlose. Similarly, after a Sussex County court in 1683 found that Cornelius Verhoffe and John Vines had illegally withheld payment for goods from "Christian the Indian," it merely decreed that the two men make proper payment within thirty days. A Chester County court summoned John Mendinghall and John Gibbons in March 1684, and charged them with selling rum to the Indians. Yet when both men offered petitions in their own behalf, the court summarily discharged them.[27]

When arbitration, mediation, compounding, peace bonds, and ancillary methods failed or were inappropriate to the case, the public prosecutor took the first step in formal prosecution by making a presentment to the grand jury. The grand jurors could decide either to indict (return a true bill or *billa vera*) or not to indict (return *ignoramus*). Few things appear as clearly in the whole justice process as the inclination of the early Pennsylvania grand juries to vote true bills. (Table 2.5) For the earliest three decades, if the province prosecuted a charge, an indictment was almost inevitable. This period of severity coincides obviously with the years of Quaker preponderance in the provincial population, and the severity is at least partly related to their preponderance. Quakers practiced rigorous discipline within the Society of Friends. If a member were accused of violating church strictures, the judicatory, called the monthly meeting, proceeded to investigate.[28] Once alleged misconduct became a matter of recorded business in the monthly meeting, the outcome was near certain: the offender either made amends for the error or was severed from membership.[29] Acquittal was almost unknown. When Quakers outnumbered other Pennsylvanians and commanded the grand juries, they probably operated in public life as they did in their own councils. It was "their" Pennsylvania, after all.

Once grand juries indicted the accused, and neither victim nor accused retreated, the cases went to trial. The outcomes of trials may be measured by the simple conviction rate (SCR), which is the percent of convictions among all charges brought to trial. The highest simple conviction rate occurred in the first two decades in Pennsylvania. (Table 2.5) That tendency of juries to convict complemented the high indictment rate by grand juries in the first three decades. And like the high indictment rate, which partly resulted from Quakers applying Quaker

TABLE 2.5. OUTCOMES OF CRIMINAL PROSECUTIONS IN PENNSYLVANIA (EACH CATEGORY'S PERCENT OF TOTAL OUTCOMES PER DECADE) 1682–1800

	N	Default	Ignoramus	Submit	Conviction	Acquittal	Escaped	Unknown	Simple conviction rate
1680s	214	7.0	0.0	25.5	38.6	4.8	3.2	20.9	89.0
1690s	304	5.3	0.4	31.9	25.1	3.8	1.9	31.7	86.8
1700s	178	13.2	1.1	21.6	28.4	10.6	0.0	25.1	72.7
1710s	209	2.0	12.0	16.5	8.5	5.7	4.9	20.2	59.7
1720s	300	8.2	15.6	28.5	21.0	7.1	0.5	19.0	74.6
1730s	633	5.0	10.3	38.8	22.2	6.9	0.2	16.6	76.3
1740s	937	2.4	16.4	39.4	15.3	7.4	0.1	19.1	67.5
1750s	1934	1.7	22.6	38.9	12.8	5.2	0.2	18.7	71.3
1760s	2796	1.2	16.9	38.7	19.4	7.9	0.1	15.8	71.1
1770s	4097	2.5	17.8	26.1	21.2	8.6	0.4	23.3	71.1
1780s	7040	5.3	21.1	26.3	18.7	7.1	1.2	20.4	72.4
1790s	12108	7.7	24.0	21.5	17.6	7.8	1.2	20.2	69.4

sectarian standards in public, the Quakers on trial juries were skeptical of the defenses that accused men and women asserted. In heavily Quaker Chester County, before 1710, the simple conviction rate was an astonishing 83.8 percent.

While it is very helpful, the simple conviction rate is too simple to measure all aspects of the justice process and to discover how zealous and effective systems were. Effective prosecution involves more than getting indictments and prosecuting indicted men and women before trial juries. Cases must be brought to resolution. At various points along the judicial path to resolution, something may go wrong and a case never gets resolved. The histories of cases vary, and the outcomes sometimes are opaque. In colonial Pennsylvania, one common problem with closing prosecutions was the accused's escape from custody—an unambiguous failure by magistrates. Inadequate jails contributed to escapes, especially from jails outside Philadelphia. Other causes went unresolved due to simple faults of the clerks of court. Cases could drag on for months, even years; harried clerks advanced them from docket to docket every three months. But some protracted cases surely fell by the clerical wayside, and never appear terminated on the record when indeed they eventually were resolved.

Another possible path taken in apparently unresolved cases occurred when public prosecutors reached an accommodation with the accused, and the accommodation escaped being recorded. One likely case for accommodation was the operation of a tippling house. If the person accused of this offense agreed to get a liquor license, the charge might disappear from the docket. Also, the court costs in license prosecutions were higher than the fine imposed by law, so the courts often dismissed these cases and took fees in lieu of fines, effectively punishing the crime.

The government also permitted cases to expire for lack of resources or interest. But since private citizens prosecuted most criminal charges in early Pennsylvania, they accounted for many of such unresolved cases. Some complainants lost their enthusiasm to push a case to its formal conclusion. Some may have never intended to persevere to the end, especially in slander and assault proceedings. For these men and women the opportunity to air a grievance in public doubtless acted as a catharsis, a social or psychological "safety value" for private tension.[30] They got their satisfaction before their case ran its judicial course. Other private criminal complaints, like civil cases, were settled by private arbitrators, "out of doors." In 1741, the renowned attorney Andrew Hamilton observed that he spent "more time in hearing and reconciling Differences in private, to the loss of his Fees, than he did in pleading Causes at the Bar."[31]

For various of the reasons cited above, unresolved charges do not necessarily mean that the justice system was ineffective. But in the historical record, unresolved charges due to blameworthy, faulty conduct by the personnel of the courts cannot be separated from intended, unresolved outcomes, and each tallied separately. The figures and percentages in the "Unknown" category contain both, and therefore must be treated as the high estimates of ineffectiveness and unresolved charges.

In the first three to four decades, the highest figures ever in Pennsylvania of grand jury indictment rate and simple conviction rate coincided with the most frequent use of arbitration or mediation. More was at work here than simple coincidence. Many of the cases that went to grand juries and trial had been sifted through a pretrial process and efforts at informal reconciliation. The trial jurors surely knew as much in this comparatively small and religiously uniform community. Magistrates were almost certainly Quakers, as were most of the jurors. After mediation failed, these informed citizens were ready to render expeditious justice and see the obstinate accusers or accused get whatever they deserved. Quakers conducted discipline in their meetings this way, and in public life they carried over their sectarian way of doing things.

When trial juries returned guilty verdicts, the final step was sentencing. The sentences and sanctions imposed upon guilty defendants in the years 1682–1718 also distinguished the period from its successors. In fact, secular variations in sentences created the equivalent of three successive Pennsylvanias. The first of these was a time when any court's inclination to act punitively or vindictively was circumscribed by the most progressive criminal code in the western world. But also, in the first period, as we have seen, there was the least need for punitive action or reaction and deterrence, because Pennsylvania experienced few serious crimes. Rarely and reluctantly did courts impose the death penalty.

The earliest period stood out in other ways. In the first three decades fines were levied in less than 40 percent of sentences. They would never again be so uncommon in Pennsylvania. Moreover, fines and amercements that were levied were more often than not remitted when defendants petitioned for redress. Although a court in the Lower Counties fined John Browne ten shillings for failing to carry out his duties as a juryman, he successfully petitioned to have the fine remitted. George Young also was successful in having his fines cancelled, when he convinced the court he had missed his scheduled appearance because he had lost his horse and was "forced to spend some time in Looking after him." William Wargent prevailed upon the court to erase his fine for the same offense by persuading the judges he had "to run after unruly Catle to put them oute of A corne Feild." When Samuel Baker of Chester County was brought to court in 1686 for verbally and physically abusing Judge John Simcock (who attracted more than his share of abuse), he found himself standing before his victim. Even under these circumstances, when Baker submitted and accepted the fine for his misdeeds, Simcock generously remitted his fine.[32]

Without belittling the impulse of early Pennsylvanians to be generous or the amity among the majority Quakers, the paucity of fines and the remission of the fines was also grounded in difficult economic times and the scarcity of money. The obvious evidence of these economic straits was the inability of property holders to pay their taxes and the reluctance of tax collectors to collect them much of the time from 1690 through 1710. Moreover, magistrates simply did not prosecute the non-paying civilians or the defaulting officers responsible for the collections.[33] Certainly in some cases, the very men in the justice system who neglected to collect taxes were the very men who declined to fine the guilty. In yet more cases, almost all the personnel of the government from administrators down to jurors understood that the times were difficult.

In a justice system often exhibiting generosity and respect, administering progressive criminal laws, one practice seemed out of place. That was the sentence of wearing of a sign. Wearing a sign or letter broadcasting one's crime seems to be a relict of English criminal justice or of Calvinist faith such as informed the laws and courts of New England. Thanks especially to Nathaniel Hawthorne, many modern laymen associate wearing a sign with early American justice—the "A" for adultery. The intention of sentencing men and women to wear a sign is to discomfort them psychologically, or put more bluntly, to humiliate deviants. That purpose seems hardly consistent with Quakerism and its foundation premise of the native goodness and spiritual equality of all people. Nevertheless, all sentences but one of wearing a sign dated from 1689 to 1718—when Quakers most clearly controlled criminal justice. The 1705 law specified wearing a "T" for six months in cases of theft. Ironically, the severe criminal code of 1718 eliminated that specification. In Chester Country, sixteen men and women had to wear a sign. The women among them were convicted of bastardy, theft, and one unknown crime (none for adultery); the men for theft (11), burglary (3), counterfeiting, and libel.

The record on humiliating punishments is messy and inconsistent, however. The appearance of other sentences having the purpose or effect of humiliation did not complement chronologically sentences of wearing a sign. The chief case in point is being sentenced to the pillory or stocks—it may be physically painful, but it definitely exposes the convict to ridicule if onlookers wish to vent. It seems likely that this sentence would appear at the same time as wearing a sign. It did not. In Chester County, the pillory was a sentence only once before 1720.

The lack of crime or the achievement of public peace and effective criminal justice in early Pennsylvania had much to do with its homogeneous population and culture. The Society of Friends comprised a majority of Pennsylvanians for two to three decades, and while the city of Philadelphia was first to lose its Quaker predominance, some rural areas preserved Quaker majorities much longer. Eastern Chester County, the best example, had a majority of Quakers until the American Revolution. Social or civil peace, if not political peace, is understandable in a land populated by Quakers—they were pacifists. How likely were pacifists to kill, assault, or rob each other? No one, including Quakers or other nonviolent people, should enjoy the presumption of blameless behavior, but when a people's historical record shows so little problem with major crime, the fact that they professed to be a nonviolent people deserves high credit.

In his study of courts in early Pennsylvania, historian William Offutt found the same successful establishment of public peace and criminal justice institutions described in this chapter.[34] He also finds that Quakerism was pivotal to that success. However, the thrust of his explanation depends upon the Quakers being an élite in Pennsylvania and the province being more pluralistic than it was. Offutt credits the success to an élite composed of wealthy Quaker men—an assertion that stands on the two legs of religion and property. Of the two, the weak leg is religion. Quakers were the majority for most of the period, and if they ran the justice system that was natural and not élitist.[35] That leaves the question of the economic and social character of the alleged judicial élite. Here there is credible evidence for some parts of the proposition.

As historian Gary B. Nash has demonstrated, William Penn was least impartial and equitable when he appointed men to high provincial offices in Pennsylvania. Penn labored to bring to Pennsylvania a landed and mercantile élite from which to draw talented judges and magistrates. He proffered large land grants and other privileges to induce his favorites to migrate. He subscribed to the theory that the obedience and deference accorded men in public offices arose especially from such men's high social status. Simply put, effective leaders must be socially eminent. Penn's early judges and administrators generally were just such men.[36]

Of the men appointed to serve as judges of the Provincial Court in the first decade of the colony's history, only John Eckley was identified as a "yeoman." The others were either "gentlemen" or substantial merchants. Five purchased more than 1250 acres in the new colony. Chief Justice Nicholas More obtained 10,000 acres, Robert Turner 6,000. William Crispin, the first to be appointed chief justice in Pennsylvania, had purchased 5,000 acres but died before taking office. The land holdings of the Quaker merchant William Welch are not known, but he apparently had resources beyond that of the common settler. James Claypoole, who eventually held several judicial offices, owned more than 10,000 acres besides a thriving mercantile business.[37]

Men such as Arthur Cooke, Andrew Robeson, John Simcock, and John Guest, who served the colony as "pryor judge" or chief justice of the Provincial Court in the seventeenth century, also were men of means and social pretensions. Cooke had been a prominent Quaker in London and a successful merchant in Rhode Island before moving to Pennsylvania. He and Simcock were close advisors to Penn and served as Commissioners of State, among other offices, for the proprietor. The merchant Edward Shippen, who also served on the high court, stood at the very top of Pennsylvania society. Reputedly the owner of a £10,000 fortune and what was considered the largest coach in Pennsylvania, Shippen acted as alderman of Philadelphia and as a justice of the peace as well as justice of the high court. His biographer observes, "the economic gap between Shippen and most settlers was immense."[38]

The youth of Pennsylvania society almost insured that the pool of eminent candidates for office would remain small and force Penn to appoint a few men to several offices. Penn was prepared to accept such pluralism; he favored it over loosening his élite standards. Nicholas More served as president of the prestigious Free Society of Traders, provincial secretary, and clerk of the Council in addition to his chief justiceship. Robert Turner secured a position on the important Board of Property, which was invested with authority to allocate land in the absence of Penn, and acted in that capacity even as he exercised his functions as justice of the peace for Philadelphia County, and served as judge of the Provincial Court. Penn's initial selections for the Philadelphia County court of quarter sessions included Welch, Turner, William Clayton, and Francis Daniel Pastorius, all of whom also exercised other official duties.[39]

Few men combined high offices, influence, wealth, and intimacy with Penn more obviously than Robert Assheton. Coming to Pennsylvania at the urging of Penn, his cousin, Assheton was quickly named town clerk, clerk of the peace, and clerk of the court. And he was effectively if not officially prothonotary of the Provincial Court in 1701. He also soon became recorder, a member of the Provincial Council (where he acted as advisor and legal draftsman to the governor), and clerk of the Secretary's Office. Yet more, he was named a judge in the court of common pleas, the Supreme Court, and the orphans' court, and appointed Naval Officer of the Port of Philadelphia.[40] But even with the use of plural appointments, Penn and his administrators could not find enough eminent men to fill all the provincial offices. Their goal of rendering the personnel and culture of American government a close reflection of English patterns mostly failed.[41]

When too few Pennsylvanians qualified to be Penn's model officers, who finally filled the offices of the justice system, and what kind of men were they? Data for the following description of the personnel of the justice system come from Chester County. There the ample records reveal who served, from the highest officials down to jurors, together with important personal circumstances like their wealth. In the three counties of early Pennsylvania (Philadelphia, Bucks, and Chester), the most exclusive office was that of sheriff; it was as close as one could come to making a vocation in the justice system. The work could be constant. The sheriff was charged with attending all court sessions in his county. He served (with constables' help) all legal writs and forms emanating from the clerk of the courts, and executed all court judgments. He listened to allegations of criminal conduct in his venue, investigated them, arrested or detained persons thought to be guilty of infractions, and supervised the care of prisoners.[42] He enjoyed impressive power over local elections by naming the clerks who supervised them, working with elected inspectors to verify qualified voters, taking the ballot boxes into custody when the polls closed, and certifying those men honestly elected. Clearly he could influence the outcome if he were disposed to do so.[43]

William Penn was able to name the sheriffs until 1701; then the Charter of Privileges made the office elective. Initially after 1701, voters in each county selected two men from whom the governor chose one, but later, counties forwarded just one name. The election of a sheriff often drew more interest among voters than did the candidates for Assembly.[44] Incumbents were limited to three-year terms, at first by law and later by custom. Sheriffs often served the three years and after a hiatus served again.[45] In terms of years and span of service, John Owen was the premier incumbent in Chester County in 112 years, with twelve years in office distributed in a variation on a common pattern: 1729–1731, 1735–1737, 1743–1745, and 1749–1751. John Taylor served the longest continuous terms, 1721–1728.

Overall, the cyclical patterns of incumbency produced a small knot of men with great experience in law enforcement: only two incumbents occupied the office in the 1720s, three in the 1730s, and two in the 1740s. Turnover was more common in the first forty years than later. Sheriffs also occupied other high county offices before and after being sheriffs. Eighteen of twenty between 1689 and 1775 were justices; twenty-three of twenty-eight between 1689 and 1800. Thereby, they worked the gamut of judicial functions: conducting grand juries, guiding trial juries, and conducting criminal and civil trials. Also, fourteen of the sheriffs

TABLE 2.6. PERCENTILE RANK IN TAXABLE WEALTH OF SHERIFFS AND JUSTICES OF THE PEACE IN CHESTER COUNTY, 1690–1800

Sheriffs[1]		Justices	
1690s	78.6[2]	1693	85.8
1720s	95.2[3]	1718	84.1
1730s	86.1	1730	91.5
1740s	77.0	1740	91.0
1750s	85.5	1750	93.8
1760s	90.6	1765	94.1
1770s	84.6	1775	86.9
1780s	80.0	1785	87.5
1790s	69.5	1799	77.8

[1]Source: Sheriffs are from J. Smith Futhey and Gilbert Cope, *History of Chester County, Pennsylvania* (Philadelphia: Louis Everts, 1881), 374. The 1700s and 1710s are missing because the sheriffs were not in the 1693 or 1718 tax lists. Averages were computed for each decade by multiplying a man's percentile by the years he served.
[2]The average was comparatively low due to one sheriff, Andrew Job, who ranked in the 34th percentile in the 1693 list. However, in the 1718 tax list he had risen to the 88th percentile.
[3]John Taylor was sheriff from 1721 through 1728. In 1718 he ranked in the 76th percentile and that figure is used in the computation for the 1720s. But by 1730 he had risen to the 98th percentile.

(1689–1775) represented Chester County in the Provincial Assembly, and so had the ability to draft, amend, construe, or repeal the laws they enforced as sheriffs and applied as justices.[46]

Before 1775, all the sheriffs were from townships within twelve miles of Chester Borough, the county seat. With two exceptions the sheriffs before 1775 were Quakers.[47] The mean rank of the taxable wealth of incumbents through 1800 put them in the 83rd percentile. It would be even higher if the mean were computed using each sheriff's highest tax levy or assessment (generally when he was a mature head of household). The position of sheriff was one of profit. The tax assessor in 1765 valued the sheriff's remuneration in that year at £100. Table 2.6 and Figure 2.1 illustrate changes in their ranking over most of 112 years. While there was only little change, they were the least distinguished by great wealth, the least élite, in the period before 1718—as well as in the Revolutionary era. Because of their plural offices and powers, their wealth, and their common religion, the men appear to be an élite, at least until the irruptions of the American Revolution. Before 1701 that élite could be credited partly to Penn. But in the 1701 charter he gave up most of his hand in selection. Thereafter, sheriffs would be an oligarchy by popular consent—if an oligarchy at all. Wealthy for that time and place, Quaker in religious faith, concentrated in the eastern county, and equipped with

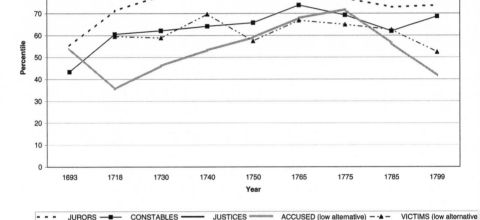

Figure 2.1. Percent rank in taxable wealth of justices, sheriffs, constables, jurors, accused criminals, and victims of crime in Chester County, 1693–1799.

extensive power, the sheriffs were vulnerable to the voters' rejection of them. Even so, the voters rarely turned any of them out of office.[48]

The men who served as justices of the peace and sheriffs were almost interchangeable. They practiced serial pluralism rather than occupying two or more offices at the same time.[49] With respect to their economic status, therefore, it is not surprising to discover (Table 2.6) that they shared approximately the same decile rank in taxable wealth, with the sheriffs outranking justices only once in nine samples between 1693 and 1799. Unlike the sheriffs, the justices in Pennsylvania were not popularly elected or popularly vetted at a community caucus before they were commissioned. The proprietor commissioned them and could have used the justice commissions to create political clients. An ambitious proprietor might have dreamed of cementing together a political party using this and other patronage. A patronage model was close at hand in British parliamentary politics and parties and was imitated in some other American colonies.[50] And yet, neither William Penn nor his sons used the commissions in a self-gratifying way, despite their undisguised impatience with opposition political parties or factions in the province.[51]

Juries are critical to the argument for élitism in Pennsylvania. In England, the aristocracy boldly packed juries. Allowing a few adjustments for a different time and place, according to William Offutt a Quaker élite in Pennsylvania substantially duplicated in Pennsylvania juries the élite character of juries in England. And the public acquiesced in it. This New World differed little from the Old, either in ideology or practice; its existence meant that if progressive justice came to Pennsylvania it had to wait until this English legacy died.[52] That such élitism should prevail in the courts of Pennsylvania by manipulating juries appears ironic in a colony fashioned by William Penn.

[margin note: élite juries]

Penn had immediate personal reason to think hard about juries. He was the accused in one of the central cases in English constitutional history involving juries, called Bushel's case or the Penn-Meade trial. In 1670 he was tried for conspiring to cause a riot. The jury returned a split decision, but the judge sequestered the jurors without food or water, and threatened them with worse if they did not bring back a conviction. Instead, they brought an acquittal, for which the court fined and jailed them. They finally were released, and another court decided that a jury could not be punished because of its verdict. Penn was only one of many Quakers who suffered from the abuse of intimidated or packed juries in England.[53] One would reasonably expect that with the power to create a justice system in Pennsylvania, Penn and Quakers would try to mend some of the faults of English juries from which they had suffered, and at least provide more autonomy for juries within the judicial system.

Pennsylvania law prescribed how jurors were to be selected. In the 1682 "Laws Agreed Upon in England," Penn described an ideal jury rather than specifying the mechanics of selecting one, stating that jurors shall be "as near as may be, peers or equals, and of the neighborhood." The following year the law required that from a collection of names of all freemen in the county—put into a hat—a child was to pull names of jurors who would serve.[54] The few sentences were a great advance beyond English practice, where local élites packed the juries as needed. Clearly Penn turned the system into a more popular or representative course. Yet there was plenty of ambiguity in Penn's succinct prescriptions. No peer is ever the exact equal of any other in the sense of being a duplicate. How many resemblances therefore satisfy the requirement of an "equal"?[55] On the other hand, a neighborhood is more precise, especially since there are useful political demarcations that beg to be used to define neighborhood, like town, township, or parish. In light of such ambiguities, jury selection in American justice systems is a recurring question, testing how closely or remotely societies comply with the spirit and outlines of progressive justice.

The jurors examined to answer the questions raised about them number 3308 from Chester County. The tests applied to the 3308 involve their distribution among the whole population eligible to serve, their repeated service on juries and the number of cases they heard at each sitting, and finally, their wealth and residence—in brief, their conduct and their personal characteristics. The outcomes of these tests reveal how well they fit into any élite characterization of them and what kind of an élite they were, if any. The first question is how extensive or limited was jury service? If it were limited to a small portion of the population, the case for élite domination of juries defying Penn's wishes gains credibility, or to the contrary, if it were widely distributed, juries look less élite and more likely to represent all adult men.

In the small population of adult men in seventeenth-century Chester County jury service was common. In 1693 it had only 281 adult taxpaying males, living in sixteen townships adjoining the Delaware River, which meant (with one exception) they lived within twelve miles of it. A large proportion of these men, 7.5 percent, were impaneled annually to serve on a grand or trial jury. Following the prescriptions of the Charter of 1682, the sheriff oversaw the choice of jurors, and in this small community he knew the persons selected. In the courtroom, the jurors probably knew some or all of their fellow jurors, the justices who presided, the accused, the victims, and witnesses. If they did not know them personally, they doubtless shared hearsay about them. By reason of this geographical intimacy, they were a jury of the accused's peers. By the same token, their minds were hardly blank regarding the accused. The modern predilection for a "blank-slate" jury was not a concern in seventeenth-century Pennsylvania. Nor had their intimacy yet been diluted by the famed pluralism of Pennsylvania. These 281 adults were mainly English and Welsh Quakers, like most of the people of Chester County before 1718.

By 1718, the equivalent population at risk had reached 994 and jury service per year involved 4.3 percent of it, still a large percent. The county was still mostly Quaker, English and Welsh, even though in 1717 a surge in non-Quaker immigration to Pennsylvania began which diluted the homogeneity of the province, including rural counties and their juries.[56] By 1750 jury service reached less than 1.5 percent of the population per year, and it remained below that mark for the rest of the century. In 1750, 3852 diverse taxpaying men were spread over forty-four townships that reached as far as forty miles west to the Lancaster County border. There is no doubt that jury service was least exclusive or élitist in the years before 1718, and arguably, at four to seven percent annual service, it was not exclusive at all.

In a population of only 281 in 1695 or 994 in 1718, taxpaying males would likely serve on juries repeatedly without this repetition raising the suspicion that someone was conniving to exclude other eligible men. In contrast, in England service was limited to a small élite, but the English

TABLE 2.7. DISTRIBUTION OF JURY SERVICE IN CHESTER COUNTY

Juries served on	Jurors serving	Percent of total jurors	Percent of all jury seats
1	2125	64.2	40.0
2	699	21.1	26.3
3	273	8.3	15.4
4	127	3.8	9.6
5	55	1.7	5.2
6	21	0.6	62.4
7	5	0.2	0.7
8	2	0.1	0.3
9	1	0.0	0.2
Total	3308	100.0	100.0

TABLE 2.8. MEAN JURY ASSIGNMENTS PER JUROR AT NINE INTERVALS IN CHESTER COUNTY, 1691–1801

Years	Mean assignments per juror	Standard deviation
1691–1695	2.8	1.7
1716–1720	1.8	1.2
1728–1732	1.7	1.1
1738–1742	1.5	0.9
1748–1752	1.5	1.0
1763–1767	1.6	0.9
1773–1777	1.4	0.7
1783–1787	1.5	0.9
1797–1801	1.6	0.9

population to be served was large. Therefore, repeat service had to be the case—which was just what the élite wished. Historians J. S. Cockburn and J. M. Beattie have explained how commonly jurors made repeat appearances in England. In three samples of grand jurors from 1690 to 1801 in the Surrey assizes, Beattie discovered that between 51.5 and 56.3 percent of them served more than once. Three samples of trial jurors from the same years showed between 14.5 and 25.7 percent serving two or more times.[57]

In Pennsylvania jurors served repeatedly, although less often than those in England. And in Pennsylvania, the repetitions occurred most often before 1718.[58] Tables 2.7 and 2.8 illustrate the repeat appearances of grand and trial jurors combined in Chester County. In the years 1693 through 1799, 35.8 percent served more than once and as many as nine times. That 35.8 percent was responsible for 60 percent of all jury service in the county. Breaking the jurors into their two categories, the trial jurors served more than once 19.3 percent of the time, while grand jurors served more than once 35.8 percent.[59] The year 1693 stands out for the highest occurrence of repetitions and the widest variation in the distribution of service among jurors, but in an eligible population of only 281, that frequency need not raise suspicion of élitism.

The broad distribution of jury service before 1718 cripples the assertion that a Quaker élite was working the justice system. However, there remains the question of the personal character of those who served in Pennsylvania, as well as in England. Who were the jurors in England and Pennsylvania? In the case of English grand jurors, since the Exclusion Crisis of the 1680s, the grand jury's power of indictment and "its right to speak for the community on matters of common interest was too powerful a weapon to fall into the wrong hands." The aristocracy sealed off the grand jury. Gentlemen were eager to serve because grand jury service was "a sign of a man's importance in the county." Any suggestion that the grand juries linked the justice system to the democracy in England does not apply to this era.[60]

In the case of trial jurors in England, Parliament recognized that repeat service on juries was a problem, but not the one of resented aristocratic control. Rather, too many humble men were serving; jury service was too widespread. Parliament rued that more substantial citizens were avoiding or otherwise escaping jury duty, and it attempted to remedy the fault. Whether due to Parliament's curatives or not, over a century or more, Beattie states, trial juror service changed from being burdensome to being a desirable token of prestige or class and probably power.[61] The question for Pennsylvania is: were the jurors there serving class and wealth, or religion, neighborhood or township, or something else? Offutt argues that the élite that allegedly packed early Pennsylvania juries was the familiar Quaker élite. But to repeat the fault with that assertion, since the majority of Pennsylvanians were Quakers, Quaker juries did not make élite juries.

The wealth of the jurors obviously bears upon their possible élitism. If they resembled contemporary English jurors they would be, as Beattie found London jurors in the 1690s, "at least relatively prosperous in that they were drawn overwhelmingly from the upper third of the rate paying population." They "were securely within the prosperous and respectable communities in their wards."[62] P. J. R. King found that jurors in the eighteenth century were men of some wealth and hardly the illiterate plebeians that captious gentlemen asserted.[63] Douglas Hay believes that Parliament, through its 1730 reform legislation, succeeded in raising the social status of jurors: By late eighteenth century, "Jurors were of much higher social standing than most of the men and women whom they tried, or indeed, of the general population." They had triple the income of the men they tried and far greater estates.[64]

TABLE 2.9. CRIMINAL CASES TRIED PER JURY IN CHESTER COUNTY

Number of cases per jury	Number of juries	Percent of all cases
1	2568	54.9
2	400	17.1
3	175	11.2
4	102	8.8
5	46	4.9
6	2	0.3
7	6	0.9
11	8	1.9
Total	3308	100.0

Figure 2.1 tracks the mean percentile of taxable wealth of the Pennsylvania jurors (grand and trial) from 1693 to 1799. It shows that they were usually from the top third or quarter of the property holders, and so were not average adult males in this population. However, the only time when their mean wealth approached the 50th was in 1693—and the median that year was at the 52nd percentile.[65] And the second lowest mean percentile rank occurred in 1718. In brief, the jurors were least élite when they were supposed to be élite. Exceptional wealth should also be the case with men who sat repeatedly on the juries—the wealthier one was, the more often he should have sat. However, for the whole period 1693–1799 no statistically significant correlation exists between the times jurors served and their percentile rank in the distribution of wealth. Not even at the time of the most repeat appearances, 1691–1695, does any exist. Wealthier jurors (top half, top third, top fifth) served at all levels of frequency and not mostly at higher frequencies, although poorer men were less likely to be impaneled after a single appearance. This mix demonstrates that wealth mattered a little but clearly not enough to exclude other possible influences upon selection. Something else was at work in jury selection.

Some jurors served at more than one meeting of the county courts, but some trial jurors also heard more than one criminal case at any sitting of the court of quarter sessions. Table 2.9 describes the frequency of that event: how many cases juries in Chester County heard from 1682–1800. Hearing more than one case seems odd to modern observers and hearing eleven, the maximum in the historical record, seems bizarre. But putting the oddity of the times aside, the question is whether the practice was élitist and whether wealth or some other distinction secured more cases for some juries. First, the large majority of juries, 72 percent, decided only one or two cases; if an élite operated, it did not pervade the justice system. Turning to the question of a wealthy

TABLE 2.10. CORRELATIONS (PEARSON'S *r*) BETWEEN JURY ASSIGNMENTS AND
TOWNSHIP POPULATIONS AND BETWEEN JURY ASSIGNMENTS AND TOWNSHIP
LOCATIONS IN CHESTER COUNTY

	Jury assignments with township populations	Jury assignments with locations of township
1693	0.7648	
1718	0.3928	0.5124
1730	0.2445	0.6795
1740	− 0.0222	0.7600
1750	0.1485	0.6217
1765	0.2989	0.5916
1775	0.5545	0.4332
1785	0.3516	0.3468
1799	0.4851	n.a.[1]

[1]Not available due to the division of Chester County

élite hearing multiple cases, no significant relationship appears between the two. Only the bottom fifth of the taxpayer spectrum appeared sparse in jury panels which heard more than two cases.[66]

The data assembled here also permits testing the influence of residence and population on the choice of jurors. Before 1718 especially, jury seats (grand and trial) were equitably distributed among the taxpayer residents of Chester County. When the distribution of jurors by township, 1691–1695, is compared with the populations of the townships a strong correlation appears. (Table 2.10) The apportionment of seats was equitable. Only after 1718 did the correlation weaken markedly and continue to weaken, until by 1740 no relationship existed between the population of the township and its share of the jurors. Were the slighted townships after 1718 more remote from the county seat than the favored townships?[67] Until the creation of Delaware County in 1789, remoteness meant the distance from the county seat at Chester Borough, on the Delaware River. Quarter session courts were held there, a location that was convenient enough for Chester countians in 1693, but which was as much as forty miles distant from later citizens living near the border with Lancaster County.

As the numbers grew, the population balance shifted westward. Growth in the county was not especially an urban phenomenon. As Table 2.10 illustrates, distance from the county seat was correlated with a township's share of jurors. For this test, the county was divided into three equal concentric zones focused on Chester Borough. In 1693, almost all the population and jurors lived within the first or innermost zone, so the correlation between distances and share is perforce total. When these jurors were proportional to the populations of townships, the townships were also conveniently close to the county seat. As the county grew, after 1718, the inconvenience of travel and communication increased. The Scots-Irish initiated the first settlement on the Susquehanna River at Donegal, in northwestern Chester County. They complained that the county seat was three weeks away by foot and three days by horse.[68]

As the distance from the county seat grew, so too did the disproportionate influence of the east. Overlying these tendencies was the fact that for the rest of the eighteenth century, the east had more Quakers and wealth than the west. Growth and prosperity eventually created problems in Chester County, and this disparate influence and alleged élitism duplicated a graver sectional problem in the whole of Pennsylvania.

In terms of equity, the operation of criminal justice in Pennsylvania for almost forty years was commendable. Penn's plans to superimpose élite direction on the system in the manner prevailing in England failed in the thinly populated, immature society of the Delaware Valley. County sheriffs and justices, as at no other time in Pennsylvania, were average men and served with either the formal or informal consent of their fellows. Juries similarly were culled from nearly average men, and the jurors resembled others who presented themselves in court—justices, plaintiffs, and defendants. These equitable practices helped produce less discontent than would appear at any subsequent time in Pennsylvania: less violence, less loss of property, more mediation and honest reconciliation, fewer punitive sanctions, and more generosity.

Compared with populations past and present—nations, provinces, colonies, counties, frontiers, mining camps, and so on—Pennsylvania had done well. It was a new society without the mature institutions that in other times and places were credited with keeping the public peace— elders and statesmen, aristocracy and hierarchy, established church and religion, government and criminal justice system, widespread servitude and slavery—and yet it created social, if not political, peace. It was a decent society in an adolescent land. The causes of its decency and civility can be clearly discerned when it is compared with populations that "failed." At the top of the list of causes were its creators, William Penn and thousands of nonviolent people, Quakers and pietists. The Quakers were aggressive and even cunning in their politics. Still, they remained an ascetic people who valued modesty, self-control, and self-restraint; who resolved many of their personal differences economically and privately; who administered severe justice to those who persisted in coming to court, but who shunned sanguinary punishment; and who valued honesty and peace with Native Americans.

Civility in Pennsylvania also benefited from the colony's physical envi-

ronment. Unlike the Chesapeake, Pennsylvania had no staple crop like
tobacco to attract the kind of people who historically stimulated disorder—single, young men, comfortable with risk, bent on immediate gain,
and oblivious of the remote future of their land. Virginians brought race
slavery to the South, with its profoundly ambiguous effect on the public
peace. Slavery had an obvious immediate benefit, but eventually it
brought violence for both blacks and whites. The founders of Pennsylvania hardly understood in their first forty years how much credit for their
felicity belonged to the unintentional exclusivity of their Pennsylvania
experiment. In the following years, as exclusivity disappeared and Europeans arrived demanding equality under the law, everyone's civility was
tested as it had not been earlier.

Early on, PA did well. Juries
and sheriffs were plain non-elites.
Jurors were elites. Quakers
controlled sheriff system though
it was elected.

Most trials never came to be
because of a strong push
for mediation. If it did
come to trial, a conviction
was likely (82%).

Chapter 3
Problems of Pluralism

> Pennsylvania cherishes the rottenest, subtlest sinners who in other
> parts of the world would be scummed off and swept out.
>
> —*Henry Melchior Muhlenberg*

In the summer of 1717 the mayor of Philadelphia, Jonathan Dickinson, was surprised at the number of immigrants arriving at the city—more than he had ever seen before.[1] He guessed there were two thousand. There were not that many, but the novelty of it doubtless caused Dickinson to exaggerate.[2] Dickinson belonged to a small fraternity of merchants and public officials who shared his surprise—including Isaac Norris, James Logan, and Lieutenant-Governor Sir William Keith. They were mostly curious that summer; Logan wondered why English administrators had not forewarned them that these voyagers, some of whom were aliens who could not speak English, would be deposited on their doorstep.[3] In as little as several months, however, their curiosity shifted to anxiety. Dickinson did not know how Pennsylvania was going to deal with them. But what they saw that year was only the beginning of the problem they would have to deal with. In the next two years, the arrivals increased—they came in "swarms," one observer remarked.[4] However impressive the numbers were, they rose still higher in the 1720s. And more: with some dips and swells, the influx continued for the rest of the century. Long-time Pennsylvanians did not relish the advent of a quality essential to the genius of America: America's openness to people who voluntarily migrated here with reasonable hopes of being treated equitably. Histories and commentators who tout that genius, like the admiring philosophes of the eighteenth century, are far easier to come by than critics.

A purpose of this history of crime, however, is to point out the cost of immigration and diversity to American society in the case of its prototype, Pennsylvania. Not all who immigrated to Pennsylvania were content to live agreeably with their fellow immigrants and indigenous peoples, gratefully enjoying their enlarged liberty, and modestly limiting their covetousness. These people—they are accused criminals in this story—never comprised a majority of the new Americans in Pennsylvania. Criminals very rarely are the majority in any society. But they were numerous enough to become the despair of statesmen, their neighbors, indigenous peoples, and others.

After the surprising appearance of immigrants in 1717 and 1718, there was a lull in the traffic in the early 1720s, after which it surged, beginning in 1727: one thousand in 1727, three thousand in 1728, and as many as six thousand in 1729. These were only the arrivals from Ulster—the men and women whom Americans labeled the Scotch- or Scots-Irish. Almost two thousand German-speaking immigrants arrived in the same three years. All came to the Delaware Valley, the large majority to Philadelphia. In 1730 Philadelphia was a city of only 7,000 people and it is little wonder that its residents were variously shocked, dismayed, and unhappy. We are being "invaded," Logan sighed, by "shoals of foreigners come and set down." Immigration continued long after the tide of 1717–1730, but Philadelphia and Pennsylvania were larger, making those later newcomers less conspicuous and alarming. No later Pennsylvanians showed as much unhappiness over immigration as those in the years 1717–1730.[5]

With surprising speed the newcomers in the 1720s raised the level of discomfort by getting politically engaged. They would not have gotten engaged so quickly had conditions in the province not impelled them, the foremost condition being economic decline, and a second, protests by poorer residents and immigrants who were led by long-time Pennsylvania politicians. A transatlantic economic depression took hold of Pennsylvania by 1722. Veteran Pennsylvania politicians such as Governor Keith and the Speaker of the Assembly, David Lloyd, adjusted their politics to take advantage of the unwelcome economic conditions. Of the two, Keith was far more colorful and charismatic. For those who disapproved of his politics, he was transparently a demagogue and the Pennsylvanians he patronized, with their alleged sufferings, were his deluded minions. To these detractors, his politics and people looked criminal and violent.[6]

Before 1722, the Penns found that Keith had performed admirably as governor; Logan credited Keith with bringing "a perfect peace" to Pennsylvania. But in 1722 Keith bolted the proprietary interest and its clique of political blue-bloods like Logan and Norris. He affiliated himself with Lloyd, the compiler of the provincial criminal code and the man who, more than anyone, deserved to be called the regnant politician and jurist of the early eighteenth century. The two of them schemed to alleviate the hardships of depression. Some of their creations, like the provincial Loan Office, became ornaments of government in Pennsylvania. Of the two men, Keith was the liaison with the restless masses and immigrants. With astonishing verve for a man who was a baronet, he posed as comrade of the people, extolling their industry and virtue, contrasting them to the dishonest, wealthy drones— Logan and Norris—who railed at his gestures toward social justice. This nemesis of the provincial elite, Norris reflected, "found us a United Peaceable people & left us by his wicked politicks & Artifice Divided & in partys."[7]

Keith curried favor with immigrants in order to add them to his and Lloyd's political front. In the division of executive authority in Pennsylvania, the governors had no ability to distribute land (the proprietary secretary, James Logan, had that authority). Nevertheless, in 1723 Keith inveigled Germans from New York to settle at Tulpehocken Creek, cheek by jowl with Delaware Indians who had a clear right to the land. The next year, Keith pushed the Assembly to naturalize four hundred Germans, Tulpehocken settlers among them. Logan believed that Keith's motive was transparent. The Germans had been soldiers in Europe and now Keith was making them into his "Janizaries."[8]

The city was Keith's bailiwick (the countryside was Lloyd's), and here he mounted his new political devices—political clubs, parades and rallies, rousing satires and calumny in the press. The élite rued all of this and interpreted the outdoor exercises as civil disorders. But in 1726 Keith and his followers outdid these innocent exercises. In the fall election campaign for the Assembly, Keith's constituents paraded the streets in unprecedented numbers and wound up on election day by burning down those humiliating instruments of criminal justice, the pillory and stocks, as well as demolishing some butchers' stalls.[9] Keith fled the province in the autumn of 1728, but the people he had galvanized politically stayed their earlier course, and exceeded their previous deeds. This time they attacked more than symbols of authority, they attacked the authorities. When the assemblymen gathered in the city for the opening of the fall session, rioters assaulted them. The assemblymen quickly petitioned the governor to move the Assembly out of Philadelphia. On a different occasion, a mob threatened to level Logan's home, but stopped short after tearing off the shutters and throwing bricks through the windows.[10]

Nervous, xenophobic assemblymen tried to stanch the disorder. In the fall of 1728 they passed a bill to restrict immigration by levying a duty on foreigners, "Irish" (Scots-Irish) servants, and Negroes, and later, added felons to the list. To better control the violent people already in the province, they enacted a bill that duplicated for Pennsylvania the Riot Act of England.[11] Because all of Philadelphia's criminal dockets from these years have disappeared, the prosecution of crimes in the city can only be inferred.

Even before the riots in 1726 and 1728, Logan complained, "The Quaker Countrey, as this is called abroad, is become a scene of the vilest, most extravagant Licentiousness."[12] Logan was a Quaker (but not a very observant one); for twenty years, Isaac Norris was clerk of Philadelphia Yearly Meeting, the preeminent office in American Quakerism; and David Lloyd too was a leading Quaker.[13] Most troublemakers in the province were not Quakers, and certainly the shoals of newcomers were not. Quakers came to feel that Keith and his minions were jeopardizing their political command of Pennsylvania, its social customs and culture, and most ominously, the public peace and personal security. In 1730, in a long supplication to Lieutenant-Governor Patrick Gordon (Keith's successor), the Philadelphia Monthly Meeting of Friends recalled that they comprised most of the people who settled Pennsylvania, and they came in order to enjoy a quiet, moral, and religious life. With God's blessing "many had enjoyed [that life] for several years." "But now," they moaned, "for some time past . . . vice and immorality greatly abounds." The Philadelphia Yearly Meeting warned all Friends to be on guard due to the increase of people in the province, not only ones born here, "but others of divers nations, customs and manners, which of late years have flow'd in upon us, so that with grief we observe vice and immorality to increase."[14]

The alien behaviors the Friends referred to included singing, fiddling, and dancing, gambling, drinking and reveling, celebrating St. Patrick's Day, and shooting off guns on New Year's Eve. But there was more, and worse. Someone had burglarized Jonathan Dickinson's home in 1719 and taken £500. Isaac Norris remarked that Dickinson's misfortune was becoming common: "Many Robberies are committed Such as never heretofore known in the Country. The people who were never before under apprehensions of the kind are now afraid of traveling the Roads." Almost ten years later, Norris found nothing had improved: "In my memory we could Safely go to bed with our doors open but now Robberies, housebreakings, Rapes & other crimes are become Common."[15] The Society of Friends in 1732 published a coarse, candid broadside that for Quakers had no equal in that century: "Remarkable and grievous is the Depravity of Manners so observable in our Streets; sorrowful enough is it to see the great Encrease of Prophaneness and Lewdness . . . much owing to the Importation of great Numbers of the vicious and scandalous Refuse of other Countries."[16]

In the 1720s the messages and reflections penned by official Quakerism and eminent Quaker politicians conveyed images of tides surging, barriers breached, and circles pierced. Absent were expressions of the liberal idealism of William Penn and other founders of the colony. If their expressions of confidence in the goodness of human character, toleration, and openness were meant to have real-world applications, they had to be applied when people showed up who were not one's own religious, ethnic, and social kin. Musing about stopping people who spoke German or looked shabby and wild, as the generation of the 1720s did, was to give up most of the rationale for the establishment of Pennsylvania. Liberality was tested in the '20s, possibly for the first time in the history of the province, and it got short shrift.

As James Logan gradually understood that he could not bar immigrants from the province, he attempted to turn some benefits from immigration. His ability to affect the immigrants depended upon his occupying the office of secretary of the proprietary land office and running the office with little supervision from Hannah Penn. With great personal discretion, he could and did direct immigrants to settle in specified locations. He personally profited from manipulating settlement, and in some cases he committed a variety of "white-collar" crimes.[17] At the same time he attempted to solve some political and diplomatic problems. Two problems loomed above all others: the disputed border between Pennsylvania and Maryland, and diplomatic relations with local Indians. The first was inescapable; the second was a problem mostly if Pennsylvania's population grew and the newcomers expanded into lands held by the Indians. The influx of immigrants after 1717 made problems with the Indians more likely.

Prior to 1717, European settlement in Pennsylvania was confined to an arc that ran southwest from the Delaware River to the (disputed) border with Maryland near Octorora Creek and the Susquehanna River. South Mountain marked the northern boundary of the arc. All of what Pennsylvanians called the Great Valley lay beyond settlement—lands between South Mountain and the next ridge to the north, Blue Mountain. This area is the present-day Lehigh and Lebanon valleys, where Allentown, Bethlehem, Reading, and Lebanon later rose. Beginning in the 1720s, settlement filled that region, with troubling consequences that endured into the 1760s.

Logan's first machination unfolded within that arc. He ejected a band of Delaware Indians from what was, in effect, their reservation in the Brandywine River valley in Chester County. Next, he attempted to allay the worst of the immigrant problem, the Scots-Irish arrivals, by posting them to the western limit of Chester County, on the east side of the Susquehanna River. There, he hoped, they would be too remote to disturb the peace of settlers to their east. There, they would also support Pennsylvania's land claim against the Calverts. Logan depended upon these

Ulster people pugnaciously defending themselves and their settlements. They were, he remarked, those who "had so bravely defended Derry and Inniskillen." They were Logan's Janissaries. But there was a third benefit. While they, being "idle trash," could not pay for the lands in the west, they would hasten development and the appreciation of nearby lands, which Logan and the Penns would sell to better-equipped migrants.[18]

Other arrivals from Ulster situated themselves on the Susquehanna in the remote northwest corner of Chester County. The Scots-Irish character of this settlement became so distinct that the township was renamed Donegal, after the namesake in Ulster. Logan did not originate these advances and railed at their impertinence. Other unsanctioned moves beyond the arc of settlement included, of course, Keith's situating the Germans from New York at Tulpehocken Creek in the northwest reaches of the Schuylkill River valley. Finally, the wealthy Philadelphia merchant and land speculator William Allen illegally placed Scots-Irish immigrants on the upper Delaware River, in the Lehigh valley. These transections of the arc raised protests from the Calvert proprietors of Maryland and from the Delaware and Shawnee Indians. The Indians either were ejected from their land or were now living intolerably close to Europeans who obstructed the Indian economy and culture. Worse, intimacy generated crime and the problem of its resolution. By 1723, crimes were common enough that the Five Nations met with Pennsylvania authorities to reach some agreement on prosecuting the offenders. The arc of settlement was becoming, in the words of historian Francis Jennings, the arc of Indian discontent.[19]

After 1732, prosperity returned and relieved most of the apprehensions of the 1720s and any concern for the new direction Pennsylvania was taking. Politics lost its combative, divisive edge, and while immigration continued, the anxiety over immigrants seemed largely spent. The public made peace with immigrants, but with some more than others. Of the newcomers, the German-speakers were problems because they were not British subjects and many did not speak English. Governor Keith suggested in 1717 that Germans undergo registration and swear oaths of allegiance to the king and proprietors. That requirement became law a decade later.[20]

Especially because of their industry and civil behavior, in as little as a decade the Germans won the goodwill of many Pennsylvanians. John Penn, the eldest son of William and Hannah Penn, ordered that German immigration to Pennsylvania not be discouraged. That was most clear in the case of the Mennonites and Amish—"Industrious and Laborius people." Governor Patrick Gordon found Germans to be "a very industrious People." Politically, "they behave themselves very respectfully to

the Government and pay their Taxes." They clamored for naturalization. They were civil, "very sober and honest." Research into provincial
German life confirms that they did indeed create a stable community
whose members gave comparatively little trouble to each other or to outsiders.[21]

The reputation of the Scots-Irish did not improve apace with the Germans'. Before they even arrived, they had a reputation that put them
beneath the Germans in public esteem. Anglo-Pennsylvanians shared a
historic English misgiving about the Scots and their kinsmen in Ulster.
The Ulster arrivals in Pennsylvania were originally from north Britain
and southern Scotland, border people who had violated the peace of
England and Scotland for centuries. Until the British repression of the
Jacobite rebellion of 1745, the border between England and Scotland
had not known fifty consecutive years of peace in more than six hundred. Where civil society hardly existed for centuries, border families
and clans defined who were friends and enemies, what passed for law
and justice, and who persisted there and who failed. Violence infected
not just relations among kings, clans, families, and classes, and not just
differences over land and livestock; it inserted itself into interpersonal
relations. Men assaulted each other without reference to one another's
larger affiliations and sometimes in everyday encounters of no discernable consequence. From the borders they had been transplanted to the
north of Ireland in the sixteenth century to further the English subjuga-
tion of Catholic Ireland. Their bellicosity, together with their unbreak-
able bond to Presbyterian Protestantism, fitted them for such a role in
Ireland. By putting them in this contested area, Ulster, England cultivated their predisposition to be violent.[22]

Then in the eighteenth century they migrated from Ulster to
America, mostly to Pennsylvania as their first destination. In Pennsylvania, James Logan found them serviceable for the same reasons and purposes that the English had more than a hundred years earlier. Thus,
writes historian David Hackett Fischer, many of the Scots-Irish who came
to America included "a double-distilled selection of some of the most
disorderly inhabitants of a deeply disturbed land."[23]

Logan and Englishmen long before him had obtusely relocated the
Scots-Irish for the expedient benefits they expected from such aggressive people. Logan and other responsible Pennsylvanians hardly gave a
thought to the difficulty, and the irony, of inserting the Scots-Irish
among a people who practiced nonviolence. (The inconsistency did not
attract comment until it appeared in the public press during King
George's War.) An incident in 1734 encapsulated better than probably
any other the issue of conflicting cultures. Representing the established,
nonviolent people was Quaker John Churchman; the Scots-Irish were

represented by Alexander Ewing, Jr. Churchman was one of the half-dozen or so most significant persons within the Society of Friends in the eighteenth century. He initiated a transformation of the Society that began in the 1750s and produced an insistently ethical, pacifist, philanthropic, and prophetic church.[24] He was respectable and respected. A surveyor, in 1750 he ranked in the 98th percentile in taxable wealth in Chester County. From the 1730s into the 50s, he was about as dutiful and productive a public servant at the Penn family could ever wish for, and they knew it. In performing their office, surveyors, like constables and sheriffs, provoked people who did not want the government or some other land claimant interfering with them and their property claims.

Alexander Ewing was a Scots-Irishman, born in County Donegal, Ulster, who had migrated to Pennsylvania only in 1727. Churchman was surveying John Christy's land near Nottingham in 1734 when Alexander Ewing, Jr., stopped him. Ewing told Churchman and his helpers that he would be the death of any man who proceeded with the survey. He pulled out a gun and threatened to shoot Churchman "through." John Barrett, an assistant to Churchman, charged Ewing and wrested the gun from him, but not before the gun discharged.[25] Churchman was not harmed, and Barrett apparently escaped unharmed too. Word of the confrontation doubtless reached Logan and others in the Provincial Council and informed their philippics against the Scots-Irish. The problem of these two cultures clashing and threatening public peace in the province reached imperial proportions in the 1750s and beyond.

By the 1730s, the Scots-Irish had pretty well exhausted any respect they had received from older Pennsylvanians. Detestation of the "Irish" now filled the air. Isaac Norris called them "ye very Scum of mankind." To Logan they were "Idle trash." What is to become of us, Logan railed, "with those additions [of more Scots-Irish] to ye Poyson in our Bowels"? It shamed Logan to acknowledge that he came from the same ethnic stock. Because of his position on the Provincial Council, "numerous and heavy complaints [were] brought to me," said Logan, "of their Violence and Injustice to each other, such as this Province till their arrival, was very much stranger to"; "they will quarrel amongst themselves and commit such outrages as no force against them will be sufficient to quell or appease."[26] Logan's point needs reinforcement; the Scots-Irish behaved aggressively not just toward alien enemies—Catholics in northern Ireland, Marylanders, and Indians—but also toward each other. Their crime disturbed not just the peace of the borders and the putative aliens across the border, but the everyday peace among their own people and non-Ulster Pennsylvanians who settled among them.

Other than homicides, much of the violence and crime in the west

TABLE 3.1. SCOTS-IRISH SHARE OF INDICTED CRIMES, CHESTER COUNTY, 1681–1799

	All indicted crimes	Scots-Irish indicted crimes	Scots-Irish percent of all crimes	Scots-Irish percent of tax list population (tax list year)
1680s	132	28	21.2	
1690s	243	64	26.3	15.7 (1693)
1700s	150	40	26.7	
1710s	180	42	23.3	19.4 (1718)
1720s	260	108	41.5	
1730s	329	162	49.2	27.3 (1730)
1740s	391	203	51.9	34.2 (1740)
1750s	471	239	50.7	35.3 (1750)
1760s	566	247	43.6	35.8 (1765)
1770s	611	281	46.0	33.5 (1775)
1780s	840	341	40.6	30.7 (1785)
1790s	950	426	44.8	32.9 (1799)

that officials in Philadelphia or Chester heard about does not appear in the records of the criminal courts. For one reason, in the 1720s and 30s, the courts hardly operated in remote Donegal Township. Some of the potentially criminal conduct showed up in the sessions of the Presbyterian Church, which tried to serve in the place of absent county government. In a quite different vein, many Scots-Irish did not consider their turbulent behavior criminal. A person who thought he was a crime victim should go to a justice or sheriff and complain about his victimizer. In Scots-Irish culture, a man with self-esteem, conscious of his public reputation or "honor," would not go to the law but rather personally avenge himself upon his detractor. Finally, violent encounters in this culture were often treated as innocent and ordinary, so that no one, either participants or witnesses, would think that any party to an assault was blameworthy. That attitude emerged in cases of assault and homicide that did get into court. There, juries tended to acquit the indicted men, the jurors working upon the presumption that aggression was natural and conflict was excusable upon almost any pretext, especially when some man's honor had been slighted.[27]

Despite the likely existence of a "dark figure" of unrecorded crime in cultures of "honor," like the Scots-Irish, recorded crime in Pennsylvania does not significantly mislead the student who tabulates it. In fact, crime tracks immigration as well as denunciations of immigrants: all three roughly grew apace and confirm each other. Table 3.1 illustrates that duplication. The table depicts the volume of crime in Chester County and the indictments of the most-often suspected criminals, the Scots-Irish.[28] In the signal year of 1718, when the disturbing numbers of immigrants began arriving, the Scots-Irish percent of all crime was only 3.7 percent greater than the percent of Scots-Irish taxpayers. By 1730, however, the difference had grown to 21.6 percent for that year and 22.3 for the 1730s.

Other tokens of the difference that Scots-Irish and other immigrants made in the years after 1717 appear in the record of homicides and assaults. There were only seven cases of homicide in Pennsylvania from 1682 through 1709, but ten the next decade and eighteen the next. (Table 2.1). The more revealing homicide rate per 100,000 population rose, too, to 4.5 in the 1720s. More interesting historically than these decadic rates are the rates in the years when Pennsylvanians complained of crime and immigrants. Those years, as we know, began in 1717–1718 and lasted until a wave of immigration in the late 1720s ebbed and economic prosperity returned in the early 1730s. Partly because of these changes, politics lost its threatening edge for the public men who railed at the out-of-doors activism in the 1720s. The focus period, therefore, is 1718–1732; the provincial rate in those years soared—and that understates the increase in some locations. The rate more than tripled from 1682–1717 to 1718–1732 (Table 2.2). Philadelphia trailed the provincial and Chester rate. However, its rate too increased, since there was only one homicide prosecution in the city before 1718.

In Chester County between the two periods, the homicide rate skyrocketed, from 0.9 to 9.0, producing the worst experience with homicide in the county's history. It was in Chester that most of the immigrants of the era were planted, including especially the Scots-Irish. Chester County is extraordinary for yet another reason: it included a population of pacifist, nonviolent people, Quakers and German pietists, which gave Chester one of the highest concentrations of nonviolent people in America in any age. Given so many pacifists, the astonishingly high homicide rate after 1717 did not occur because pacifists lost their religious scruple and began killing each other, but rather because new people without pacifist scruples did more of the killing.

In 1729, Chester County was reduced by the creation of Lancaster County from its western and northwestern regions. The effect of the division on the population was to remove from Chester a large number of recent arrivals to Pennsylvania, including the Scots-Irish in Donegal Township.[29] Pacifist Quakers were left behind, concentrated in the eastern townships of Chester (which in 1789 became Delaware County). Homicide data reflect the changes in political geography and population. The rate for Chester dropped from 9.0 in 1718–1732 to 2.2 in 1733–1754, after Lancaster was separated in 1729. The rate dropped in the province as a whole at the same time, but not to one-quarter its earlier rate, as happened in Chester.

Assault rates tell a similar story of change and immigration. Chester registered assault rates in 1728 and 1729 of 101 and 121 per 100,000. In 1730, the first year after Lancaster was separated, the Chester rate dropped to 102, and in the next four years to 86, 90, 84, and 75. This pattern reappeared over the decades elsewhere in Pennsylvania. Dauphin County was separated from Lancaster in 1785. About half of Dauphin was Paxton Township, which encompassed about 260 square miles. Paxton was home to the most infamous, aggressive Scots-Irish population of Pennsylvania, a reputation due especially to the Paxton massacres and march of 1763–1764.[30] Lancaster's assault rate in 1783, before the separation, was 57.0; after the separation, in 1786, it was 40.5. Meanwhile, the rate in new Dauphin County was 143.8 in the first year of its existence, and 98.2 in 1785–1789. Yet again: in 1789, Mifflin County was set off from Cumberland. Mifflin very likely had the highest concentration of Scots-Irish of any Pennsylvania county.[31] Its assault rates in 1794 and 1795 were 511.0 and 289.7 respectively. In 1786, three years before losing Mifflin, the parent Cumberland County had a rate of 144.2 in 1786, but only 87.2 for 1790–1795, after Mifflin was set off.[32]

Without comparing crime data from different times and places, crime data—like all quantitative data—lacks significance. Thus far Pennsylvania has been compared only with itself in the seventeenth and eighteenth centuries, but it deserves to be compared with England at the same time and with the United States after 1800. These additional comparisons permit observers to enlarge their impressions of how Pennsylvanians behaved.

For England in the seventeenth and eighteenth centuries, historian J. M. Beattie calculated homicide rates, first for a rural area, Sussex. The rates for Sussex never came close to those of rural Chester County, Pennsylvania. The highest rate in eighteenth-century Sussex only four times out of ten exceeded *lowest* rates in Chester for the same century (Table 2.2). Only three out of ten times did it surpass the lowest rate for all of Pennsylvania in the same century. Turning to urban rates, Beattie provides data from part of London. London is particularly helpful for comparisons, because it had an unsavory reputation for crime and licentiousness that persisted through the eighteenth century and later. It therefore comes as a surprise then that London did not outdo Pennsylvania. Beattie's homicide statistics for London (urban Surrey) show that Pennsylvania's 1720s homicide rate exceeded London's rates for the whole eighteenth century. Comparing cities shows Philadelphia in the 1720s as worse than London from 1720 through 1802.[33]

It helps also to compare the same location at different periods. Histo-

rian Roger Lane's seminal study of homicide in nineteenth-century Philadelphia explained that the city was at its most violent between 1839 and
1880; and yet the city in the 1720s had a homicide rate that equaled the
rates for about half that 1839–1880 period.[34] Probably the most evocative
comparison juxtaposes contemporary American homicide rates with
those in early Pennsylvania, since we experience the contemporary rates
and bemoan them. In the United States in the 1970s the homicide rate
reached the highest since it began being measured, 10 per 100,000. As
noted above, Chester County in the 1720s reached 9.0.

From the provincial statistics and comparisons, the anxieties and complaints that Pennsylvanians voiced after 1717 gain credibility. They cannot be dismissed as the carping of dyspeptic, wealthy officeholders like
Dickinson, Logan, and Norris. Nor are they easily belittled because of
another foible of crime reporting. That is, crime data can fluctuate not
only because people commit more crimes or fewer crimes, but also
because law enforcers prosecute crimes zealously, or do not. To state the
case simply, crime waves are sometimes law-enforcement waves. But the
likelihood that the data on homicide for 1717–1732 represent an
enforcement wave propelled by a few fretful men like Logan is very
small. Murder and manslaughter do not multiply because law enforcers
look for them; whether the government is studiously looking for them,
or whether it tries to ignore them, they are acknowledged more than
any other kinds of crime. And too, Pennsylvania had no professional,
full-time law enforcers to look for crime. Enforcement waves belong to
times when there are substantial criminal justice bureaucracies; early
Pennsylvania had nothing remotely like these.

The violence was real, and the complaints were not someone's inven-
tions. Another consideration of crime reporting and data is more sober-
ing: homicide rates derived from criminal justice data underestimate the
frequency of homicides, because a justice-system record arises when a
person is accused. When the perpetrator is unknown the records of the
courts do not acknowledge that a person has been killed. Other records
do, like coroners' reports, newspaper reports, or private correspondence. From such supplementary sources, we know that the homicide
rates reported here were the minimal rates—for the period after 1718,
but before as well. Chapter 4 discusses the unprosecuted homicides,
which appeared more often in Pennsylvania as time passed.

As Chapter 2 explained, the 1718 "Act for the advancement of justice
and the more certain administration thereof" ushered in a new era of
criminal sanctions in the Quaker colony. The sanctions were not created
to deal with a crime wave. The new code slightly preceded the surge in
crime. The signal departure from past practice in Pennsylvania was
enforcement, not enactment: after 1718 the justice system embraced the

newly available death penalty as fervently as previous codes and jurists had avoided it. The ink had hardly dried on the 1718 act when three individuals, two males and a female, were convicted of capital crimes and sentenced to die. Speaker of the House Lloyd personally showed how far he was moving away from his earlier liberality. In 1728, as chief justice of the province, he had urged that a convicted murderer be sentenced leniently. In 1730 he urged that a burglar be executed. Execution, he felt, would help deter crime, and the province badly needed deterrence.[35] By 1730 Pennsylvania courts had prescribed the death penalty for 21 individuals. (Table 3.2) Twenty persons were sentenced to die between 1730 and 1739, another 23 between 1750 and 1759. The next three decades saw many more people receiving sentences of death: 34 in the 1760s, 88 in the 1770s, and 129 in the 1780s. Even in view of Pennsylvania's remarkable population growth, these were extraordinary increases. Pennsylvania sentenced men and women to die with a speed that belies Pennsylvanians' alleged abhorrence of England's "bloody code" and their allegedly unwilling submission to England's imposition of the code upon them.

In the years from 1682 through 1719, Pennsylvania's rate of execution was 0.6 per 100,000 population. In the next decade, however, it more than doubled, to 1.4. That rate was not exceeded until the 1770s. The year 1750 was the first time Pennsylvania witnessed four executions in a twelve-month period. The years 1762 and 1764 each saw five persons hanged. Six died in 1768, seven in 1770, ten in 1774. In most instances the crimes attached to these capital sanctions were murder and burglary, with only a scattering of offenses such as rape, buggery, arson, counterfeiting, highway robbery, and infanticide.

Women, blacks, and youngsters did not escape capital sentences, although in all cases their numbers remained relatively low. Thirty-six women received sentences of death between 1718 and 1786. In the colony's first thirty-eight years a single female was sentenced to die and executed. In the twenty years immediately following the passage of the 1718 penal code nine women were sentenced to be hanged, and in three cases the sentence was carried out. No blacks died at the hands of the hangman prior to 1718. Twenty-one were convicted of capital crimes after that date. The death penalty was also given to youngsters convicted of capital crimes. At least a half dozen of those sentenced to be hanged in the colony after 1718 were eighteen years old, most of them women found culpable of infanticide. William Battin was seventeen when he was hanged for arson and murder in 1722, the youngest Pennsylvanian to die at the hands of an executioner. While deliberately torching his master's home, he inadvertently burned to death the man's three small children. Convicted of arson and "diverse horrid complicated crimes" in

TABLE 3.2. EXECUTION WARRANTS AND PARDONS IN PENNSYLVANIA

Year[1]	Death warrants	Pardons/reprieves
1688	1	
1693	1	
1707	2	2
1718	3	1
1682–1719	**7**	**3**
1720	3	2
1722	3	2
1724	2	1
1728	3	
1729	3	3
1720s	**14**	**8**
1730	1	1
1732	5	5
1735	2	2
1736	2	
1737	8	5
1739	2	2
1730s	**20**	**15**
1741	1	
1745	1	
1747	2	
1748	4	4
1749	2	
1740s	**10**	**4**
1750	6	2
1752	6	2
1753	3	1
1757	1	1
1758	3	2
1759	4	1
1750s	**23**	**9**
1760	2	
1762	5	
1764	6	1
1765	5	1
1766	3	1
1767	2	1
1768	9	3
1769	2	1
1760s	**34**	**8**
1770	8	2
1771	6	5
1772	13	10
1773	5	4
1774	14	4
1775	5	2
1776	1	1
1777	2	
1778	19	7
1779	15	2

TABLE 3.2. (CONTINUED)

Year[1]	Death warrants	Pardons/reprieves
1770s	**88**	**37**
1780	20	5
1781	21	12
1782	7	3
1783	18	8
1784	19	6
1785	12	7
1786	9	5
1787	7	5
1788	9	3
1789	7	
1780s	**129**	**54**
1790	1	
1791	1	1
1792	3	1
1793	1	
1794	2	1
1795	5	2
1796	1	1
1798	3	
1799	1	
1790s	**18**	**6**
1800	4	1
1682–1800	**347**	**145**

[1]Exact dates of pardons and reprieves are not always available. Some petitions for pardons were submitted late in one year and approved in another. Several reprieves were granted two or more years after the conviction. They are tabulated here as accurately as possible according to when granted by the state.

November 1721, he was sentenced to be executed "in a most public place," "hung in irons," then left on the scaffold "subject to the weather and the depredations of scavengers and cruel passersby as a warning to those who would emulate his crimes."[36]

When felons convicted of capital crimes escaped execution after 1718 they generally did so at the expense of banishment. The popularity of banishment after 1718 can probably be attributed to England's Transportation Act of that same year, whereby English felons were exiled to the colonies. Pennsylvania imitated the mother country. The Pennsylvania Council awarded the pregnant Ann Mitchell a pardon after her conviction of burglary in 1725 on the stipulation that she and her husband "depart the colony." Cornelius O'Brien and Edward Fitzgerald, facing death for burglary in 1735, were also awarded a pardon in exchange for their agreement to leave Pennsylvania and "never return." Richard

Heard, William Beatson, and John Wood, all convicted of burglary, escaped the hangman two years later when they agreed to leave Pennsylvania forever.[37]

Others sentenced to die enjoyed straightforward, simple pardons. Fifteen years after William Battin's execution, seventeen-year-old Isaac Bradford faced the hangman in Philadelphia. Sentenced to die with three others in oyer and terminer proceedings in June 1737, Bradford would have been the first person executed in the colony for robbery. But Bradford's luck held. The Council ordered that "on account of his youth" he be pardoned "under the gallows," a gesture that Councilors believed would "leave a more lasting impression on him."[38] Judges and juries after 1718 petitioned the Council for numerous pardons. Of the seventeen persons sentenced to be hanged between 1718 and 1729, eight (47 percent) were executed. (Table 3.2) Of the twenty assigned to die between 1730 and 1739, only five (25 percent) died at the hands of the executioner. Fourteen (60 percent) of the twenty-three persons sentenced to die in the 1750s, twenty-six (76.5 percent) of the thirty-four in the 1760s, fifty-one (57.9 percent) of the eighty-eight in the 1770s, and seventy-five (58.1 percent) of the 129 in the 1780s actually were executed. Of the thirty-six women given the death penalty between 1718 and 1786, seventeen (47.2 percent) had their sentences carried out. Only ten (47.6 percent) of the twenty-one blacks assigned death were actually hanged. The practice of pardoning in Pennsylvania is arguably merciful compared with executing all the convicted, but when compared with pardons in other places and times, Pennsylvania appears hardly better and sometimes worse. In one large jurisdiction in England, 1660–1800, 40.5 percent of those sentenced to die were executed. In Pennsylvania, 1682–1800, 58.2 percent were executed. In the United States, executions have declined consistently since the colonial period and capital punishment has been in disrepute more often than not.[39]

Other criminal sanctions changed, although less dramatically. For two decades after 1682, any corporal punishment for noncapital crimes had remained uncommon, averaging 8.3 percent or less of sentences. Slightly before the criminal code was rewritten in 1718, however, practice changed and anticipated the new direction of 1718. (Table 3.3) The rate of whippings quadrupled between the 1690s and 1700s. Then the 1718 code mandated corporal sanctions for more offenses, and permitted fewer instances where fines could be substituted for whippings. Charles Calahan was given thirty-five lashes for his sexual assault on a ten-year-old Philadelphia girl in January 1729/30. Martha Cash suffered forty lashes for stealing six yards of kersey in 1734. Mary Isaac received twenty-one lashes for picking a pocket in the same year. An unnamed Negro discovered as a pickpocket in June 1743 and sentenced to be pub-

Table 3.3. Selected Criminal Sentences in Chester County, 1682–1800

Guilty outcomes	Fines		Whippings		Jail		Pillory		Wear sign	
N	n	(%)	n	(%)	n	(%)	n	(%)	n	(%)
1680s 108	41	(38.0)	9	(8.3)	4	(3.7)			1	(0.9)
1690s 133	40	(30.1)	8	(6.0)					1	(0.8)
1700s 68	27	(39.7)	17	(25.0)					10	(14.7)
1710s 58	30	(51.7)	26	(44.8)	1	(1.7)	1	(1.7)	6	(10.3)
1720s 93	55	(59.1)	33	(35.5)			2	(2.2)		
1730s 148	91	(61.5)	38	(25.7)						
1740s 193	141	(73.1)	54	(28.0)	1	(0.5)	2	(1.0)		
1750s 251	189	(75.3)	51	(20.3)			4	(1.6)	1	(0.4)
1760s 305	244	(80.0)	69	(22.6)	2	(0.7)	6	(2.0)		
1770s 218	162	(74.3)	66	(30.3)	10	(4.6)	13	(6.0)		
1780s 311	209	(67.2)	43	(13.8)	64	(20.6)	8	(2.6)		
1790s 287	196	(68.3)			104	(36.2)				
Totals 2173	1425	(65.5)	414	(19.1)	186	(8.6)	36	(1.7)	19	(0.3)

licly whipped, "very heroically cut his own throat" rather than accept the lashes assigned him.[40] And on and on the whippings came.

More severe and varied examples of corporal punishment emerged after 1718. All were familiar to observers of English courts but had been used sparingly or not at all in Pennsylvania prior to 1718. One such variation was the cropping of ears. Two convicted male felons in 1726 had their ears cropped in addition to their having to stand in the Philadelphia pillory for several hours. Horse thieves routinely lost their ears by the 1770s.[41] Branding, too, became a more popular judicial penalty. In the case where a defendant was granted benefit of clergy after being found guilty of a capital crime, the branding was viewed as the lesser of two evils, but it was a painful sanction nonetheless. John Murray, convicted of manslaughter as a result of a 1725 fight he had with Thomas Williams in which Williams died, had an M burned upon his thumb. Nicholas Hentwerk, a Palatine, experienced the same fate in Bucks County following his fatal fight with the Irishman Patrick McQuin in April 1730.[42]

Faced with a rash of thefts, the Assembly revised the colony's larceny statute in 1722 in a way that showed they had been thinking about deterrence and the limitations of capital punishment. It recognized that juries hesitated to take a person's life for pilfering—as the law prescribed. Instead, juries acquitted the accused, foiling the deterrence. To get more convictions, the Assembly removed larceny from the list of capital crimes and prescribed flogging and branding instead. Next, it identified a crime of petty larceny—the theft of goods valued below five shillings. Individual justices of the peace could hear such cases and punish the convicted with a fine. Tacitly, the act opened a way to underestimate the values of stolen goods in order to ensure milder punishment for worthy and contrite defendants.

The real growth of crime and the perception of its growth brought a familiar reaction, which was to increase the severity and variety of punishments. In doing so, Pennsylvanians acted like people before and after them. They did not explain the reasons for their confidence in severity. But despite their silence, they believed in deterrence and retributive justice. They were alarmed and impatient.

Quakers became a minority in Pennsylvania at least seven years before the rise of immigration in 1717 alarmed most Pennsylvanians. As Chapter 2 explained, 1710 marked the end of the public effort to enforce victimless, nonsexual morals laws. Even before Quakers and other residents began to fret out loud about crime in the streets, they had quietly closed down the effort to make Pennsylvania a model of personal morality and propriety. They shifted from sectarian idealism to resignation to

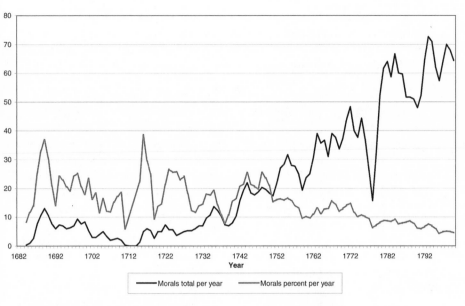

Figure 3.1. Three-year moving averages of morals accusations and morals percent of all accusations in Pennsylvania, 1682–1800.

living with some disagreeable behavior of other people. Once they dis-covered in the 1720s a need for more severe enforcement of laws against violence and property crimes, they put the sectarian past yet further behind them. When merely preserving public order taxed the capacity of constables, sheriffs, and courts, enforcement of morals laws became an insupportable burden on magistrates and the public. While they pined for the past, they could not restore it. Table 2.4 and Figure 3.1 illustrate the result: the proportion of all crime represented by morals crimes declined, although irregularly, after the 1720s and especially after 1745.

The resources of the criminal justice system devoted to morals declined. This change occurred with little contemporary comment. Amid the din of expressed concerns about other, more alarming crimes, little was said about morals crimes. Ironically, when Quakers became resigned to policing personal behavior less and tolerating others' offen-sive behavior more, they moved the original provincial experiment toward a more modern, liberal future—away from the constraining supervision they practiced in the past. Greater freedom lay at the heart of both the declining expectations of others' personal morals and the public's growing infringements upon persons and property.

At first glance, the data on morals prosecutions seem to temper the conclusion that interest and effort in maintaining morality declined after 1710. In Figure 3.1 the long-term increase in prosecutions of immorality in Pennsylvania seems to argue that interest increased while deviance too increased. (Of course, as the figure indicates, the population grew too, so that the rate of growth was not as striking as the increased frequency.) But unless these numbers are examined more closely, they can mislead. Table 2.4 breaks down the growing morals numbers into their component crimes and demonstrates that the rise in prosecutions was almost entirely sexual crimes—fornication, bastardy, and adultery. After 1710, almost all other varieties of morals crimes disappeared from the courts, but sexual crimes grew. The problem posed by the prosecution of sexual crimes is its ambiguous character as a token of moral zeal. It may or may not be a token of zeal.

For the sake of comparison with Pennsylvania, the best American example of protracted zeal is New England. New England, and New Haven, Connecticut, especially, prosecuted sexual deviance in ways that disclosed religious and moral reasons for the prosecutions. First, New England Puritans extensively explained their religious reasons for energetic law enforcement.[43] They believed that when they erected their communities, they had covenanted with God and that the covenant warranted the prosecution of deviance. Within the covenant, there were no victimless crimes, sexual or otherwise. Crime or deviance offended God. In covenanted communities, crime that went unpunished either intentionally or by neglect might bring down God's chastisement on everyone within the covenant—in this case, the chaste as well as the fornicators.

Not surprisingly, from this conception of themselves New Englanders' interest in enforcing morals exceeded and outlived such interest elsewhere in America. Earliest Massachusetts (1630–1644) was little troubled by sexual crime, but by 1671–1675, prosecutions of illicit sex comprised 15.9 percent of the total in Suffolk County, for example. Then, after almost a century, prosecutions of sexual crimes climbed in number and in their share of all crime. In seven Massachusetts counties between 1760 and 1774, prosecution of sexual crimes comprised 38 percent of the total. Over 95 percent of these were cases of bastardy. But historian William Nelson remarks that the magistrates were prosecuting fornication per se, because it offended God. Even when the guilty mother married and no innocent party was burdened with childrearing expenses, the government still prosecuted. In New Haven, Connecticut, prosecutions of married couples for fornication (and premarital conception) flourished. From 1670 through 1739 prosecutions mounted in volume. These bore witness to the longevity of New Englanders' interest in maintaining moral standards.[44] Not until the 1740s did New England begin to overlook premarital conceptions.[45] These New Haven prosecutions best typify prosecution of crimes that nonreligious people view as victimless crimes. Since the offspring of sin were born into supportive families—the parents had married—there was little or no tangible harm. From a secular point of view, no one was victimized. Even so, the perpetrators were prosecuted because they had sinned.

While Pennsylvanians, especially Quakers, shared a sense of purpose and destiny about their province, they did not subscribe to any Puritan covenant with its shared responsibility and blame for deviant behavior. Crimes were the acts of individuals, and the blame was individual too. Liberalism or individualism overbore personal identification with some shared destiny. Unlike New Haven, Pennsylvania, even in its most moralistic first thirty years, never prosecuted married couples for their premarital fornication and conception. In this respect, Pennsylvania never made an equivalent "collective commitment to a God-fearing society."[46] The persistent prosecution of sexual immorality in Pennsylvania, like New England, offers evidence of Pennsylvania's possible protracted commitment to public morality. However, these prosecutions need further examination because they are ambiguous in ways that New Haven's were not.

The increased fornication cases in Pennsylvania after the 1720s (like the earlier ones too) were detected because of pregnancy of the women accused. That was ipso facto true in cases of bastardy. Very few of the fornication prosecutions were sexual liaisons without pregnancy—and those very few cannot be identified, since the records did not detail how the offenders were apprehended. Sexual relations between unmarried men and women were so clandestine that law enforcers, even in New England or among Quakers in Pennsylvania, where privacy was minimal, did not apprehend the offenders without the evidence of pregnancy. Without pregnancy, men and women who engaged in sex easily escaped prosecution. With pregnancy, the pregnant woman was the gateway to a prosecution. Whether a male correspondent was included in the prosecution depended upon other characteristics of the times and the justice system.

But since pregnancy was almost always the case in prosecutions, when the courts in Pennsylvania recorded the offense they used different notations, either fornication or fornication *and* bastardy.[47] Why? If the couple were willing to marry, Pennsylvania did not prosecute at all. If there was a prosecution, it was because there was a bastard child and no marriage. The answer to the difference in notation is probably that cases denominated fornication did not become prosecutions for bastardy because, off the laconic docket record, child support (without marriage) from the father followed the pregnancy and birth. In these cases the courts or the interested public learned who were the male respondents and saw that the cases were resolved out of court. The women, however, were prosecuted anyway, and the perseverance of the government in their cases revealed the surviving interest in deterring illicit sex and conception—but in a very gender-biased way. Either the magistrates did not want to prosecute the male correspondents in the conceptions, or they felt uneasy about prosecuting them with less evidence than they had in the case of the pregnant women. (In the period 1690–1740 in New England, men began to object to their prosecutors' weak evidence against them.[48])

Not enough zeal for morality survived in Pennsylvania to cause the magistrates to forge ahead and prosecute the men for morality's sake despite problematic evidence against them—the way New Englanders did in public courts and Quakers did in the Society of Friends. The standards of evidence and customary practices in Pennsylvania disclose that Pennsylvanians had adopted more cosmopolitan and English ways. That adoption, with its concomitant prejudice to unmarried mothers, constituted one significant change that began in the 1720s.

When private resolution of the problems attending pregnancy failed, the province resorted to prosecuting the parents for bastardy (or, as the dockets say, fornication and bastardy). Given that women in early America were economically dependent, the courts were mostly interested in the unwed fathers, since they could be effective providers, willingly or not.[49] If a father could not be found, or, when found, persuaded to provide, the public (the township overseers of the poor) would have to take his place and support the child. Sometimes the townships had to support both child and mother. Because of its economic burden on the township and the frequency of bastardy, when an accused father refused to settle out of court, he would be prosecuted for bastardy. Prosecuting the fathers became a preoccupation of the justice system.[50] In the large view, when the volume of cases denominated only fornication falls or rises the numbers disclose (in an approximate way) the willingness or unwillingness of men to be responsible for paternity without being prosecuted for bastardy. When the volume of cases denominated bastardy rises or falls we are tracing the complement, unwillingness or willingness.[51]

In sum, when cases of fornication grew in Pennsylvania respect for older mores declined. Best if there were no premarital sex and conceptions at all. Almost as good would be a postconception marriage and a new family. Much worse was no marriage and the threat of prosecuting the father in order to get him to provide for the illegitimate child. (And the prosecution of the mother to deter more of this crime.) Worst was a full-blown prosecution of the callous father and the imposition of child support. (And the prosecution of the mother for bastardy, again, as a deterrent.) This last is the case designated as bastardy in the court records. In each of these cases, the moral state of the perpetrators was progressively less moral and respectful.

The motives of the prosecutors, however, were less clear and more complex. The public had a pecuniary interest in avoiding the support of children and the taxes it required; by itself, that was selfish. The community may also have had a moral and sentimental reason for prosecuting the irresponsible father, and that was altruistic. The first left plenty of historical evidence of itself; the latter left comparatively little. When bastardy increased, the accused fathers surely were disclosing greater apathy in the population. The prosecutors may have been disclosing continued altruism, or they may have been showing selfishness, or some combination of both.

Returning to the historical record, after 1730 and through the 1760s bastardy unmistakably increased from decade to decade (Figure 3.1 and Table 2.4). This increase betrays male Pennsylvanians' increased carelessness both toward persons they knew intimately and toward the communities in which they lived. Prosecutions of women for bastardy increased too, even though they could not provide the economic support of their children and relieve the public of that burden. The reason for prosecuting them was deterrence: other single women were expected to take notice of the unhappy fate of these mothers and avoid fornication (or at least pregnancy). Of course, the number of simple fornication cases also rose after 1730, especially those with women defendants; but they were outnumbered by the cases of bastardy. The cases of male defendants for fornication do not constitute *positive* signs of care and sympathy for their partners, but rather, signs of only less carelessness than bastardy exhibits. As a whole, the change after 1730 amounts to a worsening social situation, for children, women, families, taxpayers, overworked courts, community, and altruism.

In the period after 1718 the sentences imposed on sexual error shifted in a way that discloses that the public and courts were less offended by sexual error—as long as it did not cost the public treasury. Data on sentencing in Chester County includes 287 convictions for fornication and bastardy. Fining the convicted men and women was far and away the most common sentence (in 76.3 percent of the convictions), but guilty men and women were whipped in 15.3 percent of the convictions. Whipping is a humiliating sentence as well as a physically painful one. The courts exacted more than just the cost of child support, because illicit sex and irresponsible parenthood per se offended them. Offenders deserved to be humiliated. The period when society felt aggrieved and in a mood to retaliate was clearly the first four decades, when 38.6 percent of the whippings occurred (precisely, before 1719). After 1718 the practice of whipping went into a long decline and disappeared by 1751. By inference, the sentiment that fornication was an error for which men and women should experience humiliation declined too.

Individual cases illustrate the more selfish concerns underlying the numerical data from the decades after 1720—of accused fathers attempting to escape the responsibility for bastardy. To avoid the burdens of parenthood, accused fathers compounded the crime of bastardy with perjury, suborning perjury, bribery, assault, or abortion, while the public prosecutors pursued them. An example of adding perjury to bastardy was the case of George Gallegher and his housekeeper, Hannah Hastings. He was presented for bastardy on her but she testified that John Pim was the father, that she had never slept with Gallegher, despite attestations of other witnesses that they had seen them together in bed. Also, she denied that she had ever told anyone that she had named her two daughters, probably twins, after her mother and Gallegher's mother. Yet the court decided that she was perjuring herself and doing so at the behest of Gallegher, who was attempting to injure Pim by getting the court to assign to Pim penalties for the crime.[52]

In another case of perjury, the prosecutor presented Isaac Taylor to the grand jury for bastardy on Pheniah Way in 1785. He pled not guilty, and one William McCorkle testified on his behalf. McCorkle told the jurors that he had seen Joel Logan "lay the said Pheniah down on the ground" behind her father's barn, "and carnally know her." Furthermore, she admitted to him, McCorkle, that the bastard child she later bore was Logan's, and she begged him not to testify against her in court, nor to recount what he had seen and what she had admitted to him. If he would forbear, McCorkle continued, she promised that Logan would give him £25. The grand jury believed none of this and indicted McCorkle for perjury. A trial jury convicted him.[53]

Abortion disclosed the tribulations of bastardy and being publicly prosecuted. A servant woman, Margaret Kain, swore that when she was three or four months pregnant, Martin Rerton [Rierdon] brought her an abortifacient. She protested that she knew bastardy was a sin but that abortion was a still greater sin: "I told him I might as well go in the bed and kill one of My Masters Childer that Lay with me." Rerton assured her that it was no sin, since the child had not quickened, and that being so, she should save both their reputations by aborting. Out of her respect for Rerton, she said, she accepted the abortifacient from him. However, respecting her own conscience, she threw it away. As Rerton thought the abortifacient did not work, he brought her another. She probably did not take it either, because she bore the child, and the province prosecuted Rerton.[54]

Like bastardy, adultery and bigamy have victims and constitute both moral and religious crimes as well as secular crimes. There were only seven prosecutions for adultery before 1718 (none for bigamy), and the prosecutions did not appreciably grow in number until 1740 (Table 2.4). But the mere existence of a grievance did not necessarily cause adultery to be brought into the courts. If the public did not yet know of the adultery, for a husband to announce that he was a cuckold could be daunting. Women in general were more reluctant to go to court than men, and additionally in the case of adultery, might be too embarrassed to prosecute. They were also vulnerable in ways peculiar to women alone, which stopped them from prosecuting. Their case was illustrated in the petition of Mary Shea to the justices of Chester County in 1752. Martin Shaver, the aggrieved husband, had Mary Shea's husband jailed at Chester on suspicion of adultery with Shaver's wife. Mary Shea then petitioned the court to release her husband because he was the sole support of her and their three children. She needed him out of jail. The court granted her petition and the case ended there.[55] Almost any woman of the day would have understood Mary's predicament and her reluctance to prosecute. The several reasons for husbands and wives not wanting adultery to become a public or criminal matter mean that data on the crime understate the real volume of the crime, despite its causing harm and the state's ability to help victims.

Historically there was never any question that adultery had victims; it was rather a question of who the victim was. In English and early American society, when a wife committed adultery, the husband, as patriarch, was thought to have suffered from the infamy of it. In a more practical vein, his ability to command a family suffered equally. Since adultery fractured the family, children or others dependents might suffer too. Adultery also jeopardized patrilinearity, since the parentage of offspring was thrown into question. Thereupon, how could property and, in England, titles of nobility be transmitted securely? Adultery was easily construed as a victimizing crime, and men were identified as the victims.[56] As a result of the patriarchal understanding and intolerance of adultery, New England magistrates applied criminal sanctions in a prejudicial way. By law, adultery could be committed only with a married woman; a married man's sexual relations with a single woman were not adulterous—at least legally.[57] The upshot of such statutes and the concern for corrupted lineage was more prosecutions of women than men for adultery. The statistical bias toward the prosecution of women appeared outside New England as well, if not as well documented.[58] If the patriarchal values that usually propelled the prosecution of adultery

existed in Pennsylvania, too, the data on adultery cases should show
that bias.

When looking for signs of gender bias in the numbers, there is nothing in Pennsylvania to compare to what appeared in New England and
elsewhere—women being prosecuted more often than men (and probably convicted more often than men, although these data have not been
reported). The imbalance in New England was not the case in Pennsylvania; in fact, the opposite occurred. One hundred and forty-six men were
accused on 157 charges of adultery and bigamy versus 70 women on 76
charges.[59] The government dropped prosecutions of 28 men and
women at nearly equal rates. A large number (27.0 percent) of the
accused whom the government continued to prosecute never had their
cases come to any recorded conclusion, and of these the women clearly
outpaced the men, 43.3 percent to 24.6. The government may have
lacked the interest or the evidence, or both, to pursue these accused to
some conclusion; the fault or faults benefited women more than men,
in any case.

Grand juries returned *ignoramus* in an identical 36 percent of men
and women's presentments. Almost one in five of the indicted pleaded
guilty; 29.2 percent of the women did so and 19.7 percent of the men.
A large number went to trial, 56.7 percent, and the jurors found men and
women guilty at almost the same high rate, 60.0 percent for men and 63.4
for women. The prejudices that existed regarding gender and adulterers
in the laws and justice systems of other colonies and other times were not
present in Pennsylvania.[60] Cleary there was inequity, however, but it was
the gendered social and economic conditions that daunted aggrieved
women from ever approaching the courts to complain.

There were twenty-six prosecutions or charges of sodomy, buggery,
and bestiality in Pennsylvania against twenty-three men, but only one
before 1730. Sodomy and buggery were severely punished in Pennsylvania law after 1700, first by life imprisonment and, in the case of married
offenders between 1700 and 1706, by castration. In 1718, along with
other offenses, they became capital crimes and remained so until 1786.[61]

Discerning from dockets alone exactly what the accused did, or which
offense he committed, or with whom, would be putting too fine a point
on the data and making the language of sexual crime more precise than
the custom of the time. In the case of Isaac Waddle (alias Isaac Miles)
court papers clearly explain that he "had a veneral affair with the said
mare" and continued that he did "perpetrate that detestable and abom-
inable crime of buggery" and was indicted for buggery. And so too,
Denis McAneney was accused of buggery. John Owen swore to the court
that he saw that McAneney had a mare tied to a fence and, standing on
a stump, with the mare's tail in his one hand and his "privits" in the

other, he put his hips in motion. Contrariwise, Samuel Pettit was accused of buggery for having anal intercourse with his wife—who did not consent to it and may have been his accuser.[62] As for the eighteen other men accused of buggery, for whom there are no court papers, it is not known exactly what they did. Three other men who were accused of sodomy were probably not sodomizing animals. The word bestiality did not appear in the dockets. Hewing to the line that the Pennsylvania court papers seem to have taken, in this discussion bestiality alone means sexual relations with animals, and sodomy or buggery means illicit sex among humans, either homosexual or heterosexual.[63]

In England, prosecutions for either crime were rare—thirty for bestiality in five counties during Elizabeth I's reign and six for sodomy between 1660 and 1800 in most of England. In the early American south, they were similarly rare; there were none in the Maryland records, one case of sodomy and three of bestiality in the fragmentary records of Virginia. In colonial New England, the situation appears vividly different. Seven men were executed for bestiality between 1642 and 1674; none thereafter. Conviction effectively meant execution in the seven cases. Accusations continued into the eighteenth century, but only one man was tried before 1776. Compared with their draconian treatment of bestiality convicts, according to historian John Murrin, New Englanders were "fairly tolerant of sodomy." These numbers are not the equivalent of the numbers from Pennsylvania, the former being executions and not indictments, with some prosecutions and accusations. But it appears that magistrates in Pennsylvania responded fairly aggressively to instances of illicit sexual behavior, compared with England and the American South. With little seventeenth-century history to compare with New England, the Pennsylvanians were not slackers when measured against eighteenth-century New England.

New England makes the point that resolutions and sentences in these cases expose much about the attitudes of the communities where these crimes occurred, since New England executed so many men for bestiality. The resolutions in Pennsylvania cannot be broken down according to each kind of illicit sex, due to the imprecise language of the records; but of the total of twenty-three men involved in either sodomy or buggery, the grand juries refused to indict ten of them, and trial juries convicted eight and acquitted two. Three outcomes are unknown. Only one man among them, John Ross of Westmoreland County, was executed in 1786 for "buggery."[64]

The growing deviance and changes in the justice system that occurred after 1718 disappointed men and women who expected William Penn's vision of Pennsylvania to take root and flourish. Blame for the disappointing turn in Pennsylvania's history was general; failures abounded.

Quakers failed. When they traded their consent to new, sanguine criminal laws in 1718 for their benefit of affirming, they could have rendered
the change a cosmetic one, had prosecutors, jurors, and justices not
practically applied the death penalty. But they readily embraced capital
sentences. Immigrants who swarmed to Pennsylvania beginning in 1718
included violent, lascivious men who created unprecedented troubles.
If this were the best poor man's country, they showed little gratitude for
being here. Rather than exercising their power and intelligence on
behalf of considerate solutions to growing crime and other troubles,
Pennsylvania's statesmen, like Logan, Keith, and Lloyd, manipulated or
exploited immigrants, inventing even graver problems for the future. At
the most intimate levels of social intercourse—sex and marriage—
Pennsylvanians became more abusive and selfish. Bachelor men especially refused their responsibilities. The state, in turn, looking out for
itself and taxpayers, mounted prosecutions against the irresponsible,
while showing little new concern for the female victims. While these
changes were transpiring, there was hardly an expression of remorse
that the changes compromised or even renounced the earliest vision of
Pennsylvania. There was plenty of nostalgia for an easier past and complaints about the present, but no serious misgivings about the reactionary remedies Pennsylvanians applied to their new troubles.

The single most striking and significant fact about the accused criminals
who troubled Pennsylvania is that they were missing persons, or civilly
nonpersons. These shades from the court dockets gain almost no additional vitality when they are searched in the most reliable, best-preserved
lists of denizens of Pennsylvania. Large majorities of these accused male
criminals are not in the lists. The lists are nine tax lists from Chester
County, one tax list from Philadelphia city, and city directories from
Philadelphia.[65] In Chester, 61.5 percent of the all the accused men are
missing; in Philadelphia, 70.4 percent.[66] In the case of Philadelphia, they
may also be pursued in the city directories of the 1790s. But searching
turns up as few as the tax list: 72.1 percent of all the accused men were
missing from the directories.[67] In light of these low yields, being missing
becomes the single most common and distinguishing feature of the
accused. They had names, at least, and that is a straw at which the historian may grasp. In Chester County, 44.8 percent of the missing accused
men had Scots-Irish surnames.[68] These are the sort of men of whom
Logan, Norris, Quaker meetings, and well-established Pennsylvanians
complained. But little more can be systematically learned about them;
they are nearly invisible except for their appearance as accused criminals.[69]

These men very likely escaped the tax lists and city directories because they were poor.[70] They were also—variously—transients, indentured servants, bachelors, and young; and all of these conditions very likely made them poor. Poverty was the closest condition to a common factor. Moreover, almost all of the missing were poorer than the men and women (landowners, tenants, artisans, mariners) who did get into the tax lists and were excused from paying taxes because they had no means to do so. Typically the townships excused them due to their bad economic luck, physical accidents, or misfortunes like fire. These "community" poor, if they may be so captioned, point out that the accused poor shared some condition other than just poverty. They had to be transients or servants, and very often, bachelors too.[71] If they were long-time residents, they would have appeared on lists.

Transience pervaded Pennsylvania, showing up in urban, rural, and backcountry areas. Arguably Pennsylvania had the most transient population among the thirteen colonies and states. Research into populations in diverse, selected areas of the province—Philadelphia, Germantown, Chester and Lancaster counties, Paxton Township—consistently shows high proportions of people on the move.[72] In Chester and Lancaster Counties, 30, 50, and even 70 percent of the residents disappeared from various townships within one decade. In the western reaches of the province, stable people were few. For example, Paxton Township, an area of 260 square miles in Lancaster County (and later, Dauphin County) lost one-third of its taxpaying population every year. "Paxton, and indeed the entire backcounty region around the township, was a community of strangers, a society that had no roots."[73] When historians made the case for transience in these jurisdictions, they confined their search to men and women who left a record of their stay or passage, not surprisingly. But there were more than these; in the words of historians Lucy Simler and Paul Clemens, "a *subterranean* river of people [was] flowing through [Chester] county," for example.[74] The accused criminals who did not appear on tax lists comprised part of that subterranean river, or rather increased its size beyond what Simler and Clemens estimated. Of course, some Pennsylvanians stayed put—the Quakers, Mennonites, Amish, Moravians, and various other Germans; but to treat them as the paradigm for life and community in Pennsylvania distorts reality. Somewhat later, in Jacksonian America, Alexis de Tocqueville marveled that some Germans in Pennsylvania were stationary. He wrote eloquently, "All about them is stirring a nomad population, with whom the desire to get rich has no bounds, which clings to no spot, is arrested by no ties, but shifts wherever the prospect of fortune presents itself."[75] As this book argues in the Epilogue, this instability profoundly affected the amount of crime in Pennsylvania.

In the court papers are narratives of transience, volunteered by these elusive, accused people. They corroborate the notion that transience, and not just poverty, explains their shadowy official existence. When he was indicted for theft in 1771, William Gumley, for example, gratuitously recapitulated his transient existence. Nine years prior to his arrest, he had left London for Maryland, where he was indentured to "Colonel Fichue" in Calvert County. After three years of the five-year term, Fitzhugh sold him to Dr. John Bond of Calvert. When he finished the remaining two years, he moved to Baltimore and did menial labor for five months for Thomas Constable. Then it was back to Dr. Bond for a summer. Then back to Baltimore, where he enlisted in the 18th Regiment of the Royal Irish, which was posted to Philadelphia. After only three weeks, he was discharged. He made hay for a man named Shepperd, location unmentioned, for more than a week, after which he spent a month laboring on the wharves of Philadelphia and a month working on a shallop. Then it was over to New Jersey to thresh for a Dutchman for several days, and just the previous Saturday, back to Philadelphia. The next day he was off to Lancaster, putting him en route in Chester County when he was apprehended for theft.[76]

Transience and migration, servitude, bachelorhood, military service, and menial labor mingle or appear serially in the lives and narratives of accused men. An example is Dennis Cornealey, who closely resembled William Gumley. He had come from Ireland five years before his appearance in court, being bound to a master in Baltimore for three years. Freed, he moved to Pittsburgh for six months, whereupon he left for Philadelphia. After two months he left Philadelphia for Newport (probably Delaware) for a year. Then it was back to Pennsylvania, to West Chester to labor for Jacob Righter. He fell in with John Connally and at the latter's bidding, Dennis claimed, they stole money from Dennis's employer. John immediately headed for Lancaster, while Dennis took the road for Wilmington, Delaware, spending conspicuously along the way. He could not tell how much money he had from the theft because he was illiterate (and innumerate). He dined well and otherwise spent more lavishly than a man of his apparent social station (buying jackets, trousers, shirts, a watch, a gold brooch), all of which attracted the interest of the authorities and caused his arrest.[77] In another case, in 1782, American-born Wilhelm Clines deserted the British army and had spent a sentence in Chester jail for theft. In his subsequent indictment, he, like Cornealey, had personal possessions that provoked suspicion and his inquisition by the court.[78]

Thomas Ryan was native-born and less traveled than most. Yet he had no set residence, but rather boarded at various taverns and houses in Philadelphia and Norristown. Before Christmas, he left the city for Downingtown, headed for Miller's Tavern merely "to take a frolic," he told the court. The horse he rode caused his problem with the law. Widow Lydea Vaneredell accused him of stealing hers. Ryan lamely answered his inquisitors in court that he got the horse in question from a man in the city whose name he did not know.[79]

It is no surprise to discover that in Philadelphia even more accused were missing. Philadelphia, which had two real rivers and access to the Atlantic world, was America's largest city and busiest port. Consequently, it had possibly the largest population of transients in America. In this city in flux, historian Billy Smith found that "poor men moved more frequently than wealthier ones." Poverty and transience are at least as strongly associated in the case of Philadelphia as in Chester, and very likely much more so.[80]

Servitude appeared often in narratives, but it cannot be quantified because servants were not noted as such in court dockets and were not taxed as long as they were servants. Servants who worked off their indentures had a high rate of geographic mobility; like the accused, they went missing. Possibly as many as 66 percent from a sample population in Philadelphia disappeared.[81] Servants were also some portion of all the transients because servants regularly ran away.[82] In cases of theft the prosecution typically needed to add details about the crime that, deliberately or not, betrayed the status or situation of the alleged thief. Thieves needed access to property in order to steal it. Without access, theft is not possible, and anyone without access need not be suspected of theft. Slaves, for example, did not rob banks. House and farm servants, slaves, and free domestics, on the other hand, enjoyed easy access to their masters' or employers' property. Consequently, they were the obvious suspects when property disappeared. Servants also visited neighbors' households without dismaying anyone. To explain in court that a suspect enjoyed access by being a servant was to bolster the prosecutor's case; hence, the frequent mention of servants in court papers.

In the surviving court papers from Chester County, servants easily outnumbered all other occupations combined among men and women accused of theft, burglary, and robbery. Casual and unskilled laborers followed them at a great distance. One slave was accused, but that rarity may be explained not by their being innocent of stealing, but by their owners' choice to punish privately any suspected slave. Servants were accused of stealing from their masters and others, mostly pilfering commonplace objects, especially clothing. Social class and the setting operated in accusers' perception of servants and other suspected thieves and the discovery of stolen goods. Rural people knew their households and their neighbors' well enough that when some servants were discovered with certain goods or wore certain clothing they attracted attention and were expected to explain how they came to have such improbable things.

Others spent money more lavishly than observers thought possible for poor people. For example, Morris Obrennon told the court that servant woman Elinor Connor (Conner) was at his house and complaining about her mistress Mary Ruddel. Obrennon thought her complaints were unreasonable since he could see that she, Elinor, was wearing a new suit of clothes, which could only have come from her mistress. No, Elinor corrected him, she herself had bought the new clothes. So Obrennon asked how she, a servant, got such money. Elinor said that a Mr. Long gave her the money. But before this incident and before she had even gotten the new apparel, Connor had told her mistress that she intended to get new clothing. How will you afford it, Ruddel had asked. Connor answered that she had a gold piece she brought from Ireland.[83] From this testimony, the grand jury did not find sufficient cause to indict Connor, but the neighborhood found cause to accuse her.

Mary Wilson, a servant of Peter Worrall, had too much money. When she walked away from his house after stealing £6-10s from him, she did not have a pair of shoes to wear. On the road, she bought a pair for six shillings from a woman who became the prosecution's witness. The seller told the court that because Mary was illiterate, she had to count Mary's money and told Mary she had £5-15s remaining after buying the shoes.[84] In another case, Margaret Sweny had to explain how she came to have a bed gown, gloves, ribbon, and some money. She said that her master William Robison had given her the clothing and ribbon, and that she had earned the cash by mending stockings for a Mr. Kincade. But William Kerr had had 20 shillings stolen, and he accused Sweny of taking the money and Robison of receiving it from her. Kerr threatened to take her to the law, whereupon she claimed that Kincade had had sexual relations with her—presumably for money so that she offered a more acceptable explanation of how she got her money. Kerr confronted her with a written statement of confession and she signed it, confessing, among other things, that she had concocted the story of Kincade.[85]

In the case of a free society, without servitude and slavery, typing of criminals may nevertheless exist. However, free men and women, if typed, can more easily complain and resist than the unfree; and magistrates had to be more respectful with them than with slaves and servants. In Pennsylvania, where unfree labor continued and servants populated the criminal dockets, their necessary poverty ensnared the ones guilty of theft and bedeviled ones who appeared suspiciously out of the ordinary for their class and thus were accused of crimes.

Wilhelm Clines was a casual laborer and drifter, not long freed from service in Philadelphia. Magistrate Thomas Levis stopped him in Chester County. He wanted Clines to account for the horse he rode and the watch, chain, silver buckles, and other goods he carried. The horse was from a man west of the Susquehanna, Clines told Levis, the jewelry from a shoemaker and tavern keeper in Lancaster, and the rest was from a man in the road whom he had hailed. The man dropped a bundle of goods—the ones in question—and ran off, Clines said. Clines finally confessed to stealing geese. In another case, Hugh Tinney was quite poor but suddenly was observed with plenty of money and buying wheat with cash. He had visited Mary McClaine's house earlier, either drunk or pretending to be, and scuffled with her. She discovered £3-15s-6d missing shortly after he left and she accused him. A jury convicted him of stealing the money. Clines and Tinney were not servants when accosted, but were suspiciously poor, of the "lowest sort," and strangers, and so they were suspected.[86]

Occasional records of what was stolen supply insights into the thieves' and the victims' condition in life and motives, and the material culture of the times. Clothing easily led the list. In London, too, according to J. M. Beattie, clothing was most often stolen, while in rural Surrey and in Sussex clothing was second.[87] The significance of clothing, attested by its ranking first, may strike modern readers as too trivial an article to be so desirable. However, in eighteenth-century Pennsylvania and elsewhere, clothing and cloth were considerably more valuable than today, despite the consumer revolution that increased the supply of clothing after 1740.[88] For example, advertisements for runaway servants and slaves often described the clothes the escapees wore. The masters reasoned that escaped servants and slaves would not likely have the means of quickly changing from the clothing in which they escaped—unless they stole it.[89] Stolen clothing was almost always second-hand, often taken from washing tubs or while hanging out to dry. Ruth Simson of Chester left her laundry in her back yard to dry—two of her husband's shirts, one of hers, his trousers, and some small things. They disappeared. She suspected William Bedsen and, accompanied by her husband, she searched his house and found the trousers. And Dinah Russell discovered that the laundry in her back-yard tub was missing. She and her husband got the constable and a search warrant for Bedsen's house, and they found the clothes, Bedsen having Edward Russell's trousers "on his back" at the time. David Evans stole a tub of clothes from Isaac Lawrence's home in Chichester. Servant David Davis walked past the house of Benjamin Elliott, saw some linen hanging out to dry, and took a shirt and trousers.[90]

Used clothing was stolen in the eighteenth century because ready-to-wear garments were far less common than today; a thief could not as easily enter a store and shoplift new garments on display. On the other hand, dry goods merchants imported surprisingly large amounts and varieties of textiles (and these got stolen); three-quarters of their stock was cloth and sewing materials. Ten percent of the stock consisted of a few items of ready-to-wear, like handkerchiefs, stockings or hosiery, and hats.[91] After purchasing fabric, Americans sewed or hired tailors to fabricate their garments. Used clothing was sufficiently valuable that garments were sometimes unstitched and assembled into different ones. Inventories of the estates of decedents disclose the significance and great value of clothing.[92] Common clothing and textiles routinely appeared in inventories, and about as often as not, the various articles were listed individually. George Houser, an example of a poor farmer from Northampton County in 1774, owned a hat, a jacket, a pair of leather breeches, a pair of trousers, four shirts, a handkerchief, and a pair of shoes. Henry Smith, a thriving farmer in Philadelphia County, left a coat, two jackets, three waistcoats, a great coat, four shirts, three pairs of breeches, two hats, one pair of stockings, and two pairs of buckles. A poor widow, Mary Catherine Richerts, left seven handkerchiefs, three petticoats, two jackets, five old skirts, seven old shirts, one pair of mittens, and four pairs of stockings.[93]

In rural England, food outranked clothing and everything else among stolen goods and it occupied a large portion of the total. Men stole food both for their families to consume and to realize small profits. Either way, their crimes arose from necessity—their pinched economic circumstances.[94] In rural Pennsylvania food was rarely stolen, and one or two of those rare cases involved large or repeated thefts of food for sale, not consumption. The criminal records here reflect the different environments of crime; compared to England, food was abundant and cheap in rural America. In this respect it resembled the best poor man's country. Inventories of probated estates rarely list any comestibles on hand (while they do list livestock except for chickens). Poor or not, rural Americans needed things, but food was hardly ever one of them. Similarly, rural people did not need the markets and public exchanges for ready comestibles that urban people did, and so they did not offer potential thieves convenient venues for crime.

By comparison, Philadelphia had the produce markets and, in the last quarter of the century, people poor enough to need to steal to satisfy their daily needs.[95] Liquor and other alcoholic beverages were exceptions in rural Pennsylvania because they were stolen more often than food, but in significantly different circumstances. Alcohol was not taken by stealth, but taken aggressively from the victims by often petulant and already drunk perpetrators. The crime was often combined with accusations of assault.

Horse theft appears almost as common in Pennsylvania as the theft of clothing, and transients were repeatedly accused of it. Although numbers from Pennsylvania will not bear comparison with England, it was common in England as well, and one of the oldest capital crimes.[96] The value of horses and the seriousness of the crime distinguish it from the kinds of theft that rivaled it in frequency. In 1774 Pennsylvania inventories, horses ranged in value from £5 to £20, Pennsylvania currency. To put that amount in perspective, the estimated average annual income of a farm family in Chester and Lancaster counties was about £40 at the time. And horses were common; most farmers had one and prosperous farmers averaged five.[97] Like modern-day auto theft, stealing horses differed from other theft because the stolen object provided the means of escape. Absconding with something immobile the size of a horse would have been a problem indeed, and stealing even cattle and sheep did not make flight as easy as is the case with a horse.

David Davis, in 1757, showed the ease with which horses could be stolen, with a casualness that resembles modern joyriding. Davis was the servant who had stolen some linen hung out to dry. He ran away from his master, too, and in his wanderings took a sorrel horse he came upon in the Great Valley, visited his cousin, then went on to Lancaster County where he left the horse and stole another one. At that point, he returned to his master, riding the stolen horse. He never showed an intention to sell either horse. In a second example, Thomas Meglaughlin (McLaughlin), a laborer, stopped at a public house in Concord, Chester County. A lot of people were present that evening and horses were tied up at the shed. Meglaughlin took a dark bay horse together with a saddle and bridle and rode west across two counties and the Susquehanna River to York County. But in York he was stopped on suspicion of horse theft and was jailed. Meglaughlin's case makes the point of the ease of theft, but also the need to escape to a remote place in order not to be detected.[98] Davis at least appears to have been joyriding rather than stealing horses for profit. He could hope that the courts saw his behavior that way, too, and treated him leniently—although the crime was horse theft in any case—because the punishment for horse theft was as severe as any, short of execution. In 1780, for example, Christian Gottlieb was sentenced a fine of £1000, return of the horse, 39 lashes, an hour in the pillory, six months in prison, and his ears cut off and nailed to the pillory.[99] In its variety of sanctions, his was pretty much the standard sentence for the crime.

In the narratives of the accused, their victims appear to be men and women of at least some substance, unlike the accused, who had little or nothing. Numbers, however, do not support the inference that some economic-class contest raged between the rootless poor and the propertied denizens. In Chester County, 39.8 percent of all male, free victims were missing from the tax lists.[100] A large minority of the victims was missing, whereas a small majority (61.5 percent) of the accused was missing. The difference amounted to 21.7 percent; significant, but not a case of class conflict. The difference was larger in the case of theft and smaller in the case of assault. Poor transients had reason to mistrust poor transients, but not quite as much reason as the residents had.

A few humble men told the court their stories of being victimized on the road, illustrating what life was like for the large minority of men on the move. Edmund Cryer, born in Nottingham, England and a journeyman shoemaker from London, had led a restless life; he had traveled throughout England before migrating to America. He left England for South Carolina in 1749 and remained there until 1763, when he came to Philadelphia. In the city he worked three weeks for Samuel Ferris in Water Street and left with six dollars that Ferris had paid him. On the way to the White Horse tavern in Chester County he traveled with a George Lyon. Another traveler (so casual a companion that Cryer could not name him) joined these two on route. Cryer explained to the court that the two others beat him unconscious with barrel staves. When he awoke from the beating, he had been robbed of his six dollars and his shoemaker's tools.[101]

George Lyon told the court a different story. He argued that he was the only victim in this episode. He had just departed the ship of war *Hero* at Philadelphia, carrying with him £26 as his share of the ship's prize money. He met Cryer at the Lower Ferry on the Schuylkill, where they shared his gill of rum. Later, at the Blue Bell tavern, he again treated Cryer to drinks. Cryer, said Lyon, had been repeatedly curious about Lyon's prize money. Finally, at the White Horse tavern Cryer attacked him with a stone, then a big shoemaker's awl. Lyon begged Cryer to spare his life, but, in an amazing turn-about, Lyon asserted that he realized his grave danger and so defended himself, beating Cryer with a stone. The third transient appeared nowhere in Lyon's tale.[102] Whichever version was true, Cryer's or Lyon's, missing, transient persons certainly preyed upon each other. The suspect criminal "class" in this case did not steal from and abuse the residents of the county.

In one spectacular case, the transient was the victim of the residents of Chester County. On the Lancaster road in East Whiteland Township, one John Robinson was on his way to Philadelphia from Maryland. In the vicinity of the inn kept by Thomas Ives, he came upon Ives's daughter Elizabeth and allegedly acted rudely toward her in some manner that was never described. Ives summoned a neighborhood storekeeper, Alexander Robeson, who joined at least six men at Ives's house. Most of them thought themselves able to judge Robinson's behavior and to punish him too—although Robeson got cold feet and left when one Abel Roberts asked him if what they were about to do was legal. Ives said let's "kick the fellows arse and let him go," and they removed Robinson's waistcoat and whipped him on his knees while he roared out and asked for pardon. The mock court auctioned off his waistcoat and an extra shirt he carried to pay the "expenses" of their court.[103]

When the case came before him, Justice William Moore was not the least amused. "In contempt of all Law Justice and Humanity [and] to the great disgrace of the Neighbourhood," a poor, innocent traveler was most violently assaulted and robbed. He ordered the constables to apprehend six of those present and call eight others as witnesses.[104] However, none was presented to the grand jury, possibly due to the absence of Robinson to prosecute the assailants. By the time of the 1775 tax collection, Ives was dead but his widow ranked in the 68th percentile of payers. Two men were not on the list at all, one being the storekeeper Robeson. A fourth was an inmate (also called a cottager) in the 28th percentile, and the fifth was a landholder in the 66th.[105] Of course, Robinson was not a taxpayer, and one affidavit effectively colored Robinson as socially humble: he carried a pass with him, as a servant or slave might.[106] The lot of the assailants was mixed. The most aggressive of them and their leader, Ives, was a middle-class landholder, while most of the others owned far less. But as a group they assaulted and robbed someone clearly less wealthy than themselves.

To recall the critical point about the accused, only a minority had stood still long enough and assembled enough property to attract the attention of a tax assessor. That minority which had property, however, included men from a variety of economic and social conditions who enjoyed widely different estates. How these conditions and estates bear upon crime and victimization in Chester County and Philadelphia is the next question to examine.

The laws of Pennsylvania assigned taxpayers to one of four different categories, depending upon their tenure in their property. The first category, landowners, was the most favored economically, followed closely by the second, tenants, and then by much less favored inmates (or cottagers). A fourth category, freemen or singlemen (bachelors) differs from the three others in that freemen/singlemen were taxed because of their marital status and indirectly, their age (youth). They paid a flat tax and not a rate on their assessed property. Most owned little or no realty.[107] Only the singlemen and inmates show a tendency to appear as accused more often than they were present in the county (in tax lists), 1691–1799—but not much more often. Landowners appear only modestly, which is no surprise since men with real property and steady vocations do not burden criminal courts.[108] Tenancy, in contrast, suggests

100 Chapter Three

economic dependency, and dependency suggests possible motives or causes of crime. In the case of Chester County and much of Pennsylvania, however, these inferences are incorrect. Tenancy did not entail dependency, to begin with, and, as noted, it was not correlated with crime.[109] Tenants closely resembled landowners economically, and their law-abiding behavior differed just as little.

The fourth group, singlemen, were bachelors and of course, they headed no households. They mostly lived alone and therefore escaped the moderating influences of dependent wives and children, and of parents and siblings, who would likely have encouraged them to act responsibly, dependably, and regularly. Before 1764 the tax lists recorded only bachelors living alone; after 1764, either alone or with their parents.[110] They are especially interesting to historians and sociologists of crime because they so often appear as criminals. In his examination of disorder and crime in America's past, historian David Courtwright unequivocally blames America's young men. "Crime everywhere . . . is disproportionately a young man's pursuit," he has written.[111] More than any other historically retrievable group in Pennsylvania, the singlemen taxpayers represent the variety of men Courtwright blames. Given the sociological and historical data, the singlemen accused of crime would likely exceed their proportion in the whole population. But that was not the case; from 1693–1799 they show only a 3.2 percent tendency to be accused beyond their numbers in the taxpayer population.

Before leaving the singlemen, it must be noted that the accused who are missing from the tax lists must be revisited. The singlemen accused of crimes were not all the accused bachelors; they might be better described as *resident* accused singlemen. Some additional, unknown number of singlemen were transients—probably a sizable majority. Details from the court papers of the lives and conditions of transient accused men almost entail that the transients were bachelors. When it is recalled that the large number of missing accused men probably were transients, and the transients were bachelors, the estimate that singlemen or bachelors were the accused is significantly enhanced.

The remaining category of taxpayers, the inmates, proliferated in Chester County after 1750 and supplanted tenants in the strategies of Chester agriculturists who aspired to be more productive and prosper in the marketplace. They comprised a clearly poorer class than tenants, without the economic prospects of most (resident) singlemen. They were much more mobile geographically than tenants and landowners, but at the same time they were hardly transients. They were usually heads of families and not bachelors, and almost surely were more personally responsible and cautious since they were husbands and fathers.[112] If one expects a clear, simple correlation of poverty and crime,

TABLE 3.4. OCCUPATIONS OF PHILADELPHIANS ACCUSED OF CRIMES IN THE 1790s[1]

merchant	42	hairdresser	7	clock & watch	
grocer	28	bottler	5	maker	3
[widow]	19	ship carpenter	4	cabinet maker	3
house carpenter	17	mariner	4	coach maker	3
tavern keeper	16	blacksmith	4	drayman	2
laborer	13	cooper	4	fruiterer	2
shopkeeper	12	broker	4	coppersmith	2
boardinghouse-		bricklayer	4	jeweler/goldsmith	2
keeper	12	porter	3	biscuit maker	2
gentleman	11	saddler	3	tinman	2
tailor	9	upholsterer	3	baker	2
innkeeper	9	clerk	3	silversmith	2
cordwainer	8	sail maker	3	butcher	2
sea captain	8	minister	3	physician	2
shoemaker	8	china dealer	3	livery man	2
printer	7				

[1]Table omits occupations appearing only once.

these relatively poor men, whatever their family situation, should have populated the dockets of the accused. And yet they were little more likely to be accused of crimes than landowners and tenants. Their relative poverty did not significantly incline them toward committing crime, and their maturity and patriarchal responsibilities led them to behave prudently and cautiously.

As for Philadelphia, Table 3.4 displays the occupations (culled from city directories) of Philadelphia men accused of crime. Table 3.5 categorizes them and compares the categories with the distribution of the categories among all Philadelphians. Neither the élite nor the humble turn out to be highly correlated with crime in the city. If any groups seemed to have been inordinately accused, they were men in retail business and service and makers of small consumer goods. If one assumes that class would be correlated with crime or prosecutions for crime, laborers, mariners, stevedores, and longshoremen should most often appear. But this sample of the accused gives the lie to the assumption. In it, the rough-hewn classes of the city were not inordinately criminal—but only *if* they were residents and not transients. Missing accused, who are a population roughly three times larger than those present in these lists, were likely mariners of some sort, casual laborers, or servants and apprentices. Mobility made a critical difference, not just poverty or poorly paid vocations, in explaining the likelihood of being accused criminals. In fact, being rootless seems most important regardless of whether one lived in or outside the city.[113]

TABLE 3.5. OCCUPATIONS OF ALL PHILADELPHIANS AND PHILADELPHIANS ACCUSED OF CRIME IN THE 1790S CLASSIFIED BY ECONOMIC SECTOR AND TRADE

Occupation	All Philadelphia (%)	Philadelphia accused (%)
Government	1.7	2.8
Service & manufactures		
Professional	5.0	7.4
Retail and local wholesale	10.9	23.1
Retail crafts	17.9	3.1
Building crafts	11.3	5.8
Travel & transport	6.0	4.0
Other services	2.2	7.7
Industrial		
Textile	0.2	0.9
Leather & fur	1.8	6.5
Food & drink	0.9	4.0
Shipbuilding/fitting	1.6	2.5
Metal crafts	3.4	3.7
Furniture	1.8	2.8
Miscellaneous	3.0	3.1
Commerce		
Mariners	5.2	3.7
Merchants and assistants	21.9	15.1
Laborers	5.1	4.0

Source: Billy G. Smith, The "Lower Sort": Philadelphia's Laboring People, 1750–1800 (Ithaca, N.Y.: Cornell University Press, 1990), 214. N of accused is 325.

The valuation of men's realty and chattels is as critical as their tenure in their estates. In this study their taxes or property assessments have been translated into each taxpayer's percentile rank in each of the ten tax lists. The thousands of individuals' percentiles permit an analysis of the distribution of wealth and the average percentile of various groups, like accused criminals or victims of crime. To wit, the wealth of the accused criminals in Chester County usually ranked them above the 50th percentile at nine intervals between 1693 and 1799—even using their low alternative tax[114] (Figure 2.1). Their mean percentile for the whole period was 54.[115] They were not the poor of the county—not even close to being poor.

In the city of Philadelphia, seventy-four accused men from 1779–1781 were discovered in the 1780 tax list, and the mean percentile of their wealth was 43.6.[116] They lay a decile below the rank of all the Chester accused. Thus, whether they were transients or residents and taxpayers, the accused in the city were poorer than the rural accused.

Victims of crime (discernible only in Chester County) resembled the accused criminals in Chester; like the accused, the victims in each of the four taxpayer categories appeared as victims just about as often as their numbers in the county population statistically warranted.[117] The mean taxable wealth of all Chester County crime victims put them between the 52nd and 70th percentiles (using low alternatives) from 1718 through 1799 (Table 3.6 and Figure 2.1). At no time did they join the lower half of taxpayers. Only six percentile points separated the mean wealth of victims and accused; so, again, the two were not much different.

Because most accused criminals in Pennsylvania were not members of any community in either the countryside or the city, and because they owned little or no property that would command respect, they could have suffered from discrimination within the justice system—a system staffed by residents, who clearly enjoyed social and economic status superior to most accused (Figure 2.1). Contrariwise, did local men when they were prosecuted for crimes, enjoy the favor of their peers and community? How did strangers fare compared with residents and wealthier men? Were the personnel of the justice system partial toward economically superior persons?[118]

The first question to ask is, what judicial outcomes would privileged people have enjoyed? The most favorable outcome for them would have been the government dropping their prosecutions ("Default"), excusing them from any further distraction by grand juries and courts. The second most favorable outcome would have been the grand jury returning no indictment (*ignoramus*). The third most favorable outcome was acquittal (not guilty) by jury trial. An examination of Table 3.7 of the outcomes shows that taxed accused men enjoyed almost no advantage compared with the missing accused; the largest disparity favored the taxed by only 2.2 percent in the category of government defaulting to prosecute.

Table 3.7 also refines the test for bias by isolating the outcomes for accused men in the top one-third and top one-tenth of taxpayers. Of these select groups the top one-tenth enjoyed a tendency to exit from prosecution in the pre-trial stage, while the poorer went on to trial. Prosecutors—the least popular or most élite actors in the justice system—benefited the wealthiest ten percent more often than average by ending their prosecutions. But the top 10 percent enjoyed even greater favor from the popularly selected grand jurors. To a smaller degree, that was the experience of the top third of the accused too. At trial, the result was most thoroughly the expression of the public, since it came from trial jurors only. And there, the favor enjoyed by the wealthy disappeared. Thus, the results were inconsistent. The soundest inference is

TABLE 3.6. PERCENTILE RANK IN TAXABLE WEALTH OF ACCUSED CRIMINALS, VICTIMS OF CRIME, JUSTICES, CONSTABLES, AND JURORS IN CHESTER COUNTY

Mean percentile rank	1693	1718	1730	1740	1750	1765	1775	1785	1799	1693–1799
Jurors	55.4	71.3	78.0	78.2	77.4	81.6	77.0	72.9	73.7	75.2
Constables	43.4	60.6	62.2	64.2	65.8	73.8	69.3	62.0	68.7	65.3
Justices	85.8	84.1	91.5	91.0	93.8	94.1	86.9	87.5	77.8	86.8
Accused (low alternative)	54.0	35.5	46.1	53.3	59.1	67.9	71.8	56.4	41.7	54.0
Accused (high alternative)	56.1	44.5	48.7	53.3	59.2	73.7	72.0	61.4	49.2	58.6
Victims (low alternative)		59.6	58.9	69.7	57.5	66.9	65.0	62.6	52.5	60.0
Victims (high alternative)		59.8	66.7	75.3	61.5	68.7	71.2	62.9	59.1	64.3

TABLE 3.7. JUDICIAL OUTCOMES FOR TAXED AND NONTAXED (MISSING) ACCUSED
CRIMINALS IN CHESTER COUNTY

	Non-taxed (missing) accused[1] (%)	Taxed accused[2] (%)	Accused in top 33% of all taxpayers (%)	Accused in top 10% of all taxpayers (%)
Default	2.9	5.1	5.4	5.5
Ignoramus	32.8	34.9	37.8	43.6
Submit	22.4	22.9	25.0	27.3
Guilty	14.9	15.6	13.5	10.9
Not guilty	8.4	7.0	4.7	3.6
Unknown	18.7	14.6	13.5	9.1
	100.0	100.0	100.0	100.0

[1]$N = 1002$.   [2]$N = 315$.

that the government may have been of one mind (slightly favoring the
élite), but that the public was less certain about the accused.

In closing the analysis of accused and victims and their status and property, it is important to remark on what one does not see in the figures as
well as what one does. First, disparities between the status and the property of the accused and of the victims were not great—although victims
were marginally wealthier and more rooted in the community. What one
cannot see in the data is the number of accused consistently rising as
their wealth and status declined, nor the number of victims consistently
rising as their wealth and status increased. In other words, the poor residents were not victimizing the rich residents (and vice versa) whether or
not they had reason or inclination to do so. Nor were transients choosing
to victimize only residents. Most accused were transients, but a large
minority of victims were too. Instead, it appears likely, as is the case today,
that people victimized people whom they knew or met—on the roads, in
the taverns, near their homes, farms, or businesses.

Convenient opportunities for crime and easy access to victims
trumped distant spoils, remote victims, and malice toward unfamiliar
people. When crime and victimization play out in these ways—among
familiars and within class rather than between classes—secure men of
high rank and public power can dismiss crime as a problem, since most
of the perpetrators and the victims are not their kind. Criminals and
victims are the "lower sort." Corporate responsibility for crime or the
whole community's complicity—typically disclosed by complicated anal-
yses of impersonal causes—may appear far-fetched, distracting attention
from the immediate perpetrators of crime, in the eyes of the powerful.
Powerful Pennsylvanians did fret about crime and did not ignore it, but

they were not very curious about the situation they had created which in turn promoted crime.

The accused transients and servants reflected the society of Pennsylvania—even though they may have joined that society only shortly before they were prosecuted and may also have left it shortly after the justice system handled them. Of all the colonies in British America, Pennsylvania was more likely than any other to be the scene of their alleged crime. By way of contrast, the population of Virginia was forty percent slave and therefore forty percent immobile, sentenced to lifetime confinement. New England historically had excluded or expelled people who diverged from its religious and ethnic standards and continued to be hostile to outsiders even after it was legally obliged to open itself up. Even New York, diverse as it was, did not offer the welcoming economic prospect that Pennsylvania did. "The best poor man's country" was bound to have a lot of strangers. A colony without plantation slavery but with a thriving agricultural economy was bound to have indentured servitude, whose ranks were filled by impecunious immigrants looking for the best prospect.

An open society attracted immigrants and transients and they, in turn, contributed unmistakably to the volume of crime in such society. And immigrants were denounced for the crime. Strangers, who in the seventeenth and eighteenth centuries were mostly single, young men, with few ties, affiliations, or responsibilities—no wives, children, or other dependents, no homes, neighbors, churches, clients, patrons, or masters. Thousands of young men who arrived as servants worked out their obligations and joined the rootless and ungoverned. Others simply ran away from their masters.[119] Residents and settled men and women of Stuart England and colonial Virginia dreaded them. They were "masterless men," beyond society's grip, and dangerous.[120] In an illiberal world, governments could repress or oust such feared or dangerous people. But professedly liberal states could do so only by giving the lie to their professions of liberty and tolerance.

— Scots-Irish on border are lawless

— Transients committed crimes

— Not too many special privileges for the elite

Chapter 4
Persistent Violence

[Thomas Riley] lifted up one of his [Mathias Leamy's] Feet and
Swore he would Kick Leamy's Dam'd Guts out for one Half-Penny.

—*Chester County Quarter Sessions Papers*

The violence that alarmed Pennsylvanians in the 1720s stayed. Sometimes it grew and at other times it declined; but it never declined
enough to restore the peace that Pennsylvania had enjoyed in its first
four decades. When Pennsylvania is compared with other societies or
jurisdictions, the significance of violence swells: it amounted to a hall-
mark of Pennsylvania society, because it exceeded all other varieties of
crime, and thereby made Pennsylvania probably unique among American colonies and states. In virtually all other large jurisdictions, property
crime ranked first. In modern America, it continues to rank first. In
Pennsylvania, however, almost one-third (N = 10,133; 30.7 percent) of
all criminal charges recorded from 1682 through 1800 involved some
type of assault upon persons. In addition to these were the grimmer 513
cases of homicide. This chapter expands the examination of Pennsylvania's singular violence beyond the first four decades of its history and
considers homicide, suicide, and nonlethal aggression, perpetrators and
victims.

Through 1800, 513 homicides came before Pennsylvania courts, 1.6 percent of all crime prosecuted there[1] (Table 2.1). The number of murder
prosecutions far exceeds the total in any other continental British possession and American state except Virginia, which had a longer history
and a larger population. Even though the homicide rates were high, the
statistics do not completely take the measure of homicide in Pennsylvania. They reflect only the homicides known to the courts and prosecuted. Newspapers and coroner reports document scores of deaths that
went unsolved and unprosecuted. Because authorities could not con-

firm most of these cases as homicides, or because no suspects surfaced, these occurrences do not appear in court dockets or in our homicide statistics. A Philadelphia man digging in his garden in March 1743 unearthed the remains of an apparently slain woman. An unknown person slew Chester's William Wilson as he rode toward Philadelphia late one night in October 1751. Three men were found dead in 1733 alongside a road. Two had had their heads cut off; the third had been shot in the head. A sailor, "presumably murdered," was discovered near one of Philadelphia's wharves in June 1767. In May 1742, a Negro woman was pulled from the Delaware River. "Barbarously murder'd," she had been "cut open from her Collar bones to the lower Part of her Belly, and sewn up with double ozenbrigs Thread." The many unsolved homicides suggest that Pennsylvania was much more violent than the formal records depict.[2]

As several of the examples above illustrate, cases of homicide in Pennsylvania sometimes took an unmistakably depraved character. Henry Hander the younger, a laborer in Lebanon Township, Lancaster County, believed that Jacob Kissell had "used him ill." He stabbed Kissell in the throat and threw him out the door. Kissell screamed for Hander "to let him alone for he was most dead," but Hander pursued the fallen man, grabbed him by the hair and cut off his head. He then "threw dirt and snow on the body, laughing and talking to himself."[3] John Myriack (or Myrack or Myrick) murdered his family in 1755. Myriack, of East Caln Township in Chester County, flew into a rage and killed his wife, then burned her face so "that no Person could know her." Having dispatched his spouse, he then killed his two children and a neighbor's infant by swinging their bodies so that their skulls were "beat to peaces [sic] against a rock that was before his door." Josiah Ramage's 1786 slaying of his wife of thirty-seven years in Franklin County was equally brutal. After beating his wife to death with fire tongs, Ramage climbed upon a table and repeatedly jumped upon her lifeless body in a frenzied attempt to crush her.[4] There were more cases of supererogatory violence, but they add little more to the profile of violent murder in the province.

Murder victims generally knew their assailants—like most of their modern counterparts. Perpetrators and victims lived together or close to each other, worked together, or associated together in some capacity. Families and neighbors quarreled, workers got under each others' skins, drinking companions overindulged and conversation turned foul, masters oppressed servants and servants vowed revenge, employers and employees resented each other, and through it all, willy-nilly, passions turned deadly. Adding to these numbers also were more than six dozen single women who out of shame, fear, or ignorance slew their illegitimate offspring.

The site of much of the fatal personal violence in early Pennsylvania was its heralded families and households. Although historians celebrate the advent of the modern family of affection, tenderness, and self-discipline (albeit mostly among Quakers), the household witnessed a comparatively high degree of violence.[5] Of murder cases that led to death sentences, 23.8 percent involved persons related to the victims. Parents killed their offspring, and not always in short explosions of passion. Thirteen men faced juries for killing their spouses, and a dozen or so others were suspected of doing so. Nor were children exempt from violent parents. The systematic torture of his nine-month-old daughter by Nicholas Wyriak (or Weyriak) of Bethel Township, Lancaster County, in 1748 eventually killed her. Authorities noted that Wyriak had "broke one of her Thighs" and that "from the Crown of her Head to her toes she was cut, bruised and Mangled in the most Shocking manner Imaginable." In September 1785, Kelly Rogers of Cumberland County "with the most unheard of barbarity, murdered her son, a boy about 8 or 9 years of age, by cutting his throat from ear to ear." She did so, she told authorities after failing to commit suicide herself, to save her son from a life of poverty and "servility." Infanticide prosecutions made up a small but constant part of each decade's crime totals. Children also killed siblings. Samuel Brandt shot his brother, Valentine, following a 1773 quarrel in their Leacock Township, Lancaster County home before setting fire to the house in an effort to hide his crime. An eighteen-year-old "deaf and dumb" lad from Chester County murdered his ten-year-old brother in 1739 by slitting his throat.[6]

That almost one quarter of all convicted murderers had victimized family members is a troubling and surprising statistic. It is most surprising in light of the expectations of Penn and Quakers that they were erecting in Pennsylvania a more sensitive and peaceable society than its many predecessors. Although Quakers, Mennonites, Moravians, and others professing nonviolence were only briefly the majority in the province, few societies had even this many professors of nonviolence—this much leavening. And also because they were the wealthiest and most powerful people in Pennsylvania, their peaceful way of life could be expected to have diffused among more of the nonprofessors. But it did not happen. Pennsylvanians as a whole were as apt as others to vent their frustrations upon their kin. Compared with examples from later America and from Western Europe, the proportion of intimate homicides in Pennsylvania was striking. Some historical situations registered higher proportions than Pennsylvania—up to roughly one-half of all homicides being intimate. But these higher proportions typically coincided with low rates of homicides overall. In the case of Pennsylvania, overall rates were high but were combined with high proportions of intimate homicide.[7]

Between thirteen and twenty-five men killed their wives or intimate companions, several of them with remarkable violence. The laconic records from the eighteenth century do not permit further analysis of these murdering husbands and their motivations. However, more recent historical cases suggest what caused the earlier men to murder. To speak broadly, defense of ego and patriarchalism stimulated many of the men. Behavior that attacked the husband's ego or belittled his status sparked his violence. It may have been a wife's infidelity, but it likely was more pedestrian behavior, like her failure or refusal to meet his domestic demands—in housekeeping, child-rearing, and the like. If she did not accommodate his criticisms and demands, or even worse, candidly challenged him, she might suffer more quickly or more grievously.[8] John Ulrich Seiler (Hans Ulrich Seilor) typified such aggressive men when he stabbed his mistress to death in Philadelphia in November 1750 after she became "cross with him."[9] Actions such as seeking others' aid against a husband or lover, leaving his house, or running away have been occasions when husbands and lovers slew women.

If he killed his children as well as his wife, as John Myriack did, he fits a different profile. Men who kill their children, or children along with their spouse, show deep depression or despair rather than (or in addition to) unbridled temper and egotism. Patriarchal values may nevertheless be the culprit. Even without their wives accusing them of failure, men may have realized they failed economically or socially, at least by their own standards and goals. Failure depends upon aspirations and obligations or sense of duty. Men who internalized values of strength, command, independence, or men who aspired to achieve status became candidates for failure more readily than insensitive and narcissistic husbands and fathers. Men despondent over their unfulfilled dreams have killed not only wives but also their children, because they despaired for the children's future or prospects in life: better that the children die than face grim adulthood and the same environment that wounded the father.[10] Women too who found themselves in dire economic and social straits (but without the psychic contribution of patriarchy) and became despondent were the ones who committed infanticide, and they were common.

Pennsylvania homes also witnessed murders beyond the nuclear family, including extended relatives, servants, slaves, masters of servants and slaves, and neighbors. In Cumberland County James Anderson killed William Barnet, his son-in-law, in the summer of 1774. In 1798 Dauphin County's John Hauser (or Haner) slew his brother-in-law, Francis Shitz.

William Davis killed his master, William Cloud, in Chester County in
1728. Timothy McAuliffe was slain by his servant James Burke in 1784.[11]
Masters murdered their subordinates more often than slaves, servants,
or apprentices murdered their masters. Henry Reynolds was responsible
for the death of his maidservant in Chester County in 1685. Witnesses
testified that prior to her death Reynolds had repeatedly beaten her with
a broom and kicked her. Charles Jagler (or Seigler), a Lancaster apothecary, was convicted in November 1756 of poisoning his maidservant, Ros-
ina Holdersinger.[12] In 1772 in Lancaster County, John Nicholas beat to
death his apprentice, John O'Neil, when Nicholas discovered the lad
sleeping on the job. Even after the wounded boy mumbled, "Master, you
have beat me terribly," Nicholas continued to thrash him.[13] Lancaster
County's William Crawford apparently stabbed to death his female slave,
Dinah, in 1767. Though witnesses indicated that Crawford had threatened her life on numerous occasions and though the evidence against
him was formidable, the jury refused to convict. John and Elizabeth
Bishop of Berks County sadistically mistreated their "negro wench,"
Louisa, until she collapsed and died in April 1772. William Bullock's violent behavior toward his eight-year-old male slave "at Sundry Times" in
1742 led to the boy's death, another of many such fatalities where the
perpetrator went unpunished. On occasion, however, as in the case
where Hannah, slave of John Frederick Hillegas, tried to poison her mistress, slaves attacked their owners and their owners' property.[14]

Alcohol clearly fueled more than two dozen murders and probably
accounted for many more, although the surviving records do not always
indicate intoxication. Pennsylvania authorities perennially bemoaned
drunkenness and punished abuses flowing from it, but they did not prohibit the manufacture and sale of alcohol. Even among the most abste-
mious Pennsylvanians, drinking was a problem. Drunkenness was the
third most common violation of church discipline among Quakers and
their most intractable problem. Quakers believed that drunkenness
inexorably led to other social and personal problems. Drunkards cursed,
quarreled, slid into debt, neglected their families, and in some cases
killed.[15]

Alcohol-related homicides typically involved long-time friends and
acquaintances. William and Mary Dickson killed neighbor Allan Regan
in Lancaster County in July 1772, by hitting him repeatedly with a board
after Regan came to the Dickson home to complain of Mary Dickson's
alleged abuse of Regan's wife, Anne. Both Dicksons were drunk at the
time. Charles Reid of Philadelphia, described as "wealthy but . . . a wild,
dissolute, incorrigible young man," provoked a quarrel in February
1789, while drunk, with the boatman he knew at Market Street ferry and
killed him.[16] Alcohol and harvest work proved to be a particularly lethal

combination. Almost universally farmers supplied rum to their field hands who worked longer hours than usual to bring in a crop. While the rum was typically regarded as a refreshment to sustain otherwise weary workers, Quakers and others, like Dr. Benjamin Rush, focused on the disorder the rum provoked. In a case in point, eighteen-year-old Patrick Sherry killed John Weigert with a sickle in York County in May 1786 during one such fray, with what one onlooker characterized as "an undesigned, unlucky stroke."[17]

Emotionally disturbed men succumbed to depression, melancholia, or deep-rooted anger and murdered innocent people. Philadelphia jeweler and former army officer John Bruelman, "weary of life" in October 1760, determined to shoot the first person he should meet. His unlucky victim proved to be neighbor and billiards partner, Robert Schull. Henry Halbert (or Henrich Albers), ground down by failure and depression, also killed the first person he met on August 30, 1765. Encountering twelve-year-old Jacob Woolman, the son of an acquaintance, Halbert cut his throat and watched impassively as the boy bled to death. In Bedford County in 1795 German Reformed minister Cyriacus Spangenberg (or Spongenburgh), believing himself to be carrying out God's wishes, stabbed to death Jacob Glessner, Sr., during a church service, crying, "My Saviour did it. . . . I will die free now and go to my Jesus." Severely depressed and suffering delusions, John Lewis murdered his pregnant wife in 1760. Chester County's Terrence Rogers, who admitted to killing Edward Swainey in 1743, apparently was the first individual in Pennsylvania to seek acquittal based on a plea of insanity, but others quickly followed suit.[18] Of all the murders that occurred in Pennsylvania, murders involving insanity appear most like their modern parallels. What distinguishes the early ones from late twentieth-century shootings at schools, post offices, and places of employment is mostly the availability of handguns and automatic weapons. In the eighteenth century, demented murderers rarely had more than one victim.

Many murders arose from the proximity of Indians to whites, often went unreported to authorities, and left little more than a hint that they existed. Among the cases that did get public notice, an unidentified Indian killed one Thomas Wright forty miles from Conestoga in 1727 and escaped authorities by going "away hunting." The Delaware Mushmelon (or Mussmemeelin, among other variations) confessed to the brutal killing (and suspected cannibalism) of Indian trader John Armstrong and two of his assistants in April 1744.[19] In 1751, five Indians were arrested and incarcerated for trying to kill "an Old Indian from Germantown." Though they badly wounded the old man, when he survived they were released.[20]

Among Pennsylvania's white population, men committed murder

more frequently than women. In three principal categories of homicide used in early Pennsylvania—premeditated murder, manslaughter, and death by chance medley—men outnumbered women by large margins. Of the 321 recorded charges of first-degree murder, men were involved in 278 (87 percent of the cases). They also monopolized authorities' attention in 113 of 120 (94 percent of the trials) manslaughter prosecutions. No woman was prosecuted for death by chance medley. Only in infanticide proceedings—the fourth category of homicide—did women constitute the overwhelming majority of defendants. Even there, several men were charged with abetting the infanticides. Peter Harp was convicted in 1732 of aiding Margaret Shitts in concealing the birth, death, and burial of her illegitimate child, presumably under the infanticide statute. Negro Abraham was tried as an accessory in the infanticide prosecution of Northampton's Hilkiah Vanveyan in October 1780.[21] However, the accused in most infanticide cases were women.

In homicide cases in Pennsylvania through 1800, men tended to murder men. Of the eighty-four men sentenced to die for the crime of murder (records in cases where defendants were acquitted are less reliable regarding victims), sixty-five (77.4 percent) slew other men. In only nineteen cases (22.6 percent) of men convicted of murder were the victims female. In ten of these last cases the slain were wives of the accused. In the remaining nine instances where women were victims (and where the victim is known), four involved elderly women slain during robberies, one victim was the mistress of the accused, and one was "a squaw."

Men have been responsible for most of the murder and violence suffered by humankind. David Courtwright has reminded us that, more than just males, it is young, single, undereducated, and unattached men, naturally aggressive in both their behavior and temperament, who have been responsible for this mayhem.[22] The history of homicide in early Pennsylvania does not offer compelling evidence for Courtwright's thesis. Young men incontestably contributed to the murder rate. For example, the wealthy young Charles Reid, whose 1789 killing of a boatman during a drunken rage excited Philadelphians, and Patrick McSherry, a young harvester whose assault upon a fellow worker in 1786 proved fatal, were typical of youths accused of murder. However, the most obvious and most frequent means by which young, unattached men caused homicides in Pennsylvania before 1801 was by committing bastardy and abandoning the pregnant, adolescent women, who then killed their illegitimate newborns. Despite these examples and others, a substantial percentage—probably a majority—of Pennsylvanians accused of murder before 1800 do not fit Courtwright's profile. They include married men like Nicholas Wyriek and John Bishop who, because of religious visions, alcoholism, anger, sadism, or a sense of injured pride, resorted to murder. The names of mature, employed, domesticated men commonly appear in the list of those thought to be guilty of murder. Of those sentenced to die for the crime of murder, where marital status is known, 45 percent were married at the time of their offense. The maturity of other accused may be inferred from their professional status, an uncommon achievement among young men: Charles Jagler was an apothecary, John Nicholas a blacksmith, John Bruelman a jeweler, John Jones a lawyer.[23]

Perpetrators of homicide who acted alone and were prosecuted seldom had multiple victims. Less than a dozen cases appear where more than a single individual was slain. The rarity of multiple victims can partly be credited to the lack of modern firearms in the hands of the single perpetrators, who might have killed more than one person had they been able—which appears most clearly in the case of demented men or women. Multiple victims tend, therefore, to be helpless or trusting persons, who likely could not or would not stop or flee from their assailants. Among these was John McDonald (or McDowell) of Bucks County, who killed Catherine Kraemer and her infant son in November 1785. Elizabeth Wilson was convicted in 1786 of slaying her twin bastard sons. A case of familicide in Chester in 1755 produced four victims. In that instance John Myriack killed and disfigured his wife, then killed two of his own children and a neighbor's infant. Another familicide case accounted for two victims when John Lewis of Chester County murdered his pregnant wife in 1760. The worst prosecuted homicide, in number of victims, differed from these because it was political and ethnic rather than familiar or intimate. The case was Frederick Stump's 1768 rampage against ten peaceful Indians in Cumberland County.[24] Other multiple-victim homicides against Indians, like Stump's, went unprosecuted.[25]

For homicides that did not exhibit premeditation or calculated brutality Pennsylvania prosecuted the accused for manslaughter rather than murder "with malice aforethought." Manslaughter was the unlawful killing of a human being without malice, either expressed or implied. It might be either done voluntarily, on impulse, or involuntarily but in the commission of another illegal offense. Homicides perpetrated by individuals under the influence of extreme mental or emotional disturbance were prosecuted under this statute. Peter Lesher of Lancaster County faced manslaughter charges in May 1782, when, after becoming persuaded that Zacharias Cummer "was the devil," he slashed him to death with a scythe. And yet when a clearly disturbed John Bruelman, formerly an officer in the Royal American Regiment, killed Robert Schull in September 1760, he told the court he had "nothing against" his victim; he merely wanted to be hanged. Authorities accommodated him.[26] One hundred and twenty cases of manslaughter appear in the Pennsylvania record. Perhaps as many as one fourth of these prosecutions began as indictments for murder, but were downgraded by prosecutors or juries.

A third option open to grand and trial jurors as well as to prosecutors was to charge an individual responsible for the death of another with "death by chance medley." In criminal law chance medley is a sudden affray. This charge generally applied to any homicide by misadventure or killings done in the defense of one's self. James Hendricks, Christian Nisewanger, and Peter Sware, all of Chester County, for example, were convicted of "Homicide by Chance Medley" in the death of Albert Hendricks in May 1732. Authorities viewed Hendricks's death to be a "shooting by misfortune" and eventually pardoned all three defendants. Pennsylvania clerks of court were not always careful in distinguishing between manslaughter or murder and death by chance medley, but some two dozen deaths by chance medley do appear.[27] Deaths occurring from fistfights where both combatants participated willingly, or from physical contests where participants voluntarily joined, were prosecuted under this statute.

Pennsylvania women probably committed more homicides than their contemporaries in other colonies did. One hundred and twenty charges of murder (including infanticide) were initiated against women (2.9 percent of all accusations directed toward women).[28] In the Revolutionary generation (1763–1790) alone Pennsylvania authorities initiated murder charges against almost twice as many women as did Massachusetts in more than half a century, and more than six times the number of women prosecuted in colonial North Carolina courts for that crime. Altogether nine women were executed for murder (not infanticide) in Pennsylvania, the first being Judith Roe in 1688. It was another thirty-six years before a second woman, Chester County's Elizabeth Murphy in 1724, went to the gallows for murder under the common law. Of those executed for murder, two were black. An additional two women, Sarah Williams of Cumberland County in 1787 and Mary Dickson of Lancaster County in 1772, were among those women convicted of murder but eventually pardoned.[29]

Of those accused of first-degree murder, most were charged with slaying neighbors or individuals they knew. Mary Dickson of Lancaster joined her husband in killing their neighbor, Allan Regan, after an argument over the Dicksons' conduct toward Regan's wife. Some, like Judith Roe, killed passersby and travelers for their money. In the spring of 1688, during her husband's absence, Roe, of Kent County, killed an unnamed man with an axe while he was abed in her home. Her son reported that he saw his mother "Strike the Man and Kill him with an Ax, the man being in bed." He then saw her "take money out of his pocket, tye a rope about the Mans Middle and drag him by his owne horse Tayl" to a nearby creek. Roe was convicted on this testimony, and more, offered by her children and husband.[30]

Most women brought to court for killing someone were prosecuted for infanticide.[31] Of the seventeen women condemned to die for homicide, thirteen were convicted of infanticide and four of killing adult women. All four women in the latter cases were charged in connection with a male accomplice and appeared to be more the abettor than the principal perpetrator. Prosecutors pressed infanticide charges aggressively in Pennsylvania, but with surprisingly little success. Though indictments for infanticide rose steadily throughout the eighteenth century, especially after 1750, convictions failed to increase at the same rate. Only after the penal reforms of 1793, when capital sentences were reduced, were convictions commonplace. In the first ten prosecutions following the law's revision on infanticide, juries voted seven convictions.[32]

Any examination of infanticide must focus on mothers who allegedly murdered children in their first year. Some historians have advocated a broader definition of infanticide that would include all parents responsible for the deaths of their children if those children had not reached the "age of discretion." This definition would include all such cases relating to the deaths of children nine years old or younger.[33] However, authorities in early Pennsylvania did not employ the infanticide statute in cases of children that age. They indicted married parents for murder under the common law when children older than one year old were involved. Thus, Kelly Rogers, a poor, single women living near Carlisle who killed her eight-year-old son to prevent him from suffering from poverty, as she had done, was indicted not for infanticide but for murder.[34] Only one married women, Margaret Rauch of Northampton County, was tried for infanticide; she had conceived the child before she married by a man other than her husband.[35]

A woman who had killed her child could be prosecuted under either of two laws, murder at common law or infanticide under the 21 James I, c.27 (1624) statute. It made a grave difference. If prosecuted for murder, a woman was viewed as innocent until the court established her guilt. If prosecuted under the infanticide statute, which was "received" in Pennsylvania in 1718, a woman was viewed as guilty. The infanticide statute assumed that the child was born alive. As a consequence, if a woman's plea was that her child was stillborn, it was her responsibility to prove it, and to do so "by one witness at least." Concealing a newborn's death, even if the death was from natural causes, was punishable by death under the 1624 law.

Under the circumstances it would appear that prosecutors would have little difficulty securing convictions against women charged with infanticide. But that was not the case. Juries refused to interpret the infanticide statute literally. Because infanticide was a capital crime (1718–1786) and because invariably young women were prosecuted, jurors sought to judge each case on its own merits and to give the benefit of doubt to defendants. If defendants in infanticide cases shed tears or were found to have prepared in any way for the coming of the child ("benefit of linen," it was called), acquittal ordinarily followed. Tears and "linen" indicated to jurors that the woman presumably loved the child and regretted its demise. That alone often was sufficient to convince them to acquit.

Juries balked at assigning young women to death in infanticide cases and effectively thwarted the law. They made the prosecutors' work very difficult, sometimes impossible. Prosecutors needed to prove to the satisfaction of the jurors the condition of the newborns and the mothers' malice or willful neglect of them. Coroners could be useless to the prosecutors. The unscientific nature, or incompetence, of many of their inquests was glaring. During his investigation of the death of Alice Clifton's child in 1787, for instance, the coroner failed to question carefully either Clifton or members of the household in which she lived, and neglected to keep a written record of his findings. He permitted Clifton to be examined in her room by several people who had no official standing before he questioned her. Because of the crowded room in which she was examined, it was a long while before the coroner discovered the child's throat had been slit "from ear to ear." The coroner and a doctor who accompanied him to Clifton's room later testified that they made their initial judgment on what the defendant and several others told them rather than on personal scrutiny of the victim. When asked why he had not conducted a more careful and systematic examination of the room and its occupants, the coroner responded that he "did not know it was necessary."[36]

Other circumstances encouraged jurors to acquit in infanticide prosecutions. Everyone knew the birth experience was dangerous. Respiratory and venereal infections, unhygienic conditions, malnutrition, gastritis, congenital defects, and exhaustion on the part of birthing mothers all could contribute to infant deaths, as could an exhausted mother rolling over on a newborn child during sleep. The records of Gloria Dei church between 1786 and 1831 confirm that the birth experience was traumatic; almost one-third of all those buried were under the age of one.[37] Determining precisely to what degree natural conditions or health problems may have contributed to an infant's death was nearly impossible. The fact that young, unwed mothers often hid their infants following their deaths (or murders), and that evidence of the crime often was not discovered until long after the fact, additionally burdened prosecutors seeking to persuade juries to convict. For a number of reasons, then, ranging from the dangers of childbirth to inept forensics, convictions for infanticide were extremely difficult.[38]

Seventy-eight men and women were accused of slaying infants or with being accessories under 21 James I, c. 27 (1624) or later revisions of that statute. Seventy-three of them were women who allegedly slew their illegitimate infants. Fifty-seven (78 percent) of those seventy-three were indicted and fifty-six finally went before juries. Twenty-four of the fifty-six were convicted and eight were executed. Six went to prison and served no more than two years. Six others were pardoned. Two of the fifty-seven are known to have fled.

Patterns of prosecutions of infanticide cases shifted over time.[39] The year 1768 proved to be something of a watershed for infanticide prosecutions, although the reason is unclear. Prior to that year Pennsylvania witnessed few prosecutions, a fairly high conviction rate (eleven of nineteen tried), and the highest execution rate (26 percent of those tried) in its history. The period between 1768 and 1785 saw few convictions and fewer executions. From the time that Catherine Kreps of Berks County was hanged in 1767 to the execution of Elizabeth Wilson in 1785, only Lancaster's Catherine Fisher (1779) was convicted and sentenced to die. Fisher's defiance of the court and its personnel, her unrepentant utterances, and the undeniable damage done to her infant's skull doubtless account for her execution.[40] The year 1785 was another turning point. A third phase, between 1785 to the end of the century, produced a growing tendency to convict in infanticide cases. Five of the final eight cases prosecuted in the eighteenth century ended in conviction. This greater proclivity to convict in infanticide cases is explained in part by the changing attitudes toward women, and in even larger part by revisions of the law. After 1786 the law called for young girls convicted of infanticide to be sent to prison rather than face the hangman. Additional modifications in the 1790s permitted prosecutors much greater latitude in charging women for the deaths of their infants and gave juries greater discretion in determining their punishment.

Though there was no lack of suspicious infant deaths in Philadelphia before the nineteenth century, most infanticide prosecutions occurred outside the city. If Philadelphia women killed their newborns or let them die in numbers comparable with rural women—and in all likelihood they did—they mostly went undetected and unprosecuted. The greater anonymity of the city and the greater opportunities for hiding the corpse without raising suspicion probably account for the low numbers of infanticide cases in Philadelphia, as does the fact that urban women had more freedom of movement than did their country counterparts. Additionally, older women in urban settings viewed younger, unrelated women differently from the way rural adult women did and, thus, had less interest in bringing their actions to the attention of authorities.[41] Only thirteen allegations (17.8 percent of the total) of infanticide came before Philadelphia courts. Lancaster County prosecuted the same number of cases as did Philadelphia. Berks and Chester Counties each witnessed nearly as many infanticide cases as did Philadelphia. Northampton County with perhaps a fifth of the population of Philadelphia and Philadelphia County tried half the number of the larger jurisdiction.

Young, unmarried, pregnant women typically returned from the city to their country homes while determining what to do. Thus, Elizabeth Wilson, who ultimately was executed in Chester County in 1785 for allegedly slaying her infant twin sons, became pregnant in Philadelphia, then returned to her parents' home in Chester County to await the birth of her children. Wealthy Philadelphians like Elizabeth Drinker, upon discovering their female servants to be pregnant, often sent them to the countryside to avoid embarrassment and unwanted gossip.[42]

Differences in prosecution patterns existed despite the fact that conditions conducive to infanticide were similar in communities throughout Pennsylvania. Differences in prosecution rates are explained less by the number of infant deaths in each jurisdiction than the enthusiasm and success of authorities in pursuing those responsible. Berks, Chester, and Lancaster Counties, for instance, aggressively prosecuted infanticide cases and achieved the highest rates in Pennsylvania. Nearly half of all infanticide charges occurred in the three counties. Ethnic and religious factors—the counties were heavily German, pietist, or Quaker—clearly played a role in determining the prosecution of infanticide.[43]

Numerous cases where parents killed their infants went unprosecuted. Christ Church officials in Philadelphia in May 1769 alerted authorities to "an unknown infant" found buried "about ten inches underground" in the church's cemetery. Still another "unknown infant" was recovered later that same year after it had been tossed into the Delaware River and became lodged against a Philadelphia wharf. An unidentified female infant was found in April 1772, in the city's "Strangers' burying grounds." Another was stumbled upon "lying dead by a path," "starved," and "exposed to the weather." A coroner's jury subsequently concluded that she had "come to her death by the Cruelty of the Parents unknown."[44] Occasionally infants came to grief at the hands of stand-in parents charged to care for the children in the parents' absence. Thirteen-year-old Elizabeth Thomas of Bucks County was convicted of manslaughter in the 1730 death of an eighteen-month-old infant "over whom she had charge."[45]

In crimes of homicide (murder, manslaughter, and infanticide) it is possible that the men running the justice system in Pennsylvania discriminated against women defendants. A statistic that raises suspicion about men's impartiality is that grand juries were 18.7 percent less likely to give a woman than a man a bye (*ignoramus*) in homicide accusations. As a quantitative measurement alone, that is the greatest gender disparity across the whole range of crimes and prosecutions in Pennsylvania.[46] It could have gravely jeopardized some women's lives and liberty. In the homicides they were accused of, women were only 50 of the 440 murder and manslaughter defendants, but 73 of the 78 infanticide offenders. In those numbers lies part of an explanation for the indictment disparity. In the case of infanticide, women's likelihood of being prosecuted was patently greater then men's: childbirth linked mothers with newborns, living or dead. That obvious link would have been difficult for a grand jury to ignore, and therefore they would likely have indicted an accused mother. At the trial stage of infanticide cases, however, the trial juries could consider a multitude of other circumstances that would exculpate an accused mother. They did make such considerations, which led to acquitting 45.2 percent of the prosecuted women.[47] That rate of acquittal explains in turn a disparity that women enjoyed over men in all homicide trials: they were 20.2 percent more likely to be acquitted.

The explanation of women's disparity in indictments does not end with infanticide, however. Although women assailants were not nearly as intimate with their adult victims as mothers were with their newborn victims, they nonetheless knew their adult victims. On the exceptional occasions when women kill, they perennially tend to kill persons they know—husbands, other family, and neighbors. Theirs are "intimate homicides." That being the case, their crimes are easily detected and the women are easily indicted—little different from men who commit intimate homicides. The case against them is often compelling, and grand jurors feel almost bound to indict. But, as in the case of infanticide, trial jurors may not feel, and did not feel, equally obliged to convict, after viewing mitigating circumstances of women killing. Grand jurors believed the women had done it. Petit jurors often felt that they were not blameworthy. The upshot was that women were indicted more often than men, but convicted less often. Women were 9.2 percent more likely than men to be indicted for murder and manslaughter and 13.6 percent more likely than men to be acquitted. In cases of assault, women more often than men were not indicted, by a margin of 6.9 percent.

In archaic Anglo-American law, suicide would not deserve its own rubric. The act of taking one's own life constituted murder, self-murder, and "an offense against God, against the king, and against Nature." The case of Kelly Rogers of Cumberland County, cited above, links suicide and murder in a modern, social scientific way. Professing to have no hope for their future, Rogers killed her son, attempted suicide, and failed. She typifies how commonly despairing parents in Pennsylvania and elsewhere killed children, spouses, and then themselves.[48] Moreover, social science supplies a theoretical and psychological link between homicide and suicide that can be empirically tested. Sociologist Martin Gold has theorized that suicide expresses the frustration or thwarted hopes of the person in question, although homicide can too. The different course of action the subject takes depends upon his or her sense of guilt and blame. If he faults himself, or feels deeply held restraints on aggressive behavior, he chooses suicide. If he blames others, and blaming overbears his sense of restraint, he kills others. Gold's hypothesis is open to testing by means of examining populations from different times, places, cultures, and genders for different homicide-suicide practices and different shared values and esteem for restraint. In a modest way, Pennsylvanians can be so tested; modestly, because past people deliberately obfuscated the record of suicide.[49]

Before the seventeenth century, these self-murderers were tried posthumously by a coroner's jury, and if a conviction was returned, the victim and his family were "savagely punished." Their moveable goods, including money (and debts owed to them) were forfeited to the crown. They were denied proper burials. First exposed naked to the public, then cast into an improvised grave, the victim's body was to be pierced by a wooden stake. No prayers were allowed and no minister was to be in attendance.[50] Though the law remained intact until the nineteenth century, by the mid-eighteenth century, English coroners' juries more often than not softened its sanctions by declaring the victim *non compos mentis* rather than finding him a *felo de se*, a felon of himself.[51] By the time of the American Revolution the law relating to suicide was under severe attack.[52]

Pennsylvania practice in handling suicides closely approximated the English. If anything, Pennsylvania coroners' juries were even quicker than their English counterparts in palliating the harshness of the law. They did so in three ways. In the first, they followed the lead of English juries by finding the deceased *non compos mentis*. Increasingly in the eighteenth century, people came to believe that the act of suicide was itself evidence of insanity. The Quaker diarist Elizabeth Drinker reported a typical case, where Robert, Robert Parr's manservant, feeling "unwell and low spirited," took his own life in September 1759. Drinker noted, "the jury brought in a verdict of Non compos mentis."[53] Though this slaying, and similar ones, posed a real problem for juries because servant deaths raised the possibility of abuse-induced suicide, or murder on the

part of the master, insanity verdicts seemingly offered the least complicated solution for all concerned.

Other means of circumventing the law included the juries' choice of
finding no verdict, or of ruling the death "accidental." In April 1772,
for instance, a young mulatto woman was found drowned in the Delaware River near Philadelphia's Hamilton's Wharf. In the following
month another unknown woman and two unidentified men were pulled
from the river. Juries failed to decide whether these deaths were suicides. A jury in October 1772 believed that an unknown woman found
in the reeds along the Delaware River had died aboard ship and had
been tossed overboard "in order to save Funeral Charges," but jurors
refused to rule out suicide. Ultimately, they took no stand. Juries in 1769
were similarly reluctant to find a definite verdict of suicide. They failed
to make a determination on five adults removed from the river in that
year. When Charles Story (or Stoy), a servant, was found floating in the
Delaware in July 1769, a jury concluded only that he was "supposed to
be accidently Drowned."[54] These noncommittal findings saved victims
and their families alike from severe penalties and the scandal that might
accompany suicide. Increasingly juries seemed to be saying that death
was punishment enough; the victim and his or her family should not
suffer added burdens. Noncommittal findings on the part of coroners'
juries served that end. Another version of this strategy was simply to rule
self-inflicted deaths "accidental."

Coroners' juries blunted the intent of the law in still a third way by
failing to carry out its specific provisions even after finding that a death
was, in fact, suicide. Mary Snider, Frances Herr, and Mary Gordon were
found to have committed suicide by drowning in the fall of 1774. Ann
Waln hanged herself in December of the same year and her death, too,
was ruled a suicide. Yet the evidence suggests that these women did not
suffer the penalties of the law. Women, of course, were less vulnerable
than men to the forfeiture penalties, but apparently female suicides did
not suffer ignominious burials either. Nor did a Philadelphia man who
took his own life in July 1753, leaving behind a wife and several small
children.[55]

The only instances in Pennsylvania where suicides led to *felo de se* findings on the part of juries and the self-murderer received a profane burial
or suffered rituals of desecration occurred with convicted or suspected
felons. Phillip Cane was incarcerated in Philadelphia in 1741 under suspicion of having slain William Bunting while robbing his home. While
awaiting trial, Cane committed suicide by slashing his throat. Cane's
body was therefore "expos'd to public view [and] afterwards dragg'd out
of Town, and buried in a cross Road."[56]

Questionable deaths among servants and slaves also raise difficult questions for students of suicide in early America, for on one level there was an inclination among officials to treat deaths by abuse as "suicides," and on the other, to deny that bound laborers were driven by conditions to kill themselves. In the latter cases magistrates often found it convenient to find that the deaths were "accidental." Confusing any attempt to determine the extent of conditions leading to suicide in Pennsylvania is the fact that numerous suicide attempts were botched and do not appear in the record.[57]

The practice of magistrates, jurors, family, and neighbors makes clear that historical counts of suicide misrepresent its frequency, which was greater than can be counted from justice records. Despite the difficult of reaching a compelling figure, a rate for Pennsylvania for the 1730s appears to have been 2.7 per 100,000, a figure lower than those available for England.[58] Unofficial comments on suicide confirm the existence of the "dark figure" regarding suicide.[59] Suicide was so common in England that it came to be referred to as "la mort à l'anglaise." Pamphlets lamenting the "Frequency and daily Encrease of wanton and Uncommon self-murderers" in England appeared throughout the eighteenth century. Michael MacDonald and Terence R. Murphy, in their study of suicide in early modern England, demonstrate that foreigners held the same view of England and appeared amazed at "the nonchalance with which the English cast away their lives."[60]

Similarly in Pennsylvania, comments outside the coroners' records tell of suicides. In March 1731, a Lancaster farmer "with a design to clear Land and settle with his Family, hang'd himself . . . the first morning [they] began to work." Observers thought it "remarkable that of 7 or 8 families in that Neighborhood, there are but two who have not suffer'd by the like misfortune." In the summer of 1738, a five-year-old hanged himself on a fence after being told "vivid stories of the hanging of blacks for poisoning." Relatives believed the stories "had fill'd his Mind." He told his parents he had "dreamt about [his] Execution the Night before." A Philadelphia woman, "melancholy [for] some time before," shot herself to death in 1732. A seventeen-year-old female who had been "agitated" and "despondent" drowned herself in the Delaware River in January 1739.[61]

Black Pennsylvanians appear roughly as likely to commit suicide as whites. In their case, being minorities and unfree, their motives are less puzzling than for more common free people. Among enslaved black Pennsylvanians, the conditions of slavery took a severe psychological and physical toll and some resorted to suicide to end their misery. A slave took his own life in Philadelphia in November 1730. Another committed suicide in August 1742. A Negro woman hanged herself in September 1731. Still another black slave resorted to self-murder in July 1738. A

Negro male assigned public corporal punishment by a Philadelphia court in June 1743, preferring death to public shame, "very heroically" cut his own throat at the pillory. Maria, a mulatto woman, seemingly drowned herself in the Delaware River in April 1772.[62]

Servants shared with slaves some of the conditions of the unfree and with them the effects, including suicide. Servants constituted a substantial portion of Pennsylvania suicides. A young male servant went into the woods in the summer of 1731 and hanged himself. Eventually attracted by the smell, searchers discovered him, his "Head still hanging, but his Body had dropp'd off and was lying on the ground." Another male servant in Chester County committed suicide in June 1738. Still another Chester servant, James Reilly, hanged himself in May 1746. Charles Story (or Stoy), a servant found floating in the Delaware River in July 1769, probably was a suicide. A young male servant tried twice to kill himself in August 1730. When he first hanged himself onlookers called for a coroner's jury. Before the jury could arrive the youngster had been revived but made a second effort at ending his life. When jurors did arrive 'he was upon his Legs again.'"[63]

Young women committed suicide in surprisingly large numbers. Indeed, almost half of the recorded suicides in Pennsylvania were women. Sarah Eastman of Philadelphia drowned herself in the Delaware in the fall of 1735. In 1739, a seventeen-year-old girl ended a long period of despondency (thought to be brought on by her being pregnant) by taking her own life. As we have seen, Mary Snider, Frances Herr, Mary Gordon, and Ann Waln took their own lives in 1774. Jamima Howard, who "appeared to be for sometimes past disordered," was a February 1773 suicide. Another woman, name unknown, took her own life in May of that same year.[64]

Pennsylvanians incarcerated in jails or workhouses also looked at suicide as an escape. Confined to a Chester County workhouse in 1738, a young white male hanged himself. Five years earlier, a woman assigned to Philadelphia's workhouse also took her life. John Webster, convicted in January 1752 in a Philadelphia court for stealing a silver teapot and a silver spoon, tried to commit suicide in the city prison. When he failed he was executed as scheduled. Phillip Cane was more successful in his attempt to take his life. Convicted of murder and burglary in 1741, he died after slashing his own throat.[65]

Pennsylvania suicides chose a number of methods to end their life. Individuals seeking to terminate their lives occasionally used guns. Men turned to this remedy more often than women, but a Philadelphia woman shot herself to death in May 1732. Knives also were utilized on occasion in suicide attempts. Michael Boyle, for instance, cut his own throat in March 1731. Phillip Cane died the same way in April 1741.

Clearly the two most popular strategies for ending one's life in Pennsylvania were hanging and drowning. Women seemed to favor the latter; men the former.

Although individual cases of suicide are puzzling and idiosyncratic, when numbers of cases are examined some order appears and some insight into society emerges. An impression from suicides in early Pennsylvania is that suicide appeared disproportionately among the unfree, minorities, and women. In turn, there may well be a commonality among them that supplies a rationale for their recourse to suicide. As Gold theorized, suicide expresses the frustration of the person in question, but that it is only one among at least two ways, suicide or homicide, of expressing frustration.[66] The difference in outcome depends upon the freedom of the subject to choose between the two. Obviously, some frustrated people lacked the physical freedom and ability to commit aggression and murder—the incarcerated, slaves, servants, and many women and children. Another category, that overlaps the first, are persons who have internalized or learned inhibitions which society deems appropriate for their kind—women, children, and some blacks. They were taught docility and submissiveness and learned it so well that they could not strike out at others without violating their own ethic and feeling guilt and shame. Instead, they turned upon themselves.

As Roger Lane has aptly shown in the case of nineteenth-century Americans, altered conditions can lead masses of free adult men, who had long been apt to vent frustration upon others, to adopt ideals of self-control which enhanced the possibility that they would commit suicide.[67] Industrial labor and universal education conditioned men and boys to curb their aggression toward others and taught that respect and self-respect came from a disciplined life. In the era examined here, before the appearance of these economic and social conditions, these restrictions were nevertheless prescribed to the groups who were most likely to commit suicide, especially women. Women comprised half the suicides, but numbered only 13.4 percent of the accused murders. As for the adult men, they were freer to be aggressive and to murder, and they did.

Although the numerous assaults prosecuted in Pennsylvania make Pennsylvania exceptional, many or most assaults and batteries did not become part of any criminal court proceedings.[68] This dark figure of unreported crime was far more often the case with assault than with murders. Often victims of assault wanted to exclude public officers from their business for a variety of reasons, including the cost and time involved in judicial proceedings. Or they preferred different amends from those the justice system afforded. Some persons and whole cultures have looked upon physical violence as a part of life and no business of the state or "outsiders." Andrew Jackson, descended from Ulster migrants to Pennsylvania, recalled his mother instructing him, "The law affords no remedy for such outrage that can satisfy a gentleman. Fight."[69]

Some of the most influential and powerful men in Pennsylvania turned to fisticuffs on occasion. The 1764 fist fight between John Dickinson, author of the famous Revolutionary pamphlet, "Letters from a Pennsylvania Farmer," and Joseph Galloway, speaker of the Assembly and Quaker, is only the most notorious Pennsylvania example of a physical confrontation that did not go to the courts.[70] Other assaults appear only in the discipline records of various churches. Still others evolved into civil actions rather than criminal prosecutions and thus do not appear in criminal records. When, in 1685, John Bristol and Samuel Rowland quarreled in Chester County, Rowland attempted to shoot Bristol but onlookers wrested the weapon from him. In the process Rowland had his "haire torne and face Blood[ied]." Rather than see Rowland prosecuted in criminal court, Bristol sued and won damages in civil proceedings.[71] The numbers of such cases increased dramatically after 1750.

Similarly, criminal court records obscure the actual number of assaults because assaults frequently escalated into more serious crimes and were prosecuted as those offenses. For instance, assaults sometimes grew into riots—which in this study are not numbered with assaults. Authorities ordinarily charged those involved in such affrays with riot rather than assault. In May 1795, a scuffle broke out between workers at a Southwark ropewalk and the crewmen of a French privateer. The fight quickly escalated, and two crewmen and a worker were eventually killed. The tumult was substantial enough to warrant the calling out of troops to calm and then patrol the area. Officials deemed the development a riot rather than a series of assaults and essentially prosecuted the affair as such. A jury refused to sort out culpability and acquitted all those accused.[72] No one was convicted of the slayings.

In the case of female victims of assault, ancillary records demonstrate that complaints and indictments in the courts do not represent all the significant attacks on women. Numerous women whose names do not appear in criminal court dockets or papers were brought to the Philadelphia Alms House complaining of being beaten and otherwise physically abused by their fathers, masters, lovers, and other male acquaintances and associates.

As in the case of homicide, men vastly outnumbered women as assailants, women comprising only 10.0 percent ($N=1014$) of the total. Because women appear infrequently in public records, the predominance of men produces more public evidence about these assailants, especially their wealth and social status. As for wealth—measured by property taxes and assessments—violent men were undistinguished in the amount of property they owned; they were neither impoverished nor rich, nor much different from all accused men. The mean percentile rank of men accused of assault in Chester County was no lower than 54.0 and no higher than 59.6.[73] They do not differ significantly from all accused men respecting wealth, since they share the same mean percentile.

However, 37 percent of the assailants in Chester County were missing from the tax lists. Compared with all accused men, of whom 61.5 percent were missing, that 37 percent figure clearly raises them above the status of all accused men. Missing accused men presumably were transients, poor, or servants (or more than one of these) because these were absent from the tax lists. Assailants were less often to be found among these unfortunate men. Assailants were more rooted or stable and enjoyed more social bonds and wealth than other accused men.

Among the 975 cases from Chester County where the records specify the vocations of the men accused, the two largest groups by far were yeomen farmers and large property owners, with 57.3 percent, and second, laborers with 27.6 percent.[74] There were nine servants, too, but no slaves. Since landowners constituted 64.4 percent of the taxable population of the county and landholding tenants were an additional 6.3 percent, yeomen were underrepresented among the accused. Laborers, on the other hand, were likely overrepresented. The percent of laborers in the population cannot be easily specified because it is not a category in the tax lists. Another 61 (6.3 percent) accused were scattered among the weaving, tailoring, blacksmithing, cordwaining, and innkeeping trades. Dual occupations, combining farming and a trade, were common in rural Pennsylvania, making it difficult to segregate these and other artisans from the agricultural population and examine them for any peculiar proclivities toward assault or other crimes.

The male victims of assault appear much like their male assailants. First, their mean property rank (low alternative) was the 55.5 percentile (high alternative was 58.4), little more than one percentile away from the assailants' mean.[75] Victims who were missing from the tax lists were slightly more common than the missing assailants—44.9 percent of all victims compared to 37 percent for assailants. Assault victims were, however, rather poorer than victims in general, since the latter had a mean wealth percentile of 60.4. And slightly more of the assault victims were missing from the tax lists than were all victims (46.0 percent versus 39.8 percent). The data demonstrate that in rural Pennsylvania, the poor were not assaulting the rich (or vice versa), whether or not they had reason or motive to do so. As in modern America, assailants and victims were economic peers. Physical intimacy and convenience may have been

TABLE 4.1. Occupations of Male Victims of Crime in Chester County, 1682–1800

Occupation	All crimes[1] (N = 333)	Assaults (N = 198)
constable	31.2	48.5
yeoman farmer	12.3	11.1
laborer	9.0	0.5
sheriff	7.2	10.1
esquire/attorney	6.6	6.6
servant	6.0	4.5
innkeeper	2.7	1.0
husbandman	2.1	1.5
weaver	1.8	1.0
justice of peace	1.8	1.5
tax collector	1.5	2.5
master of servant	1.5	1.0
slave	1.5	1.0
blacksmith	1.5	2.0
wool comber	1.5	1.5
physician	1.2	2.0

[1]Left column contains occupations of 1 percent or more only.

the critical determinant of who assaulted whom. Assailants assaulted people they knew, and if they were poor, they knew other poor people.

That said, among the victims of assault with known vocations, constables swept ahead of all others, being 48.5 percent of the total (Table 4.1). Constables also were the most common victims of all varieties of crime.[76] As assault victims they had the company of other officers of the justice system. Justices, sheriffs, and tax collectors comprised another 13.1 percent of victims. Lawyers—not enforcers of the law, but at least officers of the court—comprised another 6.6 percent. In one respect, the data are not surprising. The men with easiest access to the justice system were the officers of the system, and so assaulting a law officer may have been the likeliest way to get oneself prosecuted. Yet even with that explanation of their likelihood of being complainants, the 48.5 percent share remains astonishing and needs additional examination. The percentage appears most surprising in light of populations at risk. Yeomen farmers, for comparison, were 11.1 percent of assault victims, while they were the large majority of adult men in Chester County. On the other hand, there was only one constable per township or borough in the county but they were 48.5 percent of the victims.

The difference between a constable's susceptibility and a common farmer's was vocation: almost every constable was performing his office when he became a victim. Whereas the nonconstables were victims of theft, trespass, fraud, and a variety of other crimes, the constables were assaulted, beaten, shot at, and otherwise physically and verbally abused. And this conspicuous abuse occurred in that county of Pennsylvania with the highest concentration of nonviolent people in Pennsylvania, or for that matter, all of America.

The job rather than the incumbents increased the jeopardy of constables. They had a bewildering variety of duties: attend the courts, serve writs and warrants, pursue and apprehend indicted persons, draw up property assessments, collect taxes, distrain property of delinquents, compile lists of ratepayers for jury selection, and maintain the peace and the watch. They were the closest equivalent to modern policemen before the nineteenth century, the publicly commissioned officers most apt to apprehend violators of the law and to be looking for them. Other than charges brought by private complaints, constables provided the grist for the grand juries' mill. They reported the number of "nigers," bonded servants, and "baseborn children" in their community, illegal "steels [stills] in use, "dere cilled out of Seeson," and single women suffering from "the rising of their apron."[77]

In the accounts of assaults on constables, friends and relatives of the accused commonly collaborated with the accused. They were often more violent and criminal than the principal. In November 1736, Constable George Slaton, for example, went to James McConnell's shop in West Nottingham to apprehend one Charles Patterson. McConnell swore that Patterson was not there and that he had not seen him. Unsatisfied, Slaton determined to search McConnell's house. When he informed McConnell's wife of his intent, she made a move toward the loft of the house. At that same moment, Patterson appeared from the loft and with a hanger (a hook) in hand, threatened that no man would take him. Slaton decided to guard the house while help was summoned from the nearest justice. Suddenly, Patterson broke from the house to the orchard where McConnell stood at the head of a mare on which he had just put a bridle. Patterson rode off through a gap in the fence that had just been opened.[78]

In 1697 a Chester County constable and several women sought out a woman suspected of "bringing forth a bastard child and murthering the same." The constable reported, "Upon their telling the occasion of their coming, the Sd Barbra, starting up in her bed and catching a knife out of the wall, swore if any of the women touched her she would have their hearts blood." Her brothers and sister quickly rallied to her cause "with knives and staves in their hands" and "swore the death of men or women that should touch their sister." Seventy-three years later in rather similar circumstances, Constable James Kelly was serving a warrant on William Little for committing bastardy on one Ruth Allen. Five friends, none by the name Little, attacked Kelly and freed Little, who fled.[79]

Executing distress warrants was one of the most obnoxious duties constables were expected to perform. Even when distraint was a fair application of the law, the officer who entered a man's house to seize property aroused anger. In 1789, when Lewis Gable sued George Varner (Warner?) for a debt of about £2 and Varner would not pay, Constable William Griffith was obliged to seize a cow belonging to Varner. Thomas Davis and John Elvis joined Varner in assaulting Griffith and rescuing Varner's cow. More than at any other time in Pennsylvania's history, the grim economic conditions in rural counties in the 1780s and 1790s provoked these confrontations between law-enforcers and defensive farmers.[80]

Normally, the accused and their accomplices threatened to detain the constables while the accused or his property made an escape. Bodily harm often occurred while the accomplices wrestled with the constable, but death was a prospect, too. Constable Robert Young was on the road bringing George Gibson to Justice Walter Finney on an arrest warrant. Three men, their faces blacked, emerged from the woods, one carrying a gun and the other two clubs. They ordered Young to dismount and he refused. One man grabbed him by the leg to pull him down, another hit him with a club, and someone called to the assailant with the gun to shoot Young. The gunman tried but the gun misfired. Young spurred his horse and escaped the grip of one assailant but was clubbed on the back of his head. Again, someone shouted, "Shoot him, damn him, shoot him," and Young believed he heard the hammer of the gun snap a second time. Young escaped. He did not record whether Gibson did. Young suspected that his three assailants were the laborers working in Gibson's fields when he took Gibson into custody. Accomplices were not necessary in order to escape the constable. When a constable worked alone it seemed easy for two or more apprehended men to overpower him. Thus, Thomas Jenkins and mulatto Ben Boston assaulted John Edwards, constable of West Marlboro, and made their escape.[81]

Not surprisingly, the constable's office was unwelcome, and few men served repeatedly. Among the 1,184 officeholders compiled from twenty-seven sample years between 1692 and 1800 in Chester County, only twenty-three men (1.9 percent) repeated.[82] When nominated, men petitioned the county courts to be excused from serving. The inconvenience and unpleasantness of the job and the danger that occasionally threatened was reason enough for men to want to avoid it; some sent substitutes to serve in their place. Others pleaded that they were poor choices or incorrectly chosen, or that their situations would hardly bear the demands of service. John Hunt of Westtown Township paid Edward

Thornbury to serve his year as constable in 1767. Probably one of his last remaining obligations, Thornbury omitted to send the court the list of constable-eligible Westtown men for 1768. The court, perhaps with discriminatory intent, selected Hunt to serve. Hunt felt that he had done his stint, albeit virtually, and he wanted to be relieved of what he viewed as reappointment. Thomas Bull wrote the justices that he was unmarried, a "casual renter" without property in East Nantmel township, and he expected to move on. He was not a suitable person to be constable, he felt, and he expected the justices could find some more appropriate person.[83]

One of the hardship cases, petitioner Daniel Hoopes, found himself appointed constable and overseer of the poor in the same year, surely a gratuitous burden, according to Hoopes. But more: Marple township had not even returned his name to the court for constable, but rather Nathan Yarnall's, and moreover, he, Hoopes, owned no property in the township. A second, Joseph Hancock, related to the court a timeworn story of popular guile. He missed the Marple township meeting at which officers were nominated and his neighbors selected him! It seemed inconsiderate on their part, because Hancock missed the meeting in order to nurse his ailing wife. She shortly died, and now he was the sole care of his children, while he was burdened with the constable's duty. Since there were neighbors in Marple who had never served as constable, Hancock hoped one would be chosen to replace him, and to help the justices he appended a list of them.[84]

In light of the demands and the hazards of the constables' service, the men whom the courts penalized for avoiding service appear less blameworthy. In 1778, George Jacobs was fined the healthy sum of £25 for refusing to act in that capacity in York County. Three years earlier, Stephen Foltz of that same county was required to pay £45 for "contemptuously refusing to hold the office of constable." York's John Flander agreed to be named constable, but then refused to carry out his duties. In mountainous central Pennsylvania the situation became acute in the 1790s. The years after 1791 accounted for 42.9 percent of all contempt of court (evasion of duty) offenses, and 80.0 percent of these offenses were in five counties from Cumberland (whose share alone in that period was 39.2 percent) on west and north.[85]

Sheriffs were targets of assault in 9.1 percent of the cases of identified vocations in Chester County. These involved twenty assaults or riots against four or five sheriffs. The percentage is far below that for the constables and appears unexceptional—until compared with the populations at risk. The ratio of sheriffs to constables ranged from 1 to 17 in 1693 to 1 to 60 in 1785, but the ratio of sheriff victims to constable victims was about 1 to 12 or 1 to 15. Being a sheriff was therefore at least as hazardous as being a constable. Long-tenured sheriffs especially, like John Taylor and John Owen, learned to be vigilant.

John Owen was the victim of the worst recorded assault on a sheriff in Chester County. Owen went to the house of William Downard to arrest Charley Hickinbotom (Higgenbotham?). Jean Downard threw scalding broth at the sheriff and struck him with a stone. But the government's witness described unlikely persons appearing from odd quarters adding mayhem to the scene—where Hickinbotom did not even appear. John Starr got down a gun. Daniel O'Neall beat the sheriff with his fists, and threatened to hit with a hoe anyone who approached O'Neall. John Henthorn knocked a man to the floor and caused his head to bleed. James and Mary Henthorn beat some unnamed person with sticks.[86] It was a riot.

It is baffling to recall that John Owen was a Quaker and so a pacifist. The Society of Friends prohibited all Quakers from physically controlling other men and women, and the disciplinary articles of the Society made no allowances for magistrates to use force. So, how did this Quaker gain control of a scene like the Downards' and of armed, violent characters like Starr and O'Neall? Did he reason them into submission? Did he have nonpacifist constables with him who grappled with them and disarmed them? Or did he personally use force and the Society of Friends let it pass? The court papers describe neither any Quaker magistrate personally using force, nor any armed confederate helping sheriffs. But does the absence of mention necessarily indicate the absence of arms and even Quaker magistrates' use of them? Conclusive answers are not likely to appear.

The frequent attacks on officers of the law by men and women in Pennsylvania displayed widespread contempt for the justice system. An often-employed explanation of this kind of behavior holds that before the democracy of the nineteenth century, respect for government depended upon the élite status of the men who exercised public power. Élite officerholders evoked deference from commoners that commoners did not show officials of low birth and station.[87] The explanation applies best to Europe, with its hereditary ruling aristocracies. In the American colonies, with no equivalent élites, the usefulness of the explanation becomes arguable. In the case of Pennsylvania, with its evidence of contempt for officials of the law, might the status of the officials bear upon their being so often abused? First, the case of the officials is not all the same; constables differ greatly from sheriffs. Resisting and ridiculing constables was not exclusive to Pennsylvania; at least since Shakespeare parodied Constable Dogberry in *Much Ado about Nothing*, constables have not enjoyed public esteem or evoked much deference.[88] Their low social status seems to have caused their suffering.

In Pennsylvania, constables did not fit the explanation well, because their wealth, at least, did not put them in the lower classes. As Table 3.6 and Figure 2.1 illustrate, constables almost always ranked among the top forty percent of property owners in Chester County. The only time when they did not, in 1693, was ironically in the period when they were least abused and most respected. From 1693 through 1765, they consistently improved their economic status and yet came in for more abuse.

Ever since the medieval era in England, sheriffs were the social opposites of constables and enjoyed great deference. They fully support the thesis that private status and public authority were linked. In Pennsylvania, the wealth of sheriffs (Figure 2.1) located them in the top ten to twenty percent of property owners. Moreover, all but two of them before the Revolution were Quakers—in Pennsylvania, another token of élite status. But their wealth does not separate them from constables in any degree that approaches the gap between English sheriffs and constables. The gap aside, they were nevertheless as good an élite of wealth and religion as there was in Pennsylvania. The trouble was that their social status got them none of the deference that English sheriffs enjoyed. Pennsylvanians treated their sheriffs mostly the way they treated their constables—badly. Whatever laurels a man achieved in the province respecting vocation, property, church, and family did not evoke enough honor in public life to preserve him from bodily harm.

Equating Pennsylvania sheriffs with English sheriffs because both possessed great wealth or belonged to the preferred religious faith has at least one great shortcoming: they did not get to office in the same way. In England the Crown commissioned sheriffs; in Pennsylvania the voters elected them. Originally the governor chose one from two candidates per county in Pennsylvania; later, from just one. The election of a sheriff often proved to be the most interesting poll in which voters could participate and drew more of them to vote than did the elections for the Assembly.[89] For being similar to the English élite officeholders, Pennsylvania sheriffs, to repeat, were not deferred to like English sheriffs, and on the other hand, for being popularly chosen, these same sheriffs were not popularly respected. Archaic in some ways, progressive in others, they benefited in neither way.

Courtrooms in Pennsylvania too were not always decorous. Thomas Tunneclif found himself guilty of contempt after he told a 1688 Bucks County court that "I Care not a Pin for none of you." Israel Taylor of Bucks County was convicted of being in contempt after he called members of a jury "sworn Rogues." Chester County laborer Hans Hamilton drew a fine when he told a justice of the peace in 1737 that he was "a blockhead and an ass" and that "the King hath made so many asses justices that I can't get one to ride upon." Charles Grim of York County was fined twenty shillings in January 1752 when he threw a glass of wine in the face of a grand juror. In that same year and in that same county John Proby faced a similar penalty when he "forced open the Door" of the grand jury room to scold grand jurors for finding a true bill against his wife. All in all, 280 persons were charged with "being in contempt."[90]

The crisis of public authority displayed in violence toward public officials owed much to the allure of Pennsylvania and to the kinds of people who came. Eighteenth-century migrants to Pennsylvania came in order to escape frustrations at the hands of magistrates, tax collectors, enlistment or press officers, priests, lords, landlords, and gentlemen—men who made the law, applied it, or enjoyed its partiality. Encouraged to come by Quakers who had suffered many of the same frustrations and were as ambitious personally as any of the immigrants, who had spectacularly obstructed authority in England and politics in the province, whose dress and speech daily flouted deference, Pennsylvanians became accustomed to questioning authority at often as they questioned their own impulses. The paradox of having Quaker hosts and leaders before 1776 is that Pennsylvanians might have learned nonviolence, too, from the Quakers. The evidence, however, says otherwise.

Pennsylvania women were like most women in other places and times in that they committed few assaults (or murders); they represent only one in ten of all accusations for assault. But unlike most other women, assault was the second most common crime for which Pennsylvania women were prosecuted. It was a larger proportion of their total deviance than that of women in any other jurisdiction for which there are reliable statistics. Almost one-quarter (23.6 percent) of all accusations against women involved some type of physical or verbal assault. Over one thousand charges of violent behavior were leveled against them. Pennsylvania's numbers in this respect exceed comparable figures for eighteenth-century New York, North Carolina, and Massachusetts.[91] Pennsylvania women were much less violent than men, but more violent it seems, than women elsewhere. With good reason Lewis Miller portrayed brawling women in his paintings and sketches of early Pennsylvania society.[92]

Sarah (Mrs. William) Robinson offers the best example of female boldness. Robinson operated an inn in Chichester, and Martin Reardon was a patron. Reardon befriended two drovers at Robinson's inn, shared some rounds of drinks, and invited the two to lodge at his house, five miles further on. When the drovers called for their horses to be brought from the stable, Sarah Robinson turned to Reardon and called him a sorry scoundrel for luring away her clientele. When Reardon tried to explain his innocent motive, she told him to get out or she would scald him with boiling water. As the altercation accelerated, she went to the bar and got a walnut measure with which to beat him. He grabbed it away. While her sister and maidservant joined the attack on him, Sarah returned to the bar to get salt from a cellar that she then threw in his face. As he left the house, she came at him with the saltcellar and hit him in the face with it.[93]

Assaults by women in Pennsylvania were prosecuted more frequently in urban centers than in rural areas. Philadelphia and its immediate environs experienced nearly four out of every ten (38.1 percent) assault and assault and battery prosecutions against women in Pennsylvania. The proliferation of women's assaults in urban areas contrasts sharply with the distribution of men's. Men's assaults occurred at the highest rate in isolated, central counties of Pennsylvania and among the Scots-Irish population that dominated those counties. Accusations of assault by women contributed very little to these record exorbitant rates. In the three-county Bedford-Huntingdon-Somerset population (with the highest assault rate in Pennsylvania), women's share of assault was 6.9 percent—whereas in Philadelphia city and county their share was 18.2 percent. The extreme farwestern counties of Washington and Greene showed women's shares of only 3.2 and 2.5 percent respectively.

Women usually assaulted husbands, male acquaintances, and constables. Only a minority of their victims were other women. In Chester County that minority was one-third. This was the general pattern, in the city of Philadelphia as well as in rural areas. Assault statistics also confirm Susan Klepp and Merril Smith's findings that marriage in early Pennsylvania was often an impromptu, tempestuous affair.[94] Assault was the crime most frequently attributed to married women. Spouses often communicated with each other and with each other's friends with verbal and physical violence. Women directed most of their physical and verbal attacks against members of their domestic circle—husbands, children, servants, and slaves. They also frequently attacked neighbors and acquaintances, or authorities seeking to serve warrants on members of their families and friends. About one-third of the time women had help in their acts of assault or gave it; between 1763 and 1790 in 31.3 percent of the prosecutions where women were alleged to have committed assaults, they were charged as codefendants. Women in Berks County were typical: fourteen were presented for having committed assaults; eleven of them joined men in carrying out the violence; five of the eleven with their husbands, five with male companions, and one with a brother. In Chester County a handful of the men whom women assaulted can be identified by their occupations. The women preferred the same occupations in their victims as did the male assailants. Almost half the victims were constables.[95]

Women, including the victim wives already discussed, were the targets of assault in 15.2 percent of all the cases from Chester County in which victims were identified. That percentage compares with 25.8 percent of women victims in all cases except assault.[96] When women in Chester County were the victims of assault and battery the mean wealth percentile of male assailants was 43.0 (using the lower tax alternative). That was 13.1 percentile points lower than when men were the victims.[97] Assailants of women were doing less well economically than those who attacked men.

Compared with their appearance in court dockets, women appear as victims even more often in court papers. In these short histories the aggressors display some very malevolent behavior toward them. Two pregnant women were attacked with the intention to harm them through their vulnerable pregnant condition—and in one of the two cases, because of the pregnancy. Thomas Scott, very intent upon learning whether he had impregnated a servant woman, Mary Dunlap, entered her master's house and damned her because "the last time he saw her, she sat Cross leg'd but that now he would know whether she was with Child or not." Then he demanded "some of her Water to know if she was with Child." He got no satisfaction, left, but returned more aggressive than earlier. He "took hold of her & Crushed her against the Wall & with his Hand pinched her Belly so very hard that she was obliged to cry out." She got loose and ran to the outside doorway where she vomited. She told the court that she believed the fetus was dead, owing to Scott's assault.[98]

In the second case, William Mullin, Jr., came to the house of Sarah (Mrs. William) Robinson and asked for rum. When she refused him, he impulsively called her a whore and a bitch, and even threatened to kill her husband. Robinson sent for Mullin's father—indicating that they were neighbors—and when he arrived he smacked his wastrel son, who ran from him. But Mullin, Jr. returned, grabbed Sarah Robinson by the throat and kicked her twice in her pregnant belly. Robinson's servant interposed to stop the assault.[99]

Alcohol was also a catalyst in two other attacks on women. In possibly the most melodramatic assault on a Chester woman, at the home of Griffith Jones in Willistown, Doctor Lewis David asked Mrs. Jones for some rum and she refused. He called her a "whore Bich and negro whore." She set upon him with a stick and got him out of the house. However, he crawled back in through the window, and she switched him again, whereupon he grabbed her by the arm and breast and dragged her to the door. At that point one Charles Tasey pulled him off her, put him out again, and locked the door. But David was undaunted. He broke the door down, seized Jones again, and kicked her. "Shee Beged of him for God's sake to leave her alone," but he did not do so until her husband came in and pulled him off her.[100]

The battery of Elizabeth Pownal was more violent in its effect. In October 1763, Pownal informed John Ingram, John Edwards, and William Leppard (or Leopard) that they owed her one crown for drinks they consumed at her inn. Edwards shouted, "you are a Damned lying Bitch." Mrs. Pownal slapped him, saying, "don't call me a lyar," at which point Edwards scooped up "a Piece of Board about Seven feet long & with both his Hands Struck her . . . with the edge of it on the Side of her Head whereupon she fell down as dead." Edwards then "Danc'd about the House Singing & saying the Damn'd Bitch is I hope as Dead as a Devil." John Pownall later testified that his wife "Bled mutch & was Unsensible for some Hours, & is yet very Ill."[101] Truly violent assaults like this were prosecuted as "assault with intent to kill."

In the case of rape, the data from the courts do not convey the frequency of the crime or the suffering of the victims. Rape may be the most serious case of the dark figure of crime; the number of rapes that were not prosecuted clearly outnumbered those that were. What the justice system failed to do about rape is a more important story than what it did. And too, by obviously doing too little, the system encouraged the public not to expect it to do much, which caused it to do little. Ideas of gender current in the eighteenth century suppressed the reporting of rape too. Thus, for several reasons, the official criminal record is misleading regarding the frequency of rape and the health of the culture where it occurred. To repeat, the treatment of the all-too-few women plaintiffs in court led women to avoid the courts. But the scanty court record does have its value as it helps to explain why it is scanty and to understand the reluctance to prosecute.

From a first look into the official record, rape appears not to have been a major problem in Pennsylvania.[102] Only fifty-seven prosecutions for rape appear in the court dockets, 1682–1800. Added to these are thirty-eight prosecutions of attempted rape or assault with the intent to ravish. Twenty other cases involved incest, sexual cruelty to a spouse, and child molestation. The victims of these twenty male aggressors were probably all women. All these cases do not amount to an eye-catching number—only 0.01 percent of the total prosecutions in Pennsylvania. It is conceivable that they depict the real situation, a province untroubled by sexual assault. Upon his visit to Pennsylvania, Francois La Rochefoucault-Liancourt wrote in 1793 that attractive young women could travel unattended anywhere in Pennsylvania, even at night, without fear of being attacked. But even as he made this comment, others persons in a better position to know contradicted it. William Bradford, who spent a lifetime as lawyer, judge and attorney-general in Pennsylvania, voiced what many knew: "there is scarce any crime which escapes punishment so often as that of rape." Thomas McKean, Chief Justice of Pennsylvania for more than two decades and the father of six daughters, in his charges to juries asserted that, "mothers, wives, Sisters, [and] Daughters cry out for justice" against rapists. Judge Alexander Addison of the Fifth Circuit expressed even more concern for hapless women than Mc-Kean.[103] The judicial record simply did not reflect the real danger to women. These magistrates were pointing out a recurrent problem in criminal research, the dark figure: official records undercounted some crimes and the state under-prosecuted them. [104] Rape was a real problem in Pennsylvania.

There were a number of reasons for the dark figure, and they illuminate social attitudes and behavior regarding sex, gender, and rape. For one thing, men coerced women into sexual acts and women failed to report them out of embarrassment, shame, fear, or despair. The *Carlisle Gazette* reported a case where, in October 1788, a farmer and his wife were on their way to Philadelphia for market day. Two men stopped them. While one held a pistol on the farmer, the second raped his wife. The newspaper reported that the farmer and his spouse hurried to market, dumped their goods, and returned home without notifying authorities of the assault. Whether or not it was true in this case, husbands and fathers often discouraged wives and daughters from revealing the fact of their rape to prevent scandal or embarrassment to themselves and their families. Or wives, such as Philadelphia County's Becky Cress, refused to alert authorities to her husband's rape of their servant girl, Rachel Davis, preferring instead to send the girl away.[105] Doubtless also, some women refused to report sexual assault out of a sense of their own guilt or complicity, believing they may have contributed to the attack upon themselves.

Yet, even in cases where women were inclined to bring charges, lack of corroborative evidence discouraged complaints or stalled prosecutions. Invariably the attack was committed in isolated or uncrowded locales. As a result, prosecutors (and it should be remembered that for the seventeenth century and much of the eighteenth, victims were usually the prosecutors of criminal offenses) lacked sufficient corroboration for an effective prosecution. Not wanting to waste the time of judges, jurors, or participants when evidence was lacking and convictions unlikely—or to shoulder the substantial court costs associated with prosecutions when one lost—victims opted to remain mute.[106]

Lack of agreement on what constituted rape also encouraged silence and reduced statistics for that offense. What would pass as sexual assault today was viewed then as part of the courtship ritual. In 1685 Philadel-phia's Peter and Bridgett Cock alleged that John Rambo "in the night time by force of arms did breake into the[ir] dwelling house & then & there did forcibly disquietlie, & mutinously & imprudentlie frighten & disturb manie of the . . . family." They also alleged that Rambo "at that time did keepe, force, & compel [daughter] Bridgett . . . to stay in bed with him, and did then & there promise and firmly contract himself to marrie the said Bridgett." Testimony from the other Cock daughters established that Rambo had lowered himself through a hole in the roof and insisted that the sisters leave Bridgett's bed so that he might join her there. When the sisters reluctantly complied, Rambo got into the bed with Bridgett and remained with her "until daybreake." During the night Rambo implored Bridgett to marry him "and tho she first said noe, she did finally say yes."[107] The Cock family charged Rambo with breaking and entering, and with reneging on an oral contract with their daughter "to [her] hurt and staine . . . and utter ruine," but they did not view his entering her bed and pressuring her into agreeing to a mar-riage to be rape. Numerous similar instances went unreported and unpenalized.

Later, when it was discovered that Bridgett was pregnant as a result of Rambo's visit, the family added to the charges that Rambo had "defloured & dishonoured the pl[ain]t[i]ff under the pretense of mar-riage" and requested that Rambo be ordered to maintain the child. Still, the Cocks and the attorney-general chose to charge Rambo with fornica-tion and bastardy rather than rape.[108]

The Rambo proceedings are a vivid reminder that many occurrences of what today would be considered rape were prosecuted under the rubrics of fornication and bastardy, another means of obscuring the record. This obfuscation was probably true of those cases where victims were impregnated or when the victim or her family knew the assailant. Families were naturally reluctant to admit what today is called "acquain-tance rape" and when they admitted it at all, they tended to label it for-nication rather than rape.[109]

Married women suffered from the abbreviated definition of rape in the eighteenth century. Divorce petitions are replete with wives' com-plaints that their husbands cruelly treated them. This abuse sometimes included having to have sex when uninterested or actually repelled by the prospect. In 1785 Lancaster's William Clark was charged with raping Mary Clark. Whether they were husband and wife is unclear; probably they were. In any case, the grand jury refused to indict in the case. Wives suffered rape from husbands, but few had the courage of Mary Clark or Chester County's Elenor Petit who came forward in 1750 to press charges of sodomy against her husband, Samuel.[110]

Another deterrent to wives' complaining of husbands raping them was the law's obvious prohibition of husbands and wives testifying for or against each other, "for if they swear for the Benefit of each other, they are not to be believed, because their Interest are absolutely the same." Wives could not testify against husbands because "such a law would occasion implacable Divisions and Quarrels, and destroy the very legal Policy of Marriage." Even in rape cases courts were reluctant to accept testimony by the wife, although, on a rare occasion, they did so. Judges feared that such a precedent gave wives power to initiate "frivolous charges against husbands and to create divisions in the marriage."[111]

Even when rape charges were brought, victims and their families understood the limitations of institutional remedies. Victims faced male lawyers, judges, and jurors. As formally trained lawyers became more prominent in the colony's judicial proceedings, as they did by mid-century, rape became even more burdensome to prosecute. Attorneys, with their command of the language and preoccupation with the "reliability" of evidence, often made quick work of rape victims and their allegations, especially younger victims. The very prospect of lawyers' prying in public into victims' private histories was enough to preclude victims from pursuing prosecutions.[112]

Attorneys relied upon legal technicalities to frustrate prosecutions for rape. They generally insisted that both penetration and ejaculation be proven beyond a doubt before a conviction could be returned. This strategy was effective because English law itself was divided on the issue, and judges could find both positions in English reports.[113] Orgasm became an issue in the defense's pleading. Conventional wisdom held that a woman could not conceive without experiencing orgasm, and if she had an orgasm, she had consented to intercourse, and enjoyed it. Thus argued Counsel John Ross in the case of Andrew Sullivan's alleged 1793 sexual assault upon Sarah Sutherland. Sullivan was acquitted.[114]

Lawyers, justices, jurors, and average men believed close scrutiny of purported victims of rape was warranted because the women were not the victims they claimed to be. They were not in court seeking justice as much as undeserved benefits. These clever plaintiffs were pregnant and single; they could allege they were raped in order to protect their reputations or to escape punishment for fornication and bastardy, or allege rape or paternity to guarantee financial maintenance for an illegitimate child. Some women certainly did such things, but conventional wisdom amplified the number who allegedly did. Reflecting what he heard in the street, that famous visitor to Pennsylvania, Gottlieb Mittelberger, recounted that a servant man had impregnated a servant woman (but not necessarily raped her). She asked her master—a justice, no less—for his advice. She anticipated prosecuting the servant man, but her master said there was no good prospect in that; the servant man was penniless. Prosecute a man of means, he advised; you could get a comfortable maintenance from that. She did. She named her own master as the father.[115] Such were the wiles of hapless women that men had to be alert to. Or, is it the case that such was the conventional wisdom that men shared with other men?

Some judges acted flippantly and callously toward rape victims. One of them was told that a man had attempted on several occasions to sexually assault his maidservant—even in his wife's presence. The judge "had his laugh over the affair and let the man go after he promised to do better in the future."[116] Judges controlled their courtrooms, or should have, but some took no offense when the men attending court added a note of levity over rape: the *Carlisle Gazette* reported a rape case in July 1788, which, because the assault had occurred near the Cumberland County-Franklin County line, raised some question about which county court had jurisdiction. Supposedly, someone in the courtroom asked the lawyer for the defendant "was the road in good shape?" If it was, the wag continued, it could not have been in Cumberland County.[117]

Even success in convicting an assailant could prove fleeting when the court did not support the victim. Richard Shirtliff raped Hester Painter in April 1786. Several times he threatened her *and* members of her family if she prosecuted him. Incarcerated awaiting trial, he tried to escape on several occasions. "His Ingenuity being Such," one official noted, authorities feared he would succeed in escaping. When Painter persevered in her prosecution and a jury convicted Shirtliff, the court considered granting him a pardon. An alarmed Painter again petitioned the court to remind the judges that if they released him, she and her family were in danger of their lives. Women who knew of Painter's plight and the courts' indifference to women would just as well suffer quietly as go public with their grievance.[118]

The most extraordinary event from inside the courtroom involved six defendants in 1785. Timothy Cockley, Thomas Masonry, Timothy Lane, Patrick O'Hara, Michael Snody, and Timothy Conner, all Lancaster County men, broke into the home of Benjamin Whistler in Donegal Township, and "roughed up" Barbara Whitmore (or Witmer) who was "under the Age of fifteen Years." They got her drunk, took her "to a secret place" and, apparently, took turns raping her. Unrepentant at the trial, the men told the court they thought, "a good fuck would make her a woman."[119] Their nonchalance was unique; they had incriminated themselves in a capital crime. Their victim was a minor. What were they? Too stupid to understand the gravity of what they had done and acknowledged in court? Were they defiant in the face of evidence that does not survive but which had condemned them hopelessly? Or, did they think they were speaking to a friendly audience—jurors, judges, attorneys, and laymen—who approved of men being sexually ravenous? "Good old boys," like characters from the imagination of author James Dickey? The first was not likely, and the last possibility speaks volumes about a current mentality in Pennsylvania regarding the inconsiderable stature of women and a presumption that most men would share that mentality. The six did more than presume that their behavior was not criminal; they conveyed that it was *natural* for themselves, like all men, but also, it was natural for women—a service that sooner or later, some-one or other had to perform. And so, why not them, now, for her? (Never mind that by legal convention, that initiation was to be per-formed by a husband after marriage or engagement.)

In a courtroom of skeptical or indifferent auditors, a plaintiff enjoyed a benefit if she were from the community represented by the magistrates and jurors and was accusing an outsider. Prosecutors and jurors had less difficulty in evaluating her narrative and treating her equitably if they knew her. And the defendant stranger might have to work all the harder to gain their respect. Of course, if she accused a local man of status or good repute, she increased her burden of proof. It became doubly diffi-cult if she were the outsider and charged a respected local man. The serious nature of the charge and the sanctions attached made men reluctant to prosecute or convict. The prosecution's case had to be com-pelling. The defense could make it less than compelling by attacking the plaintiff's credibility—and that, in turn, could hinge upon her past, her social and economic condition, and similarly, her family's. Servant women, slave women, and poor free women were not taken as seriously as were their wealthier, more powerful counterparts. William Bradford admitted that in most cases rape judgments were determined "by the rank, situation, and character of the victim." In cases where women were undistinguished in rank or station, juries frequently ignored "posi-tive evidence."[120] It was a harsh cycle: the most likely victims of rape were powerless women because no one would come to their aid, and because no one would come to their aid, they were apt victims.

Women servants were more likely to suffer rape than free women. Male servants in the household or unrelated men were much more often the assailants than masters of the house. Nevertheless, masters abused maidservants, some with impunity. The Rev. Henry Muhlenberg related an instance where a master, in the presence of his wife, sexually assaulted his servant girl. It was only after a series of such assaults that the wife of the perpetrator finally contacted authorities. The legal files of the Lancaster lawyer (and later state Supreme Court justice) Jasper Yeates suggests that rapes of servant girls, especially during harvest when field workers often took advantage of available women, were more often than not ignored by magistrates. Lancaster's David Robb, a married man, raped his servant girl, Rebecca McCarthy, on more than one occasion in his barn during the haying season. Robb also escaped prosecution, though the girl gave a deposition to the court. William Cress of Philadelphia County was able to continue to sexually exploit his servant girl, Rachel Davis, long after his wife knew of his first assault on her. Davis later told the court she did not complain to authorities because "she did not dare—she a bound girl & her father absent."[121]

Women of color were doubly susceptible to rape because of racism and possibly their slave status. Given her youth, the case of Alice Clifton was uniquely pathetic. She was a sixteen-year-old black girl accused of killing her illegitimate infant. Evidence in the infanticide trial made clear that Clifton had been repeatedly raped by one John ("Fat John") Shaffer, a married white man, who had earlier also "debauched" a "milk girl" near Church Alley where he assaulted Clifton. Despite serious doubts about obtaining a conviction, Pennsylvania authorities subsequently charged Shaffer with the rape of Clifton, and in a celebrated trial in February 1788, tried him. Before "a great crowd" that pushed and shoved each other until "one of the windows was broke," a jury found him not guilty. One appalled observer of Shaffer's exoneration was none other than William Bradford, who believed that white Pennsylvanians were not yet ready to see a white man hang for the rape of a black woman, even for repeated assaults upon a black youngster.[122]

Most rapes of black women did not come to the attention of authorities or were ignored if they did. The number of illegitimate mulattoes in early Pennsylvania is clear evidence of the frequency of interracial sexual connections.[123] There can be little doubt that many, perhaps most, of these encounters were coerced, either through outright force or by the implied threat of it.[124] Because courts paid little heed to black women, there was no incentive for black victims of rape to report their victimization. William Bradford observed that jurors considered the rape of black female slaves "so lightly" that they "w[ould] not let the victim herself testify." The same was true for Indian women.[125]

When accusations of rape made it into the justice system, they were, along with infanticide accusations, the most difficult cases in which to gain convictions. Of the fifty-six men formally charged with rape, almost one in four (24.6 percent) was voted *ignoramus* by grand juries. That is a high rate for Pennsylvania. It met or exceeded the rate in all but one of the major categories of crime in Pennsylvania. Another nine cases (16.0 percent) were dropped by the public prosecutor or the victims or were arbitrated out of court—a high rate of default in prosecution. Twenty-eight, half the total, went to trial; eighteen were convicted, which was 31.6 percent of all rape accusations and 64.3 percent of defendants tried. That is a high rate of conviction—but not as high as that for crimes against property. However, the cases that got to trial had been finely screened by grand jurors and public prosecutors for strong evidence of guilt and trouble-free convictions.

The first rape case to come before Pennsylvania courts occurred in the spring of 1700, when young William Smith, son of a prominent Philadelphian of the same name, sexually assaulted Elizabeth Henbury. To argue his son's case, Smith's father immediately secured the services of David Lloyd, the best-trained legal mind in the colony and future speaker of the House of Representatives. Under Lloyd's prodding, and to escape conviction and punishment, young Smith pleaded with Henbury to marry him. Henbury frustrated the eager prosecuting attorney-general by accepting Smith's proposal. She told the court she agreed to the arrangement "to save ye Man's life."[126]

In 1772 Pennsylvania executed its first rapist.[127] Chester County's Patrick Kennedy, a white man, was hanged in that year for the rape of Jane Walker of Thornbury Township. Only seven executions for rape in Pennsylvania can be confirmed.[128] Four of those seven were black men and a fifth may have been. All executions of black men occurred after the passage of the Gradual Abolition Act in 1780 stimulated the growth of the state's free black population.[129] White Pennsylvanians were less concerned with rape after 1780 than with rapes perpetrated by black men against white women.[130]

From 1718 to 1794 rape was a capital crime. Therefore, the men trying the accused might have been more careful about convicting an accused man, since they were presumably destining him to die.[131] That presumption about the scruples of the male functionaries can be tested, however: the death penalty for rape was removed in 1794, and for the rest of the century, the scrupulosity of bench, bar, and jurors would not have applied.[132] They should have sought and delivered more convictions for the last six or seven years of the century, because any mistaken judgment would not have killed the accused. Yet there was no increase in indictments or convictions.

Before 1794, grand juries indicted in 80.4 percent of the accusations; from 1794 through 1800, they indicted in 54.4. Before 1794, trial juries convicted in 34.8 percent of the cases they heard, but in the rest of the century, they convicted in only 18.2 percent. These declines in a time of less punitive laws bring into question the possible scruples of jurors and bench. Had any possible sympathy for the alleged victims of rape been tempered by the prospect of executing a rapist or executing an innocent man, the jurors and judges should have exhibited that sympathy beginning in 1794 by indicting and convicting more often. But they did not, and in fact, showed even less inclination to convict and deter rape.

Closer to the truth, the 1790s was no sympathetic era for victimized women. William Bradford's skepticism in the 1790s about rape prosecutions had numbers to support it, whether or not he knew the numbers.

In the case of attempted rape, the outcomes differed slightly from rape. In attempt to rape or ravish, prosecutors have an easier evidentiary case to make and no capital–punishment qualms of jurors to hinder them. Therefore, presuming that some sympathy exists in society or the justice system for vulnerable women and rape victims, there should be higher rates of prosecution and conviction of attempted rape. In fact, grand juries were more likely to indict for attempted rape, by an additional 14.1 percent.[133] But trial juries found only a small additional 5.2 percent guilty. These are not major differences from plain rape, and thus there is this additional reason to doubt there was enthusiasm for prosecution of sexual aggression. The justice system was not sending any messages of deterrence to the people, even if the men involved in the system had intended to do so.

An astonishing statistic on rape is the proportion of victims who were children or minors. In Chester County, there were thirty-three cases of rape or attempted rape through 1800. Seven of the thirty-three assaults, or one in five, were upon children twelve years old or younger.[134] The actions of assailants were as depraved as most times and places could supply—and this was in Chester County, with the highest proportion of nonviolent people in Pennsylvania, or all of early America. In December 1754, Mary Gordon of West Nottingham Township asked a neighbor for help in harvesting hay. The neighbor ordered his servant, Jonathan McVay, to help Gordon. Later, Gordon was away from her house, leaving behind her children and McVay. Upon returning, she heard her eight-year-old daughter Jane crying. When she got to the house, Jane told her that McVay had "murdered" her; he had climbed onto her back and penetrated her. A witness, Elizabeth Scott, testified that she came upon Mary acting bereft of her senses. Scott and Mary entered the Gordon house, where Scott saw blood on the floor and on Jane's clothes. Jane's six-year-old brother, who had witnessed the rape, recounted the assault to Scott.[135]

The youngest victim was Lydia Bird, age four. Her grandmother, Ann Babb, had put her to bed. An hour later, Patience Clayton came running to Babb to tell her that a drunken Thomas Hemphill had fallen upon the child in bed and was smothering her. When Ann ran to the child, she found Hemphill on top of Lydia with his pants down and Lydia struggling and screaming. Babb pulled him off the child and pushed him down a flight of stairs. In August 1734, Jean Smith informed the Chester quarter sessions that her daughter, "scarce six years old," had told Smith that a man had come to their house during the mother's absence "and laid upon her and was like to kill her and took a long red thing out of his trousers and hurt her belly with it." From Chester there were also Elizabeth Lewis, Mary Good, and Hannah Sugart, who were ten, and Hannah Evener and Hannah Tanner, who were twelve.[136] To make an informed guess about all of Pennsylvania, probably as many as one-third of the victims of sexual assault were eighteen years old or younger. If ever Pennsylvanians needed to erect barriers to forestall harm to its most vulnerable members, it needed to do so in the case of its children. Experiencing trepidation needed to be so common and effective that the destructive impulses of men were stopped before harm was done. Self-restraint had to be ordinary and license, an unwelcome oddity. In Pennsylvania, the justice system seemed most often to have agreed to these propositions by its prosecution of deviant men committing egregious sexual assaults. But commendable as that may be, the courts operated in a culture that failed to deter its men from preying upon its most vulnerable members.

After realizing the frequency of murder within families, it comes as no surprise that assaults too were common within families. Among the civilian victims of assault, perhaps as many as one-eleventh of all recorded assaults involved married couples.[137] In most instances the husband assaulted the wife. Hector McNeil shot and wounded his Chester County wife, Catherine, in November 1772. He had threatened to kill her, and in two previous incidents he had fired his pistol at her. Divorce petitions after 1780 provide particularly graphic descriptions of violent physical confrontations between spouses. Elizabeth Love testified in September 1793 that her husband, Benjamin, "repeatedly endangered [her] Life." Neighbor Mary Norris claimed that Phillip Heger beat his wife, Catherine, unconscious and mistreated her so badly that she often heard Catherine call, "murder, murder." Both the Prisoners for Trial Docket and the Vagrancy Docket for the city of Philadelphia are laced with cases of wife beating. The case of Henry Higgert was typical: he was jailed for "frequently" being responsible for "violent ill treatment in beating his Wife Ann [which] greatly endangered her life." Michael Bowyer not only "violently assaulted and endangered the life of Deborah, his wife," but he also attacked "his Infant child only four days old." Samuel Petit came before the Chester County court of quarter sessions in 1793 charged with first striking, then sodomizing his wife, Eleanor. The fact that the law permitted husbands to employ a degree of physical restraint or force "controlling" their wives and in maintaining the proper hierarchy within a marriage and family suggests that it took some unusual or sustained display of physical coercion on the part of husbands to bring them to court.[138]

But wives also assaulted husbands. In October 1785, Alexander McArthur accused his wife, Sarah, of continuously assaulting him "with sharp objects, bottles, etc." In September 1795, Philadelphia's John Young "charged on oath" that his wife, Ann, had assaulted and beat him "& threaten[ed] to take his life." He swore "that he believe[d] himself in danger." These cases generally were not impulsive and isolated developments but, rather, habitual behavior. The Downs family of Philadelphia illustrates the point. Margaret Downs came before the Mayor's Court for assaulting her husband, Robert, in June 1790. Six months later Robert stood before the judges for beating her.[139]

Children both suffered from violence and instigated it within their own families. On occasion children assaulted parents. Catherine Carr was jailed in July 1795 for "committing An Assault & Battery on the person of her own Mother," as was Bucks County's Robert Kennedy for the December 1768 beating of his mother. And siblings assaulted each other, as illustrated by Ann Collins's beating of her sister, Phoebe, in 1781.[140] Parents struck their children, often violently, and physically abused them in other ways. Even Quaker mothers at times turned to the rod to discipline their offspring.[141]

Occasional evidence from beyond the criminal courts illustrates, but does not measure, the dark figure of unreported violence upon children—as the divorce petitions illustrate violence to spouses. James McMeehen (or McMechen) remembered an occasion of child abuse that dismayed no one enough to interfere with the father then or later. The father's escape from criticism and correction shows how much violence the witnesses and his neighbors were willing to let pass. Forty-four years earlier, James McMechen recalled, when he was a boy of eleven, his father brought together his neighbors and with two of his sons, James and William, they all walked the property line of McMechen's Chester County farm on Whiteclay Creek. They came to an oak on the bank of the creek. James continued: "I do most perfectly Remember that my father did then & there give my brother William . . . a very severe blow on the head with a small staff he then had in his hand." His father said to his son William, "Now, sir, remember as long as you live that this is the corner tree between your couzen John Stewart's land & me." However nonplused the other walkers were, James recalled, "the Novelty of this Circumstance made Impressions on my mind never to be eras'd." [142] The activity the McMechens were performing was called "running the lines" or "beating the bounds."[143] It was customary and common in the British Isles, and it had the potential for adults' abuse of children. There was some dark figure of assaults lurking in this folk practice.

If the complaints to the courts are to be believed, masters commonly beat servants and some criminally assaulted them. Cumberland's Dominick Fishbaugh was accused of physically mistreating his servant, William Cohan, in October 1788. Lancaster County's Christopher Riegert beat his servant maid, Ann Barbara Charles, so severely throughout 1757 that the court released her from service to him. A year later, Samuel Scott of that same County "greatly abused" Ann Long, "an Infant in service to him." Because the court found that he had "cruelly treated her" she, too, was released from her indenture. Neighbors were so shocked by boarding house proprietor Elizabeth Gathers' treatment of her eleven-year-old servant girl, Mary Duffy, and protested so vigorously, that authorities forced Gathers "to give up the Indenture" and assigned Duffy to the Almshouse.[144] Ann Perin explained to the Chester court that she permitted Joseph Walker to stay at her house overnight because he feared going home after dark. For being absent overnight his master Joshua Minshall beat him until, according to Perin, "shee could not Lay a Straw in any one place from his shoulders to his waist that was free from Cuts or burses."[145] Jonas Davenport tied his servant Henry Hawkins behind a horse that kicked and dragged him until Hawkins nearly lost an eye or his life, depending upon the witness.[146] Finally, Joseph Rhoads and John Jones beat and kicked Rhoads's servant Henry Strickland until shortly thereafter Strickland died.[147]

Less often, but unmistakably, servants, especially male servants, resisted orders from their masters or mistresses and exhibited "insolent" behavior toward them. At times they moved beyond mere insolence, physically assaulting their mistresses and masters. Philadelphia's Francis McHenry was jailed in January 1795 "for threatening his Master Richard Babe and his Family in a very unjustifiable Manner." Negro Henry made similar threats against his master, John Lawrence, in June 1790. A month later Negro Peter was confined after being found guilty of "disorderly and turbulent behavior towards his Mistress." Servant Sarah Morton, while drunk, severely beat her mistress and was jailed for her actions, and for "otherwise misbehaving."[148]

The law acknowledged that systemic violence played a pivotal role in sustaining the traditional family and its service to the economy and community. Thus, handbooks for constables, justices of the peace, and sheriffs reminded judicial personnel that parents might strike children, masters might smite servants, and teachers might cuff students without incurring the wrath of the law. "Battery" (as in "Assault and Battery") was the "*wrongful* beating [of] another [emphasis added]"; it was left to authorities (and the populace in the guise of grand and trial juries) to determine at what point a husband, father, master, or schoolmaster crossed the line from properly exercising the prerogative of his station and authority to "wrongfully beating another."[149] If, as anecdotes and data on assaults suggest, this society condoned force and violent behavior even within households, the presumption has its consequences for the judicial record. In such a society, one would expect prosecutors, grand juries, and trial juries to ignore episodes that did not reach their threshold for culpable assault. If grand juries did filter out such cases, the volume of recorded assault cases in Pennsylvania courts represents a minimal number. The actual violence would be markedly larger.

Possibly one-fifth of all assaults consisted merely of threats and insults. The proportion is difficult to determine because court clerks did not carefully distinguish assault from assault and battery. Examples of verbal assaults were full of provocation to actual violence and battery. George Smith of Chester County testified in August 1763, that his neighbor Thomas Riley's "Blood Boyled . . . when he seen the Sight of Mathias Leamy," and that Riley approached Leamy and "lifted up one of his Feet and Swore he would Kick Leamy's Dam'd Guts out for one Half Penny."[150] Barnard Watters of Fayette County found himself seized roughly by neighbor Thomas Hall in the summer of 1784. Hall told Watters he "could whip any of the Family of the Watters." Moreover, Hall violently shouted in his face "By God he had fucked . . . Barnard's wife oftener than he [Bernard] had himself."[151] On the other hand, less provocative jibing than what Hall gave Watters erupted in other cases into actual fighting and wounding. Why some confrontations did not escalate when the insults seemed to warrant it, whereas lesser provocations did erupt in actual violence, cannot be answered from the meager information available on the two or more parties to assault cases.

Motives for assault ranged from easily intelligible ones, deliberate and sometimes political, to the whimsical, bewildering, or absurd. An event closely linked to the political history of Pennsylvania occurred in July 1740 when Lieutenant-Governor George Thomas moved to enlist men for service against the Spanish in the War of Jenkins' Ear. When the provincial assembly, dominated by Quakers, obstructed his plans, he and army recruiters enlisted servant men. Whiggish Assemblymen became outraged at the violation of contracts, property rights, and the political and constitutional autonomy of Pennsylvania, as they understood these. Their constituents displayed the same anger. Officer Robert Taskbury traveled to Chester County to do some recruiting. Joined by James Casey, just south of Philadelphia, the two stopped at the shop of John Weldon, where Taskbury enlisted two of Weldon's servants and John McCowley, servant of Elizabeth Connolly. While they treated the three servants to rounds of rum, Connnolly argued with Taskbury and came at him with a rake. After scuffling, Taskbury and Casey took the road for the Blue Ball tavern in Chester. But Weldon, Connolly, and others pursued, assaulted, and tied up Taskbury. Then Weldon pulled ex-servant McCowley down and held him while Elizabeth Connolly stripped him naked. Weldon kicked McCowley's hat, which had a cockade in it, into the dirt. Casey reproved him for abusing the King's colors, but Weldon cursed the King. Weldon added that the officers were "a percle of kidnapping rogues & might as well robb a mans house & if his [Taskbury's] officer were there he would geld him."[152] In other instances, Lucas and Mathias Nethermark assaulted John Wharton and John Hanley and tried to retake goods that the two had distrained from the Nethermarks when they did not pay the proprietor's quitrents.[153] In 1792, seven Chester men conspired to assault and stop, and possibly assassinate, the collectors of the whiskey revenue.[154]

Edward Hagan and Patrick Kelty battered each other in a melee that Hagan provoked for no more reason than inflating his ego. Hagan, a Scots-Irishman, illustrates young, male aggressiveness that serves no rational purpose, but is not one bit less common for that. Patrick Kelty, the victim, was helping John Smith to manufacture a mattock at Smith's shop. Hagan sallied in and began to taunt Kelty, saying that in "the old country" he had seen a man make two mattocks in the time Kelty was taking to make one. Kelty warned him to stop the abuse. Hagan not only continued but also came over to Kelty's work area and kicked him in the face! Kelty leapt upon Hagan, pinning him to the floor. When bystanders pulled Kelty off, Hagan jumped up, grabbed a hammer, and beat Kelty in the head with it, causing profuse bleeding, until bystanders then pulled Hagan away.[155] Conduct like Hagan's became endemic in America.[156]

In a second irrational episode, James Thompson met Benjamin Mendenhall in the road on a September afternoon in 1782 and without provocation, according to Mendenhall, he took Mendenhall by the collar and told him he "Could Lick all ye Mendenalls." Mendenhall asked him to let him go, which he did, but meanwhile asked him if Mendenhall would get the law after him. Thereupon he came back at Mendenhall, pinned him on the ground, and "Ordered him to Say he Had Enuf."[157]

Drunken assailants make more sense than men like Hagan and Thompson, since drunkenness suspends the reason and inhibitions everyone is presumed, or hoped, to have. Whether in homes, taverns and tippling houses, or in the workplace, alcohol led to numerous assaults. Evidence brought against James Erwin of Bucks County for running a "disorderly house" established that on one occasion "Sundry People [were] fighting & the chief of them had had too much linquer." One Christmas, his neighbors complained, "People were there Quarriling being Very Noysey & Prity much in Liquor." Drunkards in taverns frequently became victims. Alexander Butts was nearing George Overpeck's tavern in Bucks County in 1764 when Alexander Graham picked up "a large Club in both his Hands [and did] Strike down beat & wound & also rob Him." When Patrick Power, formerly belonging to a company of foot in New Jersey, stopped by Robert Cummings' Bucks County inn in the summer of 1764, one James Cummings accused him of being "a runaway Dog" and threatened to take him up "for a runaway." Though Powers denied the accusation, Cummings struck him with a whip and was quickly joined by other patrons in the tavern who "assaulted [Power] and Cut and Bruised his face, and Leggs in a most inhumane manner, and then stripp'd off all his outside Clothes" while searching him for money.[158] Even in long-settled areas of Pennsylvania, fights in taverns exhibited the kind of violence associated with the frontier. In their fight in 1788 in a Lancaster County tavern, Benjamin Williams and Henry Seeger engaged in gouging to the point that a finger of Williams's right hand was bitten off and much of Seeger's nose was missing.[159]

In the second half of the century, novel cases of assault began to appear in the judicial record, exposing aggression within Pennsylvania communities. The new phenomenon was cross-prosecutions. Here a victim prosecuted his or her assailant, but the accused assailant also prosecuted his accuser for assault (at either the same quarter sessions or a later one). Some kind of violent feud was occurring. It may also be that, in the manner of Scots-Irishmen like Andrew Jackson, personal feuds occurred that never made it into the judicial record. But the record shows that feuds existed, whatever else occurred out of sight of the law. In Chester County, in each decade beginning with 1750 (except for the war-interrupted 1770s), cross-prosecutions numbered between fourteen and sixteen, and in the years 1790–1800, they jumped to forty (Table 4.2).

Yet additional cases exposed violent feuds, although the actors were men and women other than the immediate coassailants. In the court dockets, the tokens of these feuds were last names shared among accusers and accused, but different first names. The targets of cross-prosecutions here were probably relatives of other assailants and victims.[160] (Table 4.3) An example of larger cross-prosecution occurred when Barbara Shaver prosecuted Elizabeth Meredith for assault, and Elizabeth Meredith prosecuted Barbara Shaver for assault. But Barbara and a Joseph Shaver also prosecuted a Samuel Meredith for assault and theft. And, Joseph Shaver brought charges against Elizabeth Meredith for theft. Two Merediths went at three Shavers both directly or, if they were kin, round-about.[161] In a yet larger example, Daniel McPeake prosecuted James Blallock and William Blallock for riot, and vice versa. James McPeake likewise charged James Blallock, Jr. and vice-versa. Thus far it was three paired prosecutions, but additionally there were the non-

TABLE 4.2. PAIRED PROSECUTIONS FOR ASSAULT OR RIOT IN CHESTER COUNTY

Year	Pairs	Year	Pairs	Year	Pairs
1751	0	1768	2	1785	1
1752	0	1769	0	1786	2
1753	0	1770	3	1787	1
1754	1	1771	0	1788	2
1755	2	1772	1	1789	1
1756	3	1773	2	1790	3
1757	6	1774	0	1791	3
1758	1	1775	0	1792	0
1759	1	1776	1	1793	2
1760	2	1777	0	1794	0
1761	1	1778	0	1795	5
1762	2	1779	2	1796	3
1763	0	1780	1	1797	3
1764	1	1781	3	1798	8
1765	1	1782	2	1799	4
1766	3	1783	3	1800	9
1767	2	1784	0		

paired prosecutions. First, Mary McPeake leveled allegations against Mrs. James (Agnes) Blallock for riot. And Sarah McPeake charged James Blallock. Mary and William McPeake prosecuted Jane Blallock. From the other surname group, James Blallock, Jr., and William Blallock prosecuted Sarah McPeake. Here was an amplified blood feud, the biggest feature of that summer's quarter sessions.[162]

As the end of the century approached, these shows of aggression increased. In 1795, for example, there were a total of sixty-three prosecutions at court and twenty-seven of them were for assault or riot. Ten of the twenty-seven consisted of five pairs of people accusing each other. But the ten involved here shared their surnames with thirty-five other accusers or accused that year. In 1798, thirty-four of sixty-eight prosecutions were for riot or assault, and sixteen of the thirty-four comprised eight pairs. But an additional thirty-three people that year who were accusers or accused had the same surnames—for a pool of forty-nine persons in court with the same surnames. Finally, in 1800, the numbers rose to fifty-one total prosecutions, thirty for assault or riot, and eighteen accused among nine pairs. There was a total of fifty-four persons in court sharing surnames. From all these numbers, three trends appeared in the last fifteen years of the century: the proportion of assaults and riots among all cases grew; the proportion of paired prosecutors among the assaulters and rioters grew; and the number of accused and victims who were probably associated with the paired accusers grew.

After 1718, the justice system and people of Pennsylvania did not take

TABLE 4.3. PAIRED PROSECUTIONS AND SHARED SURNAMES IN CASES OF ASSAULT
OR RIOT IN CHESTER COUNTY

Year	Pairs of accusers in cases of assault or riot	Accusers or accused (any crime) sharing surnames with paired accusers	Total accusations of assault or riot per year	Total accusations of any kind per year
1786	2	12	16	63
1787	1	3	11	60
1788	2	4	17	51
1789	1	2	12	61
1790	3	11	27	73
1791	3	14	17	35
1792	0	0	18	44
1793	2	15	13	37
1794	0	0	14	37
1795	5	35	27	63
1796	3	25	25	53
1797	3	12	18	58
1798	8	33	34	65
1799	4	39	27	66
1800	9	36	30	51

assault seriously—while, at the same time, they expected that capital punishment would deter any fatal outcomes from assaults. Neither grand jurors, trial jurors, nor judges used their power to dissuade the people of Pennsylvania from acting aggressively toward each other. Grand jurors were less likely to indict an accused assailant than any other accused criminal—followed closely by their reluctance to indict accused killers. (Table 4.4) In Mifflin County, with the highest assault rates in Pennsylvania, at 511.0 and 289.7 per 100,000 in 1794 and 1795, for example, Mifflin grand juries returned *ignoramuses* (1794–1800) at the astonishing rate of 60.1 percent for all crimes, while 43.1 percent of its crimes were assault and an additional 21.9 percent were riots. If an accused assailant were indicted, he could choose to confess and plead guilty, or he could submit to the court without confessing. Either way would bring him to the bar for sentencing. Among all accused men and women, none outdid accused assailants in confessing or submitting to the court; 37.3 percent did so. Their reason for choosing not to go to trial lay in the mild punishment the courts were imposing for assault. In a sample of 527 cases of assault (Table 4.5), nine in ten sentenced assailants were fined, but most paid small amounts: about one-third (34.5 percent) paid five shillings or less; about two-thirds (67.4 percent) paid less than a pound; and 90 percent, £5 or less. Court costs typically exceeded the prescribed punishment. Punishments other than, or in addition to,

TABLE 4.4. OUTCOMES OF CRIMINAL PROSECUTIONS BY CATEGORY OF CRIME IN PENNSYLVANIA, 1682–1800

	N	Default %	Ignoramus %	Submit %	Conviction %	Acquittal %	Escaped %	Unknown %	SCR[1]
Violence	10635	3.5	26.3	35.5	11.2	5.3	0.9	17.2	67.9%
Property	9507	2.4	16.9	17.9	35.4	13.6	0.5	13.4	72.2%
Sex/morals	2650	8.5	8.8	30.1	12.5	3.7	1.4	34.9	77.2%
Public order	7082	10.2	19.6	27.5	10.4	5.0	0.8	26.5	67.5%
Crimes against state	225	1.8	24.9	14.7	20.0	16.9	0.4	21.3	54.2%
Other	64	4.7	3.1	20.3	25.0	1.6	0.0	45.3	94.0%

[1]Simple conviction rate

TABLE 4.5. CRIMES PUNISHED BY FINES, WHIPPING, OR JAIL IN CHESTER COUNTY

	Assault	Property	Sex/ morals	Public order	Fornication/ bastardy[1]
N	527	529	346	244	287
Fines[2]	91.1%	85.4%	77.2%	88.5%	76.3%
Whipping	3.2%	65.0%	13.3%	0.8%	15.3%
Jail	3.0%	26.1%	1.7%	9.4%	1.0%
Maintenance of child/mother					27.5%
Mean fine	£5.6	£25.0	£16.7	£5.0	£9.6
Median fine	£1.0	£3.5	£10.0	£3.0	£10.0
Mean fine	$13.00	$69.20	$50.25	$33.57	
Median fine	$8.00	$30.00	$50.25	$20.00	
Mean lashes	24	20	19	30	19
Median lashes	21	21	21	30	21
Mean jail time (months)	16	24	8.5	12	5
Median jail time (months)	0.3	12	12	3	3

[1]A category of Sex/morals. [2]Both sterling (Pa. currency) and dollar-denominated fines.

fines were exceptional: seventeen assailants were whipped, sixteen were jailed, and seven were assigned the pillory. Only thirty-seven assailants suffered more than one kind of punishment (disregarding paying court costs).

Especially because of abundant confessions and submissions, trial jurors got to hear only 14.4 percent of the accusations of assault. They convicted in 68.8 percent of these cases—which, at first glance, appears to be severe justice, but which was not.[163] Jurors were convicting assailants at about the same rate that they did other crimes, and not treating it as a chronic, peculiar problem in their community that they needed to help deter. And more importantly, they were hearing only the most flagrant examples of aggression or grievous harm to the victims. In the cases they did not hear, the accused had confessed from the well-founded expectation that the aggression would not be severely sanctioned. The 14.4 percent of accused, on the other hand, expected to be severely sentenced and risked little more by going to trial.[164] Almost one-third of them chose well.

In effect, Pennsylvanians trivialized violence, and thereby encouraged it. From the perspective of most Pennsylvanians, especially the Scots-Irish, that was no problem. Any social costs of Pennsylvanians' acting inconsiderately toward each other were either unclear to them or passed over. Courtesy, self-restraint, and reserve were expected from Quakers, Mennonites, and other sectarians, while all of Pennsylvania enjoyed an exaggerated reputation for peace because of its quiet people.

But the story did not end with trivializing nonfatal aggression and its increase. Pennsylvanians created yet graver contagion, which was more difficult to shrug off. That was homicide. Assaults and homicides are, of course, related but not equivalent. All homicides are assaults, but not all assaults are homicides. Not every homicide is a successful assault. Rather, most homicides are mistakes and not the product "of malice aforethought." The dead are the unintended casualties when things get out of hand. Historian Pieter Spierenburg explains that homicides are one pole of a continuum where the opposite pole is aggressive behavior and commonplace violence that does not kill.[165] "I never intended to kill," pleaded numerous, remorseful defendants from many places and times, who seconds earlier were bent on asserting or defending their honor, reputation, manhood, or ego. To avoid homicide, things must not be permitted to get out of hand. "The tighter the situational rules . . . the less likely it is that people can murder or be murdered," historian Eric Monkkonen explains. "Social 'scripts,' comprehensive rules of etiquette, steer people away from unpredictable exchanges."[166] The discouragement of homicides required instruction in the gravity of everyday behavior and social intercourse. Men had to be brought to mistrust themselves and depend upon internalized routines, to have premonitions of disaster if they deviated from routines, and to have a foretaste of guilt. But in the civil society of Pennsylvania, there were too few instructors in mistrust, clairvoyance, and guilt—certainly too few in the courts.

— Crime happens in families

— Rape and sexual attacks often went unreported.

— Most assaults on law enforcers

Chapter 5
Enlarged Land, Shortened Justice

> Civil Officers, whose Business it is to see that [the laws] are duly enforced, cannot exert their Authority in so distant and extensive a wilderness.
>
> —*John Penn*

The migration of people to Pennsylvania after 1717—with their ethnic, religious, and linguistic differences and a penchant for disregarding authority—obliged the apprehensive lawmakers, governors, and bar of the province to work to meld these people into a better-functioning civil society. Between 1726 and 1755 Pennsylvania's population burgeoned from 40,000 to nearly 150,000. By 1755 Pennsylvania had the third highest population of the British continental colonies, behind only Massachusetts and Virginia. The means to accommodate the growth included educating the people—publishing laws and otherwise exposing the people to the laws and courts; secondly, expanding the bar and raising its sophistication; and most importantly, enlarging local government and extending it westward in the province. While clearly necessary and wise, as well as beneficial to many Pennsylvanians, the efforts fell short of what was needed. The work of strengthening government and civil society was dashed especially by the irruption of war in the 1750s and 1760s. To some minds, the Seven Years' War and Pontiac's Rebellion threatened nothing less than civil war in the province and unlimited injustice.

The governors of Pennsylvania most fondly hoped that an informed, enlightened people would act civilly toward their fellows, and for that reason they tried better informing and educating Pennsylvanians in the laws and the system of government in the province. The effort never matched, or even rivaled, that performed in New England, where the first publicly supported schools in America were erected, especially so that crime and error would be kept at bay.[1] Still, Pennsylvanians made some efforts. Assemblymen and magistrates believed, first, the newcom-

ers had to know the provincial laws in order to obey them. For the logi-
cal first step, the Assembly decreed that statutes were to be printed and
distributed, read aloud at court sessions, and taught in Pennsylvania
schools. All laws were to be copied and maintained on rolls and kept
available for official use and public scrutiny. The Keeper of the Great
Seal was to guarantee that superseded laws were expunged from the
rolls, and new laws were to be accurately and faithfully recorded. Further, he had to ensure that a true copy of each law was preserved.
Because he and his fellow officers failed in these responsibilities in the
first decade of the colony's history, citizens often puzzled over which
laws were in effect. Following 1717, these duties were carried out scrupu-
lously and overseen more thoroughly.[2]

   Though court clerks diligently executed their obligation to read the
laws aloud, there is no evidence that schoolmasters taught the law to
their charges as required.[3] Newspapers helped by frequently printing
Assembly records and noting the passage of new statutes, but they seldom provided the complete text of a bill.[4] Before 1720 the Assembly
published its laws only episodically, although it did post its written minutes in taverns and at other public sites. After 1720 publicly underwrit-
ten publications appeared more regularly.[5] Edward Hunt, hanged for
counterfeiting and treason in November 1720, complained "the laws
under which he [was] to die were not duly published."[6] Whether or not
Hunt's complaint had anything to do with it, following his hanging all
laws were published at the end of each legislative session.

   Provincial laws were compiled for the public twice before 1718, and
six more times from then to the Revolution.[7] By 1742 a single collection
of the colony's laws exceeded 500 pages. Officials also published broadsides designed to keep citizens abreast of new laws and pending legal
problems, a practice that accelerated after 1717. Broadsides touching
piracy, immorality, an escaped convict, controversies with Maryland,
rioting, the murder of Indians, illegal land possession, and the increasing incidence of public swearing were typical. In addition, print sheets
appeared detailing treaties with the Indians, legal disputes with neighboring colonies, and charges to grand juries by judges, as did governors'
proclamations related to criminal matters. Publishers expanded upon
all these by chronicling crime and criminals. A typical example was *An
Account of Robberies Committed by John Morrison and His Accomplices* (1750–
51). In 1755 Pennsylvania readers eagerly pored over *The Life and Confession of John Myrick . . . executed for the Murder of his Wife and Children*. The
particulars of John Lewis's "inhuman, barbarous and bloody Murder of
his Wife" also fascinated the public. By the late 1720s newspapers began
as well to provide at least limited coverage of oyer and terminer proceedings, cases, and dockets. In the mid-1720s, execution sermons (sermons

by local clergymen given at the site of executions) and "last statements" by condemned felons began appearing. By far the most popular of these tracts described Elizabeth Wilson's execution for the murder of her illegitimate twin sons in 1786. It was reprinted several times both in Pennsylvania and in neighboring states.

In a different vein, after 1722 the Pennsylvania press offered *The Office, Duty, and Authority of Sheriffs* and *The Conductor Generalis, or the Office, Duty, and Authority of Justices of the Peace* . . . for persons interested in learning about the procedures and duties of judicial officers. When the lawyer Ralph Assheton died in 1746, his estate included a library of over three hundred volumes, two-thirds of which were law books.[8] By midcentury the colony's booksellers routinely advertised legal works. Blackstone's celebrated *Commentaries on the Laws* quickly found subscribers in Pennsylvania and the Lower Counties in the early 1770s, and before the end of the decade was a staple at Philadelphia booksellers. These varied publications permitted citizens to learn their criminal laws and the workings of their courts—providing, of course, that they were literate in English.[9] Not surprisingly, few criminal defendants argued ignorance of the law to escape accusations.

On the contrary, court records suggest that early Pennsylvanians at least believed they also were conversant with English law—both written and unwritten. In 1687 George Davis was indicted in a Sussex County court "for falseyfying his test taken in th[e] Court[,] . . . the prisoner pleaded his Attestation was not according to the law of England and that he had not broke the Kings laws." Later in that same year Phillip Russell, charged with breaking a contract, argued that he "was overtaken in drink when he Made the said Contract . . . and that it was Repugnant to the laws of England for A drunken man to Make such contracts . . . [and have them] stand in force." Hugh Thomas and Lazurus Pugh, accused of the murder of a judge in Chester County in 1717, pointed to the fact that they had been indicted by Quaker grand jurors who had not taken oaths of office. On that basis they boasted "they knew well it was not in the power of the government to try any Capital Crimes according to the common and Statute laws of England." They asserted that the act of the Pennsylvania Assembly under which they were tried was "Contrary to the Laws, Statutes and Rights of your Majestie's Kingdom."[10] Edward Hunt, hanged in 1720, also insisted before his execution that he had not been tried "by the Laws of England on all Points, as a Church of England man ought to be."[11] Convicted persons petitioning the court for the remittance of their punishment also employed that argument to have their sentences softened, or canceled altogether. Indeed, many protested that they understood the law better than the judges before whom they stood. Eleazer Oswald's belligerent attack upon the state's Supreme Court justices in 1782 is just the most blatant example of a citizen lecturing the court on the assumed particulars of the law.[12]

In the seventeenth and early eighteenth centuries, Quakers were not likely to credit the legal profession with bringing any welcome changes to the practice of law or the access to justice.[13] They complained that lawyers fomented conflict, arguments, and delay. Some spoke more brutally, charging that lawyers had "a License to Murder and to make Mischief." In Pennsylvania, where Penn and Quakers could act upon their antipathy, "The Laws Agreed Upon in England" (1682) stipulated that litigants were not "to fee any attorney and councilor." In 1686 and again in 1690 the Council sought to prohibit the charging of any attorney fees, only to have their intentions aborted by the legislature. Even so, the Friends' sense of fairness and equity opened a crack for lawyers to slip through. The Charter of 1701 declared "all Criminals shall have the same Privileges of Witnesses and Council as their Prosecutors." The 1718 reception law applying English laws to Pennsylvania insisted that "upon all trials of . . . capital crimes, lawful challenges shall be allowed and learned counsel assigned to the prisoners." Between 1710 and 1723 a series of laws acknowledged the presence of lawyers and established fee schedules. To practice, lawyers had merely to file a Warrant of Attorney in the prothonotary's office of the court before which they wished to practice, including the colony's Supreme Court.[14]

Despite all these discouragements to a professional bar, from the very first court sessions in Pennsylvania, friends of defendants and plaintiffs in civil cases appeared to plead, as did men with a smattering of legal education (pettifoggers) who hired out for such service. John Moore, Robert Assheton, George Lowther, Thomas Clarke, Thomas McNamara (or McNemara), and Peter Evans were among the most visible practitioners in the first decade of the eighteenth century who had legal training. Several, like David Lloyd, Ralph Assheton, John Guest, and Roger Mompesson, were trained in England. David Paul Brown, a historian of the early Pennsylvania bar and a practitioner himself, observed that in the first decades of the colony's history, "if a man understood a few Acts of Assembly and knew Dalton's *Justice of the Peace*, he had all the legal education which any one could teach, and almost all that any could attain."[15]

This became less true following 1717, as men with a better grasp of English practices and forms made their presence felt. Peter Evans, John Kinsey, James Alexander, Joseph Growden, Jr., James Graeme, Andrew Hamilton, William and Francis Rawle, and David French joined the bar in the decade after 1717 and left ample evidence of their skills and success. And for every David Lloyd, John Guest, Roger Mompesson, John Kinsey, and Andrew Hamilton there were attorneys like John Remington, Charles Brockden, Francis Sherrard, and John Morris who toiled in relative obscurity. It was during this time that Benjamin Franklin resigned a minor judicial post, arguing that he was inadequately trained "to act in that Station with Credit."[16]

Even more talented practitioners like Tench Francis, John Moland, Richard Peters, and Edward Shippen appeared in the 1730s and 1740s. The 1750s and early 1760s introduced Thomas McKean, George Read, and Jasper Yeates to a Pennsylvania bar rapidly becoming among the best in the English continental colonies. Between 1742 and 1775, seventy-six lawyers were admitted to practice, doubling the number available to defendants coming before the colony's courts.[17] After 1750, "swarms" of lawyers congregated at courthouses during court term to solicit clients, to the chagrin of many observers. As Francis Hopkinson put it in a poem to his lawyer brother-in-law, "Attorneys and clients here lovingly meet, the one to be cheated, the other to cheat." So few defendants appeared in oyer and terminer proceedings without legal counsel by 1750 that clerks remarked on it when one did.[18]

In England, it was essential that the indictment be done accurately and precisely. Failure in either respect laid the indictment open to challenge and the process subject to dismissal. From the beginning Pennsylvania indictments, written or printed in English, followed a rough form, with individual variations appearing from county to county and over time.[19] In England, in civil cases, a careful lawyer could achieve his client's aim, or lay the foundation for an appeal, by spotting carelessly drawn or erroneous writs and capiases. Early Pennsylvania law specifically permitted greater leeway in drawing up legal forms, and prohibited cases being truncated on the basis of minor errors. As early as 1701 Pennsylvania law proclaimed that defects in pleas or other clerical errors should not suspend or abort the judicial process. A 1710 law called for cases to continue to completion regardless of "imperfections and omissions" in actions and pleas.[20]

This leniency did not preclude attentive attorneys from bringing errors to the attention of the court in criminal proceedings. In May 1688, Norton Claypoole, charged with issuing a false order of the court, argued through his attorney, William Emot (or Emmatt), that his indictment "was A false Copie" and desired that proceedings against him be quashed. In that same session William Bradford, accused of "Challenging Arthur Starr to fight," pleaded on the same basis for similar results.[21] And despite the law's admonition to be generous in evaluating writs and pleas, judges sometimes truncated proceedings initiated by irregular causes of action, or permitted appeals because of faults. In the William Bradford case above, "the Sence of the Court [was] that the Indictment [was] not suffitient and no[t] According to law." Hence, the case against

Bradford was "dismist" and the prosecutor ordered to pay all costs.[22] Juries, too, acted to abort faultily drawn bills of indictment. In June 1688, a Sussex County trial jury refused to convict Henry Stretcher and Phillip Russell for selling beer "at More then the law directs or allows" because "[their] indictments [were] not according to law."[23]

Among other things, the growth of a professional bar meant that procedures were more strictly observed in Pennsylvania criminal courts, and that indictments were scrutinized even more closely and routinely. And, as indictment form changed at the insistence of lawyers to accommodate new (English) norms, pressure increased both on clerks to draw more careful and sophisticated documents, and on attorneys to examine them minutely in the interest of their clients. As professional lawyers became more common in criminal as well as civil courts after the first four decades, indictments, presentments, and other court papers were scrutinized even more closely and attempts to quash them because of errors increased.

The emergence of common law lawyers, familiar with English ways, led to changes in causes of action. Writs of replevin, for instance, became more popular. The great majority of civil cases in Pennsylvania were attempts to recover goods "unjustly detained" by another. An individual initiated the common law practice of detinue, a possessory action for the recovery of these lost chattels. A trial determined the true ownership of these goods and only then would they be returned. As lawyers entered these frays, actions of replevin and trouver became the desired mode of action.[24] The first demanded that the goods in question be returned prior to trial. The second palliated the impact of the action by pretending that the goods had been "lost," then "found" and "used" by the defendant.[25]

These were significant developments in criminal justice. Civil suits often clearly dealt with incidents of theft, and were taken in lieu of criminal action. Despite earlier Quaker abhorrence of lawyers, by mid-century practitioners were offering Pennsylvanians means of resolving criminal matters in ways more consistent with conventional Quaker beliefs and attitudes. The use of civil rather than criminal proceedings in cases of theft, assault, or trespass, for instance, established the remedy as fiscal rather than incarceration or corporal punishment. It also reduced the involvement of authorities in the case and lent itself to mediation rather than sanctions. Whether this growing appeal of civil solutions represents an aversion to criminal administration solutions on the part of the authorities or society generally—or both—remains unclear. It is equally unclear why the authorities or people resented criminal justice solutions.

With professionally trained lawyers also came a more obvious use of

Latin in proceedings. It increased dramatically in the third and fourth decades of the eighteenth century on the part of attorneys as well as by clerks. "Non est inventus" (he is not found), "non cul" (not guilty), "curia advisari vult" (the court will advise), "qui tam" (an action initiated by an individual or informer), "nolle prosecqui" (the court will not prosecute), and "ponit se super patriam" (the defendant demands a jury trial) became commonplace notations in criminal dockets. So, too, did a pidgin legalese incorporating Latin and English. Thus, phrases such as "Sur rule to declare," "pleads no cul," and "security for cost or non pros," began to appear.[26] Following the Revolution, when professionally trained practitioners dominated both the bench and the bar in Pennsylvania, the usage of Latin in legal forms was so common that a serious movement arose in the first decade of the nineteenth century to eliminate it altogether. Critics of the use of Latin terms and phrases argued that they merely confused the uneducated, made the criminal justice system more complicated and mysterious than it needed to be and, naturally enough, served to permit lawyers to demand high fees for "interpreting" the law.[27]

As criminal dockets swelled and as the public's concern with crime grew, the role of court officials changed. Naturally enough, because in law crime violated the king's peace, the crown took great interest in its prosecution. In early Pennsylvania the task of prosecuting offenses in the name of the crown fell to attorneys-general or, more likely, to their deputies ("Attorneys for the King"). Frequently, local lawyers were commissioned to carry out these functions, especially in courts outside Philadelphia where the King's Attorney could not easily operate. Much earlier than historians have generally conceded, however, attorneys-general, or their representatives, managed the prosecution in criminal courts.[28] Prosecutions of minor criminal activities remained in the hands of laymen victims, but even in the first decade of the eighteenth century, agents for the king and the Proprietor, like George Lowther, managed the prosecutions of more severe crimes. As the eighteenth century progressed the attorney-general or his deputies more frequently replaced citizen prosecutors in courts of quarter sessions.

By the 1740s in the more populous—and reachable—older counties, the attorney-general shaped the makeup and order of court dockets. Tench Francis became a powerful and influential attorney-general in the middle decades of the eighteenth century and contributed mightily to the professionalism of court proceedings. He and his cohorts judged cases *non prosequi* or *non vult ulterius prosequi* when witnesses failed to appear or the facts did not warrant proceeding. They initiated writs of *certiorari* to move prosecutions into other (usually higher) courts. They quashed proceedings against offenders considered mentally retarded.

Francis, for instance, stopped proceedings against Catherine Pickering of Bucks County in 1742 because he considered the defendant "an Ideot." Peter Gift of Carlisle, charged with the murder of William Greene, also escaped prosecution when he was judged insane and "ordered to the care of the Managers of the Pennsylvania Hospital." Attorneys-general also argued that some punishments be reduced, or fines remitted, based on their assessment of the facts.[29] By the Revolution it is possible to glimpse the lineaments of the modern attorney-general's office and, with them, the growing interest on the part of the state (and other agencies of the government) to investigate, prosecute, and urge convictions in the name of the people.

Much of the pressure from within the system after 1717—from lawyers and, increasingly, from judges—was to move Pennsylvania forms and practices more faithfully into line with those of England. The push and pull between Pennsylvanians' intent on bringing local legal norms into compliance with those in England, and those desiring to maintain, and even expand, divergent American practices continued to the end of the century, and well into the next. This tug of war made it more difficult for Pennsylvanians to know the law. In the early nineteenth century, Pennsylvania Chief Justice William Tilghman observed that "By degrees, as circumstances demanded, [Pennsylvanians] adopted the English usage, or substituted others better suited to our wants, till at length before the time of the Revolution we had formed a system of our own."[30] The American Revolution naturally complicated this development.

More important than education and the growth of the bar was the effort to add courts and enlarge the bench in Pennsylvania in order to remedy the inadequate services and spotty public order that some people were complaining of—a growth in public authority which yet other men resented and resisted. The obvious first step required the Assembly to create new counties. The rush of immigrants into western Chester County forced the formation of Lancaster County in 1729. As these settlers and additional newcomers drifted west, across the Susquehanna River, York County was founded in 1749 and Cumberland County a year later. In 1752 Berks County was created to the northwest of Philadelphia County and Northampton County was born out of northwest Bucks County. Even these attempts to accommodate growth did not meet the needs of continued migration after 1750, and complaints kept coming to the government at Philadelphia. Residents of newer counties still demanded more convenient justice, nearby courts and adequately manned tribunals.[31] When Bernard Daugherty protested, he asserted that he spoke on behalf of "many Hundred Families" in western Pennsylvania that "labour[ed] under the greatest Difficulties," because the nearest court was sixty miles away. Attendance at court, he maintained, was "almost impracticable."[32]

The problem did not end with inconvenience; men and women who behaved civilly suffered from licentious neighbors, who thrived because the courts and magistrates were remote. Thus, they complained, "Rapine, Violence, and Injustice are suffered to pass unpunished, and the Laws as well as the Properties, of the Inhabitants are rendered insecure." "Delinquents escape before they can be apprehended."[33] A 1772 petition from the inhabitants of the East and West Branches of the Susquehanna observed that they still "find themselves Subject to many Inconveniences chiefly arising . . . from their being so very far removed from the Seat of Justice."[34] Punishment of "lawless and Abandoned Men" and "Disorderly Neighbors" was impossible "while Courts of Law and places for the Administration of Justice continue at the Distance of Eighty Miles and upwards from there."[35] Inhabitants of Fort Bedford in 1767 complained they "were in great Necessity for justices of the peace to reside among them." William Maclay, writing from Augusta in Northumberland County in the spring of 1773, referred to the "scandal of living entirely without any Peace or confinement or punishment for Villains." "If Hell is justly considered as the Rendivous (sic) of Rascals," he wrote, "we cannot entertain a Doubt of Wioming [Wyoming Valley] being the Place."[36]

The hell that Maclay referred to opens Pennsylvania's problem with inhabitants who did not want to see Pennsylvania's laws and peace officers and who put between a rock and a hard place the officers who did show up and do their job. These officers were responding to the pleas for local justice while meeting the fury of other local men who wanted them out of there, or never there to begin with. In the 1760s and '70s, hostility arose from Virginians migrating into the Ohio River watershed and Connecticut men moving into the Wyoming Valley of northeastern Pennsylvania.[37] They disputed Pennsylvania's colonial boundaries and challenged titles to property granted by Pennsylvania. Pennsylvania magistrates had to defend the boundaries and titles, and support the province's laws in general.

The work was always difficult and often dangerous, especially when ejecting settlers with faulty titles. Justice Arthur St. Clair of Bedford County learned in 1771 that many settlers were threatening to "oppose every of Penn's Laws" and to resist "Sheriffs and Constables and all ministers of Justice."[38] Thomas Wood, deputy sheriff of Bedford County, told his superiors in 1771 that when he sought to carry out orders to serve an ejectment on John Martin, a crowd "armed with Guns and Tomhawks (sic)" held him prisoner and told him "if he would depart out of that Settlement quietly and not attempt to execute his Office, they would allow him, but that if he would execute any part of his Office, he might depend upon the heigh of ill usage." In that same area three years later, a crowd threatened the life of Sheriff John Carnahan. Carnahan informed Penn, "I am Daily threatened of my life and property if I proceed to execute my office."[39]

Establishing new counties and courts obviously helped answer the need of western Pennsylvanians, but without resolute, qualified men to fill the magistracy and bench, founding new counties was hardly enough. When they searched for qualified men, governors found too few able and willing men to staff the new counties, and moreover, too few to fill vacancies in the older counties when retirements or deaths created a need. As early as 1750, Governor James Hamilton complained to Thomas Penn that he was having trouble; some men refused because they did not want to expose themselves to popular abuse. Nor could he easily replace aged and ill justices in the older jurisdictions.[40]

A partial solution to the problem in the west was to draw upon the officeholders in the east. Thus when Arthur St. Clair moved to Bedford County he was given the posts of justice of the peace, recorder of deeds, clerk of the orphans court, and prothonotary. Two years later, when Westmoreland County was established, St. Clair was given commissions for the same offices in the new county. His successor in Bedford County was Thomas Smith, who had previously held the same offices in Cumberland County.[41] The case with Pennsylvania contrasts sharply with that of Massachusetts. According to historian David Flaherty, a coterie of eager, élite families was planted in the west even as far as remote Hampshire County, and until the Revolution, the families (Pynchons, Partridges, Stoddards, and Williamses) monopolized offices, kept order, and received deference from the people. Pennsylvania had neither these élite volunteers nor the results that Massachusetts did.[42] In an even greater contrast, the bench in Pennsylvania never became the élite appointment that it was in England.

Men were nevertheless installed into judicial office, and some of them proved to be minimally qualified, not qualified, or plain dishonest. The public protested against magistracy often enough that the Assembly in January 1767 created a committee to hear and investigate "complaints of Persons who conceive themselves aggrieved by any public Officer of this Province."[43] The House, Council, and governor were all kept busy fielding complaints against justices of the peace. In September 1764 the Assembly heard charges of partiality against Lewis Clotz, Lewis Gordon, and John Moore, justices of the peace from Philadelphia County. A committee of grievances in May 1769 weighed accusations of incompetence against two Chester County justices, John Hannum and Richard Reilly. More substantial charges were leveled against Charles Jolly, a Philadelphia County justice of the peace who was eventually judged guilty of "diverse misdemeanors and corrupt Practices" and removed from office. In January 1771 "diverse Freeholders and Inhabitants of Lancaster" complained of "the dangerous Principles and bad Example of Isaac Sanders," another justice of the peace. Charges of incompetence also were directed toward Gilbert Hicks and his colleagues on the bench of the Orphans Court in March 1772. Lewis Klutz and Henry Koken, justices of the peace from Northampton County, were forced to defend themselves in 1773 against a variety of allegations, as were John Hannum and William Parker of Chester in the following year. Three years later "diverse Magistrates" in Northumberland County were exposed to an onslaught of charges relating to their conduct. William Plunkett of Northumberland County was said to be "ill-conditioned," "slothful," "drunk," and generally not very responsive to his official duties.[44] Subsequently, some of the offending magistrates were removed.

Without waiting for public complaints, the government initiated removals on its own. Justice of the Peace Thomas York was removed in 1761. The Penns also moved against Lancaster's William Peters once the Proprietor became convinced "the love of money has got the better of him, and . . . has led him to do many dirty things he otherwise would have been ashamed of." Cumberland County's justice, William Smith, who consorted with angry frontiersmen who fired upon the King's troops at Fort Loudon in 1765, had his commission withdrawn. A year earlier, in that same county, magistrate George Stevenson, depicted by John Penn as "a universal bad character," and "certainly as great a Rascal as ever existed," was also removed from office.[45]

Growth had its effect at the apex of the justice system as well as in the county courts. The Supreme Court came under attack in the 1760s for failing to process efficiently a growing number of cases and to bring its power and authority to outlying counties. By 1767, the court was several hundred cases in arrears, according to its dockets.[46] The proprietor sought to upgrade the court's personnel and its effectiveness. He replaced Lawrence Growden, who resigned in 1764, with Alexander Stedman, whose credentials for the office were lauded by Edward Shippen and Benjamin Chew. John Penn came to believe Stedman "the best qualified for [the office] of any man in the Province [and] strictly honest."[47] Penn, who also wanted his Supreme Court to expand its circuit responsibilities and exhibit greater energy, took advantage of the judicial bill of 1767 calling for four justices rather than three. He named a new court of William Allen, John Lawrence, Thomas Willing, and John Morton. The extra justice was badly needed, and the subsequent stability in court personnel was welcome.

But the court defaulted on its obligations anyway. It was seated in Philadelphia, but was obliged to travel on circuit through the counties. With additional counties and county seats, riding circuit became more arduous and disagreeable. The court had for some time dodged circuit duties. In 1710 justices were allowed to forego trips even into neighboring Chester and Bucks counties if no pressing cases were docketed there. This provision was extended to Lancaster County in 1729. Judges could determine for themselves what constituted pressing cases. The Judicial Act of 1722 stipulated that they also could bring to Philadelphia capital cases committed "without the certain and known bounds and limits of any of the counties." A 1744 enactment required that Indians believed to have slain white settlers be tried in Philadelphia. Appalled by the time, inconvenience, and hardships associated with the judicial circuit, the high judges found every excuse to bring cases from outside Philadelphia into the city for adjudication. Evidence suggests, for instance, that between its inception in 1729 and 1745 oyer and terminer proceedings occurred infrequently in Lancaster County, if at all.

The practice of transferring cases into the city became notorious after 1743 when John Kinsey became chief justice. Richard Peters confessed to John Penn in 1749 that it "grieved" him "to see that a Judge either from vanity or pride can countenance removals in plain & obvious cases." Thomas Penn conceded that the practice was a "grievous nuisance" to the peoples of the outlying counties, as the high court "encouraged the removing all Causes however circumstanced" to Philadelphia courts. For all his condemnation of Kinsey and the high court's reluctance to carry out much-needed circuits, Kinsey's successor as Chief Justice, William Allen, proved equally eager to adjudicate cases from afar in Philadelphia. As a result, individuals outside Philadelphia seeking to use the high court faced real hardships. Few could afford the time and expense to travel to Philadelphia in search of justice. Nor could they guarantee the appearance of others necessary for the proceedings. Because witnesses were not obligated to appear in Philadelphia, many defendants and victims who made the long trek into the city were frustrated.

The Assembly readily confessed the lack of justice in such cases, saying, "justice is not done. . . . It has been totally obstructed."[48] Even when the Supreme Court functioned in counties outside Philadelphia, the justices were seldom able to process the burgeoning dockets. There needed to be longer calendars and more judges. Not until 1767 did help come, and then by an act enlarging the court to four judges.[49] But by 1767 the province had been intermittently in deepest disorder for twelve years, and although the disorder arose from European and Indian diplomacy, it had its criminal justice component too.

In the spring of 1756, John Churchman, Quaker reformer, surveyor, and justice of the peace from Chester County, visited Philadelphia. As he walked through the city streets he came upon jingoistic Pennsylvanians carting around for public view the bodies of frontiersmen slain by Indians. Afflicted by the spectacle, Churchman asked himself, "How can this [calamity] be? Since this has been a land of peace. . . ."[50] Churchman was referring to the peace with the Indians, of course. That other peace, the civic one, had been slipping away for more than thirty years, violated in a thousand less conspicuous sites like homes, workshops, inns, roadways, and harvest fields. As a justice of the peace, Churchman knew as much. But now the iconic peace with the indigenous people of Pennsylvania had been crushed; to many Quakers then and historians since, the Holy Experiment was over. The success of Pennsylvania as an asylum to Europeans was killing the critical part of the original vision that men would live at peace there.

By mid-century, Chief Justice William Allen estimated that 4000 families, mostly Scots-Irish, were living beyond the Susquehanna River, outside the judicial reach of Pennsylvania authorities. As unprecedented numbers of settlers outstripped Pennsylvania's effective authority, they abused their newfound liberty and tested the justice system as never before. Moreover, the liberties they took and the incivility they practiced offended the indigenous peoples and caught the attention of French imperialists. Visceral suspicion and hostility between settlers and Indians became overlaid by deepening rivalry between English and French over the Ohio River valley. In 1754, American and French troops first spilled blood in western Pennsylvania. When French troops and their Indian allies defeated General Edward Braddock's English and American army in July 1755, Pennsylvanians from the Ohio to the Eastern piedmont lay exposed to Indian attack. In November of that year Indians murdered Moravians and Christian Indians on the upper Lehigh River. As raids accelerated, settlers abandoned their farms and homes and fled east and south toward Philadelphia. In April 1756, Pennsylvania Governor Robert Hunter Morris declared war on the Indians.[51]

Throughout the next two years, raids and counterraids wasted and depopulated the frontier. To Europeans in America and Europe, the conflict was national, between the French and British empires. To a growing number of Europeans in America, it was also a racial conflict, between red and white. The believers in race conflict were either mostly or wholly incorrect, and some of the contrary evidence that they ignored or dismissed bears upon the topic of justice in Pennsylvania, even in wartime. Although admittedly there are war crimes and justice does not take a holiday in war, new rules apply in wartime and the rules legitimate ordinary homicide committed by rank-and-file combatants. Whatever a soldier's personal feelings about the enemy might be, his affiliation (citizenship) keeps him from being indicted for criminal homicides.

Contemporary Pennsylvanians and some historians oversimplified the conflict in Pennsylvania, making it nation versus nation or race versus race, falling mostly under the rules of war. In the process, they ignored the clashes between Indians and whites which were personal and discriminating, not between faceless armies of blameless, anonymous soldiers arrayed opposite each other across some contested diplomatic boundary—and not even one race avenging itself on all members of another. Historian Jane Merritt explains that attacking Delawares and Shawnees in 1755 and 1756 knew their victims personally, attacked them selectively, and deliberately avoided other whites. The victim whites had done something to arouse a sense of injustice among the Indians, whereas other whites had been inoffensive or even friendly.[52] Whites also identified individual Indians who attacked them. However skewed the Indians' reasons might conceivably have been for feeling aggrieved, and however much their judgments and retributions against whites lacked the due process of law, they practiced one essential feature of civic law, that responsibility and blame are personal and not national or racial.

Among and between white Pennsylvanians too, violent speech and the possibility of violent action were usually close at hand from 1755 through 1764 or longer. In the capital, Philadelphia, the ascendant political powers in Pennsylvania, the Quaker party and the Proprietary, clinched—for years, no less—in debate over financing the defense of the colony.[53] Impatient and hurting frontiersmen, watching this dawdling (in their view) over nuances of power, threatened to "tear the whole Members of the legislative body Limb from Limb, if they did not grant immediate Protection."[54] Pennsylvanians, who did not trust each other much in peacetime, now questioned the very loyalty of various ethnic and religious groups, like German Moravians, and especially the founding Quakers, whose affinity with the Indians was as old as Pennsylvania.[55] This hostility outlasted the Seven Years' War, because although the war officially ceased in 1763, Indians were not reconciled. In the fall of 1763, in the episode known as Pontiac's Rebellion, they attacked Pennsylvania again. The furies that had only just been contained were loose again.

The return of war intensified the alienation between whites and Indians, and confirmed every prejudice born within the last decade. The dismissive opinions of whites toward Indians made considered, civil justice between peoples all but impossible. Even before the bloody events of the frontier after 1754, the search for accommodation between Indian tribes and Pennsylvania authorities in criminal matters was a record of drift and confusion. Relations between Indians and white Pennsylvanians were jeopardized when pacific Indians lived among or near more bellicose communities of Indians. The pacific Indians frequently were blamed for and suffered from the actions and crimes of their more war-like brethren. Pennsylvania leaders acknowledged that peaceful Indians often had reason to complain of their abuse at the hands of whites.

Frontiersmen generally did not care to distinguish between tranquil and warlike Indians. One of them, Edward Marshall, boasted of having killed indiscriminately at least twenty Indians. Marshall exemplified so much: he did the walking (running) in the most notorious defrauding of the Delawares, the "Walking Purchase" of 1737; the Delawares avenged themselves by killing his wife and son and wounding his daughter; and his possible twenty murders add to the "dark figure" of unrecorded homicides in Pennsylvania.[56] When, unlike Marshall, fron-tiersmen were moved to apologize for their indiscriminate murders, they argued that seemingly peaceful Indians were merely waiting the propitious moment to strike. Or, that they temporarily assumed the guise of peaceful Indians to escape retribution for their depredations, or to gain food and hard goods from Anglo society.

But justice proved elusive even when the system was engaged. An unidentified Indian killed one Thomas Wright forty miles from Cones-toga in 1727 and escaped authorities by going "away hunting." Caesar, an Indian servant of Daniel Worthington, was accused of the sexual assault of Frances Band in 1717 but averted trial in the same manner. The violent antics of an inebriated Indian in 1738 required two white men to subdue him. During the struggle both whites suffered serious knife wounds. Nonetheless, when it became clear that the victims would survive, the Indian was "released to his tribe on bail and bound." Then the case disappeared from the record.[57] From the perspective of white settlers, successes were few. An Indian called Glasgow raped two white females in 1730, one a six-year-old, and was punished by Pennsylvania authorities for his crimes.[58]

After 1740, still more incidents of this kind tattered the judicial record. When a Mohegan Indian, Awannameak, disfigured Henry Webb late in 1742, he was turned over to his tribe and as far as the record shows, escaped punishment. After the Delaware Mushmelon (or Muss-memeelin, among other variations) confessed to the brutal killing (and suspected cannibalism) of Indian trader John Armstrong and two of his assistants in April 1744, white and red leaders huddled over how best to treat the matter. Pennsylvania authorities pointed out that they had executed two of their own people (John and Walter Winters) for mur-dering two Indian women and a male on French Creek in Chester County "without provocation" in 1728. Indeed, they had invited Indians to view the execution to impress upon them the government's willingness to punish those who brought harm to the colony's Indian peoples. It was only fitting, they asserted, for the Philadelphia populace to view the execution of Indians guilty of killing whites. The Delawares agreed to turn over Mushmelon and two of his alleged accomplices to Philadelphia's judges of oyer and terminer, but only if Mushmelon alone were considered a prisoner. The final solution—forged as much by diplomats and the common sense of go-betweens as by legal personnel—saw only Mushemelon convicted and sentenced to die. He was executed one week after his trial, on November 14, 1744.[59]

A year after Mushmelon's execution, "Robin Hood," an Indian living in Lancaster County, was jailed for ravishing "a white girl." Though jailed, he was not prosecuted before an oyer and terminer court; apparently, he too was released to his tribe. Six years later a Nantycoke Indian was jailed in Lancaster for "abusing a white girl." He also appears to have been punished by his tribe, if he suffered at all for his actions. In that same year, 1751, five Indians were arrested and incarcerated for trying to kill "an Old Indian from Germantown." Though they badly wounded the old man, when he survived they were released. No formal charges resulted from their premeditated attack. Pennsylvania authorities had little interest in prosecuting cases where both assailant and victim were Indians.[60] Meanwhile, people on the frontier continued to complain that they received little protection from the government from threats trivial or grave by Indians. As George Bryan observed, westerners felt themselves "deserted by the Government and [were] dreadfully incensed," an observation echoed by minister Henry Muhlenberg.[61]

In a population infected by prejudices and served by a tentative justice system, grave yet justiciable cases slid out of control. On October 8, 1763, Indians broke into the home of John Stenton outside the "Irish Settlement" in Northampton County, near Bethlehem, and killed him in the presence of his wife. Although Mrs. Stenton affirmed several times over several days that she could not identify her husband's attackers because of the darkness and chaos and gun smoke in the small cabin, she subsequently changed her mind and identified Renatus, a local Indian, as one of the culprits. Several white citizens, including a local tavernkeeper and the wife of the ferryman at the Bethlehem Ferry, stepped forward to testify that Renatus, a Christian Indian, was not in the area of the Stenton cabin at the time of Stenton's murder.[62]

Despite compelling evidence that Mrs. Stenton "several times" admitted she could not recognize any of the Indians who broke into her cabin and slew her husband, and even more compelling evidence that Renatus was "an innocent and harmless Indian," he was arrested and confined. Though sixteen days lapsed between the time he was charged and his arrest, Renatus made no attempt to leave the community where he had lived in peace with his neighbors.[63]

Protesting that Renatus could not get a fair trial in Easton, Northampton County, Philadelphia lawyer Lewis Weiss successfully petitioned to have Renatus incarcerated in Philadelphia. Apparently, Weiss anticipated that Renatus would be tried there under the 1744 statute permitting such changes of venue. But Philadelphia authorities eventually crumbled under pressure from Northampton to return Renatus for trial. Despite outcries to hang him, a Northampton jury surprisingly voted to acquit. Feelings in the community remained strong, however, and Northampton officials kept Renatus confined, arguing it was for his own safety. While some local citizens fought to have him tried a second time, Renatus languished in jail. He was still in jail as late as July 1764.[64] When threats continued against the Moravian Christian Indians at Bethlehem, the governor ordered them removed to Philadelphia for their safety.[65]

Christian Indians in Lancaster County were less fortunate. Late in 1763, whites from Paxton (near Harrisburg) retaliated against Lancaster Indians for wrongs they had purportedly suffered at the hand of Indians. Armed men rode boldly into Conestoga Manor on December 14 in broad daylight and butchered six peaceful Indians, escaping with impunity. Two weeks later many of the same men murdered fourteen more Indians who, after the initial murders, had been herded into the Lancaster workhouse for their own protection.[66] The Paxton Boys then boasted that they would march into Philadelphia to kill some 140 Moravian Indians from Northampton who had been quartered there because of their alleged complicity in the killing of John Stenton and others near Bethlehem.[67]

These audacious daylight killings and bold public threats raised a host of questions regarding the colony's criminal justice system. Could its courts effectively prosecute murders on the frontier? Could they stop mass menaces against the public order—either real or threatened? Could magistrates function in communities hostile to the government's aims? In brief, could the criminal law be enforced in Pennsylvania outside perhaps Chester, Bucks, and Philadelphia counties?

Neither British authorities nor officials in Philadelphia missed the ominous fact that no local official sought to protect or avenge the Conestoga Indians by calling upon a company of Highlanders posted in Lancaster on the day of the massacre. Moreover, when some Assemblymen subsequently prepared a bill to punish those responsible for the murders in Conestoga, protests inside and outside the House forced its demise. The courts did not move against those responsible for the killings. Anyone in or near Lancaster rash enough to criticize the killings publicly was certain to be "thrashed to bits." Governor Penn conceded

that ten thousand of the Kings' troops could not bring a single perpetrator of the massacre to trial.[68]

The impotence of the colony's judiciary in the frontier counties
appeared again in 1765 when, in Cumberland County, settlers attacked
traders taking supplies to Indians. Convinced that Philadelphia merchants were supplying weapons along with trade goods to western Indians, they blackened their faces, armed themselves, and stormed a pack
train on Sideling Hill where they shot horses, beat mule skinners, and
destroyed goods.[69] When British soldiers from Fort Loudon pursued the
"Black Boys," they captured several and disarmed them, taking the rioters' guns to their post. Outraged by the soldiers' interference and the
confiscation of their weapons, several hundred men surrounded Fort
Loudon and demanded the return of the arms. Rebuffed, they surrounded and fired upon the fort for several days. At the forefront of the
"Black Boys" were William and James Smith, both justices of the
peace.[70] One justice of the peace who opposed the mob had his life
threatened.

Once again, protests from Philadelphians appalled by contumacious
westerners went unheeded. No one was tried and punished for either
the raid on the pack train or the siege of the British fort. Governor John
Penn told Thomas Gage, "No one was apprehended. Tho all the Witnesses appear'd and were examined by the Grand Jury, it seems they
were of the Opinion that there was not sufficient testimony to convict a
single person charg'd, and the Bills were return'd Ignoramus."[71] He
might have added, as another disgruntled witnessed pointed out, that
though in firing upon the King's troops and fort the "Black Boys" had
clearly committed treason, even "the slender offense of Riott . . . was too
high a crime and would not go down with the Jury."[72] An Assemblyman,
no less, from Cumberland County told an audience in Carlisle that if it
weren't for his seat in the Assembly he would have joined the "Black
Boys" himself.[73] Justice of the Peace William Smith did lose his commission, much to the anger of Cumberland citizens.[74]

In violation of treaties and the laws of Pennsylvania, settlers continued
to encroach on Indian lands and kept tension high in Cumberland
County throughout 1767. British military personnel were ordered to
remove these audacious interlopers and did so, burning cabins and scattering their inhabitants. To no avail. The settlers returned and rebuilt
their cabins. The persistence of "Long hunters" and families of settlers
in moving onto forbidden land and preying upon local Indians astonished and perplexed royal and Pennsylvania authorities alike. "The
many Murders committed on Indians in and on the Frontier of Pennsylvania . . . and no one being Ever punished for them," moaned one
observer, "cannot fail of exciting in the Minds of the Natives, the most

unfavorable opinion of the Justice and Strength of the Government."[75] Governor John Penn conceded that his "Civil Officers, whose Business it is to see that [laws] are duly enforced, cannot exert their Authority in so distant and extensive a wilderness." British authorities were no happier. Commander in chief General Thomas Gage confessed to Penn that because "these Lawless Settlers . . . meet with no Punishment," they quickly return "to the same Encroachments . . . in greater Numbers than ever."[76] Even in more mature Lancaster County, John Mitcheltree on several occasions threatened to murder Killbuck, a local Indian leader. Joseph Shippen, Jr. pressed Lancaster officials to take steps to control Mitcheltree. "People think it is absolutely incumbent upon the civil authority to take strict notice of such alarming villany [sic]."[77]

Believing that "audacious Encroachments" on Indian lands, the death threats and the actual "repeated murders of Indians" would lead to war with the Six Nations, the Assembly angrily warned Penn that "should crimes of the first Rank, of the deepest Dye, remain unpunished, wicked men will never be wanting . . . to take Advantage of the Time and Debility of Government to commit the like, or other Crimes." In January 1768 it began to draft a removal bill that called for the death penalty for anyone intruding on lands reserved to Indians by treaty.[78] Government became as violent as it conceivably could—ordering the taking of life—in order to get men to coexist peaceably. Even so, Pennsylvanians accustomed to seeing murderers escape the death penalty doubtless viewed this new legislation as merely hortatory. If the government had no capacity to confine, indict, convict, and punish murderers, there was small likelihood that it could succeed in the case of interlopers.

During tense weeks in 1768, Cumberland County's Frederick Stump, who had previously had his cabin burnt by British soldiers as an illegal settler, got six Indians drunk, including two women, and slew them. After scalping one of the males, he dumped the bodies in nearby Middle Creek. The following day, accompanied by a young male servant, he trekked fourteen miles to several Indian cabins and killed a woman, two young girls, and a female child. After burning the victims and their cabins, he returned home and "freely confessed" their deed to neighbors. He insisted that he had killed the original six in self-defense and the remaining four to eliminate any chance of reprisals.[79]

The initial responses by authorities promised a quick and just resolution of the matter. One Cumberland citizen, hearing Stump's confession, confirmed the details, and then reported them to Penn and the Council.[80] The speaker of the Assembly was determined to see the perpetrators punished. Nonetheless, he confessed, "We have Laws without being executed or even feard [sic] or respected. We have Offenders but no Punishment. We have a Magistracy but no justice." The Council ordered that a reward be offered for Stump's capture. It demanded that Chief Justice William Allen issue the necessary warrants for the sheriffs of Cumberland, York, Lancaster, and Berks Counties to arrest and confine the murderers. The remaining Indians had been assured that everything would be done to avenge their suffering.[81] Soon it appeared that wrongs would be righted. Cumberland's William Patterson, holding no official position, but fearing Indian reprisals for Stump's atrocities, took Stump into custody on January 23, brought him to Carlisle in chains, and handed him over to Sheriff John Holmes, who lodged Stump in jail. When Penn learned of Stump's capture, he ordered him brought immediately to Philadelphia.[82]

Despite these auspicious beginnings, little headway was made in prosecuting Stump. Bad weather, popular opposition to moving the prisoners, and disagreements among county judicial personnel delayed Stump's removal and that of his servant-accomplice.[83] On January 29 an armed mob estimated to be between seventy and eighty men entered Carlisle and broke the prisoners from jail, whisking them out of Carlisle and forever away from the prying eyes of historians.[84] The Assembly had to console itself by enacting a series of bills regarding rioting and wearing of disguises during riots, and by blaming Penn's ineptness and cowardice for the breakdown of law and order. A Cumberland County grand jury indicted twenty-three individuals for "rescue." Eight eventually stood trial in January 1769 and were very quickly acquitted. The man who had captured Stump in the first place, William Patterson, was driven from the county. None of the local magistracy was formally reprimanded. Thomas Wharton, no friend of the Proprietary government, watched all this with dismay and moaned to Benjamin Franklin that "the Lawless and Abandoned . . . do as they please."[85]

The events of 1763–1768 laid bare the difficulties facing a criminal justice system predicated originally on community consensus and popular involvement. Recriminations were shrill, and the targets for blame were everywhere. Philadelphians amplified the accusation circulating in Cumberland and nearby counties that all three events—the murders by the Paxton Boys, the Sideling Hill incidents, and Stump's escape—were accomplished through the complicity of county magistrates who shared their neighbors' marrow-deep abhorrence of Indians. In defiance of all common sense, both in the Conestoga killings and the Stump affair sizable numbers of men carried out their crimes in broad daylight and in the middle of communities without citizens or magistrates being able to identify any. The men who freed Stump did not even bother to disguise themselves. Evidence suggests that local justices of the peace, sharing community hostility toward Indians and believing that local values overrode the law when the two were at odds, aided and abetted those attacking the pack train and firing upon the fort in 1765, as well as those ensuring Stump's escape in 1768.

The Cumberland magistracy, like the Lancaster magistracy before it, defended itself by avoiding to mention the obvious likelihood that no local jury would convict a man of killing an Indian. Instead, they emphasized the issue of venue. Local justices of the peace and sheriffs alike argued that their constituents believed that the jailbreak of Stump was an act of justice on behalf of an accused man who would get no justice otherwise. Governor Penn and others wanted to remove Stump's trial to Philadelphia, they insisted, because they wanted to ensure a conviction and they feared that no jury in Cumberland or the west would ever convict one of their fellows for killing an Indian, or several Indians.[86]

Their suspicions were warranted. Both Governor Penn and Chief Justice Allen were loath to admit publicly that they harbored such thoughts, but they clearly did. Gage was less disingenuous. He told Lord Shelburne that "Unless extraordinary means are used, as well to apprehend and Secure these Lawless People, as to bring them afterwards to condign Punishment, by removing the Tryals to the capitals [sic] of the Province, where Jurys would be composed of Men more civilized than those of the Frontier, no Satisfaction can ever be obtained for any Outrages committed upon the Indian."[87]

In arguing that they should have jurisdiction over cases such as those of the Paxton Boys, the Sideling Hill particulars, and Stump's actions, westerners championed a principle that modern Americans recognize in the sixth amendment to the United States Constitution—the accused shall be tried in the "district wherein the crime shall have been committed." The Cumberland men never considered that Philadelphia lay within the district wherein the crime was committed. As the sixth amendment would have it, the accused deserved an impartial jury at this trial, but men in eastern Pennsylvania never expected a jury of westerners to be impartial—nor did westerners consider a jury of easterners to be impartial.

Some principle was bound to win and another was bound to suffer in this dilemma, just as one constituency would win and another would suffer. All parties demanded justice, including the Indians.[88] White Pennsylvanians on both sides of the issue grounded their grievances in an historical provision of Anglo-American law. Pleading from high principle for relief from one's plight, however, could not obscure the reality that this was a "zero-sum game," a dilemma as profound and unwelcome as ever faced the liberal experiment. Pennsylvania was uniquely the place in America that was open to everyone, including its indigenous people, and it would test whether different people could live together peaceably. The test was never more clearly administered than in the case of Indians and frontiersmen, and the confounding mixture of Pennsylvanians failed the test. This failure anticipated a long string of similar failures by later Americans.

Had the historical record in Pennsylvania been free of these specific clashes with Indians by men like Stump, justice in Pennsylvania between native peoples and Europeans would nevertheless have been tested. The tectonic westward shift of peoples promised no peace. When eventually the whole trans-Appalachian West became too small to satisfy the aspirations of numerous Americans for land and wealth, there is little reason to expect that white Pennsylvanians and Indians would have lived together in peace and justice, happy with what they had, reconciled to remaining only where they currently were. The expansion of European settlement is the most intractable case of injustice in Pennsylvania's past, and neither governments nor well-intentioned private persons had the remotest chance of bringing everyone to agree upon justice for all.

Frontier lacks justice

Chapter 6

Revolution

Liberty without virtue would be no blessing to us.
—*Benjamin Rush, 1777*

The events of 1776 severed government in Pennsylvania from its past
more cleanly than they did for any other colony in America. By the end
of that volatile year, Pennsylvania had a new state constitution and a government manned by new politicians, judges, and other magistrates. It
had a "revolution at home" which practically upstaged the revolution
for "home rule" from Britain.[1] Because the changes necessarily encompassed the justice system, the men who crafted this new order substantially altered the criminal laws and courts. For the first time since 1718,
the criminal code was seriously amended and new political crimes were
added. The Revolution set Pennsylvanians against each other more furi-
ously than politics ever had before and criminalized the behavior of a
large minority of previously trusted citizens.[2]

Philly had a revolu in 1776

   The revolutionaries of Pennsylvania boasted that they had erected a
new order in 1776, more democratic, just, reasonable, and moral than
any previous one. In many respects they were correct. But there was no
new order, no new leaf turned, in terms of common delinquency, no
regeneration of the people's behavior. For decades Pennsylvanians had
hardly been a law-abiding, peaceful community, and revolution did not
change that. Social behavior need not respond to political changes—
however much men in power think it does, wish it would, or promise it
will. And in Pennsylvania it did not. Crime continued after 1776 much
the same as it had before, while government struck out in a new direction.[3]

As early as 1774 the American challenge to Britain sparked widespread
attacks upon the colonial government and generated extra-legal committees that functioned like criminal courts. Among them, the Philadel-

phia Board of Safety, sanctioned by the Continental Congress, held
meetings, interrogated suspected Tories, pronounced individuals guilty,
and inflicted punishments. It incarcerated men it thought guilty of
opposing Whig policies or endangering their Whig neighbors. In January 1776, Dr. William Smith was brought before the board, examined,
and found guilty of "act[ing] an unfriendly part in the present dispute
between Great Britain and these Colonies" and "remanded to Gaol." It
ordered Thomas Austin to appear before it and face his accusers. As a
result of this hearing it ordered him to sign a loyalty oath or be jailed.
He signed the oath on February 14 and was released. Throughout the
first months of 1776 the board charged large numbers of people with
such crimes as being "enemies of America," "disaffected," "inimical to
the United States," and "unfriendly to the American cause"—and confined them.[4]

The Board of Safety worked closely with the Philadelphia city Committee of Inspection and Observation, empowered it to exercise broad judicial powers, and supervised its activities. In often noisy and contentious
public meetings, committee members interrogated suspicious neighbors, shouted down unfriendly witnesses, bulldozed political enemies,
and ran roughshod over people who questioned their legitimacy.
Typical of its behavior, the committee brought charges against Quakers
John Drinker, Thomas Fisher, and Samuel Fisher in February 1776 for
their refusal to accept Continental bills of credit, humiliating and abusing them in the process. Comparable county committees duplicated
the activities of the Philadelphia body. In Northampton County, for
instance, the committee's often unrestrained enthusiasm created "a
world of viciousness and unforgivingness, a world of unblinking enmity
and unbridled rapacity."[5] Not surprisingly, Pennsylvanians harassed and
confined by committee members railed their outrage at such activities.[6]

In May and June 1776, the radical Whigs substantially overwhelmed
the proprietary regime. After May 20, the justice system of Pennsylvania
crumbled in time with the House of Representatives and the other Proprietary institutions that the radical Whigs had maligned.[7] The Philadelphia Committee of Inspection and Observation sent a memorial on June
3 to the justices of the quarter sessions for the City and Liberties of Philadelphia. It demanded that they terminate the authority of the courts
until such time as a new government could be framed upon the "true
will" of the people. As a result, the colony's courts were suspended on
June 4, effectively immobilizing the Proprietary government.[8] The
energy and audacity of the radical Whigs transfixed men commissioned
by the Penns. Most of them withdrew from public life rather than contest
those challenging traditional leadership and conventional institutions.
In the first week of September, while the state constitutional convention

was still deliberating, an emergency ordinance named a number of prominent persons as justices of the peace for the state and other justices for individual counties to serve as interim court officials. Incumbent constables and coroners were asked to continue their work until the new government was firmly in place.[9]

The Pennsylvania constitutional convention published the results of its labors on September 10. Announcing the birth of a new government in Pennsylvania, including the creation of a state judiciary, was one thing; manning and operating it was quite another. Among those most unhappy with the constitution, lawyers quickly determined that by refusing to participate in the new system they could undermine it. Consequently, a large number of attorneys refused to hold judicial posts under the new government or to work in its courts.[10] Cumberland County's John Montgomery, who obviously opposed the new government and its supporters, asked James Wilson, who he believed was leaning toward supporting the new edifice, "Will you advise to Submit our necks to the Yoak like [an] ass?" "I am affraid if they once are alowed to open the Courts, it will be over with us."[11]

For approximately a year from the summer of 1776, the Supreme Executive Council [SEC] and a committee of safety exercised most of the judicial powers.[12] The SEC struggled to replace the extralegal committees with a state judiciary. The absence of any chief justice especially concerned it. Not until September 1, 1777, was it able to persuade Thomas McKean to assume the post, and William Atlee and John Evans to take up the posts of associate justices.[13] Meanwhile, criminal courts in Pennsylvania remained closed. Just weeks prior to McKean's acceptance of the chief justice post James Allen, son of the former chief justice, moaned, "Not one of the Laws of the Assembly are regarded . . . No courts open . . . [and] no justice [is] administered."

By July 21, 1777, however, the Philadelphia city court opened "amidst a great crowd of citizens," and a grand jury "composed of reputable and worthy citizens," returned twenty-one true bills. The *Pennsylvania Gazette* reported that the "whole business of the court . . . was conducted with the utmost good order and decorum."[14] Enough Pennsylvanians kept on boycotting, however, to keep most county courts closed. The presence of British troops also helped the closure. In Philadelphia, where the courts operated in late 1777, they closed again when the British occupied the city and did not reopen until the summer of 1778 when the British departed.

It was August 1777 before Lancaster's courts functioned. No courts were held in Chester County between May 1776 and August 1777. Following the brief August sessions, no courts were held until the spring of 1778, and even then, full routine did not return until the August 1778 term. By early September 1778, the quarter sessions and common pleas for the city and county of Philadelphia began without incident. Bedford County followed in October and Northumberland County in November. By the end of the year most of the county courts were holding sessions, at least on a limited basis.[15]

As nowhere else in America—with the possible exception of New Jersey—magistrates were toppled from office in Pennsylvania. In the first year of the Revolution, the new state regime contained not a single provincial executive or judicial officeholder from the old. Later, the only member of the colonial Supreme Court to hold a judicial position under the auspices of the new state was Benjamin Chew.[16] Most justices withdrew from public life rather than contest with the "usurpers" or controvert the charges of Loyalism employed to hustle them from office and discredit them with the people. The changes in personnel severely wounded the courts in the early years of the Revolution. Additionally, some disgruntled conservatives quietly sabotaged the progress of revolution by, for example, keeping public records from the hands of the new state government.[17]

A whole class of time-honored magistrates, the Quakers, disappeared from public office. Since the French and Indian War, various Quakers had found that the obligations of civil office compelled them to violate their religious principles or impulses, and some resigned. Revolution ended all the ambiguity among Quakers about public service. The Society of Friends ordered Friends out of office, and if they refused to leave, ousted them from the Society. When the Whigs erected a test oath in 1776, which no Quaker could take, they virtually disenfranchised the Quaker community.[18] For all these reasons, the number of Quakers serving in judicial posts dropped to zero.

While officeholders withdrew or were forced from their posts, "new men" stepped forward to replace them. The new state Supreme Court was exclusively new men, but all of them had legal training. Thomas McKean, chief justice, John Evans, and William Atlee, associate justices, were lawyers who had practiced law for more than two decades. Evans had been in practice since 1749. McKean had held a commission as justice of the peace. Each had prospered at the bar or on the bench and enjoyed respect in their communities. Yet none was part of the colony's earlier élite, nor did their children enter that élite, by marriage or otherwise. They got close to but did not enter the circle of older, more polished and refined families.[19] The same was true of George Bryan, who joined the court in 1780. Without formal legal training, Bryan had nonetheless served as a longtime justice in Philadelphia courts. Though Jacob Rush, who came to court upon the death of Evans in 1784, was a conservative and allied with men of great wealth, his own origins and social position were considerably more modest.[20]

New men surfaced in the lesser judicial posts as well. The Revolution attracted men previously inactive in their communities and drew them to the many extralegal committees that appeared after 1774. Their education and activity in these committees prepared them to take a more active role after 1776.[21] The militia, too, helped to recruit and galvanize the "lower sorts" to more active political and public careers.[22] Not surprisingly, a different group of candidates stood for the Assembly after 1776. As a result, less than one-quarter of the men who served in the 1775–1776 Assembly were elected to that house in 1776–1777. Those elected to the latter Assembly generally were younger and represented a different ethnic and religious base from that of those serving before 1776.[23] A significant number of new faces also appeared among those elected as justices after 1776.

The question of loyalty clearly took its toll on men with previous experience as justices of the peace. Seven justices elected from Cumberland County, for instance, concluded they could not in good conscience serve the new state government and refused their commissions. Two did so in Lancaster County and three more in Northampton County. In April 1778, inhabitants of Berks County complained to the SEC that their current justices of the peace refused to carry out their obligations. They desired new "appointees." Justices of the peace were not alone in refusing to hold or fulfill office. A number of clerks and recorders did likewise. Because the new government allotted more posts to counties and redistributed positions among the townships within counties, new faces on the bench appeared yet more obvious after 1776. Even in counties with the greatest continuity of personnel after 1776, half of those selected had not served the Proprietary government.[24]

Given the disorder in Pennsylvania government after 1775 and the inexperience of many of the new justice officials, it is no wonder that some proved to be unfit. Many were more adept at brawling with people coming before them than they were at adjudicating disputes. John Proctor, a candidate for sheriff, was found guilty of an assault in October 1782. Justice of the Peace Adam Tannehill of Pittsburgh was convicted of extortion. In 1779, numerous persons complained to the Assembly against magistrates Benjamin Weiser and William Atkinson. Henry Taylor, a Westmoreland justice of the peace, was indicted for assault and battery in 1783. Bucks County judge Thomas Dyer was fined and censured by George Bryan of the Supreme Court as a result of his part in an assault.[25]

Economically as well as politically, the Revolution marked changes in the status of the personnel and the clients of the justice system. Evidence

of changes comes from Chester County. Through 1765, the relative rank
in mean wealth of justices of the peace, constables, and jurors as well as
accused criminals and (most of the time) victims had been increasing.
(Figure 2.1 and Table 3.6) Ten years later, the upward trend ceased,
except for the accused, and thereafter, mean wealth declined. The greatest decline among officeholders concerned the most powerful officers,
the justices of the peace, whose mean percentile of wealth fell by 16.3
from 1765 to 1799, mostly between 1785 and 1799. That drop is no surprise, since the Quaker party had dominated Chester County before the
Revolution and Quakers were the wealthiest residents of the county.
Now the Quakers were entirely gone from public life. A larger, more
immediate drop between 1775 and 1785 would have been no surprise
given this signal change.

The 1776 constitution significantly altered the selection of justices of
the peace, ostensibly toward democracy. They were now popularly
elected. The radical revolutionaries made the franchise across the state
more generous economically so that any taxpaying male could vote for
justices of the peace, as well as for other officials. But in almost the same
stroke they disenfranchised men who resisted or renounced the domestic revolution. In Chester, the disenfranchised included at least forty
percent of the population, many of whom were Quakers. Other disaffected men, like Anglicans, shared the Quakers' fate. It should have
come as no surprise that when elections were held, the voter turnout for
years was extremely low. The newly elected magistrates were only ambig-
uously the choice of "the people."[26]

A non-élite minority of radical Whigs, probably poorer than the average resident, voted in the new judicial officials. And yet they did not pick
poorer men by 1785. After 1785, the opponents of the radical Whigs
(now called the Republican Party) regained control of county politics,
and the men elected justices of the peace declined in property rank. A
wealthier electorate electing poorer men? The evidence here for economic class upheaval is slim; the Revolution was more a case of a political and religious bourgeois overturning the political and religious men
they envied.[27]

Jurors experienced the second greatest change of economic status,
with a 9.1 percentile drop in rank between 1765 and 1799. That number
might reveal democratization, but not much. Two other measurements
of the equitable or democratic distribution of jury assignments clearly
show less a democratic tendency than the decline of wealth. In fact, they
demonstrate quite the contrary, that the Revolution caused little or only
ambiguous change. The first test is for the correlation between the distribution of jurors and the populations of the townships in Chester
County. Was each township getting its fair share of jury assignments, that

is, one man, one juror? When applied, that test shows that the correlation declined in the Revolutionary era, 1775–1785. In other words, the situation became less equitable or democratic. After 1785, it increased or became more equitable.[28]

A second test is for the correlation between jury assignments and the distance from the county seat at Chester Borough. The historical question here is, did the west get slighted in the criminal courts?—which is a lively question because the east was overwhelmingly Quaker and the western and southwestern townships were dominated by Scots-Irish, the premier revolutionaries. The numbers show a declining geographical correlation, a decline that occurred consistently after 1740.[29] In other words, the west benefited from increasingly equitable treatment until 1740 and less equitable treatment thereafter, a decline that the Revolution did not interrupt. The decline may have been remedied with the split in the county in 1789 and the removal of the seat to West Chester Borough.

Constables' highest percentile rank any time before 1800 occurred in 1765, when almost three-quarters of the taxpayers lay below them. In the next twenty years, they fell moderately, by 11.8 percentage points[30] (Figure 2.1). They finished the century by gaining status, the only group to do so. As Chapter 4 explained, constables suffered violent abuse, but they were never men of modest property, and the Revolution did not change that.

The relative rank of accused male criminals declined more than that of any other group in the justice system after 1775. The years after 1775 marked a time in Chester County when the disparity in the distribution of wealth grew markedly, although the disparity had been increasing since 1750. In these last twenty-five years of the century, the accused increasingly resembled 60 percent of the taxable population who saw their relative standard of living falling behind the rest.[31] The gap between them and the justices who tried them and the jurors who judged them was growing too (even though these two groups were declining at the same time). If these men were the relatively increasing poor of the county, they were not Quakers or Anglicans or likely any other rivals of the Whig revolutionaries.

Had politics carried into the courts and expressed itself in the prosecution of the disaffected, the wealth of the accused should have risen. But since it did not rise, the unmistakable political and religious rivalry had little or no apparent effect on the mass of men whom the Revolutionary courts prosecuted for crime. In the city of Philadelphia, seventy-four accused males from 1779–1781 were present in the 1780 tax list, and the mean percentile of their wealth was 43.6.[32] They lay a decile below the rank of all the Chester accused. But at that position, the accused in post-Revolutionary Chester would shortly join them as the fortunes of the Chester accused men declined.

More than other groups, the mean wealth of Chester County male victims of crime oscillated, between the 52th and 70th percentiles, from 1718 through 1799. The Revolution through the year 1785 depressed their status only slightly. The politically marginalized Chester Countians in those years, the richer, did not suffer from more crime, insofar as the new regime prosecuted it in these disjointed years.

The regular operation of new courts, run by new incumbents, did not guarantee that the civil rights of all Pennsylvanians would be secure. While the SEC tried to curb the Associators and their excesses, and the framers of the new state constitution ironically wrote into it the rights that Pennsylvanians had earlier enjoyed, the new regime violated rights, conspicuously the right of privacy and of habeas corpus.[33] Acting on orders from the Continental Congress in April 1777, the SEC called for all houses to be searched, all arms confiscated, and the people reimbursed for their loss. All disaffected persons were to be disarmed and taken prisoner. The SEC also permitted justices of the peace to issue "special warrants" to search "any house" for "incriminating evidence." In October 1777, the Council ordered county "commissioners" to "examine persons and papers" and "to use force and to break open doors in all Cases where the same goods may be secreted and concealed." Moreover, they were ordered to "commit such as shall absolutely Resist their Authority." After committeemen searched the home of Quaker Samuel Emlen, they reported that though they had "broke open his desk" they had found "no incriminating papers."[34]

Violations of personal rights occurred on a daily basis, in city and countryside alike.[35] Persons were incarcerated for long periods in deplorable conditions on questionable evidence. Evidence was often permitted that today's courts would find clearly unacceptable. Open-ended sentences were imposed. Many prisoners spent their entire confinement in heavy chains. Persons exonerated or discharged still faced burdensome fees.[36] All this behavior generated a reaction. Defendants submitted petitions, and their attorneys argued for appeals on behalf of the convicted. The convicted filed clemency petitions by the thousands questioning the legitimacy of criminal justice procedures.[37]

Quakers suffered most from the new state government. Their homes were entered violently and all sorts of personal effects were confiscated. More than three dozen Quakers were arrested and seventeen exiled to Virginia without trial or conviction. As historian Leonard Levy has observed, "Nothing that the British had done equaled the violation of privacy rights inflicted by Pennsylvania on its 'Virginia Exiles' in defiance of the state constitution."[38] Such stark violations diminished drastically by early 1778, although they did not cease altogether.

When the Quakers suspected of Loyalism were arbitrarily rounded up and confined throughout the summer and fall of 1777, they and other members of the Society of Friends sought redress through habeas corpus. Applying to Chief Justice McKean in September, Quakers successfully argued that the confinement was "arbitrary, unjust and illegal." McKean granted the writ, maintaining that the habeas corpus act was a long-time and integral part of Pennsylvania's legal code. When the Assembly learned of McKean's actions it voided his writs and suspended all further writs emanating from his court. The Council supported the Assembly's actions.[39] Protesting the Assembly's move as an "unprecedented measure," McKean continued to resist. McKean had opened or exposed a division within the ranks of the radical Whigs—with him on the side of moderation and due process—one that would not go away in the years to come.

Early in December 1780, McKean opposed the SEC's desire to have Tory Joseph Griswold denied habeas corpus. Upon his issuing the writ the Council demanded that he appear before them to explain his actions. McKean adamantly refused, insisting not only on Griswold's right to the writ but the right of his court to act independently of the Council and Assembly in determining the legitimacy of such issuances.[40] The McKean court continued to issue writs of habeas corpus until the SEC and Assembly grew tired of denouncing the court's obstructing their actions. With the exception of the tumultuous years between 1776 and 1780, the right of habeas corpus was never again seriously threatened in Pennsylvania.

Treason naturally became a contested issue in fractious Pennsylvania. The urge to punish the opponents of independence and the new regime in Pennsylvania was registered in a new state law of treason and in the courts. On September 5, 1776 the Pennsylvania Convention adopted a resolution defining treason as "levy[ing] war against this State or be[ing] adherent to the King of Great Britain or others of the enemies of this State or enemies of the United States of America by giving him or them aid or assistance." Punishment for such activities included the forfeiture of all real and personal property and confinement up to the duration of the war. A week later, a second ordinance made punishable seditious utterances, defined as speaking or writing with the purpose of "obstruct[ing] or oppos[ing] . . . the measures carr[ied] on by the United States of America for the defense and support of the freedom and independence of the said states." Individuals alleged to be guilty of such offenses could be convicted and imprisoned by a single justice of the peace. Should the first justice believe the individual too dangerous

to be permitted free on bail, he could, in association with a second justice, move to incarcerate the accused for the duration of the war.[41] However, one of the final acts of the colonial Assembly was to nullify this last
ordinance as a violation of the rights of Pennsylvania citizens. So far as
is known, no one was prosecuted under it.[42]

Then the state Assembly, meeting for the first time under the auspices
of the constitution of 1776, played its role in reshaping the law of treason. In January 1777, it passed an emergency act declaring that all British and provincial statutes as well as the English Common Law
heretofore binding in Pennsylvania would again be in force after February 11 of that year, except that portion of law rendered obsolete by the
current political revolution. This mandate, of course, included the
English law of treason. On February 11, 1777, the Assembly defined treason more concretely, identifying seven acts of treason and misprision of
treason, and proclaiming the penalty for treason to be death and disin-
heritance. The law called for those guilty of treason to forfeit all property, including the dower of the traitor's wife. It did make an exception
of whatever income the Supreme Court might designate for the survival
and upkeep of the offender's immediate family.[43]

This act also defined misprision of treason[44] as speaking or writing in
opposition to Whig governments, passing military intelligence to the
British, encouraging a return to British rule, hampering enlistments
into the American army, fomenting tumults to the disadvantage of Whig
forces, or attempting to discredit Revolutionary programs. Guilt in any
of these areas was to be punished by imprisonment for the duration of
the war and forfeiture of half of one's estate.[45] Harsh as the law seems at
first glance, it proved to be one of the milder treason laws passed by any
state at the time.[46] That said, criminalizing actions perceived to be either
detrimental to or critical of the existing government created a slippery
slope. Without question, it intimidated political opponents of the radical Whigs, and permitted those in power to interpret legitimate political
dissent as treasonable or dangerous behavior.

The first large wave of treason prosecutions occurred in September
1778. Attorney General Jonathan Dickinson Sergeant and his special
assistant, Joseph Reed, presented to the Philadelphia grand jury forty-
five bills, including thirty-six for treason. The grand jury refused to bring
forward twelve of the charges but indicted the remaining thirty-three.
Only two of the accused, John Roberts and Abraham Carlisle, were convicted of treason and executed. A third defendant, Abijah Wright, whose
sanity was questioned, had his trial carried over to the December term.
He subsequently was convicted and hanged.[47] The year 1778 ended with
fourteen men sentenced to death and eight executed. Both numbers
were the second highest yearly totals in Pennsylvania history.

Overall, 178 charges of treason, misprision of treason, and related accusations ("activities inimical to the Revolution," "aiding the enemy," and "behavior inimical to America") were leveled against citizens of Pennsylvania between 1776 and 1783. One hundred and eighteen persons were indicted for treason in the state. Another eighty-one were indicted under the state's misprision of treason law. The Assembly and SEC issued conditional attainders for another 500 citizens. Of those 500, 113 prevented their attainders from becoming absolute by surrendering to authorities. Sixteen ultimately stood trial. Only six of the 386 who refused to turn themselves in to authorities eventually were captured and brought to trial.[48] It should be kept in mind, however, that political crimes were often punished under charges other than treason and misprision of treason in revolutionary Pennsylvania, especially after 1780 when state authorities concluded that juries were more apt to vote convictions if the death sentence were not involved.[49] Convictions for counterfeiting, horse theft, robbery, and riot often obscured what were trials for behavior that Whigs perceived as anti-Whig or treasonable.

Because of the unstable value of the currency issued by both Congress and Pennsylvania, Whigs viewed any act that increased the currency's depreciation (including the refusal on the part of many Quakers to use it) as treasonable and capable of undermining both state and national governments. Counterfeiting too held such potential. As a result, in 1777 the Pennsylvania Assembly made both counterfeiting and the uttering of counterfeit bills capital offenses, although it did permit benefit of clergy for each offense. Because the currencies depreciated precipitously, the law was revisited. Whigs complained that Loyalists were actively encouraging the counterfeiting of state currency, so beginning in 1779 several statutes stripped both crimes of benefit of clergy, thereby mandating the death sentence.[50]

Depreciation and counterfeit bills were not the only actions that provoked Whigs to add sanctions to the criminal laws. Tories and others, for political or just selfish motives, preyed upon Pennsylvania officials holding or transporting state funds. They also stole horses designated or available for the army. In 1780, the Assembly expanded the definition of robbery to encompass a greater variety of Tory activities and to render more harsh punishments for horse theft.[51]

As a result of the new capital laws especially, a total of fifty-four men were condemned to die from 1778 through 1780. Of these, thirty-three were executed. Twenty-one were sentenced to die in 1781 and twelve did so. Only seven were condemned in 1782, of whom three were hanged. In 1778, the proliferation of prosecutions and executions triggered outbursts from Pennsylvanians appalled by the prosecutions. These protests, in turn, helped to convince officials that they ought to treat enemies and protestors even more draconically. Joseph Reed, first as special assistant to the attorney-general, then as president of the state, pushed the Supreme Court to step up the prosecution of suspected Loyalists. "New characters are emerging from security like insects after a storm," he protested, "treason, disaffection to the interests of America, and even assistance to the British interest, is called openly only errors of judgment, which candour and liberality of sentiment will overlook." Reed defended the execution of the prosperous Quakers Roberts and Carlisle, arguing, "We could not for shame have made an example of a poor rogue after forgiving the rich."[52] Throughout the duration of the war, Reed urged the courts to deal more harshly with Pennsylvanians who, he believed, opposed the state and national governments.

Reed's impatience was a symptom of the deep divisions among the people of Pennsylvania about the Revolution. Determined Whigs, like Reed, could mobilize the criminal justice system against men they judged disaffected, but they could not prevent jurors and others from siding with the putative criminals. Most of those charged with treason in September 1778 and in subsequent oyer and terminer courts in that year were acquitted or had their charges dismissed. That pattern continued throughout the Revolution. In 1779 Reed protested to Chief Justice McKean, "Too easy an Ear has been given by the Ministers of Justice to the aplication of those who are disaffected to their Country & that from a Fear of the Imputation of Rigour or giving Offense, the contrary Error of extreme Compassion." He argued that such leniency had "a tendency to weaken Government & encourage the political Sinners of the State."[53] The diarist Christopher Marshall conceded that "honest inhabitants of Philadelphia were much displeased" with the stream of acquittals in cases involving "notorious Tories."[54]

Reed did not exaggerate the strength of moderation of his state. Pennsylvania courts and juries clearly showed restraint in treason and related prosecutions. Grand juries did not blindly embrace all charges brought before them. Juries did not automatically convict defendants accused of treason. Judges did not recklessly advocate the prosecution's arguments or match its zeal. The Pennsylvania Supreme Court played a major role in ensuring that the state showed liberality toward suspected traitors.[55] It held to a high level of evidence for prosecutions and convictions. It demanded absolute accuracy in attainders and arrest writs, even to the point of tossing out cases that erred in such minor matters as whether the defendant lived in "East Bradford Township" or "West Bradford Township."[56] It sent a steady stream of petitions to the SEC requesting leniency for individuals convicted of capital crimes. Chief Justice Thomas McKean once remarked to Associate Justice William Atlee that "the application and interest that will be made by the relatives &

friends of the culprits for mercy will create respect to the rules, and the [court's] granting it on every reasonable occasion will reconcile & endear men to the Government."[57]

In a landmark case, *Respublica v. Chapman* (1781), the Pennsylvania Supreme Court held that the January 28 treason law that suspended statutes then in effect to accommodate revolutionary realities between May 14, 1776 and February 10, 1777, was badly written and poorly conceived. The court argued that the treason enactment of February 11 logically marked the point after which treason could be committed against the present state government. In doing so, it respected the fact that the times before 1777 were chaotic and in fact the early stages of a civil war. Citizens were confused about the legitimacy of governments. Only citizens who remained in Pennsylvania following the establishment of a new state government and its enactment of laws could be held accountable for behavior detrimental to the new regime. Before February 11, the court ruled, Pennsylvanians were free to resist revolutionary committees and Whig pronouncements, and even to depart the state without fear of prosecution.[58] If this decision outraged Joseph Reed and others, it saved many a Pennsylvanian from prosecution or conviction.

Despite the Supreme Court's record of moderation and Joseph Reed's criticism of its leniency, some Pennsylvanians in this divided society viewed it as bloodthirsty. They compared Chief Justice McKean to England's Sir George Jeffreys, notorious for overseeing the "Bloody Assizes" in the 1680s, and railed that he and his court trampled the rights of suspected Loyalists and Tories, and intimidated those eager to supply testimony in their favor.[59] They pointed to the number of executions that continued to rise. Fourteen persons were executed in 1779 and another fifteen in 1780, both figures the highest annual totals in Pennsylvania's history. The McKean court oversaw the execution of thirty-seven individuals through 1780.[60] The state's Quakers were among McKean's most vociferous and bitter critics in the early stages of the Revolution. The executions of Friends Roberts and Carlisle in particular stamped McKean and his associates as implacable enemies in their eyes.[61]

A variety of other, newly fashioned punishments less severe than treason law and executions increased the state's arsenal against the disaffected. The confiscation of Loyalist estates added a major weapon. Between the spring of 1779 and spring of 1783, the court upheld 182 claimants of confiscated estates.[62] Forced exile for suspected Loyalists and Test Acts, which stripped persons failing to take an oath of allegiance of their civil rights, also became part of the strategy to repress Loyalism. Pennsylvania was one of the few American states to prohibit opponents of independence and the new state government from teaching school, all schools then being private ones. The courts not only agreed with such policies, but also willingly enforced the new laws.[63]

The Revolution also brought increased sentences for convictions for both political and apolitical crimes already on the law books. The rapidly depreciating currency would have rendered fines ever less punitive had the Assembly not raised them. On the other hand, the persons fined viewed the amercements as ever more burdensome. Amercements of £50 became common after 1777, forcing many to remain in jail because of their inability to pay. Some fines were set even higher. Susannah Longacre, convicted in February 1783 of giving food and aid to the enemy, was amerced £150. Rachel Hamer of Philadelphia County faced the same punishment after being found guilty of giving food to British soldiers.[64] Nonpolitical crimes got the same treatment. Joseph Burns of Chester County in 1780 was fined £2000 for adultery with Anne McMinn. In Chester County, the mean fine in 1777 was £8. In each succeeding year it was £38, £148, and £314.

Similarly, peace bonds were set at higher levels, as were sureties used in conjunction with such devices. Eleazer Doan, who as part of the infamous Doan gang was charged with being an accessory in a robbery, was ordered to give security of £1000 and a surety of the same amount to appear at the next court term. In the September 1778 Philadelphia oyer and terminer proceedings men exonerated of treason were nonetheless placed under peace bonds of £1000 and two sureties of £500 each. In addition, the time for which peace bonds were in force was often extended. It became commonplace for judges to make such bonds valid for "the duration of the war." Several men were ordered to provide such bonds good for up to nine years. And these were individuals who had been acquitted of criminal charges.[65]

The Revolution altered the configuration of sentencing in Pennsylvania and did so broadly and not just for political crimes. In the history of sentencing in Chester County, jail sentences appeared in significant numbers only after 1765. (Table 3.3) The years 1682–1765 represent only 11.9 percent of all jail sentences. In the cases of property crimes, jail was never prescribed before 1767. After 1767 it was always part of the sentence in property crimes. It effectively replaced whipping as a punishment for theft; after 1787 whipping was never prescribed for theft (except in one case of horse stealing in 1788), due to reforms in the criminal code.[66] In earliest Pennsylvania jails were expensive to maintain, and jail sentences meant foregoing the useful labor of able-bodied men. While immigration, especially after 1740, eased such restraints on jailing, the turnabout in jail sentencing came with the Revolution. The new state government prescribed sustained confinement for an assortment of Quakers and suspected Loyalists, and various extralegal committees speedily disarmed and incarcerated those believed "inimical to the interests of the United States"—with or without due process of law. As a result, hundreds of Pennsylvanians found themselves spending long periods in jail.[67] Nonpolitical criminals more often suffered jail terms too. Men and women convicted of larceny now received six months or more in prison. Baltzer Mentzer of York County was sentenced in 1783 to one year's incarceration for that offense. Repeat offenders like Ann Winters of Philadelphia found themselves serving up to two years in prison for stealing inconsequential items. Conviction on adultery and bastardy charges brought Northampton County's Elizabeth Wilhelm a year in prison (in addition to twenty-one stripes on her bare back). The law permitted Loyalists under some circumstances to be confined for the duration of the war.[68]

Incarceration was not to be dismissed lightly. Many defendants were kept in chains. The experience of Aaron Doan while confined in 1786 was typical of many others: He was "loaded . . . the whole time with heavy Irons, and suffer[ed] every other Speicies (sic) of Misery & Distress attendant upon a Criminal Prison."[69]

Corporal punishment had been a mainstay of sentencing since 1682. In the Revolution and later, it declined. But in some few extraordinary cases, whipping became more severe. One hundred lashes were meted out to some offenders. Susannah Longacre and Rachel Hamer, both convicted of helping British soldiers, were told their fines of £150 would be forgiven if they endured 117 lashes each on their bare backs![70]

Pennsylvanians during these chaotic years sometimes withstood the impulse to bring more terror to their penal code. In this and their other concerns for mitigating aspects of their criminal sanctions, Pennsylvanians were in tune with reformers in other states.[71] It is true that horse theft was punished with unique severity among noncapital crimes. Horse thieves received a fine that varied with the value of the horse, then had to restore the horse or its equivalent value to its owner, suffer thirty-nine lashes, serve jail time, pay court costs, stand in the pillory, and have their ears cut off and nailed to the pillory. The increase in this theft during the Revolution moved the public to request the legislature to capitalize that offense. Despite this pressure, George Bryan and others argued successfully against it, and Pennsylvania appeared all the more temperate among the states for sparing some convicts from the gallows.[72]

In addition to the sanctions that the state imposed upon opponents of the Revolutionary state government, and in addition to whatever the Associators inflicted, Quakers, Tories, Loyalists, and the other disaffected persons suffered at the hands of mobs after 1776—mobs that operated without the authority of government, but in support of independence, the state constitution of 1776, and the enforcement of state laws and populist justice. The victims or objects of the mobs, naturally, claimed that the state government encouraged vigilantism or at least made little effort to restrain licentious mobs.[73]

The Revolution marked a significant change in the frequency and character of mobs or riots. There were no riot accusations before 1718. In the following thirty-six years there were 110 cases, but since there are no court records from Philadelphia before 1759, that number is too small. We know there were political protests and riots in the city in the 1720s (Chapter 3) that left no surviving justice record. Other than these events, riots before the French and Indian War were personal or communal and not intended to make any considerable political point. A typical riot of the apolitical sort occurred in 1734 when Timothy Miller and several others were coursing down the Schuylkill River in canoes. They asked "where the 'road' was" (meaning the passage through the "fishing racks"), and then began breaking up the weirs with axes—this aggression despite the fact that "one-third of the River was clear of the racks or obstructions." Arguments over the location, operation, and fees of grist mills also produced riots. Christopher Hageman, David Van Horne, and more than a dozen others "with Axes Hands Spikes and Clubs" destroyed the Bucks County grist mill belonging to John Gregg. A confrontation between a small crowd and the Boone family over procedures at the Boones' grist and fulling mills led a mob to burn the mills in September 1745. Even churches and congregants did not escape melees. They clashed over the use of buildings, for example. Frederick Rotherbuckle, Conrad Alston, and six others were charged in Philadelphia in April 1763 with "committing a riot and Disturbing the Congregation of the Dutch Reformed Church" in one such fracas.[74]

War (1754–1763) caused and coincided with increasingly frequent riots. In these ten years, prosecutions rose to 181. The next twelve years counted 223 cases and included notoriously political riots, like the Paxton march of 1764, the mob activity associated with Frederick Stump's escape, and the Sideling Hill incidents (See Chapter 5). In clashes as large as Paxton, the court records do not begin to reflect the number of men engaged, or the scale of the event. The justice system was and remains incapable of prosecuting or even identifying all the participants in mass disorders. In the Paxton march and the "Black Boys" raid of 1765, the rioters acted explicitly to publicize their political grievances and threaten the provincial government. The government branded their behavior as crime, but to the rioters it was principled vigilantism.

These political confrontations proliferated in the colonists' challenge to Britain. Due to the eventual success of American arms, Americans rarely think of these riots—the Stamp Tax riots, the Boston "Massacre," and the "Tea Party"—as crimes. Had the British won the war, they would still be crimes. But none of these venerated assaults on tax collectors, soldiers, and Tories occurred in Philadelphia. Obsessed with its paro-chial riots like Paxton, and due to Benjamin Franklin's attempt to get a royal charter for Pennsylvania, Pennsylvanians were the model of decent English subjects.[75] Thus, there was enormous irony in Pennsylvania: more riots than ever and some so great that Pennsylvanians suspected anarchy or civil war was in the offing. Meanwhile, there were almost no popular assaults on British imperialism.[76]

In the 1770s the enormous irony dissolved. With Franklin's failure to curry favor with the British, the Pennsylvania equivalent of the "Sons of Liberty" in cities like Boston were freed to protest in the streets and con-front Tories. In Pennsylvania, when conservative, orderly men faced off against these "Sons of Liberty," they discovered many of the men who had troubled them at Paxton and other riots of the 1760s. It was the case of Presbyterians, Scots-Irishmen, westerners, city artisans, and seamen versus Quakers, Anglicans, proprietary officials, magistrates, import merchants, and East India Company representatives. The provincial and the national coincided and it produced a combustible alignment.[77]

After 1775, with Associators flexing their muscles, the Congress insti-gating provincial protests, and the overthrow of the proprietary regime, events that physically resembled earlier riots now lost most of their crim-inal repute. Crowds now acted on behalf of the government and consti-tution rather than against it. Government, rightly or wrongly, looked aside when crowds became aggressive with alleged enemies of the state and nation. In the turmoil of the period 1776–1778, when courts were more often closed than open, the government could not have pro-ceeded against rioters even if had wished to do so. Quakers, common victims of riots, got into that predicament because their religious ethic required that they publicly not comply with many demands of the state and the patriot masses. They were no furtive "third-column." Their "witness" made them easy targets.

Twice yearly, in April and December, when the SEC announced public days of fasting and of thanksgiving, and called upon citizens to do no business and to illuminate their windows, mobs harassed Friends who refused to comply and vandalized their homes and businesses. Whig cel-ebrations of military victories stimulated similar attacks upon Friends. The worst occurred in October 1781, when Philadelphians spilled into the streets to celebrate Cornwallis's surrender at Yorktown. When Quak-ers refused to join their festivities, they showed their resentment. The Quaker diarist Elizabeth Drinker commented that scarcely a single Friend's house escaped at least some destruction. With axes and crow-bars, mobs broke windows, stripped off hinges, shutters, and sashes, broke down doors, entered houses, and destroyed contents. In a few cases, they fired guns into the houses or tried to torch them.[78]

The precise number of riots and rioters against Quakers and Tories cannot be determined. For one thing, more often than not, victims and witnesses sympathetic to them were reluctant to testify. Also, after 1778, when the courts were open, they were manned by Whigs and dominated by Whig jurymen. Riot victims had little hope of gaining convictions against their victimizers. Under those circumstances there was little reason to push prosecutions of such activities on the part of either the courts or the victims. Still, 221 riot accusations appeared in the record from 1775 through 1783. Of those 221, only 15.4 percent came to trial, and the simple conviction rate (SCR) for them was a very high 81.8 percent. By comparison, of all criminal accusations for the period, 28.4 percent came to trial and the SCR was 68.9 percent—which is still a high percent. Prosecutors were inefficient; juries were rigorous.

Women too were prosecuted for riot and disorder, but not as often as men. They typically rioted in conjunction with men, and more often than not officials chose to prosecute only the male rioters present. Nevertheless, magistrates prosecuted ninety-two women for riot between 1682 and 1800 (1.9 percent of all charges against women). Most of the prosecutions occurred in Philadelphia after 1775. For example, a summertime argument in 1783 between Jane Kane and Jane Monk, and Hendrick Shoemaker of Philadelphia, escalated and the two women assaulted Shoemaker. When bystanders sought to subdue the women, Kane and Monk became even more violent and eventually were charged with riot.[79] Margaret White, "an infamous character" in Philadelphia, was brought to prison for instigating a riot in September 1790. Elizabeth Murphy, also of Philadelphia, was charged with "disturbing the neighborhood" and rioting in November of that same year.[80]

The Revolution inspired women to exhibit their grievances more often and boldly in public. It gave an economic and ideological rationale to their rioting. They rioted over the scarcity of food, exorbitant prices, and other war-related distress. Whig prosecutors were reluctant to arrest women for such behavior, in part because Whig grand and petit jurors hesitated to indict and convict them. Many of the targets of the women were Tories whom the jurors despised. Nonetheless, more than half (55.4 percent) of all prosecutions against women for rioting occurred in that wartime period.

The rising pace of prosecutions of women in the Revolutionary era suggests that the Revolution affected the status and treatment of women in the justice system, even if it did not alter statutes respecting women. First, without specifying women as fit objects of prosecution, the Revolution generated criminal laws that women might violate as well as men.

How differently and forcefully laws during the Revolution affected women is the question in point.[81] Whatever the answer, it affects the characterization of this revolution and the status of women in its society: if the Revolutionaries expected women to be responsible individually for their public conduct and prosecuted them one by one for imperiling the commonwealth, then the Revolutionaries were respecting women's faculties and enlarging their lives—ironic though it may seem. If, contrariwise, they ignored individual women's record in the conflict, they were deprecating women and maintaining the gender status quo. To have done the first was to enlarge the Revolution; to have done the second was to bound it.

In practice, the new commonwealth accused and prosecuted women, like men, for behavior the government deemed political and dangerous to it or to the United States. Every such prosecution made this Revolution one degree more a revolution. Magistrates took women into custody and charged them with a variety of offenses deemed "inimical to the United States," including even "selling for hard money." Women also faced straightforward allegations of committing treason. Susanna Adams, wife of Jonathan Adams, a Philadelphia County snuff-maker, was attainted for high treason, as was her spouse. Philadelphia's Catherine Devenderfer and Mary Colley were indicted for treason but escaped conviction. In 1788 Sarah Bulla, wife of Thomas Bulla, a member of the infamous Doan gang, was convicted of being an accessory after the fact in the crimes of Aaron Doan. Jean Kerr, wife of Thomas Kerr, who was convicted of misprision of treason in June 1780, maintained that her prosecution stemmed from "malicious" witnesses. Sarah Brecht of Berks County was brought to court charged with misprision of treason in June 1778, but for reasons not entirely clear she was not tried.[82]

Women whose benevolence prompted them to succor enemy soldiers often paid the price of being criminally charged. Nine women, the majority of them single and none the wife of a patriot, were accused of "aiding the enemy." Susanah Longacre, wife of Jacob Longacre of Coventry Township, Chester County, was convicted of giving food and aid to the enemy, although she insisted her actions had been nothing more than "an act of hospitality" to men who came to her home. Rachel Hamer of Providence Township, Philadelphia County, also suffered conviction after providing food to some British soldiers. Hamer and Longacre both were sentenced to pay a £150 fine or to receive 117 lashes on their bare backs.[83] Other crimes fell under the rubric of revolutionary offenses, including giving sanctuary to those considered dangerous to the state. As a result, Sarah Buller [or Bulla] found herself in court explaining to magistrates why "suspected felons" were in her house. Barbery Edwards, "a poor Inferior Woman," came before authorities in

1776 under suspicion of harboring deserters from the American army. Jane Cooper's 1777 offense was that she had been known to "associate" with Abigail McKay, who in turn had been known to frequent spots favored by James Molesworth, a local waterman executed as a spy for the English.[84]

Personal responsibility for one's public behavior had not been an obligation of women in Anglo-American law before the Revolution, either in Pennsylvania or anywhere else in America or England. The law defined married women (who were the great majority of women between their minority and widowhood) as "femes coverts," which is to say, women with no legal identity but that of their husbands. Married women's disability was most nearly complete in the realm of property law. However, in criminal law, a woman's status was ambiguous, at least. Blackstone had pronounced, "If a woman commits theft, burglary, or other civil offenses against the laws of society, by the coercion of her husband, or even in his company, which the law construes as coercion she is not guilty of any crime; being considered as acting by compulsion, and not of her own free will." Richard B. Morris's study of early law in America convinced him that liability was "imposed upon the husband for the illegal acts of his wife which were prosecuted in qui tam actions or by purely criminal suits" including "antenuptial crimes and misdemeanors of the married woman."[85] The jurists thought that women's guilt or innocence was less important than their subservience to their spouses.

Pennsylvania's judiciary had at hand a variety of materials explaining coverture as it related to criminal proceedings.[86] The question is, did judicial practice closely follow legal theory? Both the law and practice permitted prosecutors to lay lesser charges against married women (femes coverts) accused of criminal activities in association with their husbands. Pennsylvania was not alone in this practice. N. E. H. Hull's examination of female felons in early Massachusetts persuaded her that reducing charges levied against spouses in cases where husbands were prosecuted for criminal offenses was commonplace.[87] Some prosecutors in Pennsylvania attempted to follow the law and fulfill coverture. Mary McCoy was not prosecuted for her activities in complicity with the Morrison gang in Philadelphia in 1750/51 under the assumption that she was merely obeying her husband, Francis. When Frederick Getringer of Bucks County agreed to plead guilty to assault in September 1752, the prosecutor terminated proceedings for the same charge against Getringer's wife, Susan. York County's Sarah and Michael Price were indicted for felony theft in May 1765, but in the end authorities chose to have only Michael stand trial.[88]

And women anticipated the legal benefits of coverture. When Mary Dickey of Philadelphia was convicted in 1788 of receiving stolen property while apart from her husband, she insisted that court officers had promised she would "be Liberated as Soon as her Husband appeared" to supervise her more carefully. Philadelphia's Jane Match also looked to protections presumably accorded femes coverts in criminal cases. Following her convictions for theft and for operating a tippling house in 1788, she told state officials that she customarily did business for her husband, and in his name. She maintained that she was being held responsible unfairly. She had been prosecuted "under her own name, the same as she was a widow."[89] That both citizens and judicial personnel knew the law regarding coverture and its theoretical benefits for married women in criminal courts seems clear.

Because of coverture, husbands often pleaded for their wives. Thus, John Keen appeared in the September 1784 term of the Philadelphia County general sessions to plead instead of his wife, Mildred, in a case of assault and battery. He submitted to the court and paid a small fine for her. Sarah Kuiper's husband appeared in Fayette County court in March 1800, to plead when she was prosecuted for assault and battery. He pled her guilty and paid her fines and court costs.[90] It also was not unusual for fathers to appear for their daughters. As attorneys increasingly appeared in court to plead for their clients fewer husbands and fathers appeared in the place of their spouses or daughters.[91]

Despite the occasions when coverture was employed, the tendency after 1750, and especially after 1776, was to treat women as persons accountable for their criminally wrong choices. Whatever they did, they did for their own reasons and motives regardless of their husbands' possible instigation or control of them. They became more visible as civil persons. Two hundred and seventy-six charges involving twenty-three different kinds of misdemeanors and felonies were brought against married couples in Pennsylvania between 1750 and 1800. In more than three-quarters (77.6 percent) of the cases, husband and wife were prosecuted independently on similar charges. The rate was even higher after 1776. Out of 199 prosecutions between 1776 and 1800, in 170 instances (85.4 percent) prosecutors chose to bring the same charges against each of the spouses.[92] As such, the benefits of the Revolution for most women in Pennsylvania were ambiguous. They were treated practically as empowered persons and assigned the consequences. But the statutes were not rewritten to empower them; the disabilities imposed on them in the realm of property law did not disappear.[93] The responsibilities and punishments were real and growing while the benefits remained to be worked out.

The radical Revolutionaries professed to have little use for Europe, its past, and its institutions, including monarchy, aristocracy, the English and their "mixed constitution," and the proprietary right of the Penns. In *Common Sense,* Tom Paine ridiculed and dismissed them. The new order they were raising in Pennsylvania and America would borrow little or nothing from the old. Reason would guide them, and kings and priests would be no part of this new order of the ages. That was the Enlightenment speaking. Their plans for Pennsylvania were indeed novel, which made the state constitution of 1776 famous or infamous, depending upon the observer.[94] But, for all the talk in 1776 about change, renewal, and a new order, the vision of the Revolutionaries did imitate some of the past. In Pennsylvania's remote past lay something the radical Whigs wished to revive, even if they did not admit borrowing: they respected moral community and the efforts of William Penn to legislate it and the Quakers to enforce it.

As Gordon S. Wood, Edmund S. Morgan, and other historians have explained, the founders of the United States brooded over the moral health of the republic, and they variously prescribed ancient Stoicism, Christian asceticism, Enlightenment reason, or some mix of them for whatever ailed civil society. Revolution *and regeneration,* liberty *and virtue* came coupled to their lips and pens.[95] The view of the American Revolution from France especially detected continuity between the Holy Experiment and the Revolution, and did not dismiss the Quaker experiment in Pennsylvania while embracing its successor—however much the actors in 1776 said they were creating something new under the sun.

Understandably, then, promoters of revolution in Pennsylvania, particularly Benjamin Rush and Christopher Marshall, were enthusiastic for moral reform. Rush, a physician, also became one of the premier social reformers in the new nation. He pushed for temperance and blamed drunkenness for assaults, violence, and other public ills. He opposed gambling, horse racing, cock fighting, fairs, sexual license, and profanity.[96] While Rush had been affected by evangelical Presbyterianism, Marshall was even more orthodox and rigorous, and devoutly wished to bar all but orthodox Christians from sharing politically in the new regime in Pennsylvania.[97]

When Rush began his medical practice in the 1760s he found Philadelphia "a seat of corruption." He complained, "Vice and profanity openly prevail. . . . Our young men in general . . . are wholly devoted to pleasure and sensuality."[98] "I am infinitely more apprehensive of the Contagion of Vice than the Power of all other Enemies," Rush wrote to a sympathetic John Adams in 1777.[99] Rush was no irascible prude. All he and other critics had to do was read the issues of the press after 1760, walk the streets and alleys, look into the lodgings of the poor, listen in the taverns, and treat the infirm, in order to know that with respect to public health, responsible conduct, or "virtue," Philadelphia was declining.[100] In the press beginning in the 1760s, historian Clare Lyons found a near rout of the values and prudential mores of earlier Pennsylvania. In the second half of the century, women were depicted as passionate, lustful, provocative creatures with too little reason to comprehend and stop the ill affects of their licentiousness. After marrying they purportedly became harridans, making bachelorhood more welcome for men than marriage. Premarital sex was touted as natural, healthy, and arguably licit. In newspapers and almanacs, wags used adultery as a "vehicle for humor." The haunts of pleasure in the city gained patrons if not legitimacy: taverns, fairs, vendues, playhouses, races, and "bawdy houses."[101]

Philadelphia had not become Babylon or Restoration London, but the novelties in the press and public behavior raised the threshold of offensive indecency beyond its historic provincial level. Decades before this appearance of permissive morality in the press and streets, Pennsylvania's magistrates and courts had foregone keeping sexual activity and immoral behavior within prescribed bounds. Now the press had caught up, and the people could read that modesty was no longer much esteemed in Pennsylvania.

Troubled by the immorality of their times, some of the Pennsylvania revolutionaries went to work, first in the new state constitution. Their handiwork served well the interests of liberty, independence, and the common man. But, paradoxically in some people's opinion, it incorporated its drafters' interest in restraint, reform, and regeneration, resolving that "laws for the prevention of vice and immorality shall be made and constantly kept in force." As Rush told John Adams, "Liberty without virtue would be no blessing to us."[102] In 1777 and 1778, the British interrupted when they occupied the state capital, but they also provided an additional motive for the reformers once the state government reopened fully. English society had long provided a foil for the use of American republicans bent on touting the superiority of provincial American character, or warning of the need to protect or reform it. When General Howe and the army occupied Philadelphia, their behavior confirmed reformers' opinion of the dissipation in English life. While the army of the American republic suffered at Valley Forge, a blithe Rebecca Franks averred that with the British in town, there were so many balls, plays, assemblies, and other entertainments that she had spent only three evenings alone, and was becoming fatigued from the relentless social calendar.[103]

When Howe abandoned the city, the moralists resolved to uproot pernicious customs planted during the occupation. On October 12, 1778, Congress passed a resolution encouraging states "to take the most effectual measures . . . for the suppressing of theatrical entertainments, horse racing, gaming and such other diversions as are productive of idleness and dissipation."[104] The Pennsylvania Assembly moved in March 1779 to adopt "an Act for the Suppression of Vice and Immorality" which prohibited work or any type of sport or diversion on Sunday. It also forbade horse racing, "bullet playing," shooting matches, cock fighting, or gambling of any kind. In addition, it prohibited stage plays. An act in 1786, with minor changes, carried on the 1779 provisions. In 1789 the Assembly repealed the portion of the 1786 bill that forbade theater productions and stage plays. The 1789 statute was extended by legislation in 1794.[105]

But history did not follow the route the moral revolutionaries had mapped out. For at least two years after the appearance of the 1776 state constitution, republican statesmen had not the time or opportunity to advance the regeneration of public life and private morals. Even after the state government and courts resumed operating in 1778, drunkenness, gambling, and indecent speech and conduct were seldom prosecuted. The practical outcome was that simple.

The situation may not seem that simple upon examining the data on prosecutions of sexual crimes. Accusations and prosecutions of fornication and bastardy grew consistently beginning the 1730s—but since the population grew too, the rate was not increasing inordinately (Figure 6.1). Then, in the era of the Revolution, once the courts reopened, a curious trend occurred in the prosecutions of sexual crime: accusations of fornication dropped precipitously for the remainder of the century, while accusations of bastardy soared (Table 2.4). In the 1790s there were more than eight charges of bastardy for every charge of fornication. In 1800, fornication prosecutions appeared destined to disappear sometime in the early nineteenth century.

Concurrently, the government prosecuted ever-increasing numbers of men for bastardy while women's prosecutions plummeted. As a share of all women's offenses, fornication and bastardy declined from 38.8 percent to 16.6 percent between the two periods 1682–1775 and 1776–1800.[106] And while fewer women were appearing in court, more of the ones who did appear refused to submit to the court (i.e., they preferred to go to trial).[107] Submissions by women for any and all offenses dropped from 35.7 percent before 1776 to 18.0 percent after 1775; in cases of fornication and bastardy, submissions dropped from 52.4 percent to merely 10.0.[108]

At least two changes in attitudes and social mores helped cause the obvious differences in the courts. The accused women showed a newfound willingness to contest the government's prosecution of them, even for behavior they (being unwed mothers) had obviously engaged in. In the most extreme examples of disdain, before 1776 only one

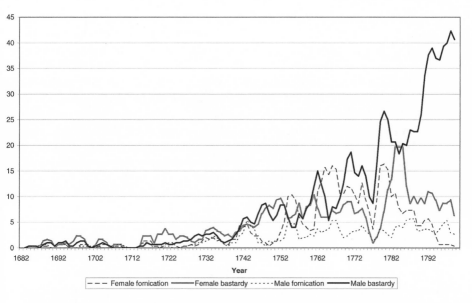

Figure 6.1. Three-year moving averages of accusations of fornication and bastardy against men and women in Pennsylvania, 1682–1800.

indicted woman fled the county and escaped the grasp of the law, but after 1775, twenty-five did so (while only nine men did!). In addition, the government was less interested in *women's* sexual conduct—less interested in humbling them and deterring future conceptions by punishment and public ritual. Underlying both of these changes, the public tolerated more sexual freedom and privacy—tolerance that the literature of the times and the press confirmed.

What positively energized the public and courts was assigning the financial support of illegitimate children (and possibly mothers). Tolerating premarital sex did not extend to public willingness to pay more taxes to support the unplanned offspring of freer sex. Nor did masters of pregnant servant women want the cost of two unproductive dependents in the household. The male perpetrators should have paid, but they too did not fancy the responsibilities of parenthood. Thus the criminal courts stepped in and obliged them to act like fathers, at least by assigning them the prolonged expenses of child maintenance. In Chester County, 88.6 percent of all the sentences of child-maintenance occurred after 1761.

Indicted men had never obliged the courts by submitting to them in the numbers that women did. In cases of fornication and bastardy (1682–1800), only thirty-five women went to trial but 297 men did so![109]

After all, the men were not pregnant, and they presumed that the prosecutors would not easily prove them to be fathers. Liking the odds or seeing little to lose, they opted for a trial. But the outcomes show they presumed too much about the ease of defending themselves, or they missed the jurors' impatience with them. For in cases of fornication and bastardy, juries convicted 78.1 percent of men who went to trial (and 85.7 percent of the many fewer women).[110] The Revolution changed men's conduct only for the worse: even fewer men submitted to the court for either fornication or bastardy, and secondly, the simple conviction rates for men for both crimes rose.[111] Again, the times showed more callousness among bachelor men and more resolve by their townships and counties to make them responsible for their callousness.

In Philadelphia, arguably the most important jurisdiction in Pennsylvania, the situation appeared to be the exception in the entire commonwealth. After 1775, Philadelphia courts prosecuted only 127 cases of fornication and bastardy or 6.9 percent of all the prosecutions in Pennsylvania. It ranked eighth among jurisdictions in the commonwealth in this respect. In the 1790s Philadelphia city counted only forty of the total 478 bastardy prosecutions. These sparse cases are seriously misleading, however.[112] Clare Lyons revealed that, beginning in the 1760s, the overseers of the poor in the city took on the responsibility of determining and assigning the financial responsibility for illegitimate children. In its records are cases that never got into the courts and explain that Philadelphians were not exceptionally continent among Pennsylvanians or responsible about paternity. Far from it. And examination of several kinds of evidence leads to the surmise that in the 1790s at least one in sixty-seven Philadelphians bore an illegitimate child.[113] To the degree that Philadelphia bastardy cases did not make it into the judicial record, the numbers on the phenomenal growth of bastardy cases for all of Pennsylvania understate the actual growth in the commonwealth.

But Philadelphia experienced growth of sexual crimes or sexually related crimes that did not escape the attention of the magistrates and the work of the courts. In the court dockets, prosecutions for disorderly houses were up from thirty-one before 1776 to 119 after 1775. Women made up most of the difference, being prosecuted seventy-four times after 1775 compared to forty-five for men. Without being able to specify the number, the prosecutions disclose more women working as prostitutes.[114] Prostitutes plied their trade in houses known for such activity. As early as June 1741, Margaret Cook was convicted in Philadelphia of "continually" receiving, entertaining, and supporting whores. Caty Mullin was brought to court for "committing fornication in the House of Ann Hill" in May 1798. In January 1799, Oley Thomson, a black female, was discovered by a justice of the peace in bed with one William McCray

... in a bawdy house." Maria Dougherty also was arrested in April of the same year for being in bed with John Marshall in a house known to be frequented by prostitutes. Rebecca Wall, a young widow with a fifteen-month-old child, claimed she was falsely arrested in July 1789 when she "accidently" was in a house "where some women were taken up." She insisted she was a victim of circumstances. It is not always possible to determine whether "disorderly house" cases involved prostitution, but clearly a good many did.[115]

Other women serviced clients in darkened alleys and doorways. A Philadelphia night watchman took up Hannah Fell in December 1795, when he came upon her in the act of intercourse with William Nand. Catherine Miller, "a vile young hussy," came before authorities a number of times on similar charges. Mary Carlisle was recognized as "a common and abandoned prostitute." Sarah Gault, another "lewd woman," was charged with prostitution, as were Margaret Miller, Margaret Jeffrey, and Ann Drain, the latter "a strapping young woman" known for her athleticism and handsome looks.[116]

A steady stream of women were also charged with profanity, breaking windows, "beating on buildings with sticks," vagrancy, throwing pebbles at passersby, begging, abusing children in the streets, "insolent" behavior, "disturbing the neighborhood," and "brawling." A large number of these aggressive women were unmarried with children living on the edge of abject poverty and ruin.[117] Yet other women disturbed the peace through their conduct with black men. In Philadelphia there were opportunities for interracial relationships and sexual intimacy. Mary Welch's 1791 arrest for "indecent behavior" involved her intimacy with a black male. The fact that Negro Charles broke into the stable of Charles Willson Peale and slept there in August 1794 disturbed the constable who apprehended him, but the constable became even more upset when he discovered that Charles's companion was Mary Hoffet, "a white girl." In February 1795, Mary Connor was confined for "cohabiting with Negroes & being an idle vagabound." Mary Shaw was indicted in April 1797, for perjury after swearing that a white lover had fathered her black child. White women who married black men or lived with them or gave birth to mulatto children were treated with undisguised contempt by those who kept the official city records and there is no reason to believe most white Philadelphians acted differently.[118]

Pennsylvania was hardly unique respecting the changes in popular morality and law enforcement. In the 1790s, Connecticut decriminalized and privatized fornication. In Massachusetts fornication prosecutions plunged after the Revolution. There, from 1776 to 1786, prosecutions averaged fifty-eight per year. There were only four indictments after 1790. According to historian William Nelson, it was during the Revolution that the Massachusetts government stopped enforcing morality—so much for Samuel Adams's wish to turn Boston into a "Christian Sparta."[119]

The moralists of the Revolution may appear to have looked at their times myopically. They were obsessive about entertainments, sobriety, vice, consensual sexual conduct, and other nonvictim behaviors. From a libertarian philosophical perspective, they and the justice system should not have busied themselves with such behavior at all; government has no business injecting itself into conduct that has apparently victimized no one.

Meanwhile, when the Revolution was building between 1765 and 1775, the homicide rate in Pennsylvania was the most horrific in its history. In Philadelphia, the murder rate was clearly its worst, at eleven to twelve murders per 100,000. (Table 2.3) With war, the rates dropped— possible perpetrators were busy killing in situations where their homicides did not count as crime. Then, after the war, homicide rates rose again. Here were plenty of victims and a problem worth all their reformist energy, to the exclusion of all other considerations.

In their defense, Rush and others did not ignore violence in Pennsylvania, but believed that the times were broadly to blame for crime and license. In a rudimentary way they looked at the times holistically. They expressed an unsystematic conviction that human behavior was much of a piece, that people did not practice self-restraint in one situation and self-indulgence in another, or were sometimes good and sometimes evil, or that the felonies were one thing and misdemeanors another. Their inexpert theory had quite a patrimony. In the eighteenth century, the gallows served as a podium for broadcasting the linkage of small and large crime, self-control and criminal license. Condemned felons about to be hanged lectured audiences how they, even as children, had scoffed at warnings that their youthful peccadilloes or carelessness forecast grave future crimes. Now, at their lives' end, they attested to the wisdom of the warnings they had been given.[120] The testimonies were mawkish, scripted, and probably insincere, but the dangers they warned of were grounded in real experience, as modern social science warrants.

From a libertarian perspective a holistic explanation of crime like this is untenable. To connect immorality, victimless behavior, and petty crime with violence and grave crimes may seem even comedic—trouble begins with "t" and that rhymes with "p" and that stands for pool. Worse, the connection threatens and deprecates personal and civil liberty. No just society could seriously consent to that in principle. Against that libertarian perspective, however, stands another opinion, which enjoys the support of modern social scientists and police. The theory, in brief, links large and small crimes rather than treating the grave ones as sui generis.[121] At the heart of such holistic views of crime lies sociologists' and psychologists' understanding that minor and major crimes alike exhibit a general lack of self-control, and are highly correlated with each other and also with still other behaviors that are licit but unwise and dangerous to the actor. The behaviors in question range from immoral and nonvictim acts—like drinking, gambling, and fornication—to harm to others. They were all similarly impulsive, insensitive, self-indulgent, egotistical, or narcissistic.[122] Within the context of this crime theory, Rush and the reformers were less myopic and more prophetic.[123] They erred not in misunderstanding human behavior and Pennsylvania's record, but in appreciating how vast a successful remedy must be—more a root-and-branch change in society than adding some laws and enforcing them.

The Revolution was, of course, also a war and war is killing—it is homicide. Men at war deliberately kill, but their killing is not treated as murder. War recasts homicide and defines it right out of the reach of a book about crime, like this one. Intolerable, unsocial impulses to kill others in peacetime shift to the battlefield, where the same impulses are at least tolerated, but much more often, encouraged and honored. Aggressive acts that in peacetime could have aroused victims to complain to king or country, prosecutors to listen, grand juries to weigh their complaints, juries to judge acts and individuals, and judges to sentence a guilty person according to the gravity of his crime, his responsibility, and his character, escape all this scrutiny in war.

The belligerents in war agree to indulge the behavior of whole categories of men. An individual killer disappears in the mass of licensed killers and none is blameworthy. Admittedly, there are rules of warfare or engagement, courts martial, just and unjust wars, and international courts of justice. They define some wartime killing as murder and prosecute the perpetrators like criminals. But in the main, declaring war redefines homicide and excuses it. Most of the Revolutionary War is omitted in this book, except for the ethical fog generated by the behavior of western Pennsylvanians in their alleged war with Pennsylvania Indians.

Among Euro-Pennsylvanians before 1776, the homicidal behavior of westerners and their indifference toward justice had been as lively a subject of debate and contention as any in Pennsylvania history. European settlers in the west denied that the considerations of criminal process applied to their alleged nemesis, the Indians, while they insisted upon due process protections when they were accused of crimes between the two cultures.[124] Infuriated British overlords and eastern Pennsylvanians argued that justice was blind and did very well comprehend behavior between Indians and whites. But this angry dialogue over justice and its proper beneficiaries disappeared into the maw of the Revolutionary War. When the Revolution dissolved British rule of the westerners and the war massively distracted far more temperate easterners from events in the west, westerner chauvinism commanded that theater of the war and informed the westerners' rendition of events.

When Americans in the Continental army or militias engaged the British army, the killing by both armies very largely fit the conventions and definition of war, so that it was not murder or criminal. Both combatants agreed to that—although the British were slower to concede it for American revolutionaries. However, the case of western Pennsylvanians and local Indians killing each other was not so simple. Most Indians allied with the British and cooperated with them in the war. The Revolution, therefore, pitted Americans against the British and their Indian allies. But Americans did not think of them as one adversary. The ways in which Indians and Americans treated (and mistreated) each other in combat were almost identical, but the ways Americans described Indians, in contrast to Americans' thinking about themselves, demonstrated a world of difference. Then words like crime and criminals flew. In the mouths of westerners, who comprised the militias that fought almost all the engagements with Indians, murder applied to *any* Indian military action, regardless of whether the Indians killed civilians or combatants. Historian Gregory Knouff writes, "In other words, the discourse of depraved crime, not warfare, was applied to enemy [Indian] acts. . . . The conflation of crime, inhumanity, and 'Indians' as a singular group was powerful."[125]

Yet it was not murder as judged in any court of law, with punishment levied by blind justice, but murder by frontier fiat. Regarding crime, Indians received neither the immunities of combatants nor the benefits of impartial judgment from civil society. Westerners had the Indians coming and going. Indians were not innocent soldiers following orders or the dictates of statecraft. They were criminals, but not criminals who deserved the benefit of law.

Most western Pennsylvania soldiers and civilians viewed Indians as innately hostile, even when the Indians were neutral and passive, or even when they assisted the American cause against the British and their allied tribes. Indians were either clandestine foes or open foes, but foes in any case. Racism had become the linchpin of the simple-minded moralizing of the westerners. "Pennsylvanians prosecuted a total war, fueled by racism, in which they sought the destruction of entire Indian societies."[126] Whereas before independence their racism had been roundly denounced, it triumphed with independence.

The Pennsylvania militia exhibited their racism most brazenly in March 1782 at the village of Gnadenhutten in future Ohio. Their victims were Christian Indians (Delawares, Shawnees, Unamis, and Munsees) living like Europeans, occasionally assisting the American cause, and therefore suspected by Indians allied with the British. Upon meeting the Gnadenhutten villagers and finding that they complied with whatever they were asked to do, the militiamen temporized and then resolved to kill them all. While they did so, the Indians sang hymns. In dispatching these peaceable people, the Pennsylvanians practiced most of the barbarities they had stamped as barbarities because supposedly only Indians practiced them. Knowledge of the massacre spread among western Indians, and either reinforced their hostility to all Americans or converted them to it.[127]

Homicide between the Indians and Americans did not end with the Treaty of Paris in 1783. Nonetheless, peace restored to the violence some of the legal and moral ambiguity that had existed before 1776. Questions of civil justice and crime reemerged, but in the new nation whites knew that their licentious conduct toward Indians would not likely put them in jeopardy with the courts. Sardonic Charles Nisbet remarked to Judge Alexander Addison in March 1796, that several whites who had committed crimes in the wilderness had "nothing to fear, except from the Indians['] Courts of Oyer & Terminer. . . ."[128] By the end of the century, the United States and the territories and states west of the Ohio River inherited most of the perplexities of Indian policy and the criminal violence that attached to the westward-tending line called the frontier.[129] The opportunity for Pennsylvania to provide justice and redeem the vision of William Penn had disappeared.

Revolution had been unmistakable in Pennsylvania. Things that had appeared solid had dissolved and monumental institutions had toppled. Most of what was gone, displaced, or in shambles, however, was political. Meanwhile, most of the social past persisted, especially crime. The Revolution did not solve the problem of violent crime in the state. But the Revolution had "authorized" the killing of Americans who were Indians—permissiveness that fixed itself firmly into the rest of American history. Riots, civil disorders, and challenges to authority continued during and after the war, as they had earlier, but with different victims and purposes. Immorality easily survived reformers' vision of a regenerate, republican people. The Revolution brought conquest of the British and an end to the old provincial regime (home rule and new rulers at home). With that conquest came more liberty than Americans had ever enjoyed before, and more abuse of it.

- Treason high
- New Magistrates
- sexual crimes history

Chapter 7

Commonwealth

Many acts of depredation, and many schemes of horror which have
occurred in this and neighboring States may, in some degree, be
traced to the extreme poverty of [the] distressed class of people.
—Gale's Independent Gazetteer

Every age betrays its identity in its crime. But at the end of the eighteenth century, Pennsylvania revealed itself also in the crime it avoided,
the crime it expected to avoid but did not, and the crime it expected
not to avoid. The Commonwealth of Pennsylvania distinguished itself by
its uniquely high rate of property crimes. Violent crimes, on the other
hand, had plagued the state for decades. Their continuation was nothing new. The novelty of violent crime in the 1780s and 90s was that concerned Pennsylvanians expected to avoid or remedy such violence, but
they did neither. Then there was novel crime that few people anticipated: the spectacular amount of public disorder that emerged in rural
areas of the state. Finally, when Pennsylvanians began working to eman-
cipate their enslaved blacks, abolitionists were warned that they if they
succeeded, freedmen would throw the state into turmoil—crime that, it
turned out, the state almost entirely escaped. These and smaller changes
illustrate a society which could not be confused with its past. During and
after the Revolution, Pennsylvanians who valued their commonwealth
asserted that it would not be like the earlier province, and that was true,
but for reasons they neither wished for nor expected.

The two decades following the Revolution in Pennsylvania were marked
by continuity confronting novelty: the persistent crime in Pennsylvania
versus the determination of prominent public men to reduce or end it.
Optimists like Benjamin Rush worked to encourage a more civil society
in which crime would respond to rational treatment and sanctions
devised by benevolent men—men, in fact, reminiscent of founder Wil-

liam Penn. In 1786, these reformers initiated a third era of criminal justice in Pennsylvania. The first legislators had written into laws the benevolent beliefs of William Penn and the Quakers about human character and their displeasure with sanguinary punishments. That era ended no later than 1718 with Pennsylvania reverting to the more typically British criminal code, which operated until the 1780s. In 1786, the Assembly overhauled the penal code and, in the 1790s, reformed it still further. Pennsylvanians, like other Americans freed from the British and able to apply their republican ideals as they wished, fastened upon their criminal laws and began rewriting.[1]

Sentiment for criminal law reforms thrived in Pennsylvania throughout the 1780s. Organizations such as the Society for Political Inquiries and the Philadelphia Society for the Alleviating the Miseries of the Public Prisons arose to create a more enlightened penal system. Members of those societies joined individual citizens in suggesting means to rationalize the penal code and to redeem offenders more readily and efficiently. The most illustrious member of the reformer circle, Benjamin Rush, published a pamphlet *An Enquiry into the Effects of Public Punishments Upon Criminals and Upon Society* (1787) that further provoked Pennsylvanians to reexamine their laws. Men of strikingly different minds collaborated to accomplish changes. Some were humanitarians appalled by the number of executions in the state between 1778 and 1786 and interested in rehabilitating criminals. Others, less idealistic, were distressed at the growth of crime and the apparent failure of past and current punishments to stop it. Such Pennsylvanians thought that a virtual army of thieves had mounted an attack upon their property.[2] Common citizens called for new means of controlling and reducing the criminal population.[3] This desire for social and legal change produced in September 1786 "An Act Amending the Penal Laws of This State," which redrew the landscape of the penal code[4] and thrust Pennsylvania in the forefront of penal reform in the young republic.[5]

The reformist aims of the 1786 law were clear: "it is the wish of every good government to reclaim rather than to destroy." The past laws had failed, the law continued, "it having been found by experience that the punishments directed by the laws now in force . . . do not answer the principal ends of society . . . to correct and reform the offenders." For those misguided punishments, it substituted "continued hard labor, publicly and disgracefully imposed" on persons convicted for many crimes previously capital. Included in the crimes rendered noncapital were robbery, burglary, sodomy, buggery, and horse theft. Earlier, concealment of the death of the infant had been sufficient to convict a mother of infanticide. Now the law demanded that prosecutors prove the child was "born alive."[6] Crimes such as blasphemy, profaneness, and swearing had their penalties considerably reduced. Conviction of such an offense brought a five-shilling fine and twenty-four hours' confinement for each offense. (By 1794 the penalty had been reduced to a fine of sixty-seven cents and a maximum of twenty-four hours confinement for each offense.) Other oaths were penalized by fines of forty cents. The 1786 legislation did make penalties for drunkenness more severe, calling for a fine of five shillings and confinement for up to seventeen days.

The authors of the new criminal justice believed that shaming guilty men and women would deter crime and recidivism and would rehabilitate offenders more effectively than corporal punishment.[7] But the public humiliation called for by the 1786 legislation differed from earlier practice of humiliation by adding "good works" to the existing feature of public exposure. Rather than sit idly in the stocks or stand for unproductive hours in the pillory, criminals were assigned tasks that would benefit society. They would clean and improve streets, repair buildings, and collect garbage and trash. Their clothing and haircut would identify these "wheelbarrow men" and remind them of their social failings. Through hard and productive labor on worthwhile projects, they would enlarge their sense of social responsibility and at the same time, their sense of their own worth, and they would ultimately be restored, valued members of society. Past sentences of shaming—wearing a sign and the pillory—had failed, reformers maintained, but shame titrated according to the new laws could even regenerate social consciousness. In addition, jails were to be made more wholesome and prisoners ensured better clothing and diet. Youthful offenders were not to come into contact with "old and hardened" offenders.[8]

Additional reforms of prison conditions came in March 1789.[9] Statutes separated debtors and witnesses from other criminals and hardened offenders from the general prison population. However, change was not entirely in the one direction, toward leniency. Some convicts after 1786 managed to commit crimes while allegedly laboring on public works projects. When the public became increasingly incensed with such behavior, a 1789 law provided the death penalty for those who, while in prison or having just been released from prison, committed crimes that were designated as capital prior to 1786.

In 1791 the Assembly also eliminated the whipping and branding of those convicted of adultery, and determined that the fine in such convictions should not exceed fifty pounds. Confinement for adultery was also reduced to at least three months but no longer than twelve months. In the past those found innocent and those whose indictments were ruled *ignoramus* by grand juries had to pay court fees (which were often burdensome). Now the counties where the charges originated were required to shoulder these costs.[10]

Confusion over the Doan gang, famous for their robberies during the Revolution, and disagreement over the treatment received by those who were outlawed in the early 1780s, led to a reassessment of the process of outlawry in September 1791.[11] First brought to Pennsylvania in 1718, outlawry had been used by the colony's courts only once before it was employed against the Doans and their accomplices in the last years of the Revolution. The 1791 bill declared that persons indicted for treason, robbery, burglary, sodomy, buggery, felonies of death, or being an accessory to those crimes, but who refused to appear or who escaped and subsequently were outlawed, could only be successfully convicted and punished if certain careful procedures were followed by authorities. By 1791 Pennsylvania legislators were persuaded that traditional outlawry procedures did not provide adequate safeguards for those attainted. They established more elaborate, clearcut and lenient procedures, repealing many of the earlier English practices embraced by the 1718 legislation.[12]

No one observed the legal reforms more intently and sought additional improvements than William Bradford, whose long career as lawyer, judge, and Attorney-General of the United States gave him a unique perspective and the raw data to argue for innovation.[13] Bradford thought the state's criminal code (1718–1786) was unacceptably severe, characterizing it as "an exotic plant and not the native growth of Pennsylvania." He conceded that it "ha[d] been endured but [it had] never been a favorite" among Pennsylvanians. He became the primary author of the reform bill of 1786. By the early 1790s he believed additional modifications in the code were warranted. The public got to scrutinize closely his proposal to reform felony law in 1793. His pamphlet, *An Enquiry How Far the Punishment of Death Is Necessary in Pennsylvania* (1793) was widely reprinted in newspapers and popular magazines. In addition, Bradford supplied data on crime and criminal justice to important publications.[14]

Bradford's influence especially brought the final modifications in the criminal code in the eighteenth century, in April 1794.[15] In that year "An Act for the Better Preventing of Crimes and for Abolishing the Punishment of Death in Certain Cases" eliminated the death penalty for all crimes except murder in the first degree. Punishment for petit treason became the same as for second-degree murder, five to eighteen years in prison; for high treason it became six to twelve years. A conviction of arson now brought a sentence of five to twelve years confinement; rape was punished by a sentence of ten to twenty-one years. A convicted counterfeiter was to suffer four to fifteen years' incarceration and to pay a fine not to exceed one thousand dollars. Conviction of maiming or of voluntary manslaughter brought from two to ten years in prison. The bill eliminated benefit of clergy for those crimes previously capital. It also provided that women who concealed the death of their infant children, upon conviction should serve up to five years' imprisonment, but juries should not construe that concealment to mean murder. However, juries now were free to consider first-degree murder charges as well as charges for concealment in such cases if the evidence merited such an interpretation.[16]

In that same month, legislators reduced the penalties for minor offenses even more. Conviction of illegal hunting, or indulging in sport on a Sunday, brought a four-dollar fine. For anyone over sixteen swearing or cursing, conviction brought a fine of sixty-seven cents per offense. A first-offense conviction for drunkenness was also a sixty-seven cent fine. Playing dice was penalized by a three-dollar fine per offense, and horseracing elicited a twenty-dollar fine. Should a Pennsylvanian be successfully prosecuted for fighting a duel or challenging someone to a duel, he faced a $280 fine or twelve months in jail. To be convicted of accepting such a challenge meant a $140 fine or six months imprisonment.[17]

The new direction in criminal justice and penology failed. Felons assigned to public works received inadequate supervision from authorities. Instead of reformed consciousness, many of the convicts opted for freedom. Eighteen "wheelbarrow men" escaped from the Philadelphia jail in March 1787. Six others from Chester County walked away from their job assignment despite being chained, as did one from Chambersburg in Franklin County. Another sought to kill his supervisor with his spade so that he might escape. A woman of "infamous character" was arrested after she sought to pass to a wheelbarrow man "a knife measuring twenty-six inches" which she had hidden in her bosom.[18]

With good reason the public accused the wheelbarrow men of a variety of violent crimes both during their work shifts and following their frequent escapes. A farmer bringing goods to the Philadelphia market on October 28, 1788, was confronted by two wheelbarrow men between Chestnut Hill and Germantown. While one held a pistol on him, the other raped his wife. In September 1789, five wheelbarrow men walked away from their work project and broke into the Market Street home of John McFarland. Finding McFarland home, they beat him unconscious and then robbed him of "a considerable amount." McFarland died of his injuries the following day. The fact that the five were quickly discovered, tried, convicted, and hanged did not assuage the public, which unleashed a chorus of protests at local officials, particularly John Reynolds, sheriff and keeper of the jail, regarding the lax supervision of dangerous felons. Critics ridiculed the naïveté of reformers who believed the program would work, in either the short run or the long run.[19]

Early hopes for the success of incarceration under reformed conditions were frustrated. Philadelphia's John Reynolds and others responsible for imprisoning and maintaining suspects and convicts were overwhelmed by the mounting numbers of prisoners and the new rules. Common debtors, who also were incarcerated, added to the unwelcome burden on the jailers in the city and county.[20] Prisons quickly again became crowded, unhealthy, and abusive, despite the best efforts of sincere and highly motivated officials. By 1790 the law required that convicts be "clothed in habits of coarse material," and that they be fed "bread, indian meal, or other inferior food," including "one meal of coarse meat in each week." Yet dockets reveal that some prisoners received "no Bread" and that others were "fed upon Bread & Water only for the space of 36 Hours." Most were forced to "work ever day in the year, except Sundays" for up to ten hours a day. Carrying out the requirements of the law proved too much for officials throughout the 1790s. The incarcerated suffered accordingly.[21]

The number of executions plummeted between 1786 and 1800, since fewer crimes were capital. Three men and a woman were executed in 1786; two men died by the hangman in 1787, and six in 1788. Altogether thirty-five individuals were executed through the year 1800. More than half that number had died on the gallows in 1784 and 1785 alone. Twenty of the thirty-five persons hanged between 1786 and 1801 were guilty of murder, often in connection with other offenses. Five were associated with aggravated rapes. One of the stranger aspects of the new laws relating to capital punishment occurred in the case of Jacob Dryer, convicted of burglarizing the home of James Gillis early in 1787. Given his choice of going to prison and becoming a wheelbarrow man under the new laws, or accepting death under the old statutes, Dryer preferred the latter and was quickly hanged.[22]

The reduction of capital crimes eased the lot of attorneys in prosecuting some offenses. Juries seemed more prepared to convict when their verdict did not translate into the defendant's death. This willingness proved especially true in infanticide cases, where, frequently frustrated in obtaining conviction before 1786, prosecuting attorneys enjoyed greater success after that date. Reforms touching infanticide in the 1780s, and additional changes in the early 1790s, permitted the courts wide discretion in fining and imprisoning accused women for less than five years "according to the nature of the cases." A 1794 statute allowed a grand jury to charge a defendant with both murder and concealment, and juries to "either acquit or convict her for both offenses, or find her guilty of one and acquit her of the other, as the case may be." Thus, though first-degree murder charges were harder to prove in infanticide cases after 1794, a defendant could still be convicted and executed if her crime were particularly heinous. On the other hand, by 1795, three counts might be encompassed in a single indictment against a female suspected of killing her infant: murder at the common law, murder of a bastard under the 1718 act (which introduced the English infanticide statute to Pennsylvania), and concealment and death of a bastard child by the mother under section 17 of the 1794 statute. Judge Alexander Addison of the fifth judicial district argued that by including the last two counts in the indictment, the court offered jurors the latitude they preferred. Most juries found defendants guilty only of the third count.[23]

The reforms failed in a more significant way than the inability to implement some of them or the lack of reformation among convicts: the laws did not deter crime or reduce it. Rather, crime grew. In Pennsylvania, the rate of all crimes (accusations) per 100,000 population was 322 in the 1780s and 361 in the '90s. Philadelphia's rate peaked in 1790 at 504; for all the 90s it was 418.[24] Chester County had 293 for the 1780s and 331 for the 90s. Homicides (accusations count) peaked in Pennsylvania in the 1780s at 154 but fell to 98 in the 90s. The homicide rate for the 1780s was second highest ever, at 4.0. The end of the century did seem to moderate the growth in killing. Meanwhile, assaults clearly grew. (Table 7.1) In populous and long-lived jurisdictions like Chester County and Philadelphia city, as well as younger and less populous Cumberland and Berks Counties, assaults multiplied. In the city, where news traveled faster and the proximity to violence alarmed residents more than crime did in the countryside, Philadelphians noticed the mounting violence. When three men died as a result of fighting in May 1795, Philadelphia Quaker Elizabeth Drinker commented that there might have been "an uproar" from the public forty or fifty years earlier, but such deadly violence had become commonplace.[25] Moreau de St. Méry, who lived in Philadelphia during the 1790s, was struck by the number of "quarrelsome" men and women who "boxed" and "brawled" in the streets.[26]

Murders in the 1780s stimulated a prolonged public discussion. William Bradford, who knew more than anyone about Pennsylvania's criminal history, was convinced by 1793 that Philadelphia was a particularly violent city. He bewailed its high murder rate and compared it unfavorably to Edinburgh and London.[27] A contemporary of Bradford, the novelist Charles Brockden Brown, thought even more deeply about the roots of violence in their society and wrote his analysis into the plots and characters of his novels. His first novel, *Wieland* (1798), bore the revealing subtitle "The Transformation." In a world of rapidly disappearing stable forms and fixed relations, the protagonist Theodore Wieland

TABLE 7.1. ASSAULT ACCUSATIONS PER 100,000 POPULATION BY COUNTY BY DECADE IN PENNSYLVANIA, 1700–1800

County/city	1700s	1710s	1720s	1730s	1740s	1750s	1760s	1770s	1780s	1790s
Chester	75		79	82	63	101	78	65	67	123
Lancaster					44	46	47	56		101
Bedford-Huntingdon-Somerset										287
Berks								20	64	117
Cumberland						74				110
Dauphin							69			185
Fayette										66
Mifflin										218
Philadelphia (city)										127
Washington-Greene										47
Westmoreland									55	
York										24

turned from loving father to a murderous madman. He bludgeoned his wife beyond recognition, slaughtered his family, and eventually took his own life. When Brown indicated that he had based Wieland's murder on "an authentic case," scholars assume he alluded to the case of New York's James Yates whose murder of his family was described in the *Weekly Magazine* two years before Brown penned *Wieland*.[28] But Pennsylvania offered Brown material enough to pen his novel from its familicide cases, reaching back to the cases of John Lewis and John Myriak. And Philadelphians had recently suffered through a series of senseless (and apparently random) murders in their own streets. Murder is a persistent theme in Brown's *Ormond* (1799), *Arthur Mervyn* (1799), and *Edgar Huntley* (1799), as well in *Wieland*. His murderers invariably lack any connection with a community and covet individual distinction and gain. Edgar Huntley, as critic Norman Grabo has pointed out, "is merely a bewildered victim of circumstances who is forced to kill."[29]

Historian Daniel A. Cohen has observed regarding those guilty of familicide in the late eighteenth century, "Their experience with American freedom was not simply incidental to their tragedies but created a matrix of social insecurity and psychological stress that is crucial to any adequate explanation of their crimes." His observation applies just as well to the other varieties of murderers. Forces unleashed by the Revolution created "new conditions of freedom" for individuals, and loosed them to rise or fall on their apparent merit alone. The Revolution expanded individual freedom and destroyed the "few remaining barriers to personal choice and achievement," but it also, as Cohen cautions, removed "excuses for personal failure."[30] The "contagion of liberty" could be deadly as well as exhilarating.[31]

Next to homicide, burglary and robbery have been the gravest of crimes in the Anglo-American past—or, it could be argued, on the basis of the energy put into prosecuting them, the gravest of all crimes. The crimes troubled Pennsylvania, where, after 1760, Pennsylvania prosecuted more cases of burglary per decade than Massachusetts did in fifty years, 1750–1800.[32] It executed sixty-one burglars in all. The trouble was localized in Pennsylvania, however. Of the total charges of burglary and robbery in Pennsylvania, 62 percent occurred after 1780 and were concentrated in the metropolitan area.

After 1759, when criminal court dockets from Philadelphia become available, the city and Philadelphia County accounted for 29.9 percent of all criminal charges, but an inordinate share of burglary and robbery charges, 53.6 percent (Table 7.2). The homes of the most prominent and wealthy Philadelphia families were not safe from burglars; Chief Justice Thomas McKean, James Wilson, framer of the Constitution, and artist Charles Willson Peale were among the victims.[33] By the 1780s, the city

TABLE 7.2. Burglary and Robbery Accusations in Pennsylvania and
Philadelphia City and County, 1682–1800

	Pennsylvania	Philadelphia City and County
1680s	4	
1690s	4	
1700s	10	
1710s	3	
1720s	14	
1730s	18	
1740s	16	
1750s	14	
1760s	53	24
1770s	105	73
1780s	323	179
1790s	105	49

had spread into the county—Southwark and the Northern Liberties—
and consequently part of the county shared the conditions of city life,
including crime. The county, odd as it may seem at first, had the highest
rate of robbery. In 1786–1800, years when the county's population may
reasonably be estimated, the rate was 6.6 per 100,000. For comparison,
that rate was higher than those for London (urban Surrey) for 1740–
1779 and 1780–1802 (5.0 and 4.1). J. M. Beattie's explanation of robbery
and its rates in Surrey may help us to understand robbery numbers in
Philadelphia County. In Surrey the city met the countryside. There,
where the road traffic entering and leaving the city stretched through
less populated areas, robbers felt comfortable confronting and escaping
from their victims. It was the optimum combination of available victims
and places to hide.[34] Similar conditions boosted robbery in Philadelphia
County.

The increased burglary and robbery alarmed Pennsylvanians to a
degree that Americans living since 1970—when armed robbery is so
common—can hardly appreciate.[35] The crimes alarmed society because
they endangered life. Armed robbery obviously threatened the victim's
life or health, but any robber had to menace his victim. A successful burglary was less dangerous because the burglar employed stealth and
wished to avoid confronting his victim. Foiling your burglar and saving
your property, though, probably meant confronting him and the danger
that that raised. But even without confrontation, the idea that your
home was being violated and your privacy invaded destroyed the victim's
peace of mind. Being vulnerable—asleep at night or off guard during
the day—in the presence of some unseen, sinister intruder, frightened
real victims and fired up the imagination of potential ones. Burglars typ-

TABLE 7.3. AVERAGE RIOT ACCUSATIONS PER 100,000 PER DECADE IN
PENNSYLVANIA AND CHESTER COUNTY, 1682–1800

	Chester County	Pennsylvania
1680s	0.0	
1690s	0.0	
1700s	2.8	
1710s	26.3	
1720s	6.9	
1730s	29.4	
1740s	11.3	
1750s	16.4	
1760s	10.1	7.1
1770s	9.0	6.4
1780s	15.7	11.6
1790s	44.0	21.2

ically cost their victims more than robbers. They usually did not work
under the time constraints that robbers did, nor have the robbers' need
to escape immediately. If they burgled an unoccupied house, they could
clean it out. Fearful Pennsylvanians took the crime seriously and punished the perpetrators severely.

Riots were as conspicuous a feature of crime after 1780 as murder and
robbery and at least as worrisome as assaults. As much as Americans in
historical memory link rioting with the American Revolution, riots were
more common after 1783 than before—at least in the official criminal
record[36] (Table 7.3). Of the 2127 charges of riot in Pennsylvania, 73.6
percent occurred between 1781 and 1800. In Chester County, the rate
of riot accusations tripled between the 1780s and 90s. Chester's rate of
44.0 per 100,000 in the 1790s was exceeded by Dauphin's at 68.4 and
Mifflin's at 53.4. But the proliferation of riot offenses was not really
localized, not just rural or isolated in the mountains; Philadelphia's rate
doubled in the last two decades and in raw numbers jumped from 17 to
96 cases between the same two decades. There can be no doubt, given
the full range of tumult and violence in Pennsylvania in the last two
decades of the century, that Pennsylvanians were troubled and turbulent
to a degree far beyond what most historians have appreciated or
depicted.[37]

Urban riots of the previous twenty years, 1761–1780, had obvious
political purposes and organization, especially in Philadelphia. Now, in
the city after 1780, many were simple, impromptu disturbances or
chance melees. The concentration of people increased the possibility
that some people would grate on each other and become aggressive,
especially when inebriated. One such incident occurred when, at the

close of a night-school session in Philadelphia in March 1788, the schoolmaster treated his charges to "Beer and Wine." The boys, "not accustomed to Strong Liquor," got into an argument with an inhabitant on their way home, which escalated into a riot. Still, one observer considered it nothing more than "an unguarded Sally of Youth." Philadelphia teemed with small-scale disturbances, which could slip into riots. Littleton Haben, a Negro, kept a notorious "riotous house" which kept the city's justices of the peace and constables busy. A fight instigated by John Flood in November 1796 led to a small riot. Henry McCoy started one when he tried to strike a black woman with a hatchet. One riot in June 1795 grew to such a size that troops were called to quell it, but three participants died before the troops extinguished it.[38]

The city was underrepresented in riot accusations, as were also the three original southeastern counties. Rioters were more common in rural Pennsylvania outside the southeast—even as riots grew more common in all regions of the state.[39] Riots did not comprise the whole trouble in rural Pennsylvania, however. Six other varieties of crime proliferated in rural counties—varieties that appear distinct at first glance, but were really complementary. The six were forcible entry and detainer, rescue, obstructing justice or showing contempt for the courts, neglecting to perform a public office, obstructing highways, and failing to supervise the maintenance of roads or highways. Forcible entry and detainer is forcing one's entry onto real property and holding it without legally owning the property. Rescue is taking unlawfully chattels that had been seized from a wrongdoer to compel him to pay a legal obligation. It may also describe forcefully removing a person from the custody of law-enforcement officers. The meanings of the other four crimes are clear, but some, especially the last two, do not appear similar to the others. This whole odd lot, however, were spokes of a wheel of farmer distress in Pennsylvania the 1780s and 90s. But before explaining the wheel, the numbers need to be disclosed.

The six crimes together produced 1987 criminal charges from 1682 through 1800 (Figure 7.1). Of the total, 72.2 percent occurred from 1781 through 1800. The three southeastern counties and the city of Philadelphia accounted for only 9.0 percent of the charges in 1781–1800. In other words, the crimes were very concentrated in the final two decades of the century and in rural areas remote from Philadelphia. Three counties alone had 37.9 percent of the six charges (1781–1800)— Cumberland, Huntingdon, and Dauphin. Forcible entry and detainer was the most common of the six criminal accusations, at 764. Eighty percent of these accusations occurred after 1780, and 93.5 percent outside the southeastern region we just defined. Forcible entry was, therefore, even more concentrated in time and location than the sum of the six.

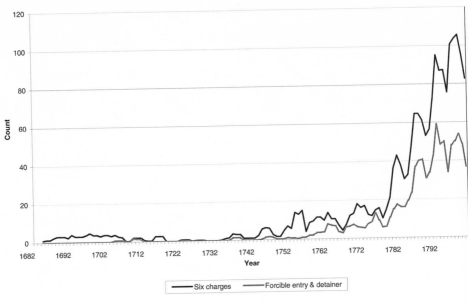

Figure 7.1. Three-year moving averages of select public order crimes in Pennsylvania, 1680–1800.

Historian Terry Bouton has ably explained the problem at the axis of these crimes: farmers could not pay their debts and taxes.[40] The preeminent cause of their inability was the scarcity of money and credit in the state after the Revolution. Before the war there was $5.33 in paper currency per person circulating in the state; by 1790, there was only $0.31. Interest rates after the war ranged from five to twelve percent per *month*. Creditors—moneylenders, bankers, merchants, landlords—wanted protection against inflation, mostly through limits on the money supply. Saddled with debt from the war, the state expected to tax its citizens to pay the public debt. The state's creditors were a relatively few men who had amassed the debt certificates, having purchased them from the original holders at a fraction of their face value. They wanted the maximum repayment that was politically possible, plus interest. Like private creditors, they did not want to be paid in depreciated paper currency. As the figures above help demonstrate, appreciation and deflation were exactly the historical case.

Taxpayers could reasonably infer that these several economic interests and historical developments expressed one overarching public agenda, and they had a candidate for its author: Robert Morris, former Superintendent of Finance of the Confederation and President of the Bank of

North America. Suspicious, aggrieved farmer-taxpayers believed in a villainous collaboration among creditors, debt holders, and state treasury and justice officials. Later, they would add authors and exponents of the United States Constitution or Federalists.[41]

Unable to meet their private and public obligations, rural Pennsylvanians were prosecuted by private creditors or the government. A tide of writs of execution rose in the counties where they lived, threatening them with the loss of their chattels or realty in payment for their delinquent debts. Bouton calculates that in some periods of the 1780s sheriffs executed more writs than there were taxpayers in a county, or enough writs in other counties to include a majority of the taxpayers.[42] The locals resisted. They or their collaborators entered the lands or buildings in question and occupied them to stop eviction or foreclosure. At other times, they retrieved property that had been distrained or sold (or sometimes rescued men who had been arrested). There were 875 prosecuted occurrences of this forcible entry or rescue after 1780.[43]

For sundry reasons, sheriffs and other magistrates, together with the private creditors and public tax collectors, did not win the day for the prosecution. Rural Pennsylvanians cleverly and doggedly obstructed the justice system and maddened the interests whom the courts served. The obstructions ranged widely in character, but grew in aggressiveness, especially after 1787. Citizens might defy the courts by not rendering ordinary service, such as not showing up for jury duty. In Berks County in 1792, when an insufficient number of grand jurors appeared, the sheriff was left to pressure spectators into filling the vacancies. Constables, sheriffs, justices of the peace, county treasurers, and tax collectors refused to execute their orders against delinquent debtors, who were their county or township neighbors. Some publicly avowed they would not follow their orders. In 1781 in York County, Stephen Foltz was fined £45 for "contemptuously refusing to hold the office of constable."[44] Judge Alexander Addison stated that David Bradford, the state prosecutor in Washington County, refused to prosecute any violators of the federal excise.[45] In refusing, the officials were acting in harmony with the large majority of rural citizens, who would not cooperate with any aggressive magistrates. The result for the judicial record is the proliferation of prosecutions after 1780 of public officials neglecting the performance of their offices. The period contained 66.2 percent of all prosecutions for those offenses from 1682 through 1800 (and 83.1 percent of all those after 1777). Eighty-seven percent of the prosecutions lay in six central and western counties, Dauphin being the one closest to Philadelphia. Only two of fifty-four accused officials ever went to trial. Among the rest, grand juries refused to indict one out of three of all accused and the state defaulted in the prosecution of another one out of five.

As the state government pressed the debtors harder the protestors grew bolder, and more physical and ingenious. Crowds in Carlisle in 1794 threatened to hang supreme court judges Thomas McKean and Jasper Yeates, but were content to burn the two in effigy when the judges left town before the mob assembled. A few days earlier the same judges had escaped death when they were attacked by a group of angry citizens in Westmoreland County.[46] More often protesters interfered in the sale or auction of foreclosed lands and chattels. A large band of York County farmers in 1787 led by Godfrey King violently disrupted a public sale of lands seized for delinquent taxes.[47] In Huntingdon County in 1788, when the court was about to proceed against delinquent taxpayers, men collected and disrupted the court. The court had several of them arrested. At the next quarter sessions, when the protestors were to be prosecuted, a crowd collected, stopped the trials, and destroyed the court's records.[48] On other occasions, farmers stopped witnesses, jurors, and prosecutors from appearing; they interdicted men expecting to attend sheriffs' sales or cart off their purchases; and, most intriguing, they dug trenches across county roads or piled trees, manure, and other debris in the roadways, stopping commerce and public business.[49]

The government of Pennsylvania responded by prosecuting the insurgents and delinquent officers for breaking or neglecting state laws, sending a judicial team into the rebellious region to oversee the punishment of the insurrectionists. Still, few perpetrators were tried, possibly because they could not be identified or because if identified, no witnesses would testify to their crimes. An obvious, culpable group to prosecute was the township supervisors of roads, who either would not stop the protests because they supported them or did not exert themselves sufficiently if they did disapprove of protests. Whereas only fifteen men were prosecuted for obstructing highways (1781–1800), 323 road supervisors were prosecuted (two out of three of them in the 1790s). Only five ever went to trial, and in 60.7 percent of the cases no resolution was ever reached or the state voluntarily quit the prosecution. In all, the state made a feeble figure in its attempt to marshal power against the protesters.

The frustration felt by state officials—and additionally the public and private creditors and bankers who were spurring the officials to act—vented itself in the movement for a national government that could secure their interests and quell the rural insurgency—insurgency which was more alarming in the case of Massachusetts and Daniel Shays. The men of property needed some national or federal force in the place of the force that rural magistrates sympathetic to their farmer colleagues would not exert. And too, they needed a federal prohibition on the issuance of state paper currency. The United States Constitution provided both. In Pennsylvania, the contest over the constitution and its ratification separated voters along the lines of the economic protest. That contest had its crimes too: in Carlisle, seat of Cumberland County, a large group of hostile opponents of the Constitution fell upon their neighbors who had gathered to celebrate the ratification of that document in 1787, causing numerous injuries.[50]

Among the hundreds of events and strategies that rural Pennsylvanians contrived to foil the civil and criminal courts, one or two have nearly monopolized the attention of historians, the Whiskey Rebellion of 1794 and Fries Rebellion of 1799. The socalled rebellions are misunderstood because, as Bouton points out, historians have not located them within the context of fifteen or more years of rural resistance to public economic policy. Despite the character they share with hundreds of less conspicuous protests, the two uprisings need attention because they showed two distinct historical twists that lesser, unnamed protests did not.

First, the burdensome taxes that the Whiskey and Fries Rebellions protested were federal, not state. To elaborate, the debt that the excise taxes on whiskey were to support was the national debt that Alexander Hamilton had the nation assume, in part from assuming the debts of the states. Nevertheless, the same old taxpayers, and more, were taxed. Now, however, the enforcement of the taxes lay also with the national government, Hamilton, and others, and not merely with magistrates of the state of Pennsylvania. Here was a remote, daunting power that could better "open the Purses of the people."[51] Second, the national government won the two contests, Whiskey and Fries—although they helped contribute to the failure of the Federalist Party in the 1800 presidential election. The protesters were dispersed or captured by federal soldiers and some were criminally prosecuted. A few were convicted in federal courts in Philadelphia—not in rural or western courts in the vicinity of the crimes and the accused criminals.

Federalist leaders like Alexander Hamilton and Washington had gone to great cost to make their point about the authority of the law over populist obstructions. Looking back on the extended record of disorder, it is wonderfully appropriate that a charismatic leader of the whiskey rebels in 1794 was David Bradford, who had been prosecuted in 1791 and 1792 for obstructing highways and dereliction as a highway supervisor.[52]

As noted earlier, state and federal justices were often scorned and sometimes physically attacked, including even the most eminent men, like

McKean, Pickering, and Yeates. Although they were more at risk in rural Pennsylvania, attacks occurred in the city too. In January 1789, one Michael Connor of Philadelphia was found guilty of "assault with intent to kill" Justice Plunkett Fleeson. Eleazer Oswald, editor of Philadelphia's *Independent Gazetteer,* was so incensed in 1788 by a state supreme court ruling against him that he threatened to kill the chief justice. Authorities characterized Oswald's threats to "beat or Kill the Chief Justice" as "attended with great vehemence" and as "Of the most extravagant Dangerous nature." In November 1778, William Thompson, too, believing that the chief justice had wronged him, first sought to engage him in a duel, then publicly grappled with the high judge, yelling, "Damn you, I will make your bones ake."[53]

In more subdued ways, in conversation and print, the whole judiciary and state constitutions suffered in the 1780s and 90s. In the 1780s especially, justices were ridiculed as uneducated rubes. For example, the *Carlisle Gazette* entertained readers with a story of a young justice of the peace who, having read his law books too hastily, became convinced he must arrest citizens who "fry any bacon." He subsequently arrested an elderly woman for this "crime," only to learn that the law book had read, "fire any beacon" instead.[54] The *Philadelphia Aurora* reported a justice of the peace in Whitemarsh, Montgomery County, who in the course of legal procedures needed a writ of *certiorari* but asked instead for "a writ of *aurora borealis.*" The lawyer William Rawle poked fun at postwar justices of the peace: "Our Tom is a wit, at the bar he will drudge,/ Our Will is a fool, and we'll make him a judge." Stephen DuPonceau, a prominent and successful lawyer, noted "ignorant judges" were "not a rarity at that time."[55]

More sober philippics accused the bench of dishonesty. Writers stormed against "trading justices," who earned their living from legal fees. They warped the system in order to exact higher fees than the law allowed and to issue more costly legal papers than necessary. Their victims were the poor, the naïve, and the uneducated who came before them expecting impartiality and justice. While very few public criticisms of trading justices appeared before the Revolution, complaints were common by the late 1780s. Philadelphia personnel were "rapacious wolves, who look on all classes of their fellow-citizens as their common prey," wrote one angry critic. It was "the common people," "the poor and friendless," who generally suffered at the hands of these "monsters."[56]

Other commentators rued inefficiency and ineffective policy in the courts. William Bradford pointed to the willingness of judges to shorten the sentences of convicted individuals and of executives to pardon criminals. He examined the judicial fate of sixty-eight persons convicted of theft between 1786 and 1790, only to discover that thirty were accorded pardons and another twenty-nine escaped from jail! Other observers joined Bradford in remarking on the ease with which criminals could gain pardons. François Alexandre, the Duc de La Rochefoucauld, who visited Pennsylvania between 1795 and 1797, observed that pardons were readily available to all offenders.[57] Charles Brockden Brown, trained in the law, also attacked the tolerance exhibited by the courts, but with very different villains in mind. Wealthy and influential persons were the criminals and the beneficiaries of official leniency—"young men of fashion," the sons of the gentry, who out of boredom or arrogance "trampl[ed] on the rights and feelings of others." In the city, according to one report, they "join in mobs, beat down the watchmen, break open doors, take off knockers, and disturb the quiet of honest people." Their rural counterparts found their own ways to wreak havoc, including committing robberies.[58]

Critics of the bench existed on both the radical, more populist wing of politics and the conservative, more élitist wing. Under the 1776 state constitution, judges were popularly elected and the judiciary was less independent than it had been in the provincial period. A considerable change occurred in 1790 to limit the earlier public influence upon the bench and raise the independence of the judicial branch. Élite critics were more common before 1790; thereafter, the 1790 change stimulated more criticism of the judiciary from the populists.[59]

In 1790 Pennsylvania replaced the 1776 state constitution. The new constitution of 1790 critically changed the state judiciary, and "An Act to Establish the Judicial Courts of this Commonwealth," passed in 1791, fleshed out the changes called for in the new constitution. The changes moved the judiciary in a less democratic direction and toward the colonial past, giving it greater independence from the popular will. The selection of the state's justices of the peace was taken from the polls of the people and returned to the governor. The governor was empowered to name three or four justices for each county to serve both in the quarter sessions and the common pleas. The powers of the quarter sessions were extended considerably to include capital crimes. Its justices also were empowered to move cases to the oyer and terminer court or to the Supreme Court by writs of *certiorari*. The former county justices of the peace (as distinguished from state justices of the peace) were also appointed by the executive, and were stripped of their judicial functions. Unlike their colonial counterparts, they no longer could settle minor civil suits or punish petty criminal offenses. The state was divided into five circuits or districts, with a president judge named by the governor to preside over from three to six counties. These presidents were to be persons "of knowledge and integrity, skilled in the laws." They were required to sit in on quarter sessions and on those oyer and terminer proceedings not overseen by Supreme Court justices. Equally noteworthy, the Supreme Court was now to be staffed by judges formally trained in the law and worked by similarly well-prepared lawyers.[60]

The new state constitution finally called for the state's judges to serve during good behavior rather than at pleasure—another recourse to the colonial past that bolstered the independence of the judiciary. On several occasions, particularly in the 1750s, the Pennsylvania legislature had pressed to change the colony's judicial tenure from commissions *durante bene placito* ("as long as it pleases") to commissions *quamdiu se bene gesserint* ("as long as they conduct themselves properly"). In each instance it had been frustrated by English authorities. Royal and proprietary officials favored commissions based on the king's or proprietor's "pleasure" so judges could be quickly removed when they became incompetent or troublesome. Legislators argued that commissions based on pleasure rendered judges cowardly and likely to routinely support crown and proprietary interests against those of the people. Only with more secure commissions, they argued, would judges truly be independent and impartial. The 1776 constitution, in one of its selectively democratic ways, retained service at pleasure, since it was the voters' pleasure and not the king's. The upstart "new men" on the bench were content with that and delayed the change to more secure commissions until 1790. By the last decade of the century, with professionally trained practitioners dominating both sides of the bench, the Assembly approved new judicial commissions based on good behavior.[61]

The reorganization in 1791 brought a very different set of judges to the state's bench. At the Supreme Court, McKean was retained as chief justice, but Edward Shippen, Jasper Yeates, and William Bradford, each of whom was a highly trained and highly successful lawyer, now joined him on the high bench. Moreover, each was highly conservative and remarkable for his "wealth and connexion." Thomas Smith, also a longtime and successful practitioner, joined the court when Bradford left after several years to become attorney-general of the United States. Hugh Henry Brackenridge pointed out in his *Law Miscellanies* (1814) that after 1795, the court seemed more monolithic than it had ever been, for Shippen, Yeates, and Smith were related, shared a single political philosophy and party affiliation, and belonged to the "aristocracy."[62] Other prominent legal and political figures in the state, such as James Wilson (and even Chief Justice Thomas McKean), scrambled to secure positions in the new federal courts, and first-rate lawyers such as William Lewis, Alexander James Dallas, William Bradford, Jr., Jared Ingersoll, and Jonathan Dickinson Sergeant lined up to ply their trade there.[63]

The modifications to the judiciary and the new appointees to the bench raised one of the most persistent issues in Pennsylvania and national politics in the Federalist era. First, locals protested the appointed judges who replaced elected officers. In Mifflin County in 1791, a host of men including the sheriff marched on the courthouse and demanded the resignation of a brash new justice, who had mouthed something about "ruling" the people. The crowd then got into a fight with some local Federalists.[64]

It comes as no surprise that many justices and successful lawyers in the state and federal courts were members of the Federalist Party. Alexander Addison, of the Pennsylvania fifth circuit court, for example, was a noisy Federalist whom the Jeffersonian Republicans succeeded in impeaching.[65] But others who were not Federalists, and indeed were renowned and combative Republicans, like McKean and Dallas, were social and economic conservatives at heart. Increasingly their conservatism roiled rural Republicans, debtors and tax protestors, and Philadelphia radicals like Dr. Michael Leib and William Duane of the *Philadelphia Aurora*. In the next decade, when the Republicans were the ascendant party in the nation and less preoccupied with combating the Federalists, the philosophical differences within the Republican Party led to a split, the conservatives carrying the nickname the Quids.[66]

In the critique of state government and politics authored by the more radical Republicans, the number one grievance was the judiciary: nothing more inhibited the progress of democracy and equality than the independence of the judiciary. Two reforms especially were tendered to remedy the evils of the élitist justice system: empowering of justices of the peace with the authority and functions they had had in colonial times, and creating a permanent arbitration system to undercut the power of lawyers and formal courts.[67] The authors of the reforms naïvely yearned to restore the past a century removed.

The last two or three decades of the eighteenth century were distinctive for at least two additional developments, both were related to property crime in Pennsylvania. Property crime flourished especially in these decades and especially in greater Philadelphia. Also, property crime appeared distinctly often within the African American population of the city. Theft became a token of black crime. Women too enter the picture when property crime is examined. Pennsylvania women (again, especially in the city, late in the century) were most often accused of property crime, which distinguished them from their early American peers (Tables 7.4 and 7.5).

The single best discriminator between urban and rural crimes in Pennsylvania was that only in Philadelphia did property crime rank first in volume. The geographical and temporal concentration of property

TABLE 7.4. ACCUSATIONS OF PROPERTY CRIMES IN PENNSYLVANIA BY COUNTY BY DECADE, 1760–1800

County	1760s	1770s	1780s	1790s	Total
Philadelphia (city)	252	203	499	997	1951
Philadelphia	182	161	438	525	1306
Chester	150	188	342	241	921
Cumberland	149	175	169	212	705
Lancaster	83	230	240	137	690
York	66	179	219	78	542
Bucks	58	89	150	111	408
Berks	9	43	104	148	304
Westmoreland		93	75	53	221
Bedford		49	52	96	197
Northumberland		39	73	19	131
Northampton		4	24	3	31
Dauphin			85	222	307
Huntingdon			22	147	169
Washington			77	62	139
Fayette			35	93	128
Franklin			3	12	15
Luzerne			1		1
Montgomery			9	3	12
Mifflin				61	61
Somerset				36	36
Wayne				24	24
Greene				18	18
Total					8317

TABLE 7.5. PROPERTY CRIMES PER 100,000 POPULATION IN CHESTER COUNTY AND PHILADELPHIA BY DECADE, 1700–1800

	Chester County	Philadelphia (city)
1700s	117	
1710s		
1720s	66	
1730s	54	
1740s	58	
1750s	52	
1760s	59	150[1]
1770s	71	191[2]
1780s	107	163[3]
1790s	81	204

[1]Represents 1760–1763 and 1767–1769. [2]Represents 1770–1771; [3]Represents 1780–1785.

crimes occurred especially because in late-eighteenth-century Philadelphia there was more property to steal, burgle, rob, or swindle than in other places and times in Pennsylvania and because of the city's poor, whose need and relative deprivation had grown more acute than ever.

Philadelphia's extant court dockets begin in 1759.[68] Counting the property crimes (including burglary and robbery) from that date through 1800 for all of Pennsylvania, Philadelphia's share comprises 23.8 percent—even though a few years' records from the city after 1759 are missing. Philadelphia County's share in the same period was an additional 15.7 percent of the Pennsylvania total, despite ten years of missing dockets. Rural Chester County, with no records missing, ranked third in volume with 11.2 percent for the same period. Philadelphia County's high volume and second rank support the generalization that property crimes were especially urban crime, because Philadelphia County contained the suburbs of the city of Philadelphia, the Northern Liberties and Southwark. The two suburban districts grew from estimated populations of 6,944 in 1767 to 13,998 in 1790, equal to 44 percent and 49 percent of the city's population respectively. In 1800 the two districts numbered 26,591 people—equal to 65 percent of the population of the city and 30 percent of the population of Philadelphia County. The Northern Liberties became home to poorer workingmen of Philadelphia because they could more easily afford the rents there.[69] Some portion of that 15.7 percent property crime of Philadelphia County can therefore be assigned to the urban crime category. A better indication of how common all property crimes were in the city is the rate per 100,000 (Table 7.5). In the 1790s the city's rate of 204 almost doubled Chester's highest rate at any time in the century.

Markets and exchange in the city enhanced opportunities for crimes that were less practicable in rural society and more subsistence-level economies. Thus, crimes of the eighteenth century that most closely resemble modern "white-collar" crimes of the marketplace proliferated in Philadelphia in the last two decades. After 1781, 43 percent of all the charges in Pennsylvania of forgery and counterfeiting, fraud, extortion, embezzling, receiving stolen goods, and usury occurred in Philadelphia city and county. These twenty years account for 63.3 percent of these charges in Pennsylvania history; the last decade of the century accounted for 41.1 percent.

The availability of property to be stolen is an obvious necessary condition of high rates of crimes against property, but it is not the only cause of the high rate. Unless a thief intended to consume the stolen property himself, he very likely expected to dispose of it and make a profit from an exchange. He expected to participate in the market, to become a merchant of sorts. In the city the likelihood of finding a market for stolen goods, linking up a seller with a purchaser, or using a "fence" or pawnbroker (the more professional disposal agents) was better than in the countryside. City markets and public vendues outnumbered those in the country. More goods were moving around.

In the country residents more easily identified stolen goods and accused the bearers of theft. People in the rural community who were known to be poor could be suspected of theft if they showed up with costly articles. Strangers and vagrants did not escape scrutiny either. They were suspected if someone's property was missing. These kinds of situations amount to what today we call criminal "typing" or "profiling." In the eighteenth century, without police, civilians and neighbors did the accusing.

In the city, however, the proliferation of goods made them anonymous, obscured the ownership of stolen ones, and gave pause to anyone who was inclined to accuse their bearers of theft. Goods came in from the countryside for sale and export and were imported from abroad for distribution in the country. Although strangers abounded in the country, they were even more common in the city.[70] By the late eighteenth century, Philadelphia had become America's largest, wealthiest city and experienced an average annual growth rate of 3.4 percent from 1750 to 1801. Trade permeated it. "Everyone in Philadelphia deals more or less in trade," an English visitor remarked.[71] In the years 1758–1762, the average sterling value of imports into the city from England and Wales was £365,400.[72] Commerce grew by fits and starts after 1750, declined in the Revolution and much of the 1780s, then reached its acme in the 1790s with the stimulus of European wars.[73]

Prosperity stimulated what historian T. H. Breen calls a "consumer revolution" in Pennsylvania, and in much of America at the same time. Pennsylvania's consumption of British exports increased by 380 percent between the 1740s and 1760s.[74] Thomas Doerflinger calculates that the average rural family spent £12 (Pennsylvania currency) annually on European goods in 1758–1762. And if Pennsylvanians did not have the cash, in the 1760s and 1780s especially, they consumed on credit which British and Continental merchants readily supplied.

In the last half of the century, wealth in Philadelphia grew and reached unprecedented heights in the mid-1790s. Men were able, says historian Billy G. Smith, to amass wealth "far beyond the dreams of an earlier generation." The proportion of taxpayers designated as "gentleman" or "esquire" multiplied by three times between 1756 and 1772 and then increased by another five times in the next twenty-five years. Many of the gentlemen spent lavishly. A visiting Englishman with a sure feel for irony observed, "amongst the upper-most circles in Philadelphia, pride, haughtiness, and ostentation are conspicuous; and it seems as if nothing could make them happier than that an order of nobility should be established, by which they might be exalted above their fellow citizens."[75]

But wealth was not equitably distributed among Philadelphians. Between 1756 and 1798, the richest decile of city taxpayers owned between 47 and 72 percent of the taxable wealth. The Revolutionary War brought mixed results, improving the lot of some of the lower sorts but apparently bringing dislocation, poverty, and despair to more. The postwar years added to the woes of the laboring poor. There was a steady decline in the number of jobs for mariners (the largest occupational group in the city) and for those whose work was closely tied to maritime commerce. There was also a serious decrease of workers in textiles, ship-building, and food and drink processing which offset the growth of craftsmen and artisans stimulated by the war. Not until the mid-1790s, according to Smith, did some of the city's laboring people experience better conditions and rising prospects. But overall, the expansion did not keep pace with the growth of the population in Philadelphia, and that growth was due to immigration more than any other single cause. The result was that "For many laboring Philadelphians, life was nasty, short, and brutish."[76]

With their hopes and prospects stymied for much of the half-century, laborers lived through an era of mass importation and consumption of foreign goods, increased production of luxuries at home, and of ostentation and self-gratification in dress, housing, and diet. With an ethos of entitlement, competition, and envy, the times supplied motives for theft—together with the opportunities. This was no republic or commonwealth. Some Pennsylvanians reasoned that poverty was the problem. "What may not be expected from him, who is pushed forward into sin by the impulse of poverty, who lives in continual want?" one observer asked. "Many acts of depredation, and many scenes of horror" could be "traced to the extreme poverty of [our] distressed class of people," concluded another.[77]

Charles Brockden Brown brooded over the conditions in end-of-the-century Philadelphia that generated crime, and particularly over the connection between poverty and crime. Poverty transformed many of his most fascinating fictional characters into villains. It was not simply poverty, but rather the obvious imbalance of wealth. Brown insisted that this economic injustice promoted crime and that the political system and ideology protected the interests of the wealthy and powerful even as they celebrated equality of opportunity. False promises and real defeats, poverty and immobility frustrated and angered men, even drove them insane.[78]

Brown was particularly incensed by "reputable" criminals—urban merchants, bankers, and lawyers, men with money, reputation, and influence—who committed crimes of avarice and ambition, usually with impunity. He accused the moneylenders and businessmen in Philadelphia of criminal offenses every bit as pervasive, destructive, and venal as those committed by the city's drunks, toughs, and pilferers. He believed that such crimes, and the subsequent manipulation of the law by those in offices of trust and influence to escape retribution, shattered the people's faith in the law to protect the innocent and to punish the guilty.[79] Others shared Brown's opinion. The architect of the national capital, Benjamin Latrobe, wrote of Philadelphia: "The importance attached to wealth, and the freedom which opens every legal avenue to wealth to every one individually has two effects, which are unfavorable to morals: it weakens the ties that bind individuals to each other, by making all citizens rivals in the pursuit of riches; and it renders the means by which they are attained more indifferent."[80]

Although the tycoons of this newly flush class acknowledged that property crimes troubled the city, they refused to blame themselves or question their conceits about society. Instead, they verbally thrashed the "criminal element," calling for its eradication—by which they meant common thieves, toughs, drunkards, and blacks. They wanted order, community, and regularity from those miscreants, while they spared the "better sort" from shouldering any obligations to others. "White-collar" criminals were every bit as venal as any felon in the dock and stole just as obviously as the common pickpocket, but meanwhile destroyed the public's faith in equal justice. The early American printer and economist Matthew Carey saw this same egotism in the tycoons. He began his *A Short Account of the Malignant Fever* (1793) with a searing portrait of a Philadelphia society of extravagance, "reckless speculation, unsteady financial institutions, and widespread ruin." When blamed, the men of commerce merely sought to "shift its losses to the unsuspecting."[81]

While their detractors claimed to know very well who they were, the men accused of theft, burglary, and robbery are more elusive to historians. From the pool of them in 1779–1781, only one in five shows up in the Philadelphia tax list of 1780 (Table 7.6). That makes them more transient and/or poorer than those accused of all other crimes, since of the latter, two of five are in the list. Also, in the city directories of the 1790s, 84.0 percent of the accused male thieves, burglars, and robbers are missing (compared with 72.1 percent of all accused—including property criminals—being missing). Because immigrants, mariners, and servants were especially mobile or inconspicuous in the public record, they are likely candidates for the missing accused.[82] Immigrants especially swelled the population of the city in the 1790s. They were overwhelmingly Scots-Irish or Irish, and secondly blacks, including foreign-

TABLE 7.6. ACCUSED PROPERTY CRIMINALS IN PHILADELPHIA AND CHESTER COUNTY TAX LISTS AND THEIR PERCENTILE RANK IN TAXABLE WEALTH WITH NONCRIMINAL COMPARISONS

	Philadelphia	Chester County
Accused property criminals present in tax lists	21.3% of 94	24.2% of 182
Mean (low/high) percentile of property criminals present	32.9/41.5	47.8/52.3
All other accused criminals present in tax lists	39.1% of 133	42.9% of 602
Mean (high/low) percentile of all other accused	45.8/50.4	53.5/57.8

and American-born. Out of all the people convicted in Philadelphia of any crime—and not just property crimes—from 1794 to 1800, 31.7 percent were born in Ireland and 31.8 percent were black. Only six percent were born in Philadelphia.[83]

As for the one in five men property criminals who are in the tax list, their mean wealth rank put them in the third decile from the bottom. No other major category of accused criminals ranked lower. Of the sixty-eight men found in the city directories of the 1790s, 31.0 percent (counting conservatively) followed unskilled or poorly remunerated occupations. Of all accused criminals except these property-crime categories, 18.0 percent followed the same occupations. By these measures, men accused of theft, burglary, and robbery consistently appeared less fortunate than the other accused criminals.

In the case of accused thieves in urban and rural English parishes, J. M. Beattie pursued the question of whether the accused amounted to what public opinion claimed they were: immoral, idle, unproductive people, who largely constituted a "criminal class." The index that Beattie used to test the question was the recorded occupation of the accused, and whether they had a skill or business (of any size) or were unskilled laborers and more apt to use crime to provide for themselves. He found that in urban Surrey (London), two-thirds of the accused claimed a skill or business. Rather than constituting a class—having little or no economic identity and activity but as criminals—these men moved in and out of property crime according to the economic exigencies of the times.[84] Whatever the public thought and said, no criminal class, subculture, or long-lived professional gangs plagued London.

The self-reported occupation data that Beattie had for the accused at the Surrey assizes do not exist for Philadelphia. Instead, it is possible to produce a collation of two lists: one containing the accused, and the second the men in the city directories. The collation shows that four of five accused had no known occupation or livelihood. Thus, if the missing have no occupation, and are not even counted as transient mariners, they end up a different class from the accused in London, a class that had fewer alternatives than the English to following crime as a livelihood. Did these men constitute a criminal class, professionals, and gangs?

Certainly there was talk of gangs in Philadelphia. A series of burglaries and thefts in 1750 caught the public's attention and were solved only when a brewer who suspected his servant of receiving stolen goods helped to unravel "the Morrison gang." The gang's ability to steal large amounts of goods and fence them was impressive. Ultimately, officials identified and convicted John Morrison, Betty Robinson, John Crow, Francis McCoy, and John Stimson. Although relatively young, several, like Morrison and Robinson, were characterized as career criminals.[85] The press believed that similar gangs of thieves commonly troubled Pennsylvania after 1750, especially Philadelphia, where they could operate clandestinely in its crowded streets and alleys.[86]

Did the Morrison gang and others constitute a criminal class? When London, with its size, population, and wealth, did not support such a class it is not likely that Philadelphia did. Unlike London, many accused thieves in Philadelphia had no other identifiable source of income. But these certainly included a proportion of mariners and immigrants who had vocations but were too transient to be taxpayers or in city directories. Add to them Philadelphia's indentured servants, who also would not appear in any city directory. These latter unfree men and women did not have the liberty to act as full-time professional burglars, robbers, or thieves, while they certainly could act as opportunistic thieves, and infuriate masters and other propertied victims, who readily railed at them for being immoral, idle, unproductive, and a criminal class.

The degree to which Pennsylvanians punished property crime betrays how greatly it troubled them and how concern for it exceeded that for other varieties of crime, short of homicide. They punished property crimes plurally, by fines, whipping, and jail, and sometimes more. They did that for no other crime. The persons they fined paid more than other kinds of sentenced criminals, although partly because of the value of the property they stole. (Table 7.7) The courts sentenced them to longer stays in jail. Courts may have several different motives for the punishments they inflict: the enormity of the crime, the personality of the criminal, retribution, deterrence, or the rehabilitation of the criminal. Justices can make the penalty fit the crime or fit the criminal. While the sentences alone are too little help to pin down the motives of the courts, they can point toward the priority of a particular crime in the

TABLE 7.7. AMOUNTS OF FINES IMPOSED FOR CRIMES IN CHESTER COUNTY.[1]

Top 10% of fines in value (N of crimes = 131)		Top 30% of fines in value (N of crimes = 393)		Bottom 30% of fines in value (N of crimes = 935)	
	% of N		% of N		% of N
Felony theft	45.8	Bastardy	43.8	Felony theft	25.6
Larceny	17.6	Felony theft	21.4	Assault	22.4
Assault	17.6	Larceny	9.2	Bastardy	18.8
Riot	5.3	Fornication	8.7	Larceny	9.8
Adultery	5.3	Assault	8.4	Tippling house	6.2
Tippling house	1.5	Riot	2.0	Riot	3.3
		Tippling house	2.0	Contempt	1.2
		Adultery	1.8		

[1]Crimes included amount to at least 1.0 percent of respective category. Fines were rarely adjusted for inflation or currency depreciation and do not require a deflator.

minds of anxious citizens and magistrates. In this society, punishments say that property crime was the highest priority.

In the period 1682–1800, women in Pennsylvania were accused of committing 4,352 crimes. These amounted to 14.2 percent of all accusations in Pennsylvania.[87] Property crime was the one most often leveled at the women, and represented nearly one-third (34.0 percent) of all their charges (Table 7.8). Their second most common category of offenses consisted of assault and homicide (26.1 percent), followed by sexual and morals offenses (25.0 percent). These proportions are odd because, among early American populations, only in Pennsylvania did property crime and violent crime rank first and second. Outside Pennsylvania, sex and morals crimes universally exceeded all others. That was the case for New England, where immorality long remained a vital concern, but also in rather primitive and disorderly North Carolina and seventeenth-century Maryland. It was probably true in neighboring New York.[88]

The geographic concentration of women's crime is as pronounced as the frequency and variety. Philadelphia and some smaller towns witnessed most of it. Twenty-three (22.6) percent of all criminal activity charged to women between 1682 and 1800 occurred in Philadelphia. When Philadelphia County, which contained the city's suburbs, is added, the figure is 40.1 percent. That far exceeds, by the most apt comparison, the share that women in New York City comprised of all crime in that colony. Upon summing the accusations after 1759 (when surviving Philadelphia records begin), the 40.1 percent rises to 45.1. Also, market towns like Chester, Lancaster, Reading, Carlisle, and York added numbers of female prosecutions.

238   Chapter Seven

TABLE 7.8. CRIMINAL ACCUSATIONS AGAINST WOMEN IN PENNSYLVANIA

Assault and homicide	Count	Percent
Assault	1000	23.0
Infanticide	70	1.6
Murder	43	1.0
Manslaughter	7	0.2
Scold	5	0.1
Libel and slander	4	0.1
Attempted rape	2	0.0
False imprisonment	2	0.0
Poisoning	1	0.0
Accessory to murder	1	0.0
Subtotal	1135	26.1

Sex and morals	Count	Percent
Fornication and bastardy	1009	23.2
Adultery	59	1.4
Bigamy	17	0.4
Incest	2	0.0
Witchcraft and magic	2	0.0
Drunkenness	1	0.0
Subtotal	1090	25.0

Property crimes	Count	Percent
Larceny	723	16.6
Theft	562	12.9
Burglary	49	1.1
Receiving stolen goods	44	1.0
Forcible entry/detainer	35	0.8
Fraud/deceit	17	0.4
Counterfeiting/forgery	16	0.4
Arson	16	0.4
Robbery	8	0.2
Trespass	7	0.2
Servant escape	2	0.0
Extortion	1	0.0
Subtotal	1480	34.0

Public order crimes	Count	Percent
Tippling house	240	5.5
Disorderly house	168	3.9
Riot	92	2.1
Rescue	20	0.5
Nuisance	12	0.3
Contempt/obstructing Justice	9	0.2
Perjury	8	0.2
Marrying contrary to law	6	0.1
Harboring	5	0.1
Breaking peace	2	0.0
Subtotal	562	12.9

Table 7.8. (Continued)

Crimes against the state	Count	Percent
Revolutionary crimes	15	0.3
Treason	4	0.1
Misprision of treason	1	0
Subtotal	20	0.5

Other	Count	Percent
Unidentified	65	1.5
Subtotal	65	1.5
TOTAL	4352	100.0

The concentration of women's crime in the city and its concentration in the category of theft and other property crimes explain each other. Theft, as we have seen, flourished in the city because the goods that it required proliferated there. Far more remarkable is the fact that women as well as men succumbed to the allure of those goods, not only desiring and enjoying them, but also getting them illegally. But there were other causes for the urban predominance among women, ones that J. M. Beattie discovered among urban English women.[89] The foremost cause was freedom. Rural life limited the movements of women, their anonymity, contacts with diverse people, choices of work or employment, and even dress and pastimes. City life enlarged all of these and enlarged them more than it did for men. Within clear limits, it liberated women.

A measure of the enlarged lives of urban women is the property they owned. Women in Philadelphia were almost two and a half times more likely to own taxable property than rural women. These urban, taxpaying, single women were, for all practical purposes, honorable and law-abiding, and had very little need to steal. Their mean wealth exceed the men's mean.[90] Their relevance to crime is their concentration in the city and their familiarity with property and trade. Women who were not on the tax rolls experienced propinquity with trade and portable property similar to that the taxpayers did, and experienced some of the additional liberty that the city extended.

But urban life added insecurity to liberty; employment and viable households were at least as precarious for poor women as they were for poor men. Women who paid taxes were on average wealthier than male taxpayers, but these were the fortunate few women. Historian Karin Wulf explains that women heads of households were usually too poor to pay taxes; others experienced even deeper distress than household heads. The latter, usually widows, struggled to maintain a household but found the necessary resources too hard to obtain.[91] They adjusted by

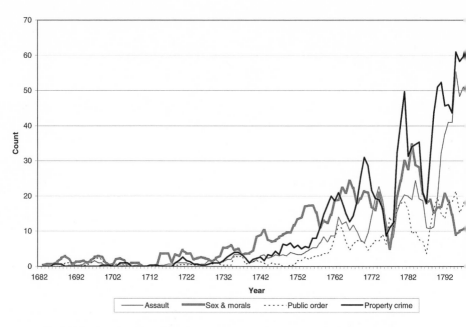

Figure 7.2. Four categories of accusations against women by decade in Pennsylvania, 1682–1800.

TABLE 7.9. FOUR CATEGORIES OF ACCUSATIONS AGAINST WOMEN AS PERCENTAGES OF ALL ACCUSATIONS IN EACH CATEGORY (PERCENT)

	1682–1720	1721–1760	1761–1800
Assault	15.0	18.0	24.9
Sex/morals	53.1	46.5	20.6
Property	8.8	25.4	36.9
Public order	13.3	7.8	14.1

placing out their children and going into domestic service, which would at least keep them all fed and housed. But too, some desperate women stole, just like desperate men. Opportunities for freedom, economic need, and crime all coalesced in the city, causing women there to violate laws more often than women in the countryside.

The predominance of property offenses among women had not always been the case. (Figure 7.2 and Table 7.9). The volume of women's offenses remained relatively stable until the 1720s, and the rate probably declined as population slowly grew (Figure 7.3).[92] In this period, women were far more likely to be accused of committing sexual

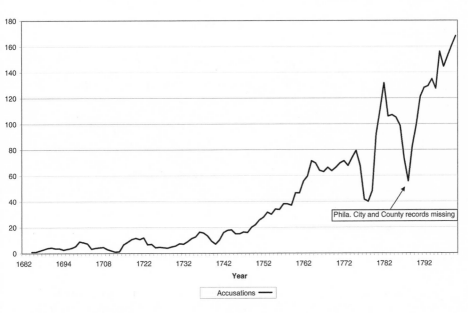

Figure 7.3. Three-year moving averages of accusations against women in
Pennsylvania, 1682–1800.

crimes. After 1720, offenses began to grow, still led by sex. After 1740,
property offenses leapt upward and then surpassed all other varieties
after 1760. That switch in rank was assisted by an artifact of the records.
In 1759, for the first time, records from Philadelphia city are represented in the totals for Pennsylvania (due to disappearance of Philadelphia records before 1759). And in Philadelphia, property crime
surpassed all other varieties. There property crime amounted to 60.8
percent of women's crime in the last forty years of the century.

The most common property accusation against women involved the
theft of what one judge called "tryfling" items. Thirteen-year old Elizabeth Baker was convicted in Huntingdon County for stealing "a check-
ered handkerchief" in 1787. Margaret Iseet of Carlisle was convicted
and jailed in February 1783 for "stealing small amounts of Bees wax and
tallow." Mary Crothy was arraigned in Chester County in February 1773
for purloining "a blanket, a Handkerchief [and] a ball of yarn."[93] Ann
Winter stole two loaves of sugar. Negress Ellen pilfered a shift and a
handkerchief. Mary Baker stole small amounts of cheese, milk, and
bread. Mary Carlisle managed to abscond with twenty dollars in coin.[94]
Three women were publicly whipped in Philadelphia in 1734 for
theft. For the combined sixty-six lashes they suffered, the three had

obtained—at least temporarily—eleven pounds of tallow, six yards of kersey, and "a piece of cloth."[95]

Some women became habitual thieves of "tryfling items." Ann Winter (who often employed the aliases Mary Flood, Ann Davis, and Ann Spencer) was a frequent visitor to Pennsylvania's criminal courts. She appeared first in December 1764, charged with felonious theft, and suffered corporal punishment upon being convicted. She was once again convicted in 1773 and pleaded guilty to a third charge of theft in September 1777. She was convicted of three counts of larceny in 1779 and received thirty-nine lashes on her back. Once again convicted of larceny in March 1780, she pleaded guilty to still another count of theft in April 1784. Her luck was better in January 1782 and October 1784 when juries exonerated her of additional larceny accusations. She also escaped another appearance when a 1785 grand jury refused to indict her on a charge for stealing, but by the 1790s this now aged and badly scarred "Notorious Thief" made endless appearances before the magistrates for petit theft, drunkenness, and riot.[96]

Elizabeth "Betty" Robinson was another Philadelphian familiar to judicial personnel. Originally brought to Maryland as an English convict, she migrated to Philadelphia, where she was arrested for theft and imprisoned numerous times. It was Robinson who helped to put together the infamous Morrison burglary gang that plagued Philadelphia authorities throughout 1749 and 1750. Morrison later confessed that she was one of his most creative and successful operatives. She was executed with Morrison and other members of the gang in February 1750/51.[97]

Few women committed burglaries or robberies. When they did, they very often carried them out in Philadelphia or its suburbs. Forty of the forty-nine burglaries attributed to women occurred in the city or its outskirts. Catherine Connor of Philadelphia, hanged in 1737, was the first female to be convicted and executed for burglary in Pennsylvania. It was another thirteen years before a second woman, Elizabeth Robinson, also died for that crime. Between 1750 and the end of the century only one other female was convicted and executed for burglary, Negress Phoebe of Chester County, in 1764, although several others were convicted.[98]

When women were involved in burglaries, invariably they were accomplices of male burglars. Here again is a gauge for how far women had or had not departed from a more deferential and submissive gender role: they usually passed up the more aggressive and dangerous behavior of burglary, and the few who did attempt burglary joined men in doing so. Courts tended to assume in such cases that their male companions coerced the women and to offer them leniency upon their conviction. Mary Hall of Philadelphia, who joined James Cannon and James Green in a 1781 burglary, was one such case. Courts also came to believe that women convicted of burglary were driven to such extremes by poverty or desperate conditions, and thus were candidates for the state's mercy. Elizabeth Grant, who burglarized the Philadelphia home of John Plankinhorn in 1771, and Martha Cash, who accompanied Margaret Ingram during their 1739 burglary in the city, were typical of those who, convicted of burglary, escaped the hangman. The judges observed that Cash was "very penitent." Ingram was described as "very aged."[99]

Female robbers were even rarer. Although eight women were accused of committing robberies, none died for that crime. Philadelphia's Ann Huson stood before the oyer and terminer court for robbing the widow Green in 1720 after she pleaded guilty to the charge. Despite her confession, she escaped the gallows when judges found "her to be a very weak and ignorant woman."[100]

Women more often received stolen goods than menacingly took them. Seventy-year-old Ann McGriggor of Philadelphia, her husband dead and her son in the army, turned to fencing stolen goods in 1781 to make a living. Several women in Philadelphia became notorious as fences for thieves and earned reputations for their ability to collect and efficiently redistribute stolen items. Bridget Edgeworth received great attention in 1787 when she was found to have in her possession the items wheelbarrow men had stolen from the home of Judge James Wilson. Mary McCoy, wife of Francis McCoy, was one of Philadelphia's busiest and most successful fences in the late 1740s and early 1750s. Mary McCoy became acquainted with Betty Robinson, thief and fence, during several transactions, and it was Robinson who began to introduce her friends, including the notorious John Morrison, to the McCoys. The McCoy home eventually became a center for receiving and selling stolen goods as well as a haven for thieves. Morrison was finally captured once he was traced to the McCoy home. Mary McCoy escaped execution with Morrison and members of his gang because—despite considerable evidence to the contrary—it was assumed her husband had coerced her.[101]

Historians have been slow to appreciate the link between the rise in property crimes, particularly the commission of such crimes by women, and the "consumer revolution" described compellingly by historians Breen, Doerflinger, and others.[102] After 1740, English manufactured items such as Sheffield knives, buckles and buttons from Birmingham, Stafford ceramics, looking glasses, cupboards, and teapots, in addition to clothing items and cloths and clocks, proliferated in the colonies. Households became showcases where wives could demonstrate their cultural sophistication and increasing status.

They also were exhibiting the new consumer items that tempted women to steal.[103] Denied the silks and porcelain increasingly found in

Pennsylvania homes, and a whole range of other goods that found their way from English factory towns to Pennsylvania, poor and disadvantaged women often took what they could not buy. As Breen has written of John Morrison's last statement at his execution, "It would have been improper form, of course, for [him] at that moment to have expressed satisfaction at having distributed so many consumer goods at low prices to ordinary people who hoped—like the members of the gang themselves—to acquire the newest material comforts of the age."[104]

For a large number of woefully poor women in Philadelphia, the influx of luxury items after 1740 was a cruel daily reminder of what they lacked. The temptation to take what they could not honestly earn was too great for many. Elizabeth McKenzie, convicted of larceny in 1785, described herself as a "poor wretched friendless woman." Isabella McKeever, pregnant and convicted of larceny—her first offense—was observed to be "really friendless and distressed." Alice Eddleton, a Philadelphia thief, was reduced to begging in the streets and "cursing those who refused to give." The dockets are filled with comments about women thieves being "objects of charity," "under utmost distress," "destitute," "without means," "a poor Strolling Woman," "a poor helpless wretch," "without means of support."[105]

Some of these women became intermediaries of a sort between the city's black and white populations. Letitia Clarke and Rebecca Buchanan, both white, were charged in May 1795 with receiving stolen goods from Negro Harry Sawyer. Ann Brooks was convicted in October 1749 of "dealing with Negroes and of receiving stolen goods" by a Philadelphia court. Mary Dickey, Phoebe Duglis (or Douglas), and Catherine Ingram were others deemed guilty of receiving stolen goods in the city, some of them from black thieves. Women like Clarke and Buchanan saw to it that the large quantity of rum stolen from financier Robert Morris by five slaves in 1780 ultimately found its way into the hands of white Philadelphians. Black women performed the same services. Negress Sarah Craig, the slave of James Oellers, was convicted of being a fence in 1790, but she had long before earned a reputation for that enterprise.[106]

Finally, urban property crime at the end of the eighteenth century opens a perspective on race and crime in Pennsylvania. Only at the very bottom of Philadelphia society were there wide-ranging and intimate relations between black and white Philadelphians.[107] More than any other Pennsylvanians, African Americans were city people, and they were newcomers to the city, immigrants, and emphatically poor. Crime and liberty are closely related. Criminals "take liberties"; they refuse to be bound by the rules that civil society erects. And if and when they are caught, modern criminals usually find that society punishes them by taking away their liberty. But taking liberties with the laws and forfeiting your liberty does not fit well the situation of most African Americans before 1865. For much of America's past, African Americans were not at liberty to commit crimes in the number and variety that free men and women were. And, too, the punishment for slaves' crimes was not the loss of liberty, which most never enjoyed. Of course, there were black crimes before 1865—homicides, thefts, arson, and more—but for all that, theirs was not the experience or record of white crime in America. This anomaly of African American life, one of many, this exclusion from the majority experience of crime and punishment, receded once they were liberated or emancipated, especially after 1865. The thirteenth amendment, abolishing slavery, therefore, opened a new chapter in the history of law enforcement and crime among African Americans, a chapter very different from the previous one.[108]

Before emancipation, Americans had always been acutely conscious of the difference that emancipation would make, if and when it came. Hardly anyone was more aware of that than Thomas Jefferson. "We have the wolf by the ears," he wrote, "and we can neither hold nor safely let him go." Looking to a hypothetical future that included free black men and women, Jefferson became frightened, because he feared blacks. So many centuries of slavery, Jefferson believed, had created so much hatred and resentment among blacks that there could never be a peaceful biracial society in America, at least in Virginia, where more than half of all African Americans lived. Other Virginians and other Americans shared Jefferson's fear. "Slaves are devils," wrote planter Landon Carter, "and to make them otherwise than slaves will be to set devils free."[109] For men who deplored slavery and wished it had never arisen and thrived in Virginia, the dilemma of abolishing it was that of freeing the wolf. From this fear flowed the logic of Jefferson's only proposal for emancipation, in 1776; it provided for the expulsion from Virginia of freedmen when they attained adulthood. But when they were expelled from Virginia, where would they go? Whose angry blacks would they become then? From the perspective of the history of crime, the specter of freedmen was the specter of a criminal class—in fact, the preeminent candidate for a criminal class in America. These liberated men and women, especially because of the abuse they had endured, would not respect the limits and laws that white society had erected.

The fear of crime and some criminal class was not confined to Chesapeake society or even the whole South. As Edmund S. Morgan so disarmingly asked, "Is America still colonial Virginia writ large?"[110] Would freedmen from the South, whenever emancipation came, move to the North? Would they become the North's angry, poor class who might easily turn to crime? Northern states, once they had emancipated their own slaves, had an interest in maintaining Southern slavery in order to stop or postpone their potential problem of crime and poverty, allaying their greatest fear. When blacks perforce remained in the slave South, they could not commit crimes in the North. The frightening actuality of newly freed African Americans fully and finally arose in 1865. But it surfaced first in Pennsylvania in 1780 with the first abolition law in the United States.

Opponents of abolition in Pennsylvania defended slavery for many different reasons, some of them quite familiar then and since. One reason was the crime they predicted would follow the manumission of slaves in Pennsylvania. Whether they sincerely feared a wave of black crime or were cynically whipping up Negrophobia among whites is not clear. In any case, in the press in Pennsylvania in 1780–81, there was the forecast of increased black crimes. In the *Pennsylvania Journal*, for example, a writer predicted:

we may fear [emancipation] will be a greater injury than all the service they [Negroes] have ever been to America; and that a new kind of bondage would be introduced, viz. White people reduced to perpetual fear and distress by the blacks. . . . We could not otherwise than expect ill consequences from having a large number of free Negroes in the heart of this country, especially if freed upon a supposition that justice required it. . . . We might expect the free [Negroes] and the bound would colleague together, connive at and conceal theft, murder, rapine, etc. etc. We might readily expect a great increase in mulattos . . . we might look for perpetual contests and broils, and to hear a country ringing with their quarrels [between whites and blacks].[111]

Abolition came to Pennsylvania, but whether this predicted infernal future accompanied it depends partly upon the record of black crime in the state and the interpretation of the record.

In the beginning, liberty had not been intended for African Americans in Pennsylvania. Slavery came to the colony in 1682, and Pennsylvanians who owned slaves started with William Penn and continued through Benjamin Franklin. In subjection these Pennsylvanians, like their peers in the South, raised few problems for the justice system (whatever was the case for the masters). On the other hand, at all times before 1780 some black Pennsylvanians were free, and in theory, liable to be prosecuted for their crimes like white men and women. While defining crime for them is less perplexing than for slaves, counting their violations of the law is impossible. Before 1780, individual justices handled minor offenses involving blacks and they left almost no evidence of their judicial business. The more serious crimes of free blacks and slaves were overseen by "Negro Tryals"—special courts for trying African Americans—for which there are even fewer records.[112] Unless comments regarding black crime appeared in Council or Assembly records, newspaper accounts, or private papers, offenses ascribed to individual blacks are almost entirely lost. The extant records contain forty prosecutions of blacks before 1780.

Highly visible cases of black crime dot the legal landscape before and after 1780. In 1690 a Sussex County (later Delaware) slave killed his master, a man named Futcher, and was burned to death for his crime, the only such burning or lynching in Pennsylvania's first century and a quarter.[113] Between 1700 and 1703 two blacks were brought to court on suspicion of murder, triggering sustained debate over the proper forum before which to try them. The first was "a Certain Negro named Jack" accused of murdering the son of William Rakestraw in December 1700.[114] Slaves Quashy and Tony were exiled after being convicted of burglary in 1707. In August 1737, a black man was convicted of "willfully setting on fire a dwelling House" in Bristol Township, Philadelphia County.[115] These were highly visible cases; cases of more commonplace crimes attributed to blacks cannot be retrieved.

White Pennsylvanians expected criminal behavior from blacks and watched them closely. Many viewed them as inferior, congenitally disobedient, mutinous, and habitually drawn to theft and disorder.[116] Routinely there were rumors and accusations of stealing pigs, chickens, butter, eggs, vegetables, buckles, handkerchiefs, coins, jackets, and other household or clothing items. Blacks were accused of being drunk and away from masters without a proper pass. "Negroes in and about the City" persisted in participating in illegal and unruly gatherings and in exhibiting "insolent Behaviour" and were periodically brought before authorities to answer for their conduct. In one instance, James Logan, whose house had been torched by a black man, questioned the arson trial, which convicted the suspect. He urged the man—guilty or innocent—be executed anyway, as a lesson to the increasingly "insolent" blacks within the city.[117] Blacks were frequently convicted of being pickpockets. Probably the most typical crime by Pennsylvania's black population, however, was running away. Even governors fell victim to this crime. Two of Governor Sir William Keith's young male slaves ran away from him in April 1723.[118] Newspapers were filled with ads seeking the return of such runaways.[119]

Some violent crimes were charged to blacks. An unnamed black male was executed in 1721 for housebreaking. Two slaves were exiled after committing burglary in February 1707.[120] Another black male was convicted of attempting to ravish an eleven-year-old white female in July 1735. A year later Negro James, a slave, was sentenced to die for rape. Negro Sampson was confined under suspicion of burning a building in August 1737. In March 1738/39 an African American man threw pebbles against the Philadelphia home of John Boyd. When asked to leave, "he gave [Boyd and his neighbors] fancy and very unbecoming Language," and when pressed further he killed Boyd with a brick. During an argument in March 1741, a young Negro male threw a chisel at a seventeen-year-old white male and struck him in the groin, causing him to bleed to death.[121] Four blacks were executed before the Revolution. But all told, this thin surviving record of black crime before 1780 hardly warrants the prediction of internecine conflict served up by the writer in the *Pennsylvania Journal* and others.

The arrival of the Revolution and the new state constitution of 1776 confused the prosecution of crimes by African Americans. The constitution provided "that in all prosecutions for Criminal Offenses a Man hath a right to . . . a speedy Tryal by an Impartial Jury of the Country." Some Pennsylvanians, among them the state's first attorney-general, apparently interpreted that provision to include black as well as white offenders. Between 1776 and 1778 courts were closed. However, when courts reopened late in 1778 blacks were prosecuted there rather than in "Negro Tryals." Two black males and a black female were tried on misdemeanor charges in a Bucks County court of quarter sessions in June 1778. The following August Chester County officials prosecuted two black males, one for assault and the other for felony theft. In November of that same year a Lancaster court was the scene of the indictment and trial of Negress Hanna.[122]

In 1780 legislation ended the confusion. Pennsylvania formally abolished its "Negro Tryals" and thereafter prosecuted blacks in its mainstream courts.[123] The law provided that black and mulatto Pennsylvanians be granted "the common blessings they were by nature entitled to," including "equal justice." Among the new legal rights bestowed upon the state's black and mulatto population, whether free or unfree, was the right "to be adjudged, corrected and punished in like manner as . . . the other inhabitants of [the] state."[124]

For African Americans the public record of prosecutions equivalent to that of whites begins with the 1780 change. The most sweeping revelation from the data is African Americans' share of all criminal charges (1780–1800), 2.8 percent. In the 1790 census African Americans probably numbered 2.4 percent of the state population and in the 1800 census, 2.7 percent.[125] They were charged, in sum, just about as often as their numbers would warrant. In the official records they differed little from other people. Nonetheless, their 2.8 percent share could be questioned as misleading because of some dark figure of unrecorded black crime. Such a question might arise from the fact that they were a socially marginalized people. In most other times and places they and people like them, when they committed crimes against each other, found that magistrates ignored them and their violations of the law. Yet the possibility that whites did not proceed against black offenders and that magistrates did not prosecute them flies in the face of the contemporary narrative record.

In that record whites had broadcast that they were anxious about black crime. The novelty of the first American manumission law in 1780, the continuing private manumissions in Pennsylvania, and an influx of blacks from other states and beyond raised an unmistakable furor about the consequences of freeing blacks. Without the constraints of slavery, blacks would run amok, proslavery writers claimed. Ignorant and unacculturated, or angry and vengeful, for various reasons the freedmen and women would boost the crime rate. Experiences with them during the early years of the Revolution had shown, the critics argued, that blacks were rebels, enemies of the new America.[126] They were political as well as personal criminals. This public abuse revealed and advanced Negro "typing"—that is, raised expectations that some people are especially criminal and require close observation and energetic prosecution.

Detractors of black freedmen and women were not alone in scrutinizing the conduct of African Americans. Abolitionists and other friends of black Pennsylvanians had a monumental point to prove about the relative effects of nature and nurture upon black behavior. In this place and time, the first known to Western reformers where chattel slavery was being abolished, former slaves could prove their ability to transcend the limitations of slavery upon their conduct and intellect. If African Americans in Pennsylvania satisfied some arguable standard of accomplishment, allegations of the inherent inferiority of black people could be exposed as groundless and thereafter impeached as white prejudice or greed.[127] Black crime would figure into any such estimate of blacks' civilized, acculturated, or trustworthy condition. From either hostile or friendly quarters, then, black Pennsylvanians were monitored. There are, therefore, good reasons to expect that the criminal prosecutions of these African Americans more closely approximated their violations of law than did the prosecutions of whites. In fact, black prosecutions may have exceeded their violations.

The black crimes that the public experienced and prosecuted were overwhelmingly property crimes—three-quarters of the black total. And the number appears all the more striking when compared with the number for whites; the property portion among blacks was two and a half times larger than it was among whites (Table 7.10). Among blacks, all other varieties of crime had minor significance; that includes violent crimes, the most common variety of crime among white Pennsylvanians.

Tables 7.11 and 7.12 display the other two most conspicuous facts about the criminal record of African Americans—that prosecutions of them rose abruptly after 1793 and that they occurred very largely in Phil-

TABLE 7.10. CRIMINAL ACCUSATIONS BY RACE AND GENDER IN PENNSYLVANIA, 1780–1800

	African American		White		African American	White
	Men	Women	Men	Women	Subtotal	Subtotal
Assault and homicide						
N	80	9	6317	701	89	7018
% of row	92.1	7.9	90.4	9.6	1.3	98.7
% of column	16.5	4.3	36.3	28.5		
% of race					15.8	36.7
Property						
N	313	112	4973	851	425	5824
% of row	73.6	26.4	85.4	14.6	6.8	93.2
% of column	73.8	79.4	29.5	37.3		
% of race					75.2	30.5
Sex/morals						
N	12	5	828	389	17	1217
% of row	70.6	29.4	68.0	32.0	1.4	98.6
% of column	2.8	3.5	4.9	17.0		
% of race					3.0	6.4
Public order						
N	19	15	4640	328	34	4968
% of row	55.9	44.1	93.4	6.6	0.7	99.3
% of column	4.5	10.6	27.6	14.4		
% of race					6.0	26.0
Crimes against state						
N	0	0	79	13	0	92
% of row			85.9	14.2	0.0	100.0
% of column			0.5	0.6		
% of race					0.0	0.5
Column total	424	141	16837	2282	565	19119
% of grand total	2.2	0.7	85.5	11.6	2.9	97.1

adelphia.[128] Philadelphia and its urbanized county precincts accounted for 68.1 percent of all prosecutions of blacks in Pennsylvania, 1682–1800.[129] York County, with the second largest black population in the state, prosecuted only eight. Of the western or frontier counties, Westmoreland and Northumberland harbored the largest number of black inhabitants; together they tried only seven crimes by blacks. Bedford County charged none. The low levels of prosecution were also caused by the composition of the black population in the rural counties; the counties had high numbers of females and youngsters. In 1783, for instance, 24 of 55 slaves in Lancaster were female and most of the 55 were children.[130] Moreover, the black population of rural Pennsylvania was moving to Philadelphia.

Between 1780 and 1800, the black population of Pennsylvania became

TABLE 7.11. ANNUAL CRIMINAL ACCUSATIONS AGAINST AFRICAN AMERICANS IN
PENNSYLVANIA, 1780–1800

	Count	Percent	Cumulative percent
1780	19	3.3	3.3
1781	16	2.8	6.1
1782	11	1.9	8.1
1783	4	0.7	8.8
1784	11	1.9	10.7
1785	6	1.1	11.8
1786	10	1.8	13.5
1787	12	2.1	15.6
1788	21	3.7	19.3
1789	9	1.6	20.9
1790	14	2.5	23.3
1791	16	2.8	26.1
1792	16	2.8	28.9
1793	11	1.9	30.9
1794	28	4.9	35.8
1795	49	8.6	44.4
1796	74	13.0	57.4
1797	48	8.4	65.8
1798	52	9.1	74.9
1799	76	13.3	88.2
1800	67	11.8	100.0
Total	570	100.0	

TABLE 7.12. GEOGRAPHIC DISTRIBUTION OF CRIMINAL ACCUSATIONS AGAINST
AFRICAN AMERICANS, 1780–1800

County/city	Accusations	Percent
Philadelphia (city)	250	43.9
Philadelphia	138	24.2
Chester	41	7.2
Cumberland	27	4.7
Lancaster	25	4.4
Bucks	23	4.0
Dauphin	21	3.7
Franklin	9	1.6
York	8	1.4
Fayette	6	1.1
Huntingdon	6	1.1
Berks	4	0.7
Northumberland	4	0.7
Westmoreland	3	0.5
Washington	2	0.4
Northampton	2	0.4
unknown	1	0.2
Total	570	100.0

largely urban. The free black population of Philadelphia increased four times over between 1783 and 1790 and reached 2,000 persons, according to Gary B. Nash. In 1790, black men and women in the city represented 20.3 percent of the black population of the state. In 1800, the African Americans in the state probably numbered 16,270, and 43.8 percent of them lived in Philadelphia. Between 1790 and 1800 the city's black population had grown 210 percent.[131] The city was the confluence of many streams of black migration, the deliberate choice of most blacks and the providential destination of others. First and largest was the movement of freedmen and women from the Pennsylvania countryside. But Philadelphia also became, in Nash's words, "the destination of and endless stream of . . . fugitives from slavery" from Pennsylvania and states up and down the Atlantic seaboard. As Southerners and Southern slave states became more hostile toward private manumissions and freedmen, Southern abolitionists sent manumitted freedmen north to Philadelphia to begin a better life, they hoped.

By far the greatest influence on black population and society in the city in the 1790s was the flood of blacks from Saint Domingue. In 1793, Black rebellion had broken out in the French colony—which became the independent nation of Haiti in 1804—and Creole French planters fled the island, often bringing their slaves with them. Between 1792 and 1798, about 900 black Saint Dominguans arrived in Philadelphia, increasing the black population of the city by about 25 percent. There were slightly more women than men and they were overwhelmingly young—Nash estimates that less than one-sixth were over 21 years old. Their youth makes them more apt to turn up as criminals than if they were in their thirties, forties, or older.[132]

Figure 7.4 illustrates the relative numbers of accusations in city and countryside and the exorbitant growth of accusations that began after 1793. Closer inspection of the city accusations in the 1790s offers clues to the condition and behavior of black Philadelphians. As exhibited in Table 7.13, the crimes were overwhelmingly thefts, and thefts were very unremarkable behavior from people who were new to the city, inexperienced, ill-equipped, some speaking no English, and as poor as anyone was likely to be in that time and place.[133] An acute observer of the poor in the city recorded that "the most afflictive and accumulated distress" was found among "the Irish Emigrants and the French Negroes."[134] The soaring number of thefts after 1794 coincides especially with the arrival in Philadelphia of exotic peoples from Saint Domingue and the slave South. It follows, too, the immense distraction from normal public business that the yellow fever epidemic of 1793 created. Philadelphia publications averred that blacks committed an unduly large portion of the city's crime, but they put the blame precisely upon newly arrived and

TABLE 7.13. CRIMINAL ACCUSATIONS AGAINST AFRICAN-AMERICANS IN
PHILADELPHIA, 1780–1800

	Assault	Sex/ morals	Public order	Property crimes	Homicide	Total
1780					9	9
1781	3		3	1	1	8
1782				3	2	5
1783	2					2
1784			1	3		4
1785	2			2		4
1786				3		3
1787				1		1
1788						0
1789				2		2
1790	3			4		7
1791			1	8		9
1792				6		6
1793	1			4		5
1794	2			20		22
1795	3	1	3	26		33
1796	4		4	55		63
1797	2		1	36	1	40
1798	3	2	1	38		44
1799	1		3	66		70
1800	4		2	43		49
Total	30	3	19	330	4	386

poor "foreign" blacks rather than Pennsylvania's "domestic" blacks.[135] A few names of the accused in the dockets show them to have been Dominguans—Lacourt, Lurvee, Cherbland, Delphine, Tuossant, Jacque. But most docket names are English. Quantifying the names proves little, since the black newcomers or court clerks Anglicized French names, much as Germans themselves and court clerks did with German names.[136]

Among rural African Americans in Pennsylvania, property crimes comprised 52.8 percent of their total crimes (1780–1800), but among urban blacks, 85.5 percent. Among urban whites property crimes comprised 40.2 percent of their total in the same years. However, in the years 1793–1800, the property-crimes percentage for urban whites declined to 33.6 percent. Meanwhile, that percentage for urban blacks rose to 88.1. Table 7.14 represents the rough rate of all crimes and property crimes for the two races.[137] From these data a dramatic change appears after 1794 in the rate of prosecutions for all crimes for the two races. For the first time the black rate exceeded the white—and that is in comparison with earlier years when the white rate doubled or even tripled the black

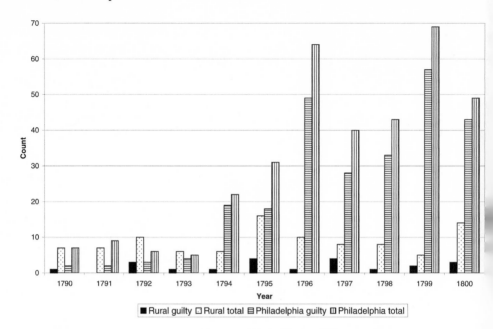

Figure 7.4. Judicial outcomes of accusations against African Americans, 1790–1800.

TABLE 7.14. CRIMINAL ACCUSATIONS PER 100,000 POPULATION BY RACE BY YEAR IN PHILADELPHIA CITY AND COUNTY, 1790–1800

| | African Americans | | Whites | |
	All charges	Property	All charges	Property
1790	337	192	717	355
1791	358	318	690	355
1792	203	203	673	212
1793	148	118	453	132
1794	576	523	642	256
1795	775	611	691	223
1796	1364	1172	917	243
1797	780	702	455	189
1798	791	683	601	247
1799	1167	1100	746	250
1800	761	668	358	93
1790–1800	709	622	611	221

rate. After 1794 the black rate handily outpaced the white. As for just property crimes—the crimes indigent blacks were most likely to commit—early in the decade (1790–1794) these did not exceed the white rates. Then the black rates outdid the white rates even by multiples of six! This increase was the effect, again, of the endless and penniless "stream of fugitives of slavery." For the 1790s, it would be more appropriate to call it a flood rather than a stream. The figures complement what Philadelphians related about the prospects of black men and women. In 1790, when their crimes were less a problem than those of whites, the Pennsylvania Abolition Society recorded that "the negroes [of the city] have been so universally employed that the [assistance] committee has had little to do." Benjamin Rush said that white employers preferred black workers to white. Free blacks, writes Nash, "were remarkably successful in finding employment."[138] That happy situation did not last long.

Property offenses, and especially the more serious ones like burglary, show that African Americans had ample opportunity to associate or collaborate. Accused black men seldom acted alone, and in most instances they associated with other blacks. Four slaves joined Negro Daniel, for instance, during the 1780 theft of four hundred gallons of rum owned by Robert Morris. But whites figured in their schemes, too. Of the sixteen burglaries for which blacks were prosecuted, ten of the cases involved white collaborators. Black thieves often turned to whites to fence their stolen wares.[139]

Of the other crimes by African Americans recorded in Pennsylvania, violent crimes ranked second to theft or property crime. But black violence was not a problem, especially when compared with that of whites, among whom it was the most common infraction, and two and a half times more common than black violence (Table 7.10). It is conceivable that violent crimes by blacks against blacks were overlooked. White detractors of blacks may not have cared what blacks did to each other, and the friends of blacks, from the opposite concern, may have hidden these crimes in order to preserve their argument about black civility. But such conduct was not likely. And as for blacks assaulting whites, these crimes would not have been overlooked.

African Americans were accused in seven murders after 1776, including several prosecutions for infanticide. In five of those cases other African Americans proved to be the victims. There is no record of any slave killing his or her master or mistress during this period. Negro Peter was convicted in September 1782 for stabbing Negro James to death. Bob Waldren (who appeared in the dockets as both Negro Bob and Mulatto Bob) killed Negro David, a New Jersey slave, with an axe in 1795. Alice Clifton and Mulatto Elizabeth were tried for killing their own children.[140] Only five African Americans were prosecuted after 1776 for rape and one for attempted rape. From all the extant data, cases of rape did not increase during and after the Revolution. What did increase was public concern for rapes of white women allegedly by black males. Although only seven executions for rape can be confirmed from all of Pennsylvania, four of those clearly were black men and a fifth probably was—and all their purported victims were white.[141]

When an oppressed or subservient population commits violent crimes it is reasonable to ask whether the violence arose from their condition or from motives of revenge or rebellion against their oppressions. Fearful white Pennsylvanians certainly believed that African Americans had cause to be vengeful and recited their fears in arguments before 1780 against manumitting black men. Homicide and assault obviously qualify as violent and malicious acts of revenge and rebellion, and rape may too. Rape of white women has been interpreted as a form of rebellion and revenge by oppressed black males. In this case, rape may be understood as blacks wresting from white oppressors something the whites highly valued, their women.[142]

How many African Americans accused of these violent acts were motivated by racial oppression is difficult to discern from laconic records. In the majority of black homicides whites were not the victims. In the case of assault, victims were rarely named. But the foremost consideration is not the identity of the victims, but the pacific record of the black community in the eighteenth century. African Americans had reason to be angry, but anger provoked few of them to act upon it in an overt, threatening way toward whites—whatever whites believed and said about the blacks among them.[143]

The argument on behalf of black resistance, revenge, or rebellion, may be taken to a more subtle level in the case of nonviolent offenses. Historians Gerald Mullin, Peter Wood, and Eugene Genovese, among others, have reminded us that those rebellious blacks, slaves especially, can act more subtly than murdering, assaulting, raping, and burning. Such subtle acts include work slowdowns, verbal abuse, and feigning ignorance or incapacity. None of these was subject to prosecution. The theft of property was. The pilfering of property was one means by which a black man or woman could attack those possessing what he or she did not. Raids upon the corncrib, the chicken coop, the smokehouse, the hog pen, and the still may indeed have bolstered the self-esteem of black thieves, and narrowly challenged white autonomy.

However, the evidence that the Pennsylvania thefts were deliberate, calculated acts of malice, revenge, or rebellion is meager. The purpose of the theft appears partly in the nature of the goods stolen by desperately poor people. Blacks generally purloined life's necessities: cloth, clothing items, food, small amounts of money, or property that could easily be turned into cash, like watches, rings, and other jewelry. The actions of Chester County's Jesse Shriver, the mulatto slave of Edward Vernon, were typical of most black thieves. In 1784 he was accused of stealing items described by the court as "of a Tryfling Nature." Secondly, delinquency that challenged or rectified imbalances of power appears all the less likely when one discovers that the victims of black thefts seemed most often to be housewives, small storekeepers, yeomen farmers, and mechanics, and not any élite. Robert Morris, who lost a large quantity of rum to slaves, was among the few truly wealthy Philadelphians victimized by black thieves—though black fences handled goods taken by whites from the homes of James Wilson and Charles Willson Peale. Additionally, most blacks charged were not repeat offenders. Less than five percent of them were prosecuted more than once.

Real, unambiguous acts of rebellion by African Americans were rare after 1776. No black faced charges of treason, misprision of treason, aiding the enemy, conspiracy, "being inimical to the Revolution," or of "actions detrimental to the American cause." None was attainted. Arson has been regarded as an expression of blacks' desire for rebellion and revenge. White Pennsylvanians alluded to it as "the crime of slaves and children." Lewis Miller, who captured early Pennsylvania in paintings and sketches, included a dramatic scene of Negroes torching York in 1803.[144] In the 1790s Americans all along the coast feverishly suspected that arsonists were abroad. Philadelphians were as much stricken as the troubled people in other ports and towns. Quaker diarist Elizabeth Drinker recorded rumors of arson in New York and elsewhere and the existence of a conspiracy among blacks to spread conflagration. Because other Philadelphians shared her fear city patrols were mounted and increased. Finally, the finger of blame and fear was pointed at the St. Dominguans—"those missionaries from hell."[145]

The judicial record, however, has nothing to corroborate these fears; cases of arson were almost negligible. The more suspicious or paranoid Pennsylvanians probably would have questioned the record, by arguing, for example, that arsonists are elusive, so that the thin judicial record underestimates the real danger. Nevertheless, the real and thin record points toward the opposite conclusion, since it contained only eight African Americans charged with arson, six of them after 1780. Cumberland's Negress Sukey was hanged for deliberately torching her master's barn and several smaller outbuildings in 1781 after, she alleged, he abused her verbally. Of those eight, three were females. Earlier, a black arsonist tried to fire the home of James Logan, one-time Chief Justice of Pennsylvania. When former slave Barrick Martin became angry with Susannah Morris of Lower Dublin Township, Philadelphia County, in

1784, he burned her barn.[146] None of the arson cases appeared related to the Revolution and politics.

Slaves and black servants running away from their masters did exemplify criminal rebellion. Philadelphia, as we have seen, became the destination of runaways from near and far. Newspaper advertisements attest that slaves in Pennsylvania had long run away, like slaves elsewhere. But running away increased after 1776 as confusion and dislocation racked Pennsylvania. Gary Nash has explained that Pennsylvania African Americans quickly absorbed the language and spirit of protest and freedom after 1765, and accordingly during the Revolution some ran to the British, convinced that they would be freed.[147] African American men and women in Pennsylvania also had even more artful means of defying the dominant white society and its conventions, which means sometimes tested prohibitions of the law and the tolerance of white society and magistrates. They did so by the way they dressed, gestured, shouted, sang, and played at dances, funerals, parades, and demonstrations, and through their language. In 1796, and periodically thereafter, the Pennsylvania Abolition Society warned them that their loud public appearances and fancy dress were offending whites.[148]

Blacks' behavior after dark seemed yet more suspect and troubling or threatening. After the first thirty years in Pennsylvania, whites were not prosecuted for lascivious, scandalous, or rowdy behavior. In fact, after 1760 such behavior became much more common among whites and almost entirely ignored by magistrates. Yet, if blacks indulged in the same behavior, some Pennsylvanians became anxious. Philadelphian Charles Biddle, for example, while trying to trace his runaway black servant boy, was shocked to discover numerous parties where "whites, blacks, and mulattos [were] all dancing together."[149] Some slaves verbally tested their masters and mistresses and argued with them or disobeyed them. Philadelphia's Vagrancy Dockets are sprinkled with blacks confined for quarreling with masters or mistresses, or for being belligerent. Negro Henry, confined in June 1790, was typical of those incarcerated for "misbehaving himself toward his Master," as was Negro Dick who ended in jail after "conducting himself very disorderly and absenting himself from his master."[150] The slaves of the white Dominguans typically became indentured servants to their prior owners, and these masters found some to be insubordinate. Madame Magnan, in probably the best example, committed four of her servants—Andre, Amades, Bunno, and Zemire—to hard labor for being "disobedient, stubborn, and untractable; and utterly refusing to obey their said mistress."[151]

It is possible that in some respect or respects African American women deserve more attention than what they receive from being considered just black or just women. The combination of color and gender may have particularities associated with it respecting crime. That possibility appears most clearly in the case of property crime. As a portion of all their criminal accusations, property crime occupied a much larger share than in the case of white women—79.4 percent compared with 37.3 (Table 7.10) Among crimes by their race, black women had a larger share of all black property crime than white women had of all white property crime—26.4 percent compared with 14.6. Property crime, which was overwhelmingly petty larceny, described black women as no others in late-eighteenth-century Pennsylvania. They were almost certainly as poor as black men, but also had even fewer options for maintaining themselves than black men had.

Their distinctiveness appears also in violations of public order. Here they did not exceed white women in their respective shares of that crime, but within their race they had 44.1 percent of the charges, whereas white women had merely 6.6 percent of white violations. Broken down into the precise charges, thirteen of the total fifteen were cases of disorderly houses (8) and tippling houses (5). The disorderly houses may have involved prostitution, although that was not specified. Here the case may have been black women gaining a living on the periphery of respectable society when choices were few.[152]

Since property crimes loomed so large among black women's crimes compared to white women, they had a smaller share in other categories. This smaller share appeared first in assaults and next in sexual offenses. Compared with white women they appeared neither violent nor sexually delinquent. In neither of these cases, however, were the ratios among black women's offenses distinctive from those among black men's.

In the years after the 1780 abolition law, abolitionists and friends of African Americans labored on behalf of justice and mercy for black defendants. Jurymen and judges called to weigh their alleged crimes also petitioned the Supreme Executive Council in their behalf, a proclivity that doubtless they would have tempered had blacks posed a greater threat to the stability of Pennsylvania society. Numerous white neighbors of Barrick Martin sought mercy in his behalf after his conviction for arson in 1784. When Negress Sarah was convicted of larceny in the city court in 1785, white jurors asked that she be shown leniency because of "the severity of the Service she was oblig'd to perform, the helpless and destitute Situation she was in, and some harsh treatment which . . . she had received of her mistress." Alice Clifton did not die for her infanticide conviction in 1787 because influential white citizens in Philadelphia rallied to her cause. During her trial this young, poor, uneducated black woman had not one but two of the city's best attorneys acting in her behalf. Only four blacks were executed between 1776 and 1783.[153] This exemplary philanthropic work has obscured somewhat the workaday operation of the justice system in Philadelphia, where most blacks in Pennsylvania were prosecuted. There the prospects were not happy for most of the indicted, black or white.

The anxiety or even phobia that the new black population of Philadelphia generated among white residents had a quick, obvious effect in the resolution of charges brought against blacks in the city. Figure 7.4 shows the change that distinguished the years 1794–1800 from earlier ones: indictments soared and convictions of blacks did so as well. Just as clearly, however, the change occurred only in the city. Rural Pennsylvanians did not share the anxiety of city residents over black crime and new black immigrants, because they did not experience increasing numbers of blacks. In many ways, the countryside was demographically, socially, and economically more stable than the city.

Philadelphia grand juries from 1794 through 1800 indicted in 81.8 percent of the charges brought against whites whereas they indicted in 94.7 of charges against blacks.[154] Then, in the workings of the trial juries a more glaring disparity appeared: juries convicted blacks of 76.7 percent of the charges against them but only 22.1 percent in cases of whites (1794–1800). The juries were almost surely all white men and, in that pool, were probably picked in a reasonably unbiased manner. Their opinions and suspicion of blacks very likely represented the opinion of the white men generally in the city. Later in the judicial process, almost one in five of the charges against whites came to no recorded resolution. But blacks enjoyed no such lapse of attention by prosecutors or other functionaries in the justice system; only 3.4 percent of their charges escaped judicial resolution.[155] Meanwhile in the rural counties nothing similar occurred. Prosecutions rose, but also fell, and there were comparatively few. In most years after 1793, conviction rates of blacks were below 25 percent. The rural black population was, to repeat, declining. Rural blacks evoked little fear of crime and rebellion.

In the era of emancipation in Pennsylvania, the population of free African Americans grew beyond what the emancipation law would have led observers to expect.[156] Had the growing numbers of free blacks been native Pennsylvanians only, there are good reasons for expecting that far fewer white Pennsylvanians would have become agitated about black crime. The growing black population, however, free and not free, did not remain exclusively old Pennsylvanians; the immigrants from abroad and the southern states added impressively to its numbers. As a result, Philadelphians discovered, to their minds, plenty of black crimes and energetically prosecuted the suspected criminals. This problem was as much one of immigration and poverty as it was of race. White racism may have been merely latent when, before the 1790s, there was so little to object to about black behavior, or the racism may have largely originated then. In any case, immigrant poverty in the late 1790s either resuscitated or initiated racism and discrimination.

The possibility that emancipation in Pennsylvania would prove that racism was baseless suffered a severe blow. The emerging public record of black theft and other crime raised the burden of proof upon abolitionists and friends of equality who intended to show that environment decisively determined behavior of black men and women, as it did with whites and all races. Would the accuser of a black thief "cut him some slack" because the accused was poor and new to the city? Or, would he accuse the black man or woman of congenital criminality? Decades earlier Quaker abolitionist John Woolman explained that confusing physical conditions with character had started or extended racial prejudice: when blacks are dressed in rags, work for others at drudgery and in the dirt, and have no property or power, people come to think they are beneath others "in nature."[157] In the 1790s visibly more African Americans came to fit the physical description that Woolman penned, and whites treated them as though they deserved that condition.

The 1790s were too short a time to see how records of crime, race, equality, and prejudice would play out, or to see whether the black crime "wave" would recede and African Americans enjoy equitable treatment and a better civic reputation. Historians Gary Nash and Roger Lane have provided the sequel, however. Nash found that African Americans' experience in the early nineteenth century "shattered the hopes of those who had believed they were approaching a new era of racial unity." "Hostility toward free blacks," "racial tension and sporadic violence" only increased.[158] Slowly, over the first thirty years of the century, blacks were excluded from economic opportunities in incipient industries like textiles and shoemaking. With the new Irish immigration of that century, blacks were ousted from the mainstays of their employment, like stevedoring and the service trades.[159] That was the upshot of the first emancipation.

In some respects, the problem of black crime—or the perception and fear of black character and crime—is not a problem unique to African Americans. In America before 1800, there was a problem of Scots-Irish and their violent and criminal ways; in the nineteenth century there was problem of Irish crime; and in the twentieth, Italian crime.[160] They were all problems of immigration and poverty, like those of poor Caribbean and southern black migrants. And yet, black crime, like the black experience generally, is unique in America. The "waves" of crime generated by Scots-Irish, Irish, Italians, and other newcomers to America receded as the newcomers assimilated and were employed in American commerce, industry, and government. But they were different. As Lane concludes, economically "Germans, Irish, Italian, and Jewish . . . moved past the blacks;" blacks "were not only denied a chance to grab at the fabled American 'ladder of opportunity' but in many cases were actually kicked off."[161] And whereas the other ethnic groups on the ladder put their criminal record behind them, many blacks, Lane argues, did not have that choice. Making a life on the periphery of the legitimate economy, and supplying "legitimate" people with whatever they demurred at supplying themselves, blacks lived at risk of arrest and punishment, bad health, bodily injury, and violent death.[162] For black men and women, the past appears to be cycles of enthusiasm and frustration, from which escape was futile.

At the end of the eighteenth century, Pennsylvanians agreed that they were suffering from an abundance of crime—probably more than Pennsylvanians had ever suffered, they believed. They agreed on little else. Pennsylvanians carped over the blame for their crime. The system was to blame—the magistrates or the courts or the justices or the constabulary; or if it were not the system, it was the naïve reformers who loosed convicts upon the public; or, if neither of them, then it was the poor and the many, or the rich and the few; or it was the city environment. Blaming was political too; élitist or Federalist critics favored one analysis, and populist or republican critics favored another. In this respect the end-of-the-century debate over crime anticipated so many public, political brawls over the causes of crime in America in the next two centuries.

No one contended that there were no problems, or that the problem had been solved, or that there was no conceivable solution to the problem—this in the colony and state which had experimented with solutions more than any other in America. But few or none regarded crime frankly as the price Pennsylvanians had to pay for being what they were and wished to continue being—free, liberal, expansive, and acquisitive. Rather, crime was exceptional, morbid, and despicable. In the coming century, they would continue trying to solve the problem, recycle some past remedies, and attempt new ones—like professional police and penitentiaries—but with no more satisfaction than they felt in 1800.

Epilogue

> [Pennsylvanians must] not . . . give away any thing of Liberty and
> Property that at present they do . . . enjoy.
> —*William Penn, 1687*

Crime violates social order, harmony, and peace. Society is the contested
ground where the forces of disorder like crime, famine, disease, war,
and death contend with order. Crime is the omitted fifth horseman. In
some societies, crimes occur so seldom that men and women scarcely
need to pause in their daily routines. Elsewhere crime destroys routines,
fractures society, and creates anarchy. In the worst cases, obtaining food,
clothing, and shelter, bearing and rearing children, and other vital activities are so obstructed that men and women quit trying. In different ways
people work to resist disorder and bring peace, harmony, and productiv-
ity into their marriages, families, neighborhoods, companies, nations,
and world. The most obvious and least subtle way to preserve order is to
rely upon laws, courts, police, and armies to stop criminals and alien
enemies. But there are more subtle ways to encourage order and
peace—ways that are equally as important as laws, typically less intrusive,
and far more ubiquitous than courts, police, and armies.[1] These forces
include custom (in its linguistic, familial, ethnic, religious, and many
other expressions) and commerce. Whether a society is orderly and
peaceful or disorderly and criminal, social scientists who explain the
peace or disorder must examine these subtle forces of custom, political
economy, and commerce as well as the obvious inhibitors like police,
courts, and punishment.

   This work depicts early Pennsylvania as a society belonging to the second category, a society troubled by crime and disorder, and it has tried
to specify how custom, political economy, and commerce affected crime
in Pennsylvania. Most of the conditions of life in Pennsylvania that
affected crime belong under the rubric liberalism, not surprisingly,
since Pennsylvania was a liberal society by design and historical coinci-

dence. Liberalism prescribes how power should be apportioned in civil society among the venerable entities of government, religion, custom, economics, and the people as they participated in any of these. Lockean liberals presumed that the impulses of human behavior were more often altruistic and constructive than selfish and destructive. Therefore, they anticipated more benefit than loss from freeing men and women from the historic constraints upon their behavior. Liberalism pointedly subordinates government, established religion, and authoritarian structures in general, while it encourages men and women to order their lives and communities voluntarily. In the seventeenth and eighteenth centuries liberal reformers were reacting against the immediate past, in which churches and governments had generated intolerable conflict and misery and had suppressed individual liberty.

The power that the reformers withdrew from established churches, hierarchical governments, and hereditary castes, they expected to distribute among the people, who would enjoy personal liberty and self-determination. Commerce too deserved to be freed from historic constraints. Enlightenment thinkers found nothing objectionable in increasing the reach and sway of free markets in society. Quite the opposite: they extolled them.[2] So, liberal Pennsylvania was open and tolerant, exceptionally free of authoritarian élites in public and religious life, unburdened by a military hierarchy, juridically humane for its day, and physically bountiful enough to win the acclaim of residents and visitors and to attract thousands hopeful of pursuing happiness.[3] This liberal society provided the context for surprisingly abundant crime in Pennsylvania. This intersection of liberalism with abundant crime was more than coincidence. Liberalism supported and stimulated crime. While it solved many past problems, it disclosed new ones.

Liberals may have misunderstood human nature and credited people with too much altruism or too little selfishness. That question will not be resolved here or by investigating only the case of Pennsylvania.[4] But Pennsylvania did not reckon with the number of base and selfish men and women who came to Pennsylvania. Pennsylvania's leaders had no adequate ideology, institutions, or fortunate conditions to solve their problem with crime—nor should they have. After all, they were liberal reformers. Typically when societies suffer disorder beyond tolerating, the impulse of their magistrates and citizens is to adjust liberal arrangements they had favored. They empower institutions they previously belittled, like the magistrates, courts, police, and armies, and constrict behavior and speech deemed destructive or disorderly. Much less often do anxious citizens think to rearrange their lives—their residence, mobility, religious commitments, education, and especially their gainful employment—in order to restore order. Pennsylvania's solutions were mostly of the former set, and hardly any of the latter.

With the insights afforded by centuries of experience and the revelations of the social sciences, the alternative for liberal states to curtailing personal liberties was to get potential criminals rooted socially, to hedge their liberty and license *with their consent*: bind them using the innumerable loyalties, obligations, routines, and "scripts" that come with settling into a community, following a vocation, marrying, starting a family, professing a religion, and expecting a better personal future. These sinews would push out of mind thoughts of quick, criminal gratification. To have accomplished this, eighteenth-century governments would have had to move beyond classical or Lockean liberalism and free-market economics and precociously taken on obligations to the public that modern social democracies perform. When no nation in the western world was doing so and when philosophers and economists were still infatuated with liberalism, one can hardly have expected Pennsylvania to have leapt a century and erected a social democracy.[5] All that Pennsylvania did was discover before the others the inadequacies of the Enlightenment.

Troubled by crime and disorder, Pennsylvania solved its problem neither by giving up its liberal premises, nor by erecting some authoritarian regime, nor by altering its customs and commerce. Had it done so, the necessary first step would have been closing itself to its nemesis, unlimited immigration. Immigrants constituted most of the transients, and transients constituted most of the criminals.[6] It was necessary either close Pennsylvania, or else deeply engage the men and women who arrived in order to meld them into a decent society. Community and decency could not thrive with the amount of transience present in Pennsylvania. Self-determination, freedom of choice, and geographical movement damaged long-term commitments to township, church, extended family, and affinity groups. All these institutions are capable of bringing stability and peace to society and have historically done so, as in the case of colonial New England. But in the open civic culture of Pennsylvania the institutions, and especially the churches, were shorn of their ability to counter the forces of disorder. Without physical stability, community suffers, not only in townships but also in churches and families. More subtly, the cultural situation in Pennsylvania obliged the institutions to eschew the work of creating stability(albeit reluctantly, according to some clerics and others).

More than any other institution, religion takes on the responsibility of correcting people's baser impulses. The mainstream churches in Pennsylvania, however, did too little correcting and prevention. Like other voluntary affinity groups in liberal society, they were open and most were evangelical, seeking converts as much as performing any other function such as education or nurture. In fact, they competed for members and created a marketplace of religion. Adam Smith himself drew the analogy between a market and religious choice in Pennsylvania.[7] The trouble for a decent society with making a market in religion was the essence of a market itself—the quid pro quo ethic of the buyer. A buyer does not desire to limit himself, subject himself to a group, or commit his property and energy to an institution without a calculated return. An organization composed of men and women who joined because of this ethic does not inspire fellow members to enhance their commitment to it. The ethic also rationalizes easy exit when benefits from belonging disappoint members and rival institutions proffer a more beneficial "deal" to them. Joining, exiting, treating people and groups instrumentally, or, on the other hand, living privately or singly, stripped most social institutions of "the incentives and penalties they can offer for socially prescribed or proscribed behavior." These behaviors made organizations anemic, and none more conspicuously than churches.[8]

Pennsylvanians committed little time and energy to the organizations that constitute civil society or to government service. They devoted themselves to few groups larger than their families. Most did not bother even to vote regularly. They were content to let a benevolent élite, mostly Quakers, run the province for almost a century. Above all else, Pennsylvanians wanted privacy and to be left alone. Their inclination to avoid voluntary, cooperative work outside the family was reinforced by the pervasive market economy. Collaborating with others in community takes work and compromise on behalf of an uncertain outcome. By comparison, economic transactions (quid pro quo) are precise and easy when markets are at hand. As is said of modern America, early Pennsylvania appears as "a society of people alive to what they can obtain effortlessly from the market and dead to what collective choice will yield only uncertainly."[9]

In the liberals' rebalancing of the components of human activity (government, custom, religion, and economics) and encouraging markets and commerce to grow at the expense of other institutions, the outcome should have been better. Voltaire, Montesquieu, Hume, and Adam Smith had asserted that commerce and free markets would produce the wholesome effects that commonly were expected from more familiar political reforms.[10] In particular, the free-market system of commerce would raise the standard of living, personal liberty, self-determination, individual dignity, and social peace. How? First, as Adam Smith explained, market systems were more efficient and increased wealth. When people began to enjoy greater abundance, achieving a higher standard of living than ever in history, a reasonable observer could predict that these better-off people would be less inclined to harm their fellows and more content to obey the laws. Beginning at least with Montesquieu and continuing to the present, some social philosophers and social scientists have linked markets and commerce with peace—not the peace of repression, but one based on contentment and the democratic will.[11] This surmise applies to early Pennsylvania, with its reputation as "the best poor man's country." All the more surprising then is the amount of crime in Pennsylvania and the United States—more than in some societies despised for their poverty. If the poor, the unfree, and the immigrants were to be afforded alternatives in their lives to committing crime, it would have taken more than the unimpeded operation of markets.

Smith also believed that men who participated in free markets behaved rationally, learned self-control, caution, and deferring gratification for the sake of their own fortune. They learned sociability. When all men follow their example, when all people become merchants, said Smith, the result is a decent civil society.[12] Finally, in the marketplace people treat each other as equals rather than as masters and servants or slaves, patrons and clients, or superior and inferior in general. "Nothing," Smith wrote, "tends so much to corrupt and enervate and debase the mind as dependency." No one is humiliated in the market, dispelling many motives for revenge and criminal behavior.[13]

That the public good would result from traders not caring about the butcher, baker, or brewer is probably the most successful counterintuitive assertion in modern times. But Smith failed to persuade some readers. "The war of each against all," Hegel called the market; "mutual pillaging is at its base," said Marx.[14] The market itself puts traders "under no obligation of candor, reasoned discussion or communication, compassion, sympathy, or responsibility except in those circumstances when, and to the degree that, it pays." Rather than thinking expansively and prudently, the trader is "small-minded, petty in calculation of advantage. He is more cunning than thoughtful or wise."[15] Making the point more simply, another modern critic concludes, "If we organize all our social relations by the same logic we use in seeking a good bargain, we cannot even have friends, for everyone else interferes with our ability to calculate conditions that will maximize our self-interest."[16]

Smith was no Pollyanna. He understood that the human impulses that drove the market and produced its efficiency—desire, covetousness, and rivalry—could jeopardize peace and community. And he provided that to keep these qualities in check, men and women use laws and government, family ties, and religion (rightly understood). The market ethic had to be confined to the exchange of goods and services and not employed in families, neighborhoods, churches, and other intimate realms. It must not become a universal ethic.[17] In early Pennsylvania, the market ethic grew beyond the exchange of goods and services and filled the recesses left by languishing social and public institutions. The social theorists of the Enlightenment addressed the paramount evils of their time—churches and regimes that had harmed men and arrested progress for centuries. They gave free commerce and markets a pass. Nevertheless, Pennsylvania quickly revealed how the redistribution of power in liberal society encouraged market-model aggression and a new set of misfortunes. Commerce became the lingua franca of Pennsylvania because, according to Hector St. Jean de Crèvecoeur, men and women who differed from each other in their place of origin, ancestry, language, ethnicity, or religion—or all of these—got along admirably and indeed, thrived. They did so by keeping their religious and cultural preferences voluntary and private, avoiding even raising them in conversation.

Instead, they talked about their crops, orchards, barns, and all the goods and services that comprised their economy. Commerce became the subject of their discourse and the medium through which they interacted. Commerce was the universal topic and the popular ethic.[18] Richard Jackson, Pennsylvania's agent to the British government, in 1755 described to Franklin the baneful effect of the commercial spirit. It tends to destroy government and enervate manners: "Steady virtue, and unbending integrity, are seldom to be found where a spirit of commerce pervades everything." And the commercial spirit did in fact infect almost everything. It would not cease "until everything has its price." "Things that *boni mores* are forbid to be set to sale, are become its objects, and there are few things indeed *extra commercium*."[19] Meanwhile, what would make them be decent toward each other? their townships and villages? their churches? their somnolent government and harassed magistrates?

Pennsylvania had no satisfactory solution to the indecencies its people inflicted upon each other. It did not fail the wealthy or other Pennsylvanians who thought they were the beneficiaries described in the caption "the best poor man's country." It certainly failed the victims of crime—Indians, African Americans, and various men, women and children. Moreover, it failed criminals whom (servants, ex-servants, runaways, transients, and immigrants) it left upon their negligible resources and options for pursuing and gaining a decent and peaceable life. It, and Americans almost ever since, deemed that allowing the people the freedom to rely upon their personal resources was a sufficient benefit to the recipient and a benefaction by the giver—felicity all around. By these gestures, Americans disclose their faith that liberal society is self-healing, needing no hospital or physicians.

Pennsylvania was precocious. America would follow its pattern, intentionally or coincidentally, and recapitulate its troubles and their causes. The inadequacies uncovered before 1800 in Pennsylvania reappeared after 1800 in all of America. Before and after 1800, immigrants and transients were linked to crime, not only as perpetrators but also as victims. After 1800, immigrants plagued America, as well as suffered in America, as spectacularly as they had earlier in Pennsylvania—especially when African Americans are included, as unwilling immigrants. To focus on them is not to assert that immigrants *necessarily* caused crime or that all immigrants committed crimes. Nor is it to assert that immigrants convicted of crime bore all the blame for their crime. But in Pennsylvania and subsequent American history, waves of immigration were extraordinarily correlated with crime, and scholars need to understand why.[20]

In the United States after 1800, the problems of an open, pluralistic society, immigrants, the abuse of labor, and crime reappeared with the Irish migration. From the end of the Napoleonic Wars to 1855, perhaps two and a half million Irish emigrated to the United States. Like the Protestant Scots-Irish from Ulster, the Catholic Irish from the southern counties of Ireland brought with them a history and culture of physical violence. No other immigrants of the nineteenth or twentieth centuries were as "collectively pugnacious." They fought, killed, joined gangs, rioted, commandeered neighborhoods, and populated the criminal dockets and prisons. Conditions in America selectively favored their historic aggressiveness. A newcomer explained to a correspondent back in Ireland, "The people here can far beat your country [for] killing one another"; "The people here think as little of killing others as you would of killing the mice in a cornstack. . . . if ever you get into a fight here you must either kill or be killed [with] . . . pistols or large knives which they use instead of fighting with their fists."[21]

Like the accused in Pennsylvania, these immigrants were transients— mostly young men spending years on the tramp looking for work. Like many African Americans moving to Philadelphia in the 1790s, they were abjectly poor, either unemployed or employed at the least-paying, most menial, most dangerous, and intermittent work.[22] For the jobs they got—as longshoremen, coal-heavers, canal-diggers, railroad laborers— they often competed violently with African Americans, who already stood on the bottom rung of the job ladder. Exposed to injuries and worn by hard labor, the life expectancy in the United States of a Famine-immigrant Irishman was estimated at six years. The Famine Irish simply overwhelmed the capacity of American economy to employ them, philanthropy to care for them, and the criminal justice system to apprehend and correct them.[23]

Conventional wisdom of the times held otherwise. The United States allegedly continued as "the best poor man's country," a place where the least fortunate immigrants could work for wages higher than those in Europe. Publications authored by Federalist- or Whig-party capitalists explained that years spent at wage labor led to personal economic independence and entrepreneurial careers (provided only a man had the requisite ambition). Out of concern for the obvious poor in the United States, some privileged Americans challenged the conventional wisdom passed down from Benjamin Franklin through Abraham Lincoln, that any man could improve his status in America.[24] From a different motive, America's most polemical, home-grown critic, slavery-apologist George Fitzhugh, put the reality this way: "The elevation of the scaffold is the only moral or physical elevation that they [the bourgeois defenders of free, wage labor and enterprise] can point to which distinguishes the condition of the free laborer from his servile ancestor."[25] The most obvious cases in point for his taunting of Northern capitalists were the Irish and free black laborers of the North.

At the end of the nineteenth century, the pattern repeated itself, substituting Italian immigrants. Italian migration totaled more than three million from 1900 through 1914.[26] Like the earlier waves of immigrants, the influx began with young bachelor men escaping hopeless situations in Europe. Like Scots-Irishmen and Irish, the Italians brought with them a culture of violence, from southern Italy and Sicily. The homicide rate for these Italians in the years 1900–1907 was an astonishing 26.5 per 100,000 annually.[27] It gained them a briefly deserved but unshakable reputation for violence. Like the Irish, Italians came mainly to lay rails, excavate canals, dig coal, bring in harvests, and in short, toil at the least skilled, lowest paid, most punishing jobs.[28]

Here, however, appears a critical dissimilarity: the Italian homicide rate from 1908 through 1917 declined to 11.4, a remarkable improvement over the preceding eight years. Furthermore, as Roger Lane discovered in Philadelphia, of the 909 people jailed for killings over the first twenty-eight years in the twentieth century, only ten were *second-generation* immigrants with Italian surnames.[29] What accounts for the plummeting homicide rate and the peaceful acculturation of second-generation Italians? The immigrants to turn-of-the-century United States came to an economy that needed them and encouraged their migration. They flooded in but they did not overwhelm the capacity of the economy to employ them. Their futures were more secure than those of ante-bellum laborers. They arrived in the United States in the midst of its urban, industrial revolution, a revolution that must be credited with civilizing and diverting these and other immigrants—as well as native-born masses—from the crime and violence that troubled earlier

America. And the Irish, already in America when the urban industrial revolution began, benefited from it like the Italians, before the Italians.

Irish, Italians, eastern Europeans, and other immigrants moved out of the mudsills to which skeptics like Fitzhugh had permanently assigned them. It appeared that the Whig-Republican boomers of liberal capitalism finally stood vindicated. In detail, with incomes and secure jobs, they married, put money into savings banks, bore children, took out mortgages, bought homes, sent their children to public or parochial school, and realized, above all, that ungoverned, unsocial conduct jeopardized all they had achieved or expected in their lifetimes and their children's. It was not only the money they regularly earned that made the critical difference in their behavior. It was the manifold links to other people that secure employment brought that changed them. They had wives, children, churches, schools, fraternal organizations, and savings banks and life insurance companies to whom they felt obliged. They had reputations to maintain among people from so many different quarters in their lives. Sociologist Alan Wolfe abstracts from such experience an axiom about all human conduct: "We are not social because we are moral; we are moral because we live together with others. . . . Morality matters because we have reputations to protect, cooperative tasks to carry out, legacies to leave, others to love, and careers to follow."[30]

However, one group of Americans never benefited from the urban, industrial revolution: African Americans. Missing the benefits of secure and honorable employment, they illustrate the transforming power on men and women of those benefits, whatever produced them—free markets, social democracy, or luck. At the close of the eighteenth century, Pennsylvania barely afforded a glimpse of the future of free African Americans in the United States. The bottom of the social ladder was their exclusive station before the Irish arrived. Thereafter, they had to contend with the Irish and others for either the bottom or one level above it. Practically, that meant keeping their jobs on the wharves, warehouses, streets, or canals, or relinquishing them to the more aggressive Irish. Practically, defending themselves meant fighting and dying, and fending off gangs invading black neighborhoods. What they shared, however, was just as important as the contest between them to avoid the bottom—both were impoverished, insecure in the jobs they got, ill-paid, and, after 1795, inordinately suspected of and prosecuted for crime.[31] The least fortunate among the black Philadelphians were immigrants too, the Saint Dominguans. With the passage of decades, crime became a more constant feature in the lives of African Americans than of any other group. Of all Americans, they were most often accused and convicted of crime, most often incarcerated, and most often the victims of crime. The Irish and Italians moved up and out of poverty and crime.

They passed a test, but the United States did not. Uniquely among Americans, black Americans remained behind.

However bountiful the eighteenth century in Pennsylvania was, however much contemporaries remarked upon its orchards, sturdy barns, waves of grain, busy markets, and enterprising citizens, and reckoned it "the best poor man's country," it was not beneficent enough to have duplicated the transformation accomplished by the urban, industrial revolution of the nineteenth and twentieth centuries that lifted all but African Americans out of crime and misery. The transients and faceless accused men of Pennsylvania anticipated their counterparts in the nineteenth century. Their crime rates rivaled or exceeded their successors', poor urban masses existed in Philadelphia before the Irish arrived there, violations of the law at times overwhelmed the ability of the justice system to apprehend them, and schemes to reform or deter criminals failed or were discarded.

It may be close to preposterous to expect that Pennsylvania, Britain, or any state in the preurban and preindustrial age would have created a social welfare and education system that attacked crime at its origins.[32] In this rural situation, to address the problem, the nation needed to provide men and women with opportunities and vocations in agriculture. For that, land was needed—as Thomas Jefferson and agrarian republicans well appreciated. The land, in turn, had to come, and did come, from its original American owners, the Indians.

Americans' continued confidence in their liberal ways supports their unsympathetic view of crime and criminals.[33] Crime is alien. Criminals are defective people. They chose what they did in a free society that offered them noncriminal options. But despite the vaunted availability of options, the country has exceptionally high rates of crime and is perplexed by them. Crime threatens cherished American "exceptionalism": Americans do not deserve such trouble—in the way that dictatorships, Third-World countries, the poor anywhere, and less pious, more secularized democracies deserve it. For the crime for which we think we are only the victims, we prosecute African Americans, the poor, transients, and the latest immigrants and incarcerate them at rates far exceeding those in nations we disrespect.

To solve the problem of crime in the United States, academicians, pundits, preachers, stumping politicians, and demagogues urge us to imitate our ancestors, who, infused with morality and values, practiced civility (real or imagined). At least since Sam Adams and Benjamin Rush, Americans have urged their countrymen to become like Spartans, Stoics, republican Romans, New England Pilgrims, and yes, the founders of Pennsylvania. Becoming Spartan, puritan, or Quaker, however, is demanding; you must not treat society like a marketplace where you expect quid pro quo. Not that the pretended physicians of the nation's ills really want or demand equal sacrifice. Depending upon whether they speak from the political left or right, they demand someone else forfeit a benefit of liberalism, some "right" or civil liberty—gun ownership versus media freedoms, for example. Iconic liberal William Penn warned Pennsylvanians not to give away any liberty and property that they enjoyed. His instruction—don't yield anything unless obliged to—fits far better the temperament of Americans. If we want to remain liberals rather than becoming Stoics, we had best come to understand our predicament, especially our perplexing deviations from our professed ideal behavior. Our problem is not with others; we are the problem. Philosopher Charles Griswold asks: "Might the seeds of our manifold troubles also, paradoxically, be the very same seeds that have yielded the fruits we enjoy?"[34] Since 1682 they are the same seeds.

- Liberalism causes crime
- The market promises to fix it but doesn't
- PA citizens only really connected through market
- Immigration causes crime as immigrants are violent
- Liberalism left blacks behind
- At the end of the day it's a trade off: more freedom for a risk of more crime.

Abbreviations and Short Titles

AJLH	*American Journal of Legal History*
Alexander, *Render*	John Alexander, *Render Them Submissive: Responses to Poverty in Philadelphia, 1760–1800* (Amherst: University of Massachusetts Press, 1980)
AHR	*American Historical Review*
AWM	*American Weekly Mercury* (Philadelphia)
Beattie	J. M. Beattie, *Crime and Courts in England, 1660–1800* (Princeton, N.J.: Princeton University Press, 1986)
Biddle, *Extracts*	Henry D. Biddle, ed., *Extracts from the Journal of Elizabeth Drinker, from 1759 to 1807* (Philadelphia: J.B. Lippincott, 1889)
Biddle	Charles Biddle, *The Autobiography of Charles Biddle* (Philadelphia: E. Claxton and Co., 1881)
BCHS	Bucks County Historical Society, Doylestown, Pennsylvania
CCHS	Chester County Historical Society, West Chester, Pennsylvania
CCQSD	Chester County Quarter Sessions Dockets, Chester County Archives, West Chester, Pennsylvania
CCQSP	Chester County Quarter Sessions Papers, Chester County Archives, West Chester, Pennsylvania
CG	*Carlisle Gazette*
Charter	*Charter to William Penn and Laws of the Province of Pennsylvania* (Harrisburg, 1879)
CJH	*Criminal Justice History*
FJ	*Freeman's Journal* (Philadelphia)
FG	*Federal Gazette* (Philadelphia)
GUS	*Gazette of the United States*
HSP	Historical Society of Pennsylvania, Philadelphia
Horle, *Lawmaking*	Craig W. Horle et al., eds., *Lawmaking and Legislators in Pennsylvania: A Biographical Dictionary*, 2 vols. (Philadelphia: University of Pennsylvania Press, 1991–1997)
Horle, *Quakers*	Craig W. Horle, *The Quakers and the English Legal System, 1660–1688* (Philadelphia: University of Pennsylvania Press, 1988)
Horle, *Records*	Craig W. Horle, ed., *Records of the Courts of Sussex County, Delaware, 1677–1710*, 2 vols. (Philadelphia: University of Pennsylvania Press, 1991)
IG	*Independent Gazetteer* (Philadelphia)
JAH	*Journal of American History*

JER	*Journal of the Early Republic*
JSH	*Journal of Social History*
Lane, *Murder*	Roger Lane, *Murder in America: A History* (Columbus: Ohio State University Press, 1997)
Lane, *Roots*	Roger Lane, *Roots of Violence in Black Philadelphia, 1860–1900* (Cambridge, Mass.: Harvard University Press, 1986)
Lane, *Violent Death*	Roger Lane, *Violent Death in the City: Suicide, Accident, and Murder in Nineteenth-Century Philadelphia* (Cambridge, Mass.: Harvard University Press, 1979)
LJ	*Lancaster Journal*
LHR	*Law and History Review*
Marietta, *Reformation*	Jack D. Marietta, *The Reformation of American Quakerism, 1748–1783* (Philadelphia: University of Pennsylvania Press, 1984)
Nash, *Crucible*	Gary B. Nash, *The Urban Crucible: Social Change, Political Consciousness, and the Origins of the American Revolution* (Cambridge, Mass.: Harvard University Press, 1979)
Nash, *Forging*	Gary B. Nash, *Forging Freedom: The Formation of Philadelphia's Black Community, 1720–1840* (Cambridge, Mass.: Harvard University Press, 1988)
Nash, *Quakers*	Gary B. Nash, *Quakers and Politics: Pennsylvania, 1681–1726* (Princeton, N.J.: Princeton University Press, 1968)
Nash and Soderlund	Gary B. Nash and Jean R. Soderlund, *Freedom by Degrees: Emancipation in Pennsylvania and Its Aftermath* (New York: Oxford University Press, 1991)
NYHS	New-York Historical Society
Offutt	William M. Offutt, Jr., *Of "Good Laws" and "Good Men": Law and Society in the Delaware Valley, 1680–1710* (Urbana: University of Illinois Press, 1995)
Ousterhout	Anne M. Ousterhout, *A State Divided: Opposition in Pennsylvania to the American Revolution* (Westport, Conn.: Greenwood Press, 1987)
PA	Samuel Hazard et al., eds., *Pennsylvania Archives*, 9 series, 138 vols. (Philadelphia and Harrisburg, 1852–1949), 1st ser.
PC	*Pennsylvania Chronicle* (Philadelphia)
PCR	*Minutes of the Provincial Council of Pennsylvania*, 16 vols. (Harrisburg, 1851–1853)
Pennypacker	Samuel Pennypacker, *Pennsylvania Colonial Cases* (Philadelphia, W.J. Campbell, 1892)
PG	*Philadelphia Gazette*
PH	*Pennsylvania History*
PJ	*Pennsylvania Journal* (Philadelphia)
PMHB	*Pennsylvania Magazine of History and Biography*
PMHC	Pennsylvania Museum and Historical Commission
Poore	Ben Perly Poore, ed., *Federal and State Constitutions, Colonial Charters, and Other Organic Laws of the United States*, 2nd ed. (Washington, D.C.: Government Printing Office, 1878)
PP	*Pennsylvania Packet* (Philadelphia)

PWP	William Penn, *The Papers of William Penn*, ed. Richard S. Dunn and Mary M. Dunn, 5 vols. (Philadelphia: University of Pennsylvania Press, 1981–86)
Rowe, *Bench*	G. S. Rowe, *Embattled Bench: The Pennsylvania Supreme Court and the Forging of a Democratic Society, 1684–1809* (Newark: University of Delaware Press, 1994)
Rowe, *McKean*	G. S. Rowe, *Thomas McKean: The Shaping of an American Republicanism* (Boulder: Colorado Associated Press, 1978)
Statutes	James T. Mitchell and Henry Flanders, eds., *The Statutes at Large of Pennsylvania from 1682–1801*,18 vols. (Harrisburg, 1896–1908)
Thayer	Theodore Thayer, *Pennsylvania Politics and the Growth of Democracy, 1740–1776* (Harrisburg: Pennsylvania Historical Museum Commission, 1953)
Tully, *Forming*	Alan Tully, *Forming American Politics: Ideals, Interests, and Institutions in Colonial New York and Pennsylvania* (Baltimore: Johns Hopkins University Press, 1994)
Tully, *Legacy*	Alan Tully, *William Penn's Legacy: Politics and Social Structure in Provincial Pennsylvania, 1726–1755* (Baltimore: Johns Hopkins University Press, 1977)
WPHM	*Western Pennsylvania Historical Magazine*
WPHS	Western Pennsylvania Historical Society, Pittsburgh
WMQ	*William and Mary Quarterly* 3rd ser.

Notes

Introduction

Epigraph. For a discussion of *The Tempest* and Shakespeare's vision of the New World, see Leo Marx, *The Machine in the Garden: Technology and the Pastoral Ideal in America* (New York: Harper, 1964), chapter 2. We are indebted to Jay Marietta for the reference.

1. The authors are aware that the area where Penn and the Quakers recruited—Wales and the midlands of England—were infamous for personal and property crimes, and that sailors, servants, artisans, and young men, who are apt to commit crimes, accompanied the Quakers to Pennsylvania. Penn knew as much, but withal expected to minimize, if not eliminate crime. Many observers sincerely believed that he succeeded.

2. Edith Phillips, *The Good Quaker in French Legend* (Philadelphia: University of Pennsylvania Press, 1932), 53–54, 68, 96, 100, 210; Dennis D. Moore, *More Letters from the American Farmer: An Edition of the Essays in English Left Unpublished by Crèvecoeur* (Athens: University of Georgia Press, 1995), 51; George Whitefield, *Journals (1737–1741)*, intro. William V. Davis (Gainsville, Fla.: Scholars' Fascimiles & Reprints, 1969), 384, 386–87; Durand Echeverria, *Mirage in the West: A History of the French Image of American Society to 1815* (New York: Octagon Books, repr., 1966), 17–18; Oscar Handlin and John Clive, eds., *Journey to Pennsylvania by Gottlieb Mittelberger* (Cambridge, Mass.: Harvard University Press, 1960), 93; James T. Lemon, *"The Best Poor Man's Country": A Geographical Study of Early Southeastern Pennsylvania* (Baltimore: Johns Hopkins University Press, 1972).

3. Thomas A. Bailey and David M. Kennedy, *The American Pageant*, 9th ed. (Lexington, Mass.: Heath, 1991), 39–40; Paul S. Boyer et al., *The Enduring Vision: A History of the American People* (Lexington, Mass.: Heath, 1990), 89; Bernard Bailyn et al., *The Great Republic: A History of the American People*, 2 vols., 3rd ed., (Lexington, Mass.: Heath, 1985), 69; John W. Davidson et al., *Nation of Nations: A Narrative History of the American Republic*, 2 vols. (New York: McGraw-Hill, 1990), 99.

4. *PCR*, 1: 116, 371, 473; 2: 13, 598; 3: 110, 260, 593; 4: 116; 5: 428–30, 9: 408–10, 455, 564; *AWM*, June 29–July 6, 1738; *PG*, April 12, 1729; January 20, 1730; January 8, 1734; September 5, 1751; *PC*, January 4–11, 1768; Kenneth and Anna Roberts, eds., *Moreau de St. Méry's American Journey, 1793–1798* (Garden City, N.Y.: Doubleday, 1947), 281.

5. Echeverria, *Mirage in the West*, 17–18. Phillips, *The Good Quaker*, 100. Doubtless Pennsylvania appeared tame to observers cognizant of the criminality and brutality associated with slavery in the southern colonies.

6. Bradford to Madison, 1774, in James Madison, *The Papers of James Madison*, ed. William T. Hutchinson and William M. E. Rachel, 17 vols. (Chicago: University of Chicago Press, 1962–1991), 1: 109.

7. Tully, *Forming*, 378. This summary of Pennsylvania government is informed by several well known histories: Nash, *Quakers*; Tully, *Forming*; Tully, *Legacy*; and James H. Hutson, *Pennsylvania Politics, 1746–1770: The Movement for Royal Government and Its Consequences* (Princeton, N.J.: Princeton University Press, 1972).

8. John Murrin, "Political Development," in Jack P. Greene and J. R. Pole, eds., *Colonial British America: Essays in the New History of the Early Modern Era* (Baltimore: Johns Hopkins University Press, 1984), 439.

9. Tully, *Legacy*, 94.

10. Stephanie Grauman Wolf, *Urban Village: Population, Community, and Family Structure in Germantown, Pennsylvania, 1683–1800* (Princeton, N.J.: Princeton University Press, 1976), 177.

11. J. William Frost, *A Perfect Freedom: Religious Liberty in Pennsylvania* (Cambridge: Cambridge University Press, 1990), 27, 46; Sally Schwartz, *"A Mixed Multitude": The Struggle for Toleration in Colonial Pennsylvania* (New York: New York University Press, 1987), 33.

12. Frost, *Perfect Freedom*, 46; Wolf, *Urban Village*, 230–31. Wolf writes that "the ministers of the traditional churches and the preachers of weightiest members of the sects almost never became the most influential voices within the community." "The pastor [of the Reformed Church], poor and mendicant much of the time, was patronized rather than respected by his parishioners, who tended to regard him as an object of charity rather than authority." Two outbursts between ordained Anglicans and lay Quaker leaders did inject clergy into politics: the Keithian schism in the Society of Friends in 1691 and the Quaker-Anglican contests over oaths and other matters, the latter treated briefly in Chapter 1 of this book. A third outburst joined Presbyterian clergy with Anglicans against Quakers in the 1740s over provision for military defense. Nash, *Quakers*, 147, 149, 156–57; J. William Frost, "The Affirmation Controversy and Religious Liberty," in Richard S. Dunn and Mary Maples Dunn, eds., *The World of William Penn* (Philadelphia: University of Pennsylvania Press, 1986), 317; Gilbert Tennent, "The Late Association for Defense Encourag'd or the Lawfulness of War" (Philadelphia: William Bradford, 1748); "The Late Association Farther Encourag'd . . . In a Reply to . . . The Doctrine of Christianity, as Held by the People Called Quakers, Vindicated" (Philadelphia: B. Franklin, 1748).

13. Patricia U. Bonomi, *Under the Cope of Heaven: Religion, Society, and Politics in Colonial America* (New York: Oxford University Press, 1986), 80; Frost, *Perfect Freedom*, 44–46; Schwartz, *"Mixed Multitude"*, 74.

14. Mittelberger, *Journey to Pennsylvania*, 47–48.

15. Whitefield, *Journals*, 384, 386–87; Wolf, *Urban Village*, 45; Lemon, *The Best Poor Man's Country: 216;* Mary M. Schweitzer, *Custom and Contract: Household, Government, and the Economy in Colonial Pennsylvania* (New York: Columbia University Press, 1987), 55.

16. Henretta was making a "Malthusian" point when he wrote this. American farmers did not have an entrepreneurial attitude because the rewards to their labor were not encouraging. That was certainly more the case in New England than it was in Pennsylvania. Henretta, "Families and Farmers: Mentalité in Pre-Industrial America," *WMQ* 35 (1978): 14.

17. A lively debate arose between Lemon, who has long espoused the entrepeneurial and liberal character of the economy of southeastern Pennsylvania, and James Henretta, who believes in the subsistence character and mentality of American farmers. See Lemon as cited above, and James A. Henretta, *Origins of*

Capitalism, 71–120; Henretta, "Families and Farms," 3–32; Lemon, "Comment on James A. Henretta's 'Families and Farms: Mentalité in Pre-Industrial America,'" *WMQ* 37 (1980): 688–95; Henretta, "Mr. Henretta Replies," *WMQ* 37 (1980): 696–97. Another early exposition on the private and capitalistic character of the area is Sam Bass Warner, *Private City: Philadelphia in Three Periods of Its Growth* (Philadelphia: University of Pennsylvania Press, 1968, 2nd ed. 1987), xi–xii, 3–4. Since 1980, research by Mary Schweitzer, Lucy Simler, Thomas Doerflinger, and Adrienne Hood has advanced the discussion beyond the bounds and evidence used between Lemon and Henretta. Schweitzer, *Custom and Contract*; Lucy Simler, "Tenancy in Colonial Pennsylvania: The Case of Chester County," *WMQ* 43 (1986): 542–69 and "The Landless Worker: An Index of Economic and Social Change in Chester County, Pennsylvania, 1750–1820," *PMHB* 114 (1990): 163–99; Thomas Doerflinger, "Farmers and Dry Goods in the Philadelphia Market Area, 1750–1800," in Ronald Hoffman et al., *The Economy of Early America: The Revolutionary Period, 1763–1790* (Charlottesville: University of Virginia Press, 1986), 186–91; Adrienne D. Hood, *The Weaver's Craft: Cloth, Commerce, and Industry in Early Pennsylvania* (Philadelphia: University of Pennsylvania Press, 2003). Recently George Rappaport supported Henretta, but omits extensive examination of household and public records that might advance the determination of rural Pennsylvanians' market participation. George David Rappaport, *Stability and Change in Revolutionary Pennsylvania: Banking, Politics, and Social Structure* (University Park: Pennsylvania State University Press, 1996), 3–42. For a review of the historiography of markets and mentality, see Jack P. Greene and J. R. Pole, eds., *Colonial British America: Essays in the New History of the Early Modern Era* (Baltimore: Johns Hopkins University Press, 1984), 67–68, 102, 111–12, 239–41.

Chapter 1. Criminal Laws and Courts

Epigraph. William Penn, *PWP,* 2: 142.

1. *Charter,* 83–84. The Charter provided that laws proposed by Penn must have the advice and assent of the freemen of Pennsylvania in assembly.

2. *Charter,* 92, 97; Caroline Robbins, "Laws and Governments Proposed for West New Jersey and Pennsylvania, 1676–1683," *PMHB* 105 (1981): 373–92. Penn complained that the current English system punished individuals (including himself) for activities that were not "crimes." He referred of course to religious activities. During his incarceration in 1667 he wrote, "Religion is at once my crime and mine innocence." *PWP,* 1: 89.

3. *PWP,* 1: 89. Samuel Janney, *The Life of William Penn* (Philadelphia: Hogan, Perkins and Co., 1852), 49–50.

4. Penn to Lord Arlington, June 19, 1669, in *PWP,* 1: 91; Janney, *The Life of William Penn,* 62–63.

5. Sheridan, *A Discourse of Parliament, of Laws* (London, 1677).

6. See, for instance, David Veale, *The Popular Movement for Law Reform, 1650–1660* (New York: Oxford University Press, 1970); Mary Cotterell, "Interregnum Law Reform, the Hale Commission of 1652," *English Historical Review* 88 (1968): 689–704; Stuart E. Prall, *The Agitation for Law Reform During the Puritan Revolution* (The Hague: Martinus Nijhoff, 1966); C. R. Niehaus, "The Issue of Law Reform in the Puritan Revolution" (Ph.D. dissertation, Harvard University, 1960); and Barbara Shapiro, "Law Reform in Seventeenth Century England," *AJLH* 19

(1975): 280–312. Horle, *Quakers* is a particularly good account of these issues and Quaker responses to them.

7. The best treatment of England's reaction to the events of 1676—and those of the Glorious Revolution which followed—is Stephen Saunders Webb, *1676: The End of American Independence* (Cambridge, Mass.: Harvard University Press, 1985). But also see J. M. Sosin, *English America and the Revolution of 1688: Royal Administration and the Structure of Provincial Government* (Lincoln: University of Nebraska Press, 1982) and Richard R. Johnson, *Adjustment to Empire: The New England Colonies, 1675–1715* (New Brunswick, N.J.: Rutgers University Press, 1981). The quote is from Sosin, 186.

8. *Charter,* 92–93.

9. *Charter,* 91, 92–93. Here Penn employed the Biblical text that was a mainstay of Quaker political ideology, Paul's Epistle to the Romans, chapter 13.

10. Paul Cromwell, "Quaker Reforms in American Criminal Justice: The Penitentiary and Beyond," *CJH* 10 (1989): 78. Documentation can be found in Jean R. Soderlund, ed., *William Penn and the Founding of Pennsylvania, 1680–1684: A Documentary History* (Philadelphia: University of Pennsylvania Press, 1983), 3–140.

11. *Charter,* 99–103.

12. *The Colonial Period of American History,* 4 vols. (New Haven, Conn.: Yale University Press, 1937, reprint, 1967), 3: 286.

13. *Charter,* 99–103.

14. *Charter,* 10, 14–15. The Duke's Laws had been in force since September 22, 1676.

15. Background of settlement in the Delaware region is provided by C. A. Weslager, *The English on the Delaware, 1610–1682* (New Brunswick, N.J.: Rutgers University Press, 1969). See also Carl Bridenbaugh, "The Old and New Societies of the Delaware Valley in the Seventeenth Century," *PMHB* 100 (1976): 143–72.

16. See, for instance, *Records of the Court at New Castle on Delaware, 1676–1681* (Philadelphia, 1904); Horle, *Records.*

17. Robert W. Johannsen, "The Conflict Between The Three Lower Counties on the Delaware and the Province of Pennsylvania, 1682–1704," *Delaware History* 5 (1952): 96–132.

18. *Charter,* 107–27.

19. *Charter,* 84.

20. *Charter,* 107–16. There remains some question about how many (and which) laws were passed in December 1682. See Marvin W. Schlegel, "The Text of the Great Law of 1682," *PH* 11 (1944): 276–83.

21. Kathryn Preyer, "Penal Measures in the American Colonies: An Overview," *AJLH* 26 (1982): 336.

22. *Charter,* 110–15.

23. It was discretion, not harshness, that was allowed, and this was primarily a function of a system of magisterial justice.

24. *Charter,* 113–16.

25. *Charter,* 168. Justice of course was not guaranteed by jury trials. Penn understood that, and so did his contemporaries. What jury trials ensured was due process, procedural fairness, a barrier to arbitrary treatment. And that represented "justice" for most common citizens.

26. *Charter,* 117, 120–21, 123.

27. Herbert W. K. Fitzroy, "The Punishment of Crime in Provincial Pennsylvania," *PMHB* 60 (1936): 244–45.

28. *PCR*, 1: 106; *Charter*, 128–29. This practice continued into the 1750s and beyond. See, for instance, "Peter Grubb v. Jacob Perkle," April 10, 1745, Supreme Court, Eastern District, Appearance and Continuance Dockets, 1740–1751, microfilm, reel 1, PMHC, Harrisburg.

29. See Paul Lermack, "Peace Bonds and Criminal Justice in Colonial Pennsylvania," *PMHB* 100 (1976): 173–90.

30. Frederick B. Tolles, *Meeting House and Counting House: The Quaker Merchants in Colonial Philadelphia, 1682–1763* (New York: W.W. Norton, reprint, 1963), esp. 251–52. Contributing also were the use of benefit of clergy and the propensity to remit fines and to grant pardons on the part of the Council, both of which will be discussed elsewhere.

31. Asking parties to pay for writs and imposing a fee system was well established and generally fair in that it did not favor the wealthy over the poor. Moreover, it was easily understood by all and each bond was evaluated at the next court session. In addition, the employment of credit rather than immediate cash reduced opportunities for judicial oppression. The alternative, billing by the hour, has doubtless enriched the bar far more. In this sense the system was neither oppressive nor unfair. Still, Pennsylvanians, particularly western Pennsylvanians, frequently denounced it as onerous. See Offutt, 197.

32. Leon de Valinger, ed., *Court Records of Kent County, Delaware, 1680–1705* (Washington, D.C.: GPO, 1959), 279, 305–6, 312.

33. Christopher K. Seglem, "A Legal History of Early Pennsylvania" (Senior Thesis, Princeton University, 1968), 69, 70–71, 76–77.

34. See Lawrence H. Gipson, "The Criminal Codes of Pennsylvania," *Journal of the American Institute of Criminal Law and Criminality* 6 (1915): 323–44.

35. Penn to Arlington, June 19, 1669, in *PWP*, 1: 91.

36. Nicholas More to William Penn, Dec. 1, 1684, in *PWP*, 2: 608.

37. *Records of the Courts of Quarter Sessions and Common Pleas of Bucks County, Pennsylvania, 1684–1700* (Meadville, Pa.: Tribune Publishing Co., 1943), 21, 80–81.

38. James Claypoole, *Letter Book: London and Philadelphia, 1681–1684*, ed. Marion Balderston, (San Marino, Calif.: Huntington Library, 1967), 175.

39. *Records of the Courts of Common Pleas and Quarter Sessions of Bucks County*, 75; Pennypacker, 79–82, 113.

40. *PCR*, 1: 104–10; *PA* 8th Ser. 1: 46–58.

41. Edwin B. Bronner, *William Penn's "Holy Experiment": The Founding of Pennsylvania, 1681–1701* (New York: Temple University Publications, 1962), 155–58.

42. Roy Lokken, *David Lloyd: Colonial Lawmaker* (Seattle: University of Washington Press., 1959), 53–55. Fletcher informed the Pennsylvania Assembly that his commission superseded, and thus negated, the royal charter of 1680/81, the Frame of 1683, and all acts of Assembly passed before the date of his commission.

43. *PCR*, 1: 406, 409–13, 416–18, 426.

44. *PCR*, 1: 250–55, 277, 386, 388–89.

45. *PCR*, 1: 473.

46. *PCR*, 1: 528.

47. "Papers of the Governors, 1681–1747," *PA* 4th Ser. 1: 108–9.

48. Quoted in Fitzroy, "The Punishment of Crime in Provincial Pennsylvania," 249.

49. *PCR*, 1: 596.

50. Durand Echeverria, *Mirage in the West: A History of the French Image of American Society to 1815* (Princeton, N.J.: Princeton University Press, 1957), 17–18.

51. *PCR*, 1: 596; 2: 13.
52. *Statutes*, 2: 4–14; Lawrence H. Gipson, "Crime and Its Punishment in Provincial Pennsylvania," *PH*, 3 (1935): 9.
53. John D. Cushing, ed., *The Earliest Printed Laws of Pennsylvania, 1681–1713* (Wilmington, Del.: Michael Glazier, 1978), 6, 11–12.
54. The criminal laws that the Privy Council vetoed were only part of 104 laws that the Assembly enacted or reenacted in 1700, about half of which were vetoed. Horle, *Lawmaking*, 1: 31–32, 810–17. *Statutes*, 2: 1–293, 489–97; Fitzroy, "The Punishment of Crime in Provincial Pennsylvania," 250.
55. Four attempted rapes were prosecuted. Also, there were only four robberies and four burglaries. Most of the prosecutions are from Chester County, where the court dockets are complete. By characterizing the Privy Councilors as offended by the harshness of the Pennsylvania laws, Fitzroy accentuates the callousness of the Pennsylvania legislators. But they wrote that the inconsistencies with English law aggravated them, and not especially the harshness of the law. Castration may have seemed harsh to them not because it was more onerous than execution, but because it offended masculine and patriarchal sensibilities, like the unequal punishment of men for bestiality. Fitzroy, "Punishment of Crime," 448–50.
56. Horle, *Lawmaking*, 1: 122.
57. Horle, *Lawmaking*, 1: 45–49; Bronner, *William Penn's "Holy Experiment"*, 201–2.
58. *Statutes*, 2: 172–84; *The Earliest Printed Laws of Pennsylvania*, 36–38, 40–44.
59. *Statutes*, 2: 233–36; *The Earliest Printed Laws of Pennsylvania*, 68–69.
60. *Statutes*, 2: 133.
61. *Statutes*, 2: 498; Bradley Chapin, "Felony Law Reform in the Early Republic," *PMHB* 113 (1989): 177. Gipson, "Crime and Its Punishment," 7, puts the figures at 53 of 104. See also Joseph H. Smith, *Appeals to the Privy Council, from the American Plantations* (New York: Columbia University Press, 1950), 243; Kermit L. Hall, *The Magic Mirror: Law in American History* (New York: Oxford University Press, 1989), 21.
62. Joseph E. Illick, *Colonial Pennsylvania: A History* (New York: Scribner's, 1976), 101; Thomas Wendel, "The Speaker of the House, Pennsylvania, 1701–1776," *PMHB* 97 (1973): 3–21.
63. J. William Frost, "The Affirmation Controversy and Religious Liberty," in Mary Maples Dunn and Richard S. Dunn, eds., *The World of William Penn*, (Philadelphia: University of Pennsylvania Press, 1986), 303–22; Horle, *Lawmaking*, 2: 30–33.
64. *Charter*, 116.
65. *Charter*, 247; Illick, *Colonial Pennsylvania*, 81.
66. *PCR*, 2: 40–41. Joseph E. Illick, *William Penn the Politician: His Relations with the English Government* (Ithaca, N.Y.: Cornell University Press, 1965), 229–37.
67. Winfred Trexler Root, *The Relations of Pennsylvania with the British Government, 1696–1765* (Philadelphia: University of Pennsylvania Press, 1912), 253–54.
68. *Votes of the Assembly*, 2: 1223; Norris to Henry Goldney, Nov. 25, 1719, Isaac Norris Letterbook, 214, Historical Society of Pennsylvania, Philadelphia.
69. Lokken, *David Lloyd*, 89ff.
70. *Votes of the Assembly*, 2: 233–34. Even as the Assembly worked to produce the new legislation, Quaker jurors helped to convict and to execute two notorious criminals tried in a Chester court.
71. Frost, "Affirmation Controversy," 317.

72. Fitzroy, "The Punishment of Crime in Provincial Pennsylvania," 250.

73. *Statutes*, 3: 199–214.

74. Ibid.

75. *Charter*, 83.

76. *Charter*, 99–103.

77. *Charter*, 97.

78. *Records of the Courts of Chester County*, 3–6, 10.

79. William H. Loyd, *The Early Courts of Pennsylvania* (Boston: Boston Book Co., 1910), 42, 46–47; Leon de Valinger, Jr., ed., *Court Records of Kent County, 1680–1705* (Washington, D.C.: GPO, 1938), i–xxii; H. Clay Reed, "The Court Records of the Delaware Valley," *WMQ* 4 (1947): 192–203.

80. *Charter*, 117, 120, 128, 129, 167, 225. Disputes over the equity powers exercised by county courts arose quite early. Complaints surfaced that county justices were using equity powers to reverse jury verdicts in their own tribunals by simply "changing hats" to function as an immediate board of appeal. The Council wrestled at length with this problem in 1687, but protestations continued. By 1693 county courts were given power to exercise equity jurisdiction only in cases involving less than £10. However, members of the Assembly, annoyed that justices were still at liberty to overturn verdicts, asked that justices be commanded "not to decree anything in equity" to the prejudice of "judgment before given in law." Even after the Council determined that county courts could not reverse their own verdicts through their equity jurisdiction, equity powers in these courts remained the center of controversy. Arguments over where the center of equity power should be lodged—whether in the county courts or in the governor and Council—continued into the third decade of the eighteenth century.

81. For a history of the early Pennsylvania Supreme Court, see Rowe, *Bench* (1994).

82. Ibid., chap. 2.

83. *Charter*, 507. The Assembly rejected this proposal. See *PA* 8th Ser. 1: 38, 58.

84. *Charter*, 129. As we have documented in Chapter 4 and as William Offutt, Jr., has observed, the frequency with which the same people were selected for jury duty undermines a completely random selection by a child. See Offutt, 54–55.

85. *Charter*, 128; *Records of the Courts of Quarter Sessions and Common Pleas of Bucks County*, 25. For examples of arbitration panels being employed, consult Supreme Court. Eastern District. Appearances and Continuance Dockets, 1740–1751, Microfilm, reel 1, passim, PMHC.

86. *PCR*, 1: 43, 85, 93; Pennypacker, 32–34, 35–37.

87. *PCR*, 1: 79, 380.

88. *PCR*, 1: 43, 85, 93; Pennypacker, 32–34, 35–37.

89. Pennypacker, 29–31.

90. *PCR*, 1: 104–10; *Votes*, 1: 46–58.

91. See, for instance, Pennypacker, 89, 90, 98–99.

92. For general surveys of the period which treat these themes, see Nash, *Quakers*; Illick, *Colonial Pennsylvania*.

93. Lokken, *David Lloyd*, passim.

94. Ibid., chapter 8.

95. Ibid.

96. Ibid., 86–87.

97. *Charter*, 311–19; Lokken, *David Lloyd*, chapter 9.

98. *Charter,* 316.

99. Greater equity jurisdiction than they had heretofore exercised was assigned to justices of the county courts. It was to become an important component of their original jurisdiction. This provision made concrete the trends of the past decade or so. Though the Council and, indeed, the proprietor had exercised chancery functions, in the last decade of the century county courts had usurped more and more of those powers. Legislation in 1693 granted to county courts equity jurisdiction in all cases involving less than ten pounds. The 1701 act eliminated that restriction and provided that county courts should "hear and decree, all such matters and causes of equity as shall come before them" and "to force obedience to their Decree in Equity, by Imprisonment, or Sequestration of Lands, as the case may require." *Charter,* 312.

100. *Charter,* 314–15; Lokken, *David Lloyd,* 106.

101. *Charter,* 315.

102. See Erwin C. Surrency, "The Evolution of an Urban Judiciary System: The Philadelphia Story, 1683–1968," *AJLH* 18 (1974): 95–123.

103. *Statutes,* 2: 159.

104. Nash, *Quakers,* 250; George Lowther, "State of a Case about the Power of this Government to make a Law to try Life by Affirmation," Logan Papers, vol. 3, HSP.

105. Lokken, *David Lloyd,* 135, 164–67; Loyd, *The Early Courts of Pennsylvania,* 77–80. The Assembly also favored judges holding commission during good behavior, while governors would have judges removable at the pleasure of the proprietor.

106. *Statutes,* 2: 77–79, 233–36.

107. *PCR,* 2: 18, 112, 160.

108. A. Leon Higginbotham, Jr., *In the Matter of Color: Race and the American Legal Process: The Colonial Period* (New York: Oxford University Press, 1978), 281, 288.

109. Horle, *Records,* 2: 691.

110. See G. S. Rowe, "Black Offenders, Criminal Courts, and Philadelphia Society in the Late Eighteenth Century," *JSH* 22 (1989): esp. 685–88; Higginbotham, *In the Matter of Color,* 272, 281, 288.

111. *Charter,* 323–44.

112. *Charter,* 323, 342.

113. *Statutes,* 2: 331, 548–49. Arguments against the legislation included criticism that the appellate structure would encourage suits and "make proceedings at law more dilatory and expensive." It was argued that the equity procedures would do the same. Finally, it was charged that by allowing individual justice of the peace to bind a person by sureties upon the charge of an individual, when that individual was not under oath, gave the justice of the peace "very arbitrary power."

114. *Charter,* 356–61.

115. *Charter,* 304.

116. Quoted in Joseph J. Kelley, Jr., *Pennsylvania: The Colonial Years, 1681–1776* (Garden City, N.Y.: Doubleday, 1980), 141.

117. *Charter,* 387–94.

Chapter 2. "While we lived not broken in upon"

1. See Edwin B. Bronner, *William Penn's "Holy Experiment": The Founding of Pennsylvania, 1681–1701* (New York: Temple University Publications, 1962);

Joseph Illick, *Colonial Pennsylvania: A History* (New York: Scribner's, 1976); Nash, *Quakers.*

2. Horle, *Records,* 1 691; *PCR,* 2: 405.

3. Rowe, *Bench,* chapter 1.

4. *PCR,* 2: 5, 275, 405.

5. See generally Lane, *Murder* (1997).

6. The Assembly passed forty laws between 1682–1709 which treated morals. In the period 1710–1756 it passed only six. Horle, *Lawmaking,* 1: 810–11; 2: 18, 1131; John D. Cushing, ed., *The Earliest Printed Laws of Pennsylvania, 1681–1713* (Wilmington, Del.: Michael Glazier, 1978).

7. Marietta, *Reformation,* 55–56.

8. William Evans and Thomas Evans, eds., *Friends Library* (Philadelphia, 1837–1850), 6: 200. For more evidence of Quakers' judgments on the behavior of non-Quakers, see Jack D. Marietta, "The Growth of Quaker Self-Consciousness in Pennsylvania, 1720–1748," in J. William Frost and John M. Moore, eds., *Seeking the Light: Essays in Quaker History* (Wallingford, Pa.: Pendle Hill Press, 1986), 79–104.

9. J. William Frost argues emphatically that the first generation of Quaker Pennsylvanians expected that their personal religious ethics would apply universally in the province. Without that expectation it hardly makes sense that, as happened, the governor's council deliberated upon restricting all inhabitants to two suits of clothes, one for winter and the other for summer. Frost, *A Perfect Freedom: Religious Liberty in Pennsylvania* (Cambridge: Cambridge University Press, 1990), 18–19.

10. We include among morals crimes rape and attempted rape, which we also include among violent crimes when we consider that topic.

11. Edgar J. McManus, *Law and Liberty in Early New England: Criminal Justice and Due Process, 1620–1692* (Amherst: University of Massachusetts Press, 1993), 28.

12. William E. Nelson, *Americanization of the Common Law: The Impact of Legal Change on Massachusetts Society, 1760–1830* (Cambridge, Mass: Harvard University Press, 1975), 36–37; William Nelson, *Dispute and Conflict Resolution in Plymouth County, Massachusetts, 1725–1825* (Chapel Hill: University of North Carolina Press, 1982), 23. McManus's records are of cases tried. Nelson's are prosecutions. Cornelia Hughes Dayton, *Women Before the Bar: Gender, Law, and Society in Connecticut, 1639–1789* (Chapel Hill: University of North Carolina Press, 1995), 160. In New Haven County from 1710 to 1750, fornication was 69 percent of all cases.

13. 7 month 1688, 10 month 1688, 4 month 1689, 13–7 month, 1692, 12 September 1693, 9–4 month 1696, 8–10 month 1696, CCQSD.

14. It is possible that prosecutions of "petty" immorality became the responsibility of single justices. Such single-justice prosecutions were not courts of record, and if any records were kept, it was at the choice of the justice. Only three such documents exist, and the paucity of such records, and their incompleteness, argues that few such courts operated. And too, the very fact that cases of immorality were relegated argues that such crimes were not as important as they earlier were, when the county courts heard them.

15. See Chapter 3 for additional treatment of bastardy.

16. For the calculation of Quaker population and sources for Pennsylvania population, see Marietta, *Reformation,* 47–48.

17. In the Society of Friends, the procedure was called "Gospel Order" and is

described in Jack D. Marietta, "Ecclesiastical Discipline in the Society of Friends, 1682–1776" (Ph.D. dissertation, Stanford University, 1968), 106–10.

18. *PCR*, 1: 106.

19. *PCR*, 2: 34, 51; David Paul Brown, *The Forum, or Forty Years Full Practice at the Philadelphia Bar*, 2 vols. (Philadelphia, 1856), 1: 214–15.

20. *Records of the Courts of Chester, Pennsylvania* (Philadelphia: Patterson and White, 1910), 192, 302.

21. *Records of the Courts of Quarter Sessions and Common Pleas of Bucks County, Pennsylvania* (Meadville, Pa.: Tribune Publishing, 1943), 80–81.

22. Although peace bonds were employed in all other colonies, the practice was more widespread and extensively used in Pennsylvania.

23. *Records of the Courts of Bucks County*, 61, 25, 59; *Records of the Courts of Chester County*, 56, 60; Brown, *The Forum*, 1: 217–18; Jasper Yeates, ed., *Reports of the Cases Adjudged in the Supreme Court of Pennsylvania with some Selected Cases at Nisi Prius, and the Circuit Courts*, 4 vols. (St. Louis, 1871), 1: 71–74; 2: 513–14; 3: 479–80, 521–26, 584–86; 4: 127.

24. See, for instances, cases in Supreme Court docket, 1740–1764, PMHC.

25. Horle, *Records*, I: 455, 463.

26. For the ability of clerks and justices to summarily resolve cases—and under what conditions—see Offutt, 45, 223, 226–27.

27. Horle, *Records*, 1: 96–97, 243, 286; *Records of the Courts of Chester*, 51.

28. For Quakers the monthly meetings were not an alternative to the criminal courts, but rather an addition. For civil justice matters—debts, contracts, etc.— the meetings were an alternative where disputes *among* Quakers had to be arbitrated.

29. Marietta, "Ecclesiastical Discipline," 5.

30. Bradley Chapin, *Criminal Justice in Colonial America, 1606–1660* (Athens: University of Georgia Press, 1983), 20.

31. *AWM*, July 30, 1741.

32. *Records of the Courts of Sussex*, 285, 297; *Records of the Courts of Chester*, 89.

33. Nash, *Quakers*, 253–55, 260–61.

34. ". . . this region achieved a remarkable level of social peace and economic opportunity despite political turmoil." Offutt, 5.

35. Even for Chester County, Offutt rejects most historians' conclusion that Friends were a majority possibly as late as 1710. Evidence indicates that Friends were a majority. Chester Monthly Meeting, which was one of four in Chester County, had 72 adult male members in 1688. Five years later, there were only 281 taxpayers in the whole county. The total adult male Friends in the county (multiplying 72 by as much as four, and allowing for five years of growth) could not have been a minority in 1693. These numbers are incompatible with the thesis of Quakers being a legal élite in a pluralistic settlement. Also, by 1720 the Baptists, Anglicans, Presbyterians, Lutherans, and Reformed in Pennsylvania together had only sixteen congregations. A Chester-County Anglican wrote in 1712 "that Quakerism is generally preferred in Pennsylvania, and in no county of the province does the haughty tribe appear more rampant than where I reside, there being but by a modest computation 20 Quakers . . . to one true Churchman." Offutt, 60; W. F. Dunaway, "The English Settlers of Colonial Pennsylvania," *PMHB* 52 (1928), 317–41 and Dunaway, *A History of Pennsylvania* (New York, 1935), 336–52; Edwin Scott Gaustad, *Historical Atlas of Religion in America* (New York: Harper and Row, 1962), 25.

36. Nash, *Quakers*, chapter 1; also Frederick B. Tolles, *Meeting House and*

Counting House: The Quaker Merchants of Colonial Philadelphia, 1682–1763 (New York: W.W. Norton, reprint, 1963), chapter 3; and Bronner, *William Penn's "Holy Experiment"*, 47.

37. Nash, *Quakers*, 24–25.

38. Ibid.; Randolph Shipley Klein, *Portrait of an Early American Family: The Shippens of Pennsylvania Across Five Generations* (Philadelphia: University of Pennsylvania Press, 1975), 14, 17–19, 21.

39. Nash, *Quakers* and Tolles, *Meeting House* trace early Pennsylvania office holders.

40. Edwin Wolf, 2nd, "The Library of Ralph Assheton: The Book Background of a Colonial Philadelphia Lawyer," *Papers of the Bibliographical Society of America* 58 (1964): 346–48.

41. Nash, *Quakers*, 50–54, 110–11, 176–78; Nash, "The Early Merchants of Philadelphia: The Formation and Disintegration of a Founding Elite," in Richard S. Dunn and Mary Maples Dunn, eds., *The World of William Penn* (Philadelphia: University of Pennsylvania Press, 1986), 337–62.

42. Clair W. Keller, "Pennsylvania Government, 1701–1740: A Study of the Operation of Colonial Government" (Ph.D. dissertation, University of Washington, 1967), 226; *Statutes*, 2: 272; Tully, *Legacy*, 112.

43. Keller, "Pennsylvania Government," 226–27; *Statutes*, 2: 214, 272; 4, 10, 183; 5: 16; 7: 32; 8: 334; Wayne L. Bockelman, "Local Politics in Pre-Revolutionary Lancaster County," *PMHB* 97 (1973): 46.

44. Tully, *Forming*, 323–324, 328.

45. *Charter*, 97; Tully, *Legacy*, 112; J. Smith Futhey and Gilbert Cope, *History of Chester County Pennsylvania* (Philadelphia: Charles H. Everts, 1881), 374.

46. Two sheriffs, John Hoskins and Henry Worley, oddly turn up in no tax lists or histories of the county. The sheriff incumbents did not appear in the lists of incumbents in one other significant county office, the commissioner. After 1722, the three-man county commissions were popularly elected annually. Only two sheriffs were commissioners.

47. John Morton was an Anglican, and his Quaker supporter Philip Ford had to reassure important Quakers, like Joseph Pennock, Sr., that Morton was to be trusted as a friend of liberty and the Pennsylvania constitution. John Morton to Joseph Pennock, Sr., June 23, 1764, CCHS, as quoted in Tully, *Forming*, 324–25.

48. Pennsylvania was a democracy in so far as a population of free, white, adult, taxpaying males is considered. In his intensive examination of Pennsylvania politics and government, Alan Tully concluded that the franchise was generous, that discrimination against non-English minorities did not exist and they voted as commonly as the longer-established English and Welsh, and that many enfranchised men skipped voting but when they did it was due to "the indifference of the satisfied." Nor were the electoral practices a diluted version of English deference or an exhibition of some patron-client obligation. Officeholders were responsive to their constituents, who in turn were content with their officials. Tully, *Legacy*, 92–94, 99–102; Tully, *Forming*, 347, 368–70, 370–81.

49. Since there were fewer sheriffs than justices, the more precise case is that all sheriffs were justices but not all justices could become sheriffs.

50. See, for instance, Stanley N. Katz, *Newcastle's New York: Anglo-American Politics, 1732–1753* (Cambridge, Mass.: Harvard University Press, 1968).

51. Tully, *Legacy*, 109–10.

52. Offutt, 54–60.

53. Horle, *Quakers*, 116–19.

54. *Charter*, 100, 117, 129.
55. See Chapter 6 for accused's challenges to juries on the bases of their character as peers or equals.
56. Marianne Wokeck, "The Flow and the Composition of German Immigration to Philadelphia, 1727–1775," *PMHB* 105 (1981): 258–59.
57. J. S. Cockburn and Thomas A. Green, eds., *Twelve Good Men and True: The Criminal Trial Jury in England, 1200–1800* (Princeton, N.J.: Princeton University Press, 1988), 165–66; Beattie, 327–28, 386.
58. Jurors served at different convenings of the courts and, secondly, they might hear several cases at each sitting of the court and jury.
59. Mean service for trial jurors was 1.47 and standard deviation, 0.92; for grand jurors, 1.73 and 1.09 respectively. This population of jurors includes all who served in the years 1691–1695, 1716–1720, 1728–1732, 1738–1742, 1748–1752, 1763–1767, 1773–1777, 1783–1787, and 1797–1801.
60. Beattie, 321–22; Beattie, "London Juries in the 1690s," in Cockburn and Green, *Twelve Good Men*, 244.
61. Beattie, 385–90.
62. Beattie in Cockburn and Green, *Twelve Good Men*, 240, 242, 244.
63. P. J. R. King, "'Illiterate Plebians, Easily Misled': Jury Composition, Experience, and Behavior in Essex, 1735–1815," in Cockburn and Green, *Twelve Good Men*, 304.
64. Douglas Hay, "The Class Composition of the Palladium of Liberty: Trial Jurors in the Eighteenth Century," in Cockburn and Green, *Twelve Good Men*, 310–11, 351.
65. Offutt also discounts the influence of wealth: "Wealth as measured by the 1693 tax and by an inventory at death did not make a statistically significant difference in the number of [jury] assignments." Offutt, 57.
66. Nor was the residence of such jurors related to the number of trials they heard. For jurors who traveled to court from remoter townships, personal wealth would have eased their duty, but sheriffs or others selecting jurors appeared not to mind the wealth of those whom they chose. The mean percentile of taxable wealth for jurors from the zone immediate to the county seat was 73.6; it was 76.5 for those from the two more remote zones. See the next several paragraphs of the text for an explanation of the geographic zones.
67. Beattie found that jurors were called "in disproportionate numbers from the towns and hundreds in which the court was sitting." Beattie, 382–83.
68. Donegal Township was immense. It encompassed all of modern Lancaster and Dauphin Counties. It became part of Lancaster County when it was created in 1729. And later, it became part of Dauphin County in 1785. George W. Franz, *Paxton: A Study of Community Structure and Mobility in the Colonial Pennsylvania Backcountry* (New York: Garland, 1989), 110. For the complaints see Patrick Griffin, *The People with No Name: Ireland's Ulster Scots, America's Scots-Irish, and the Creation of a British Atlantic World, 1689–1764* (Princeton, N.J.: Princeton University Press, 2001), 110.

Chapter 3. Problems of Pluralism

Epigraph. Henry Melchior Muhlenberg, January 9, 1752, quoted in Paul A. W. Wallace, *The Muhlenbergs of Pennsylvania* (Philadelphia: University of Pennsylvania Press, 1950), 35.
1. Dickinson to Ezekiel Gomersall, September 2, 1717, Jonathan Dickinson

Letterbook, 1715–1721, 135, HSP. For information on Dickinson, see Horle, *Lawmaking*, 2: 309–27. The next several pages on immigration and ethnicity have benefited greatly from the following excellent works: Aaron Spencer Fogleman, *Hopeful Journeys: German Immigration, Settlement, and Political Culture in Colonial America, 1717–1775* (Philadelphia: University of Pennsylvania Press, 1996); David Hackett Fischer, *Albion's Seed: Four British Folkways in America* (New York: Oxford University Press, 1989); Patrick Griffin, *The People with No Name: Ireland's Ulster Scots, America's Scots Irish, and the Creation of a British Atlantic World, 1689–1764* (Princeton, N.J.: Princeton University Press, 2001); Maldwyn A. Jones, "The Scots-Irish in British America," in Bernard Bailyn and Philip D. Morgan, eds., *Strangers Within the Realm: Cultural Margins of the First British Empire* (Chapel Hill: University of North Carolina Press, 1991), 284–313; Sally Schwartz, *"A Mixed Multitude": The Struggle for Toleration in Colonial Pennsylvania* (New York: New York University Press, 1988); and Marianne S. Wokeck, *Trade in Strangers: The Beginnings of Mass Migration to North America* (University Park: Pennsylvania State University Press, 1999).

2. The numbers in 1717 seem small compared with the numbers of immigrants who came later, but the small population of Philadelphia at the time made the immigrants conspicuous. In 1720, Philadelphia had 4,883 inhabitants. Billy G. Smith, "The Population of Eighteenth-Century Philadelphia," *PMHB* 99 (1975): 366; Wokeck, *Trade in Strangers*, 41n.

3. Logan to Henry Goldney and others, September 25, 1717, Logan Papers, James Logan Letterbook, 4: 60, HSP; Schwartz, *"A Mixed Multitude"*, 86.

4. Jonathan Dickinson to John Askew, November 22, 1717, Jonathan Dickinson Letterbook, 1715–1721, 163; Isaac Norris, Sr. to William Wragg, September 13, 1717, Norris Papers, Isaac Norris Letterbook, 1716–1730, 99, HSP; Schwartz, *"A Mixed Multitude"*, 85–86.

5. Griffith, *People with No Name*, 92, 102, 200n; Smith, "Population of Philadelphia," 366; Wokeck, *Trade in Strangers*, 45; Logan to Springett Penn, 8 December 1727, Logan Copy Book, 5: 168, HSP.

6. The politics and economics of the 1720s can be followed in the following: Thomas Wendel, "The Keith-Lloyd Alliance: Factional and Coalition Politics in Colonial Pennsylvania," *PMHB* 92 (1968): 289–305; Nash, *Crucible*, 129–57; Mary Schweitzer, *Custom and Contract: Household, Government, and the Economy in Colonial Pennsylvania* (New York: Columbia University Press, 1987); Tully, *Forming* (1994).

7. Isaac Norris to Joseph Pike, 28–2 month 1728, Isaac Norris Letterbook, 1719–1756, 515–16, HSP.

8. Francis Jennings, "Incident at Tulpehocken," *PH* 35 (1968): 335–55, and his *The Ambiguous Iroquois Empire: The Covenant Chain Confederation of Indian Tribes with English Colonies from Its Beginnings to the Lancaster Treaty of 1744* (New York: W.W. Norton, 1984), 293–94, 305; James Logan to Andrew Hamilton, February 12, 1724/25, Logan Papers, James Logan Letterbook, 2: 255, HSP.

9. Because criminal records from Philadelphia do not exist for the early eighteenth century, we cannot know when and how often the pillory and stocks were employed before 1726. In Chester County, they were not used at all in these decades and were used most often between 1766 and 1788.

10. Wendel, "Keith-Lloyd Alliance," 301; James Logan to John Penn, October 17, 1726, Penn Papers, Official Correspondence (PPOC), 1: 237; Patrick Gordon to John Penn, October 22, 1726, PPOC, I: 247; Nash, *Crucible*, 152.

11. Jack D. Marietta, "The Growth of Quaker Self-Consciousness in Pennsyl-

vania," in J. William Frost and John M. Moore, eds., *Seeking the Light: Essays in Quaker History* (Wallingford, Pa.: Pendle Hill Publications, 1986), 85–86.

12. Logan to John Wright, 25–11 month 1725/26, *PA* 2nd ser., 7: 88.

13. For more information on Norris and Lloyd, see Horle, *Lawmaking*, 1: 490–505 and 2: 760–784.

14. Philadelphia Monthly Meeting minutes, 21–1 month 1730, 29–3 month 1730, 31–6 month 1733, 28–7 month 1733, Friends Historical Library, Swarthmore; Philadelphia Yearly Meeting minutes, 17–7 month 1733, Friends Historical Library.

15. Isaac Norris to Henry Goldney, 25–9 month 1719, Norris Letter Book, 214.

16. *Advice and Caution from Our Monthly Meeting in Philadelphia* (Philadelphia, 1732).

17. Jennings, "Incident at Tulpehocken." The best explanation of Logan's political and land affairs is Joseph E. Johnson, "A Statesman of Colonial Pennsylvania: A Study of the Private Life and Public Career of James Logan to the Year 1726" (Ph.D. dissertation, Harvard University, 1943).

18. Jennings, *Ambiguous Empire*, 271; Griffith, *People with No Name*, 104–6.

19. Jennings, *Ambiguous Empire*, 348, 273; Griffith, *People with No Name*, 107.

20. Wokeck, *Trade in Strangers*, 38.

21. Schwartz, *Mixed Multitude*, 96; Griffin, *People with No Name*, 102–3; Fogleman, *Hopeful Journeys*, 99.

22. Fischer, *Albion's Seed*, 605–39, 765–82, and Keith M. Brown, *Bloodfeud in Scotland, 1573–1625* (Edinburgh: John Donald, 1986), treat the Scots and Scots-Irish culture in the British Isles and America. Griffith, *People with No Name*, 101, 103–4, 111–17 reports the instances and reputation for violence of the Ulster immigrants in Pennsylvania.

23. Fischer, *Albion's Seed*, 630. James H. Webb recently explained the deep and enduring effect of the Scots-Irish on public life in America. See "Secret GOP Weapon: The Scots-Irish Vote," *Wall Street Journal*, October 19, 2004, and *Born Fighting: How the Scots-Irish Shaped America* (New York: Broadway Books, 2004).

24. Marietta, *Reformation*, 32–39.

25. John Churchman, *An Account of the Gospel Labours and Christian Experiences of a Faithful Minister of Christ, John Churchman* (Philadelphia, 1779), 34; Examinations of John Barrett, Robert Porter, Thomas Churchman, and John Churchman, February 1734, CCQSP. Churchman was also from Nottingham Township, and therefore no alien intruder to the neighborhood. The Ewing genealogy is at the website http://freepages.genealogy.rootsweb.com/~mysouthernfamily/myff/d0013/g0000026.html. (August 17, 2005).

26. Isaac Norris to Joseph Pike, 28–2 month 1728, Isaac Norris Letter Book, 1719–1756, 516; James Logan to John Penn, 14 May 1729, Logan Letter Book, 2: 229 and to Joseph Howston, 14 April 1730, Logan Letter Book, 3: 150–51; Logan to Adam Boyd, 29 February, 1731/32, Maria Dickinson Logan Family Papers, Dickinson-Logan Letterbook, 41, HSP; Logan to James Steel, 18 November 1729, PPOC, 2: 101; Griffith, *People with No Name*, 105, 111.

27. Griffith, *People with No Name*, 110, 114, 116–17; Fischer, *Albion's Seed*, 765–71; Steven Pinker, *The Blank Slate: The Modern Denial of Human Nature* (New York: Viking, 2002), 328–29; Richard E. Nisbett and Dov Cohen, *Culture of Honor: The Psychology of Violence in the South* (Boulder, Colo.: Westview Press, 1996), 41–54 and passim.

28. Scots-Irish were identified in the lists of indicted criminals and in nine tax lists from Chester County by searching for Scots-Irish surnames listed in Robert Bell, *The Book of Scots-Irish Family Names* (Belfast: Blackstaff Press, 1988). In both cases, the indicted and the taxpayers, the figures for Scots-Irish are the maximum ones, because some surnames that were common among in Ulster, England, and non-Ulster Ireland were counted as Scots-Irish. The reason for counting Scots-Irish in the tax lists is to control for any overcount in the indicted—both figures are maximum ones so the difference between the two better indicates the criminality of Scots-Irish. See note 65 below for information on the nine tax lists.

29. At its creation in 1722, Donegal Township encompassed all of the future Lancaster County and amounted to some 1500 square miles.

30. George W. Franz, *Paxton: A Study of Community Structure and Mobility in the Colonial Pennsylvania Backcountry* (New York: Garland, 1989), 106 and chapter 3. See also chapter 5 of this book.

31. In the 1790 census, Mifflin County had the largest percentage of Scots-Irish in Pennsylvania. Thomas L. Purvis, "Patterns of Ethnic Settlement in Late Eighteenth-Century Pennsylvania," *WPHM* 70 (1987): 115. By an examination of a sample of 884 heads of families in Mifflin in the 1790 census, we found Scots-Irish were 55 percent.

32. We obviously disagree with Thomas P. Slaughter, who wrote, "There is no discernable sense in which people of Scots-Irish or Irish ancestry, two cultures often labeled 'more violent' than others, were responsible for acts of interpersonal mayhem disproportionate to their numbers in the population. . . . [T]he function of both ethnicity and race in violent encounters is not recoverable from the eighteenth-century records." Slaughter, "Interpersonal Violence in a Rural Setting: Lancaster County in the Eighteenth Century," *PH* 58 (1991): 102.

33. Beattie, 108.

34. Lane, *Violent Death*, 60.

35. Marietta, "Growth of Quaker Self-Consciousness, 85–86.

36. *PCR*, 3: 193; 4: 209, 224; *AWM*, November 11, 1721, August 16, 1722.

37. These cases and others are discussed in Rowe, *Bench*, 83–84.

38. *PCR*, 3: 193; 4: 209, 224.

39. The English sample is Surrey. Beattie, 129, 197, 257–58, 340. Lane, *Murder*, 307, 310–311, 340.

40. *AWM*, January 13, 1729/30; January 15, 1734; June 16–23, 1743; *PG*, December 23, 1729, January 13, 1731.

41. November 1780, CCQSD. Also, *AWM*, January 18, 1726.

42. *AWM*, February 16, 1724/25; April 3–10, 1730.

43. David H. Flaherty, "Law and the Enforcement of Morals in Early America," *Perspectives on American History* 5 (1971): 226.

44. Edgar J. McManus, *Law and Liberty in Early New England: Criminal Justice and Due Process, 1620–1692* (Amherst: University of Massachusetts Press, 1993), 201–10; William E. Nelson, *Americanization of the Common Law: The Impact of Legal Change on Massachusetts Society, 1760–1830* (Cambridge, Mass.: Harvard University Press, 1975), 37. Nelson calls the 95 percent cases fornication rather than bastardy, but explains that they involved births of illegitimate children. Cornelia Hughes Dayton, *Women Before the Bar: Gender, Law, and Society in Connecticut, 1639–1789* (Chapel Hill: University of North Carolina Press, 1995), 174, 182, 8. Dayton found "only twenty-eight cases of illicit consensual sex" in the history of New Haven Colony (1639–1669), although she does not specify what percent of

all cases these were. Dayton's data are from New Haven County, Connecticut. She writes that the end of the seventeenth century marked a change in the character of courts and society in Connecticut; "By then a collective commitment to upholding a God-fearing society through the courts had been abandoned." But the prosecution of couples continued for decades. From the perspective of Pennsylvania, and with respect to morals prosecutions, Connecticut appears more interested in and persistent in keeping a God-fearing society alive than she realizes.

45. Dayton, *Women Before the Bar*, 159. There were two prosecutions of couples in the 1690s, and these dates are not surprising since they complement prosecutions of other kinds of victimless crime before 1700 (4 month 1693 and 10 month 1699, CCQSD). In Pennsylvania the dockets rarely identify spouses and rarely have the occasion to do so, because men and women sharing the same surname are rare. The possibility of undetected married couples being prosecuted for fornication exists if we presume that at the time of prosecution the courts chose to use the maiden name of the wives. We believe that is highly unlikely.

46. Dayton, *Women Before the Bar*, 8.

47. The Pennsylvania criminal courts' manner of proceeding in cases of illicit sexual relations creates a problem of tabulation and interpretation. When the courts recorded two charges, fornication *and* bastardy, we tabulated only one charge, bastardy, in order not to exaggerate the volume of illicit sexual actions. When the dockets or court papers recorded a verdict of guilty of fornication (or the accused's submission to the court) and a sentence of child support, it too was tabulated as bastardy, and not fornication.

There are occasional clues that fornication cases were also cases of bastardy, even though the accusation does not read as such. First, once in a rare while, in a case denominated fornication, there was evidence of pregnancy and a birth. For example, servant Margaret Butler was indicted for fornication in Chester County in November 1747 and later pleaded guilty. In February 1748, her master, George Moore, asked the court to add eighteen months to her service because she bore a child (November 1747, CCQSD).

48. Dayton, *Women Before the Bar*, 194–96.

49. Gottlieb Mittleberger recognized this. See his discussion of bastardy and his conclusion that "Fornication as such is not punished." *Journey to Pennsylvania*, ed. and trans. by Oscar Handlin and John Clive (Cambridge, Mass.: Harvard University Press, 1960), 70.

50. Flaherty, "Law and the Enforcement of Morals," 226–27, 230–31, 246–47.

51. See Chapter 6 regarding the great changes in the rates of prosecution of fornication and bastardy in the last quarter of the eighteenth century.

52. Indictment of George Gallegher, August 1792, CCQSP.

53. Affidavit of Elinor Murphy, November 1786, CCQSP. William McCorkle was prosecuted two years later for killing two horses of John Baily "in A Barborous manner by thrusting a Sharpened Stick upwards of three feet into their Bodyes." Order to goaler, September 2, 1788, CCQSP.

54. Statement of Margaret Kain [Kuin], 21 August 1739, CCQSP.

55. Petition of Mary Shea, 28 May 1752, CCQSP.

56. Flaherty, "Law and Morals," 248; Roger Thompson, *Sex in Middlesex: Popular Mores in a Massachusetts County, 1649–1699* (Amherst: University of Massachusetts Press, 1986), 128, 141–42; Lyle Koehler, *A Search for Power: The "Weaker*

Sex" in Seventeenth-Century New England (Urbana: University of Illinois Press, 1980), 147–48; McManus, *Law and Liberty in Early New England,* 23; Dayton, *Women Before the Bar,* 165.

57. McManus, *Law and Liberty,* 23; Koehler, *Search for Power,* 147; Dayton, *Women Before the Bar,* 165. In Connecticut, men were not prosecuted officially for adultery, but if bastardy were the case, they were fined and made responsible for childrearing expenses anyway.

58. Mary Beth Norton found in an examination of adultery cases in Maryland that all but one involved unfaithful wives and single men and that women were prosecuted ten times while she lists none for men. Norton, "Gender, Crime, and Community in Seventeenth-Century Maryland," in James Henretta, Michael G. Kammen, and Stanley N. Katz, eds., *The Transformation of Early American History: Society, Authority and Ideology* (New York: Alfred Knopf, 1991), 127, 135. Koehler supplies figures for six colonies which show women outnumbering men in five, but not exorbitantly so. *Search for Power,* 149.

59. Among the prosecuted were 32 couples, 29.1 percent of the total. Dockets do not link the men and women; we included as couples a man and women who appeared in the same court session in the same county, and in two cases in consecutive sessions. Thirty-two couples is therefore a maximum number.

60. In Connecticut, the bias against women showed in punishments, which were harsher for convicted women than for men. Dayton, *Women Before the Bar,* 166–67. We are unable to provide precise sentences for the convicted in Pennsylvania.

61. *Statutes,* 2: 8, 183–84; 3: 202 and our Chapter 2.

62. Indictment of Isaac Waddle, alias Isaac Miles, November 1800, CCQSP. Examination of Robert Owen, 5 September 1749, CCQSP, February 1793, CCQSD. In the Chester County Dockets of 1705, the court recorded that William Pusey "one young black heifer . . . did carnally know & . . . the horrible sin of buggary did then and there feloniously commit." Dorothy Lapp, ed., *Records of the Courts of Chester County, Pennsylvania* (Danboro, Pa., 1972), 2: 143–44.

63. John M. Murrin uses a different definition in his "Bestiality in Early America," *Explorations in Early American Culture* 65 (1998): 36.

64. J. Thomas Scharf and Thompson Westcott reported in 1748 that Thomas White and Arthur Maginnis were hanged in Philadelphia for sodomy. The authors erred in one of the two cases and very likely in both. Arthur Maginnis was a murder victim in 1748, not a criminal. White cannot be found in any judicial record in Pennsylvania, nor do newspapers or other historical sources report any execution of White—and newspapers did report such events. J. Thomas Scharf and Thompson Westcott, *History of Philadelphia, 1609–1884,* 3 vols. (Philadelphia: Louis H. Everts, 1884), 3: 1827.

65. The data here on people in the justice system were obtained by the following means: We compiled names, taxpayer classification, taxes, and when possible, tax assessments from nine Chester County tax lists between 1693 and 1799, for a total of 33,210 taxpayers. From Philadelphia we obtained the taxpayers in the 1780 city tax list, a total of 6,065. These data were analyzed to discover the distribution of wealth in the county and city and the relative rank of each taxpayer. From the criminal records (mostly dockets) of Chester County and Philadelphia we drew the names of all accused persons in the years of the compiled tax lists, plus the year before and year after each list. We eliminated the names of women and minors, since they appeared rarely or not at all in the tax lists in Chester and were few in the city. Victims' names were culled from Chester court

papers for the same dates; Philadelphia had no papers. The two databases, of wealth and court appearances, were then collated, producing the summary figures in this chapter and elsewhere. We obtained a high and low figure for the wealth percentile of each man, because the tax lists contain men who shared one name and paid different taxes. We recorded both and derived a mean figure for both the lower and upper alternatives. Triplicates and beyond we discarded completely. For more detail, see Jack D. Marietta, "The Distribution of Wealth in Eighteenth-Century America: Nine Chester County Tax Lists, 1693–1799," *Pennsylvania History* 62 (1995): 532–45. For a discussion of the completeness or reliability of the tax lists, see ibid., n. 28.

66. The Philadelphia accused are from the 1779–1781 dockets and were searched in the 1780 Philadelphia tax list.

67. We used the directories of 1791, 1793, 1794, and 1796–1800 and the accused in those years. Of 1284 indicted, 357 appeared in the directories. The directories can be found in Charles Evans, *American Bibliography* (Chicago: Blakely Press, 1903–1959).

68. *N* of accused men = 767. Again, this is a maximum percent and should be compared with the populations in Table 3.1.

69. An unspecifiable number of the accused were indentured servants. There are no lists of servants in which to search for these accused. One may search for them in court records and elsewhere, but the effort would produce an undercount.

70. After 1750 impoverished men increasingly appeared before Pennsylvania courts, or at least Philadelphia courts. In 1761 James Hamilton, lieutenant governor of the province, argued that the accused were "in general, the most indigent of Mankind, and consequently unable to pay" the court fees. The consequence was that the attorney general, Benjamin Chew, was working without compensation. *PA* 8th ser. 6: 5266. John K. Alexander has demonstrated that ten Philadelphia men who escaped from jail in December 1766, whose occupations were listed, were for the most part from the laboring poor. This trend appears to have accelerated in the two decades following the Revolution. At least, admittedly fragmentary evidence and the observations of foreign and domestic observers seem to indicate as much. *PJ*, December 18, 1766; Alexander, *Render*, 63, 66–67, 69.

71. The records offer very few indications that the accused were juveniles.

72. Billy G. Smith, *The "Lower Sort": Philadelphia's Laboring People, 1750–1800* (Ithaca, N.Y.: Cornell University Press, 1990), 151–52, 173–75, 177, 214–15; Stephanie Grauman Wolf, *Urban Village: Population, Community, and Family Structure in Germantown, Pennsylvania, 1683–1800* (Princeton, N.J.: Princeton University Press, 1976), 72–81, 94–95; James T. Lemon, *The Best Poor Man's Country: A Geographical Study of Early Southeastern Pennsylvania* (Baltimore: Johns Hopkins University Press, 1972), 73–87.

73. George W. Franz, *Paxton: A Study of Community Structure and Mobility in the Colonial Pennsylvania Backcountry* (New York: Garland, 1989), 106, 127, 157.

74. Simler and Clemens, "The 'Best Poor Man's Country'," 245. Emphasis added.

75. George Wilson Pearson, *Tocqueville and Beaumont in America* (New York: Oxford University Press, 1938), 544. The Germans who fascinated Tocqueville may have been Mennonites or Amish.

76. Examination of William Gumley, no month, 1771, CCQSP.

77. Examination of Dennis Cornealey, December 1798, CCQSP.

78. Examination of Wilhelm Clines, May 1782, CCQSP.

79. Examination of Thomas Ryan, February 1797, CCQSP.

80. Smith, *The "Lower Sort"*, 137, 150–52, 173, 177.

81. Sharon V. Salinger, *"To Serve Well and Faithfully": Labor and Indentured Servants in Pennsylvania, 1682–1800* (Cambridge: Cambridge University Press, 1987), 119.

82. Salinger calculates that at least ten percent of the servants indentured in 1745 ran away within five years. The runaways at all times, and not just 1745, escaped mostly from rural masters and were heavily Scots-Irish immigrants. *"To Serve Well and Faithfully"*, 103, 105, 112. Simon Newman found that in the Vagrancy Dockets of Philadelphia "the large majority of runaway whites were . . . indentured servants." *Embodied History: The Lives of the Poor in Early Philadelphia* (Philadelphia: University of Pennsylvania Press, 2003), 51.

83. Examination of Morris Obrennon, May 3, 1735; Examination of Mary Rudell, May 2, 1735, CCQSP.

84. 3-month 1749, CCQSD and CCQSP.

85. Examinations of William Kerr, Alexander Fisher, and William Cey, August 20, 1751, CCQSP.

86. Examinations of Wilhelm Clines, May 1782; Examination of Mary McClaine, February 2, 1749, CCQSP.

87. Beattie, 186.

88. Adrienne D. Hood, *The Weaver's Craft: Cloth, Commerce, and Industry in Early Pennsylvania* (Philadelphia: University of Pennsylvania Press, 2003), 1–2, 134. Hood comments that, "wealthy eighteenth-century Philadelphians' fabric was worth more than their wrought silver."

89. Newman, *Embodied History*, 97.

90. Examinations of Ruth Simson, wife of George, and Dinah and Edward Russell, 20 November 1732, CCQSP; Examination of David Davis, August 16, 1757, CCQSD.

91. Thomas Doerflinger, "Farmers and Dry Goods in the Philadelphia Market Area, 1750–1800," in Ronald Hoffman et al, eds. *The Economy of Early America: The Revolutionary Period, 1763–1790* (Charlottesville: University of Virginia Press, 1986), 177–78.

92. Hood, *Weaver's Craft*, 120–23, 135.

93. Alice Hanson Jones, *American Colonial Wealth: Documents and Methods*, 3 vols. (New York: Arno Press, 1977), 1: 84, 161–63.

94. Beattie, 186.

95. Alexander, *Render Them Submissive*, 80, 124.

96. Beattie, 168. It was removed from benefit of clergy in Tudor times.

97. Lemon, *Best Poor Man's Country*, 180. Doerflinger believes that Lemon's number for annual average income is too low and £70 is more accurate. Doerflinger, "Farmers and Dry Goods," 188.

98. Examination of David Davis, 16 August 1757; examination of Thomas Meglaughlin, April 11, 1771, CCQSP. Davis was fined 60 shillings and given 42 lashes. Meglaughlin was fined £19-1s, whipped 39 lashes, and sentenced to three months in jail.

99. November 1780, CCQSD.

100. Here again, these are adult males, rarely women, and never servants, because of custom and law. Victims were from Chester County alone, because the court papers in which victims are identified are mostly missing in the case of Philadelphia.

101. Examination of Edmund Cryer by Justice Paul Jackson, 6 May 1763, CCQSP.

102. Examination of George Lyon by Justice Paul Jackson, 6 May 1763, CCQSP.

103. Examinations of Alexander Robeson, Abel Roberts, Benjamin Walker, Evan Anderson, Thomas Cuthbert, and James Martin, January 1772, CCQSP.

104. "To Any Constable of this County" from William Moore, January 1772, CCQSP.

105. The incensed Justice Moore ranked in the 99th percentile and owned two slaves.

106. There was no indication that Robinson was black.

107. See Marietta, "Distribution of Wealth," 532–45 and John Gilbert McCurdy, "Taxation and Representation: Pennsylvania Bachelors and the American Revolution." *PMHB* 129 (2005): 283–316 for explanations of how singlemen were treated in compiling wealth data.

108. Singlemen appeared as a percentage of accused 3.2 percent more often than they appeared as a percentage of taxpayers. Similarly, inmates appeared 1.3 percent more often. N of singlemen in nine tax lists (1693–1799) = 5850 and N of accused singlemen = 63; N of inmates in same lists = 3834; N of accused inmates = 39. Landowners appeared 2.1 percent less often as accused, and tenants 2.3 percent less often. N of landowners = 21,282 and accused landowners = 188. N of tenants = 2067 and N of accused tenants = 12. Jack D. Marietta and G. S. Rowe, "Violent Crime, Victims, and Society in Pennsylvania, 1682–1800," *Explorations in Early American Culture: A Supplemental Issue of Pennsylvania History* 66 (1999), 38.

109. Lucy Simler, "Tenancy in Colonial Pennsylvania: The Case of Chester County," *WMQ* 43 (1986): 569. Tenancy seems to be a condition quite remote from enjoying the independence of freehold ownership of land. While dependency may be the case for farm tenants in Europe or elsewhere, Pennsylvania tenants were not like these dependent peoples. While tilling or otherwise using land they leased, some Pennsylvania tenants owned and cultivated land next to or removed from their leaseholds. Still others were tenants, freeholders, and landlords all at the same time. The lawmakers of Pennsylvania certainly treated all tenants like landowners, assessing and taxing them alike—in tax lists they were all landholders. In her close examination of landholding in Chester County, Lucy Simler has explained that the condition, interests, and prospects of the two were very similar. Consequently, whatever one can ascertain about their criminal or their law-abiding behavior should not be attributed to any clear economic distinction between tenants and landowners or to any state of dependency. Tenants' appearance can be tracked for only thirty-five years, because they are distinguishable in tax lists only beginning in 1765. Among the nine tax lists in this work, the first observation of them comes in the 1765 tax list. Marietta, "Distribution of Wealth," 533.

110. Marietta, "Distribution of Wealth," 534.

111. David T. Courtwright, *Violent Land: Single Men and Social Disorder from the Frontier to the Inner City* (Cambridge, Mass.: Harvard University Press, 1996), 2, 14.

112. Simler, "The Landless Worker: An Index of Economic and Social Change in Chester County, Pennsylvania, 1750–1829," *PMHB* 114 (1990): 163–99.

113. Because court papers from the city, which name victims, have not survived, no analysis of victims was possible.

114. The way in which wealth is reported in the tables and figures needs to be explained. Without middle names or initials to distinguish each and every taxpayer from all others, and without other identifying tokens, like residence, as many as four or five taxpayers in a single tax list share the same name. In that case, a person in the criminal records cannot be linked inerrantly with his entry in the tax lists. In order not to exclude from analysis persons in the criminal records who appear twice in a tax list (i.e., the same name appears twice), data for such duplicates are included—but not names appearing three or more times. The product is two figures for the mean wealth and mean percentile rank for any group: one using the lower tax for ambiguous cases and a second for the same group using the higher tax. Also, we were able to associate thirteen women assailants with their husbands and get figures for their taxable estates. The women assailants (or their husbands) ranked in the 42.5 percentile.

115. $N = 302$; standard deviation $= 30.5$.

116. The high alternative mean for the 74 was 49.5. Twelve accused women in the city could be associated with their husbands and their rank determined. It was the 28.6 percentile—obviously lower than that of the accused men in Philadelphia and much lower too than the few women accused in Chester County.

117. Marietta and Rowe, "Violent Crime, Victims, and Society," 38.

118. The aggregated grand and trial jurors (who were on the tax lists) were always from the top 30 percent of the taxpayers, significantly superior to both indicted and nonindicted accused men.

119. Billy G. Smith and Richard Wojtowicz, *Blacks Who Stole Themselves: Advertisements for Runaways in the Pennsylvania Gazette, 1728–1790* (Philadelphia: University of Pennsylvania Press, 1989).

120. A. L. Beier, *Masterless Men: The Vagrancy Problem in England, 1560–1640* (New York: Methuen, 1985); Edmund S. Morgan, *American Slavery, American Freedom: The Ordeal of Colonial Virginia* (New York: W.W. Norton, 1975), 235–37.

Chapter 4. Persistent Violence

Epigraph. May 1763, CCQSP.

1. The 513 figure includes all homicide cases that came to the attention of the courts. It includes infanticide, first- and second-degree murder, manslaughter, and murder by chance medley (an affray or misadventure). It does not include suicides.

2. Coroner's Inquisitions, 1751–1796; *AWM*, March 1–10, 1743; *PG*, September 26, 1733, May 20, 1742, July 14, 1784; *PC*, June 22–29, 1767.

3. Oyer and Terminer Papers, Lancaster County, 1761, RG-27, PMHC, Harrisburg.

4. *PG*, August 21, 28, 1755; Biddle, *Autobiography*, 209–10; Oyer and Terminer Court Papers, Boxes 1–4, Philadelphia County; *AWM*, November 12, 1730.

5. For two works on the advent or the modern family, see J. William Frost, *The Quaker Family in Colonial America* (New York: St. Martin's Press, 1973); Barry Levy, *Quakers and the American Family: British Settlement in the Delaware Valley* (New York: Oxford University Press, 1988). The theme of household violence is developed more fully and illustrated more profusely in G. S. Rowe and Jack D. Marietta, "Domestic Violence in a 'Peaceable Kingdom:' Pennsylvania, 1682–1801," in Christine Daniels, ed., *Over the Threshold: Intimate Violence in Early America, 1640–1865* (New York: Routledge, 1999), 24–54.

6. *PG*, August 11, 1748, August 21, 1755; Court of Oyer and Terminer Papers:

Lancaster County, #4030, RG-33 Records of the Supreme Court, PMHC, Harrisburg (hereafter Oyer and Terminer Papers); *PG*, October 18, 1739.

7. The figure for Pennsylvania is convicted and sentenced murderers, not indicted murderers, which means that it is the low number that is being compared with the other jurisdictions, which use a higher number, indictments or murders known to the police. One-quarter of convicted murderers in Pennsylvania roughly equals the proportion in Chicago in the late nineteenth and early twentieth centuries; one quarter is half that in the United States in the 1950s; and is half that of modern England. Pennsylvania and Chicago appear similar, therefore, with high proportions of intimate homicide and high overall homicide rates. The U.S. in the 1950s did enjoy and modern England still enjoys the best of times, due to their low overall homicide rates. In modern England the overall homicide rate is only 1.0 or less per 100,000; the Chicago rate was at least 8.0; and the rate in the 1950s in the United States was at its historic low, less than 5. Medieval England displayed very high homicide rates, but very low proportions of intimate homicide. Jeffrey S. Adler, " 'We've Got a Right to Fight: We're Married': Ethnicity, Race, and Domestic Homicide in Chicago, 1875–1920," *Journal of Interdisciplinary History* 34 (2003): 27–48; Lane, *Murder*, 16, 229, 231, 258–59, 308.

8. Adler, " 'We've Got a Right to Fight' "; Jeffery Fagan and Angela Browne, "Violence Between Spouses," in Albert J. Reiss, Jeffrey A. Roth, and Klaus A. Miczek, eds., *Understanding and Preventing Violence: Social Influences*, (Washington, D.C.: National Academy Press, 1994), 121, 209; R. Emerson Dobash and Russel Dobash, *Violence Against Wives: A Case Against the Patriarchy* (New York: Free Press, 1979), 34–64.

9. Negley K. Teeters, "Public Executions in Pennsylvania, 1682–1834," in Eric H. Monkkonen, ed., *Crime and Justice in American History: The Colonies and Early Republic*, 2 vols. (Westport, Conn.: Meckler, 1991), 2: 814.

10. Adler, " 'We've Got a Right to Fight.' " Adler found a clear correlation between the Chicago fathers who slew children and wives and German culture. German culture far more effectively imbued these men with patriarchal values and obligations, which they failed. In light of the several egregious family murders committed by German fathers in Pennsylvania, the Chicago correlation suggests such a possibility existed in Pennsylvania.

11. Teeters, "Public Executions in Pennsylvania, 1682–1834," in Monkkonen, *Crime and Justice in American History*, 2: 814.

12. *PCR*, 5: 488; *PG*, October 18, 1750; *Record of the Courts of Chester County, Pennsylvania* (Philadelphia: Patterson and White, 1910), 52–53; *PCR*, 7: 343–44, 398.

13. *PCR*, 2: 513; Oyer and Terminer Papers: Lancaster County, #4030. The boy had run away on two occasions.

14. Oyer and Terminer Papers, Boxes 1–4, Lancaster, 1767, Berks, 1772; *PG*, February 24, 1742, January 8, 1734; Merle G. Brouwer, "The Negro as Slave and as a Free Black in Colonial Pennsylvania" (Ph.D. dissertation, Wayne State University, 1973), 190.

15. Marietta, *Reformation*, 107–8; Levy, *Quakers and the American Family*, 253.

16. Oyer and Terminer papers, Boxes 1–4, Lancaster County, 1772; *PCR*, 9: 745–46; Teeters, "Public Executions in Pennsylvania, 1682–1834," in Monkkonen, *Crime and Justice in American History*, 2: 814.

17. *PG*, July 16, 20, 1730; Clemency Records, 1775–1783, RG-27, PMHC, reel 37. Also *AWM*, August 22, 1745.

18. Teeters, "Public Executions in Pennsylvania, 1682–1834," in Monkkonen, *Crime and Justice in American History*, 2: 804; *PCR*, 8: 506; Halbert, *The Last Speech and Confession of Henry Halbert who was Executed at Philadelphia* (Philadelphia, 1765); Yeates Papers, Miscellaneous Legal Papers, folio 3, 1795, HSP; *AWM*, March 5, 1734; Cases of Peter Gift (1778) and Magdelana Fetter (1779) in Supreme Court (Eastern District) Miscellaneous Dockets, 1743–1749, RG-33, PMHC. Prosecutors often refused to charge obviously mentally ill defendants. See Tench Francis's response in 1742 in the case of Catherine Pickering who was clearly "an Ideot." Bucks County Quarter Sessions Docket, 1742, BCHS.

19. *PCR*, IV: 675, 676, 678, 680–81, 682–85, 698, 702; *PG*, April 26, November 8, November 15, 1744; *AWM*, November 8–15, 1744; Joseph J. Kelley, Jr., *Pennsylvania: The Colonial Years, 1681–1776* (Garden City, N.Y.: Doubleday, 1980), 233–34. Teeter does not list Mushmelon's hanging in his study of public executions in Pennsylvania.

20. *PCR*, 5: 543.

21. These cases can be followed in Teeters, "Public Executions in Pennsylvania," in Monkkonen, *Crime and Justice in American History*, 2: 756–835.

22. David T. Courtwright, *Violent Land: Single Men and Social Disorder from the Frontier to the Inner City* (Cambridge, Mass.: Harvard University Press, 1996), 13–14, 16, 18–19, 27–34. See also Lane, *Murder*, 3, and this book, Chapter 3 above.

23. See Negley K. Teeters, "Public Executions in Pennsylvania, 1682–1834," in Monkkonen, *Crime and Justice in American History*, 2: 803, 810, 832; *PCR*, 5: 119, 125, 134; 7: 343–44, 388–89; Records of the Supreme Court [Eastern District] RG-33; Court of Oyer and Terminer Papers, Lancaster County, 1772, Boxes 1–4; Biddle, *Extracts*, 16.

24. For the familicide cases, see *PG*, August 21, 1755; John Lewis, *A Narrative of the Life, together with the Last Speech, Confession, and Solemn Declaration of John Lewis* (Philadelphia, 1760). The *Short Title Evans* contains a ghost copy of *The Life and Confession of John Myriak* (Philadelphia, 1755). For a discussion of familicide, see Daniel A. Cohen, "Homicidal Compulsion and the Conditions of Freedom: The Social and Psychological Origins of Familicide in America's Early Republic," *JSH* 28 (1995): 725–64.

25. Details of the Stump case are provided by G. S. Rowe, "The Frederick Stump Affair, 1768, and Its Challenge to Legal Historians of Early Pennsylvania," *PH* 49 (1982): 259–88.

26. Yeates Papers: Legal Papers, folder 2 (April-May 1782), HSP; Biddle, *Extracts*, 16.

27. Teeters, "Public Executions in Pennsylvania, 1682–1832," in Monkkonen, *Crime and Justice in American History*, 2: 827. Jane Farrell pleaded guilty to killing George Teaffe "by Misadventure" in April 1746 in oyer and terminer proceedings.

28. The 120 figure is a minimum count; a maximum of 135 is possible.

29. G. S. Rowe, "Women's Crime and Criminal Administration in Pennsylvania, 1763–1790," *PMHB* 109 (1985): 343.

30. Teeters, "Public Executions," 779; William Markham to William Penn, May 2, 1688, in PWP, 3: 191–92; PCR, 1: 227, 252, 254.

31. This, and following paragraphs, rely heavily upon G. S. Rowe, "Infanticide, Its Judicial Resolution, and Criminal Code Revision in Early Pennsylvania," *Proceedings of the American Philosophical Society*, 135 (1991), 200–232.

32. Juries after 1793 were not required to choose between the two extremes of freedom for the accused or death.

33. See Peter C. Hoffer and N. E. H. Hull, *Murdering Mothers: Infanticide in England and New England, 1558–1803* (New York: New York University Press, 1981), esp. xiii.

34. Rogers unsuccessfully attempted suicide by slashing her own throat after killing her son. She was jailed but never tried. In all probability the court found her *non compos mentis. CG,* September 21, 1785.

35. Oyer and Terminer Papers, RG-33, Boxes 1–4, Philadelphia (1772).

36. *The Trial of Alice Clifton* (Philadelphia, 1787), 1–2, 4–8.

37. Simon P. Newman, *Embodied History: The Lives of the Poor in Early Philadelphia* (Philadelphia: University of Pennsylvania Press, 2004), 126, 133.

38. These ideas are developed more fully in Rowe, "Infanticide," 205–6.

39. These changes are traced carefully in Rowe, "Infanticide," 200–232 and discussed in Merril D. Smith, " 'Unnatural Mothers': Infanticide, Motherhood, and Class in the Mid-Atlantic, 1730–1830," in Christine Daniels and Michael V. Kennedy, eds., *Over the Threshold: Intimate Violence in Early America* (New York: Routledge, 1999), 173–84.

40. *PCR,* 11: 780; Fisher, May 3, 1779, Clemency Files, roll 36.

41. See Rowe, "Infanticide," 211–15; Sharon Ann Burnston, "Babies in the Well: An Underground Insight into Deviant Behavior in Eighteenth-Century Philadelphia," *PMHB* 106 (1982): 151–86. Lane, *Murder,* 119.

42. *A Faithful Narrative of Elizabeth Wilson* (New York, 1786), 1–4; Elaine Forman Crane, ed., *The Diary of Elizabeth Drinker* (abridged ed., Boston: Northeastern University Press, 1994), 146–47, 148, 152.

43. Rowe, "Infanticide," 214–15.

44. Records of the Supreme Court (Eastern District): Coroner's Inquisitions, 1751–1796, RG-33, PHMC. For other cases see *PG,* March 4, 1735; October 21, 1736; August 11, 1737. Many of the young corpses showed signs of systematic abuse and torture.

45. *PG,* November 17, 1730. Two months later Thomas was found dead in her own bed under mysterious circumstances. *AWM,* January 5, 1730/31.

46. To discover disparities or inequities we examined all case outcomes for significant differences by gender. (Our arbitrary rule of thumb was to regard as significant any difference of five percent or more.) From a matrix of data treating two genders, seven major varieties of crimes, and as many as six junctures in the progress of a case, significant differences appear only six times, two of them in the homicide category. The maximum number of events where gender disparities could appear is 84—the product of two genders by six junctures (not counting unknown outcomes) by seven major categories of crime. Abuses and injustices might also be discovered in the narrative records of trials, but these records have very largely disappeared.

47. The 45.2 percent was of cases resolved, and the number was 28. All four men accused of infanticide were convicted.

48. Adler, " 'We've Got a Right to Fight: We're Married.' "

49. Martin Gold, "Suicide, Homicide, and the Socialization of Aggression," *American Journal of Sociology* 62 (1958): 651–61.

50. Michael MacDonald and Terrence R. Murphy, *Sleepless Souls: Suicide in Early Modern England* (New York: Oxford University Press, 1990), 15.

51. Ibid., 16, 109–10, 114, 125.

52. See, for instance, *Considerations on Some of the Laws Relating to the Office of a Coroner* (Newcastle, 1776); also John Adams, *An Essay concerning Self-Murther* (London, 1700).

53. Biddle, *Extracts*, 11–12.

54. All cases are found in Records of the Supreme Court (Eastern District): Coroners' Inquisitions, 1751–1796, PMHC, RG-33.

55. Ibid; *PG*, July 5, 1753.

56. *PG*, April 2, 1741.

57. See, for instance, *PG*, February 10, 1730, August 27, 1730, December 24, 1733; Billy G. Smith, ed., *Life in Early Philadelphia: Documents from the Revolutionary and Early National Periods* (University Park: Pennsylvania State University Press, 1995) 43, 47, 73.

58. P. E. H. Hair says the suicide rate for sixteenth-century Nottinghamshire and Essex was between 3.4 and 4.0 per 100,000 population, a figure commensurate with J. A. Sharpe's findings for Tudor England. Michael Zell offers a rate of 10.0 per 100,000 for sixteenth-century Kent. See Hair, "A Note on the Incidence of Tudor Suicide," *Local Population Studies* 5 (1970): 36–43; Zell, "Suicide in Pre-Industrial England," *Social History* 11 (1986): 309–10; Sharpe, "The History of Violence in England: Some Observations," *Past and Present* (1985): 209–11. MacDonald and Murphy put little faith in suicide rates (240–41) but see *Sleepless Souls*, 244, where they say there were probably 50 suicides per year in the 1730s. The Pennsylvania suicide rate per 100,000 is based on 18 reported suicides and a projected cumulative population of 666,850 (an assumed population for 1730 of 51,700 and for 1739 of 81,670).

59. For a general discussion of the difficulty of computing suicide rates, see David Lester, *Why People Kill Themselves*, 3rd ed. (Springfield, Ill.: C.C. Thomas, 1992), 85–88.

60. *Self-Murther and Duelling the Effects of Cowardice and Atheism* (London, 1728); G. Cheyne, *The English Malady; or, A Treatise of Nervous Diseases of All Kinds*, 3rd ed., (London, 1734); MacDonald and Murphy, *Sleepless Souls*, 307–14.

61. *PG*, March 25, 1731, May 4, 1732, June 15, 1738, January 25, 1739.

62. *AWM*, August 19–26, 1742; *PG*, November 5, 1730, September 1, 1731, July 13, 1738; October 28, 1743. Other examples of suicide by blacks are provided by Brouwer, "The Negro as Slave and as a Free Black in Colonial Pennsylvania," 330–33, where he argues that blacks employed suicide as a means of resisting slavery.

63. *PG*, August 27, 1730, February 2, 1733, June 1, 1738, May 15, 1746.

64. Records of the Supreme Court (Eastern District): Coroners' Inquisitions, 1751–1796, PMHC, RG-33, Harrisburg; *AWM*, September 11–18, 1735, October, 2–9, 1735; *PG*, August 27, 1730, May 4, 1732.

65. *PG*, December 24, 1733, April 2, 1741, January 21, 1752, May 7, 1752. Religious hysteria also occasionally prompted Pennsylvanians to mutilate themselves, sometimes fatally. Charles Brockden Brown's *Theodore Wieland* is the most famous literary example of this from the period, but Wieland's sister, Clara, also exhibited a persistent suicidal morbidity. Real life parallels appear in the records. Motivated by religious zeal, John Wainwright castrated himself in February 1730. John Leek also emasculated himself "for the Kingdom of Heaven's Sake" in October 1743. Both Wainwright and Leek survived their mutilations. *PG*, February 19, 1730; October 28, 1743.

66. Gold, "Suicide, Homicide," 651–61.

67. Lane, *Violent Death*. See also Lester, *Why People Kill Themselves*, and McDonald and Murphy, *Sleepless Souls*.

68. That is typical of recorded versus unrecorded assaults. See Beattie, *Crime and the Courts*, 74–75.

69. Bertram Wyatt-Brown, *The Shaping of Southern Culture: Honor, Grace, and War, 1760s-1890s* (Chapel Hill: University of North Carolina Press, 2001), 73.

70. Charles Pettit to Joseph Reed, September 20, 1764, Reed Papers, NYHS. Dickinson was born a Quaker and married a Quaker but did not attend meetings. Following the fisticuffs, he challenged Galloway to a duel. Milton E. Flower, *John Dickinson: Conservative Revolutionary* (Charlottesville: University of Virginia Press, 1983), 42; Benjamin H. Newcomb, *Franklin and Galloway: A Political Partnership* (New Haven, Conn.: Yale University Press, 1972), 89. Another slugfest, between Joseph Borden McKean, son of the Chief Justice, and publisher John Fenno (1799) is just one of the many possible examples. Elizabeth Drinker seemed amused that "Joe McKean and John Fenno have had a fighting match." See Biddle, *Extracts,* 343.

71. *Records of the Courts of Chester County, Pennsylvania* (Philadelphia, 1910), 65–66.

72. Crane, *Diary of Elizabeth Drinker,* 150; *GUS,* May 30, 1795; Mayor's Court (Philadelphia) Dockets, June, 1795.

73. $N = 147$. Standard deviations were respectively 33.2 and 32.5 respectively. Cases of riot were included with assaults in this calculation; assault cases alone produce means of 53.9 and 58.6.

74. Women were identified as "spinsters" or were without vocations listed. When their spouses were named and found on tax lists, such women were entered into the property rank computations.

75. $N = 91$. The standard deviations were 30.7 and 30.4 respectively.

76. The vocations of the victims in 333 crimes in Chester County were established; the victims in 104 of those crimes (31 percent) were 58 different constables. Contrariwise, only two constables were among the assailants. Vocation should not be confused with tax list status (landowner, tenant, singleman, inmate). For example, landowners were probably farmers, but may have had other vocations or dual vocation.

77. Reports from constables, Fayette County, Fayette County Courthouse, Uniontown, Pennsylvania.

78. Affirmation of Thomas Rogers, November 29, 1736, CCQSP.

79. 8–4th Month, 1697, August 3, 1770, CCQSP.

80. February 1789, CCQSP. See Chapter 7 for more on the 1780–1800 confrontations.

81. June 14, 1792, May 1788, CCQSP. They were accused of assault on Enoch Speakman. There was never a mention of constables being armed with either some kind of firearm or a staff or stick.

82. Periodic sampling is not the best way to catch repeaters. Ours is a sample of three continuous years usually separated by a decade, so it catches men who repeat within those three years, but not earlier or later.

83. May 1770, CCQSP.

84. May 1770, May 25, 1762, CCQSP.

85. "Pennsylvania v. Adam Keffer, December 1795," in Alexander Addison, ed., *Reports of Cases in the County Courts of the 5th District and the High Court of Errors and Appeals of the State of Pennsylvania* (Washington, Pa., 1800); York County Quarter Sessions Dockets, 1775, 1778, 1780, York County Courthouse, York; Berks County Quarter Sessions Dockets, November 1792, Berks County Courthouse, Reading. A considerable portion of these refusals were part of an organized rural resistance to state government after 1780. See Chapter 7 for more about the topic.

86. Examination of Sarah Southby, November 16, 1736, CCQSP.

87. One of the most significant examples in American historiography of this interpretation is Bernard Bailyn, "Politics and Society Structure in Virginia," in James Morton Smith, ed., *Seventeenth-Century America: Essays in Colonial History* (Chapel Hill: University of North Carolina Press, 1959), 90–118.

88. Until recently what historians wrote about constables confirmed rather than revised Shakespeare. As historian Joan Kent explains, in the historical literature they appear disrespected, uneducated, too poor or shiftless to avoid the job, and sometimes criminal. Recently, Kent and J. A. Sharpe have read the historical record more sympathetically. According to these scholars, English constables were from substantial families in the parishes and were often small property owners of middling fortune. Kent, "The English Village Constable, 1580–1642: The Nature and Dilemmas of the Office," *Journal of British Studies* 20 (1981): 26–49. On page 27, Kent provides an extended survey of the historiography of constables. Sharpe, "Crime and Delinquency in an Essex Parish, 1600–1640," in J. S. Cockburn, ed., *Crime in England, 1550–1800* (Princeton, N.J.: Princeton University Press 1977), 95–97; Sharpe, *Crime in Early Modern England, 1550–1750* (New York: Longman, 1984), 34, 39, 76–77; Sharpe, "Enforcing the Law in the Seventeenth-Century English Village," in V. A. C. Gatrell, Bruce Lenman, and Geoffrey Parker, eds., *Crime and the Law: the Social History of Crime in Western Europe since 1500* (London: Europa Publications, 1980), 107–8.

89. *Charter and Laws*, 97; Tully, *Legacy*, 112; J. Smith Futhey and Gilbert Cope, *History of Chester County Pennsylvania* (Philadelphia: Louis H. Everts, 1881), 374; Tully, *Forming*, 323–24, 328.

90. *PCR*, 1: 93; *Records of the Court of Quarter Sessions and Common Pleas of Bucks County*, 21, 80–81, 111, 211; 1737, CCQSP; York County Quarter Sessions Dockets, 1752; Rowe, *Bench*, chap. 12.

91. Women were accused of only 6.3 percent of assaults in North Carolina, 12.1 percent of all attacks upon persons not leading to death in New York, and less than 5 percent of assaults in Massachusetts. Donna J. Spindel and Stuart W. Thomas, Jr., "Crime and Society in North Carolina, 1663–1740," *Journal of Southern History* 49 (1983): 238; Douglas S. Greenberg, *Crime and Law Enforcement in the Colony of New York, 1691–1776* (Ithaca, N.Y.: Cornell University Press, 1976), 50; N. E. H. Hull, *Female Felons: Women and Serious Crime in Colonial Massachusetts* (Urbana: University of Illinois Press, 1987), 84.

92. See Donald A. Shalley, ed., *Lewis Miller: Sketches and Chronicles* (York, Pa.: Historical Society of York County, 1966), 34, 88. Also Hull, *Female Felons*, 29, 35, 44.

93. Examination of Martin Reardon, 28 September 1742, CCQSP.

94. Susan Klepp, "Philadelphia in Transition: A Demographic History of the City and Its Occupational Groups" (Ph.D. dissertation, University of Pennsylvania, 1980), 100ff; Merril D. Smith, *Breaking the Bonds: Marital Discord in Pennsylvania, 1730–1830* (New York: New York University Press, 1991); Marietta, *Reformation*, 24.

95. The vocations of only eighteen victims of the women were identified. Constables were eight of the eighteen.

96. Of the total of 1227 identified victims of assaults in Chester County, 187 were women and 1040 were men. Of the 1780 identified victims of all other crimes, 459 were men and 1321 were women.

97. *N* for women victims 16; *N* for men, 107.

98. Examination of Mary Dunlap, 12 January 1757, CCQSP.

99. May 1735, CCQSP; examination of Sarah Robinson, undated, CCQSP; examination of Elizabeth Bray, 27–12 month 1734, CCQSP.

100. February 1724/1725, CCQSP; examination of Charles Tassey, 8–11 month 1724/1725, CCQSP.

101. Bucks County Quarter Sessions Court Criminal Papers, BCHS.

102. Scholars have found the same pattern elsewhere in early America. See Bradley Chapin, *Criminal Justice in Colonial America, 1606–1660* (Athens: University of Georgia Press, 1983), 126; Barbara S. Lindermann, "'To Ravish and Carnally Know': Rape in Eighteenth-Century Massachusetts," *Signs* 10 (1984): 81–82.

103. François La Rochefoucault-Liancourt, *Travels Through the United States of North America* (London, 1799), 2: 396. William Bradford, *An Enquiry How Far the Punishment of Death Is Necessary in Pennsylvania* (Philadelphia, 1793), 29–30. Bradford estimated that Pennsylvania had a higher incidence of rape than Scotland. Notes of Charges Delivered to Grand Juries by Chief Justice Thomas McKean, 1777–1779, HSP. [The title is misleading in that notes up to 1794 are here]; Alexander Addison, *Reports of Cases in the County Courts of the 5th Circuits, and in the High Court of Errors and Appeals, of the State of Pennsylvania* (Washington, Pa., 1800), 144.

104. For excellent treatments of this issue, see Cornelia Hughes Dayton, *Women Before the Bar: Gender, Law and Society in Connecticut, 1639–1789* (Chapel Hill: University of North Carolina Press, 1995), chapter 5 and Sharon Block, "Lines of Color, Sex and Service: Comparative Sexual Coercion in Early America," in Martha Hodes, ed., *Sex, Love, Race: Crossing Boundaries in North American History* (New York: New York University Press, 1999), 141ff.

105. *CG*, November 19, 1788. Block, "Lines of Color, Sex, and Service," 141, 144–45, 148–49.

106. For an unusual case, see the rape of Dorcas Hemphill by David Long and James Wilson of Lancaster. There ten individuals provided depositions of the assault, six of them women. Oyer and Terminer Court Papers, RG-33, Boxes 1–4: Lancaster County, PHMC.

107. Peter and Bridgett Cock [or Cook] v. John Rambo, November 8, 1685, Philadelphia County Quarter Sessions, PMHC. Testimony of Peter and Bridgett Cock, and daughter Margaret.

108. Pennypacker, 79–82, 112–13. Entered into the court's record were "the proceeds of ye ecclesiastical Court held at wiccaco [within Philadelphia]" on July 26, 1686 which held that Rambo was guilty of taking Bridgett's maidenhead. Like the civil court, the ecclesiastical body did not lay rape charges to Rambo.

109. Dayton, *Women Before the Bar*, 262 discusses this phenomenon.

110. Oyer and Terminer Dockets: Lancaster County, May 1785, PMHC; February 1793, CCQSP.

111. Geoffrey Gilbert, *Law of Evidence*, 5th ed. (Philadelphia, 1788), 133–34; Blackstone, *Commentaries on the Law*, 1: 442.

112. Dayton, *Women Before the Bar*, 246, 249–56.

113. Dayton, *Women Before the Bar*, 246. J. M. Beattie describes the transformation in the Anglo-American criminal trial in the eighteenth century that required the novelty of lawyers acting for the defense. The effect of defense counsel is mostly commended: it brought about the right against self-incrimination and the right to remain silent. But defense counsel also expanded the disabilities of gender in rape cases. Beattie, *Crime and Courts*, 340–76.

114. Michael Dalton's *The Countrey Justice* (London, 1655), 350–51, main-

tained that in instances where conception occurred "consent must be inferred." See also Else L. Hambelton, "The Regulation of Sex in Seventeenth-Century Massachusetts: The Quarterly Court of Essex County v. Priscilla Willson and Mr. Samuel Appleton," in Merril D. Smith, ed., *Sex and Sexuality in Early America* (New York: New York University Press, 1998), 96; "Pennsylvania v. Andrew Sullivan," June 1793, in Addison, *Reports of Cases*, 143.

115. Gottlieb Mittelberger, *Journey to Pennsylvania*, trans. and ed. Oscar Handlin and John Clive (Cambridge, Mass.: Harvard University Press, 1960).

116. Muhlenberg, *Journals*, 1: 265.

117. *CG*, July 30, 1788. The details can be found in Oyer and Terminer Dockets: Franklin County, July 8, 1788. Durham, the man accused of rape in this case, was convicted and hanged. Mittelberger, *Journey to Pennsylvania*, 38–39.

118. See relevant petitions, dated June 5, 1786, June 24, 1786, August 12, 1786, Clemency Records, reel 39. Petitions in favor of John McDonough (June 14, 1786) and Richard Shirtliff (June 24, 1786), ibid., reel 39. Shirtliff was saved from execution and exiled.

119. Clemency Records, May 29, 1786, PMHC, reel 39; Yeates Papers: Legal Papers, folder 4, May–June, 1786, HSP.

120. Mittelberger, *Journey to Pennsylvania*, 75; *The Columbian Museum, or Universal Asylum* (Philadelphia), Janunary 1793, 44.

121. David Robb, April 20, 1787, Yeates Legal Papers, March–April, 1789, folio 2, HSP; Frederick G. Tappert and John Duberstein, eds., *The Journals of Henry Melchior Muhlenberg*, 3 vols. (Philadelphia: Muhlenberg Press, 1945–1958), 1: 265; 2: 265; Block, "Lines of Color, Sex, and Service," 141, 156; Mittelberger, *Journey to Pennsylvania*, 71; "Respublica v. Michael Hevice, Frederick, Gelvix, and His Wife," in 2 *Yeates*, 114–16; Jasper Yeates, Legal Papers, folio 7, April–May 1783; folio 2, March–April 1789; folio 4, May–June 1786, HSP.

122. *The Trial of Alice Clifton* (Philadelphia, 1787), especially 1, 9–10, 12–13. For petitions to save her life, including one from the judges, see April 1787, Clemency Records, 1775–1790, RG-26, PMHC, reel 39. Oyer and Terminer Dockets: Philadelphia, February 18, 1788; *IG*, February 19, 1788. Bradford's comments are in *The Columbian Magazine* (Philadelphia), January 1793), 44.

123. See, for instance, Brouwer, "The Negro as Slave and as a Free Black in Colonial Pennsylvania," 113–14, 116–18; Susan Klepp, *Philadelphia in Transition: A Demographic History of the City and Its Occupational Groups* (New York: Garland, 1989), 33. A minister commented that "these frequent mixtures will soon force matrimonial sanction. . . . a particoloured race will soon make a great part of the population in Philadelphia." Susan Klepp and Billy G. Smith, "The Records of Gloria Dei Church: Marriage and Remarkable Occurrences, 1794–1806," *PH* 53 (1986): 136.

124. Block discusses the context of these attacks in "Lines of Color, Sex, and Service," 141–63. Also see Annette Gordon-Reed, *Thomas Jefferson and Sally Hemings: An American Controversy* (Charlottesville: University of Virginia Press, 1998), especially 158–209.

125. *The Columbian Museum, or Universal Asylum* (Philadelphia), January 1793, 44.

126. Horle, *Records*, 1: 17; *PCR*, 1: 589; 2: 11. The attorney-general said prosecution was impossible because Smith and Henbury were "now one flesh." Also Joseph J. Kelley, Jr., *Pennsylvania: The Colonial Years, 1681–1776* (New York: Doubleday, 1980), 107.

127. *AWM* reported in the July 29–August 5, 1736 issue that Negro James, a

slave, had been executed for rape. We cannot confirm that execution. In his study of public executions, Negley Teeters, "Public Executions in Pennsylvania, 1682–1834," in Monkkonen, *Crime and Justice in American History*, 2: 756–835, does not list James as being executed, pardoned, or exiled.

128. Dockets indicate that Cumberland County's James Paxton (1783) and Philadelphia County's Frances Courtney (1785) were convicted of rape and sentenced to be hanged, but no evidence of the resolution in those two cases has yet been discovered.

129. Gary B. Nash, "Forging Freedom: The Emancipation Experience in the Northern Seaports, 1775–1820," in Nash, *Race, Class, and Politics* (Urbana: University of Illinois Press, 1986), 284, 288, 301, 307.

130. Nash, "Forging Freedom," 288; Kenneth and Anna Roberts, eds. *Moreau de Saint-Méry's American Journey* (Garden City, N.Y.: Doubleday, 1947), 291, 302–3, 309.

131. Only two rape indictments dated before 1718.

132. In 1794 the Pennsylvania legislature removed the capital designation from rape proceedings. In April of that year, "An Act for the Better Preventing of Crimes and for Abolishing the Punishment of Death in Certain Cases," eliminated the death penalty for all crimes except murder in the first degree. Rape hereafter was to be punished by a sentence of ten to twenty-one years in prison. *Statutes* 15: 180–81.

133. *N* of attempted rapes is 38.

134. There may have been more than seven, since the age of victims was not uniformly recorded.

135. Examination of Mary Gordon, December 26, 1754, CCQSP; examination of Elizabeth Scott, April 28, 1755, CCQSP.

136. Examination of Ann Babb, November 23, 1792, CCQSP; deposition of Jean Smith, August 5, 1734, CCQSP; examination of Hannah Evener, March 1, 1734, CCQSP; May 1757, August 1723, March 1775, and February 1734, CCQSD.

137. This is based on a sampling of four counties: Bucks, Chester, Lancaster, and York.

138. Records of the Supreme Court (Eastern District), Divorce Papers, 1786–1815, RG-33, PMHC; Chester County, Criminal Papers, Hector McNeil, 1772, Samuel Petit, April 1793, HSCC; Smith, *Life in Early Philadelphia*, 67, 71, 78, 86; Prisoners for Trial Docket, 1790–1797, November 1, 1796. See also Jane Hahn, "'We Never Lived Happily Together': Spousal Murder in Philadelphia, 1760–1835" (Ph.D. dissertation, Lehigh University, forthcoming).

139. Divorce Papers, 1785–115; Smith, *Life in Early Philadelphia*, 76; Mayor's Court Dockets, June, December 1790, City Archives, Philadelphia.

140. Smith, *Life in Early Philadelphia*, 64, 73; Bucks County Quarter Sessions Dockets, December 1768, BCHS; Philadelphia Mayor's Court, January 1781.

141. For numerous cases of parental abuse of children, see the Prisoners for Trial Dockets and the Vagrancy Dockets for the city of Philadelphia. Also Barry Levy, *Quakers and the American Family: British Settlement in the Delaware Valley, 1650–1765* (New York: Oxford, 1988), 227.

142. Deposition of James McMeehen, March 1796, CCQSP.

143. The practice involved the officers of an English parish walking the parish boundaries all the while striking boys with willow wands to teach them the bounds of their parish. Ebenezer Cobham Brewer, *Dictionary of Phrase and Fable* (London: Cassell, 1981).

144. Cumberland County Quarter Sessions Dockets, October 1788, Cumber-

land County Courthouse, Carlisle; Lancaster County Quarter Sessions Dockets, November 1757, September 1758, Lancaster County Historical Society, Lancaster; Smith, *Life in Early Philadelphia*, 45.

145. Examination of Ann Perin, February 1727, CCQSP and CCQSD.

146. Examination of Ester Burt, February 1724, CCQSP and CCQSD.

147. Examination of Daniel Broom, May 1720, CCQSP and CCQSD.

148. Smith, *Life in Early Philadelphia*, 66–67, 77, 79, 83.

149. See *Conductor Generalis, or, the Office, Duty and Authority of Justices of the Peace, High Sheriff, Under Sheriff . . .* (Philadelphia, 1749), esp. 18–19.

150. May 1763, CCQSP.

151. Fayette County Quarter Sessions Dockets, June 1784, Fayette County Courthouse, Uniontown.

152. Examination of James Casey, Robert Taskbury, and John McCowley, July 1740, CCQSP.

153. March 1743, CCQSD.

154. Examination of Samuel Behal, John Finney, Robert Young, and Robert Fletcher, August 1792, CCQSP.

155. Examination of Patrick Kelty, August 15, 1742, CCQSP.

156. Lane, *Murder*, 127, 350–351. For many examples, see Geoffrey Canada, *Fist, Stick, Knife, Gun: A Personal History of Violence in America* (Boston: Beacon Press, 1995). Steven Pinker, *The Blank Slate: The Modern Denial of Human Nature* (New York: Viking, 2002), 328–29.

157. November 1782, CCQSP. Deposition of Benjamin Mendenhall, September 16, 1782, CCQSP.

158. See depositions under those names and dates in the BCHS.

159. Lancaster County Quarter Sessions Papers, 1788, cited by Thomas P. Slaughter, "Interpersonal Violence in a Rural Setting: Lancaster County in the Eighteenth Century," *PH* 58 (1991): 117. For more on gouging, see Elliot J. Gorn, "'Gouge, and Bite, Pull Hair and Scratch': The Social Significance of Fighting in the Southern Backcountry," *AHR* 90 (1985): 18–43.

160. Only genealogical research, which we have not done, will settle the question of the exact family relationships, but we believe the family connections did exist based upon shared surnames.

161. March 1747, CCQSD.

162. August 1766, CCQSD.

163. The simple conviction rate (SRC) was 68.8 percent, while that rate for property crime, for example, was 72.2.

164. The mean fine for those who confessed or submitted was £2.10, but the mean for those convicted was between £20 and £21. Similarly, $6.50 versus $16.50 for dollar-denominated fines.

165. Pieter Spierenburg, "Long-Term Trends in Homicide: Theoretical Reflections and Dutch Evidence, Fifteenth to Twentieth Centuries," in Eric A. Johnson and Eric H. Monkkonen, eds., *The Civilization of Crime: Violence in Town and Country since the Middle Ages* (Urbana: University of Illinois Press, 1996), 74.

166. Eric Monkkonen, *Murder in New York City* (Berkeley: University of California Press, 2001), 81.

Chapter 5. Enlarged Land, Shortened Justice

Epigraph: John Penn to Thomas Gage, December 15, 1767, PCR 9: 406.

1. Lawrence A. Cremin, *American Education: The Colonial Experience, 1607–1783* (New York: Harper, 1970), 124–25, 180–82, 305–10.

2. These developments are charted in Rowe, *Bench*, Chapters 2–3.

3. Horle, *Records*, passim.

4. Note publication of titles of laws passed by the Assembly in *AWM*, April 4, 1723 and preceding issues.

5. These publications are listed in Charles R. Hildeburn, ed., *A Century of Printing; The Issues of the Press in Pennsylvania, 1685–1784*, 2 vols. (New York: Burt Franklin, 1968).

6. *AWM*, November 24, 1720.

7. In 1701, 1714, 1728, 1740, 1742, 1760, 1762, and 1775.

8. Edwin Wolf, II, "The Library of Ralph Assheton The Book Background of a Colonial Philadelphia Lawyer," *Papers of the Bibliographical Society of America* 58 (1964): 350–52; 354–79; also Wolf, "Lawyers and Law Books" in his *The Book Culture of a Colonial American City: Philadelphia Books, Bookmen, and Booksellers* (New York: Oxford, 1988), 131–63.

9. The most convenient source of these records is Clifford K. Shipton and James E. Mooney, eds., *National Index of American Imprints Through 1800: The Short-Title Evans*, 2 vols. (Worcester, Mass.: American Antiquarian Society, 1969), and Hildeburn, *Century of Printing*.

10. Horle, *Records*, 1: 455, 483; Rowe, *Bench*, 60, 61; Frank Eastman, *Courts and Lawyers in Pennsylvania*, 4 vols. (New York: American Historical Society, 1922), 1: 181.

11. *AWM*, November 24, 1720.

12. Details of the Oswald case are found in Rowe, *Bench*, 195–98.

13. Contrary to the Quaker presumption, in England lawyers were critical to establishing the rights of the accused, especially, according to J. M. Beattie, the right against self-incrimination. Beattie, 280, 352–56, 375. Quakers, however, did not shun the English justice system, but used it as adeptly in their defense as any Englishmen. Horle, *Quakers*, 18, 268.

14. Felix Rackow, "The Right to Counsel: English and American Precedents," *WMQ* 11 (1954): 17–18; *Charter*, 11, 99–103; *Statutes*, 2: 128, 148–59; April 1759, September 1767, Supreme Court: Appearances and Continuance Docket, 1740–1764, 1764–1776, RG-33, PMHC.

15. David Paul Brown, *The Forum, Or Forty Years Full Practice at the Philadelphia Bar*, 2 vols. (Philadelphia: R.H. Small, 1856), 1: 224, 227.

16. J. A. Leo LeMay, ed., *Benjamin Franklin: Writings* (New York: Viking, 1987), 1421.

17. The growth of the Pennsylvania bar can be traced in various dockets. John Hill Martin, *The Bench and Bar of Philadelphia* (Philadelphia, 1883); and Anton-Herman Chroust, *The Rise of the Legal Profession in America*, 2 vols. (Norman: University of Oklahoma Press, 1965), 1: 206–33.

18. Francis Hopkinson, *Miscellaneous Essays*, 3 vols. (Philadelphia, 1793), 3: pt. 2, 158; "Court Houses," *The Philadelphiad; or, New Pictures of the City*, 2 vols. (Philadelphia, 1784), 1: 8; Appearance and Continuance Docket, 1740–1764, 256 ("the Defendant Personally appears").

19. Horle, *Records*, 1: 476, 514, 550–51, 591.

20. *Charter*, 311, 314, 334.

21. Horle, *Records*, 1: 549–50, 551; Bucks County Quarter Sessions Dockets, December 1788.

22. Horle, *Records*, 1: 551.

23. Horle, *Records*, 1: 568.

24. The victim in theft cases could draw upon three methods of originating

proceedings against the perpetrator. The first and least threatening was a court summons. The second was by replevin, which permitted authorities to seize the goods in question before trial, and the third, the most threatening to the alleged perpetrator, was the arrest of the suspect. For an elaboration of these approaches, see Offutt, 63.

25. Frederick W. Maitland, *The Forms of Action at Common Law; A Course of Lectures by F. W. Maitland*, ed. A. H. Chaytor and W. J. Whittaker (London, 1909; reprint Cambridge: Cambridge University Press, 1968). Offutt, 85–89, traces these changes in the county courts of the Delaware Valley.

26. For a discussion of this change, see Rowe, *Bench*, 76–77. Non-Quaker-dominated courts in early Pennsylvania moved more quickly than did their Quaker counterparts to employ Latin in their records and proceedings. See, for instance, *Court Records of Kent County, Delaware, 1680–1705* (Washington, D.C.: GPO, 1959), 8, 13, 44, 123, 147, 154, 163, 282, 301.

27. See, for instance, Elizabeth Henderson, "The Attack on the Judiciary in Pennsylvania, 1800–1810," *PMHB* 61 (1937): 114–36; G. S. Rowe, "Jesse Higgins and the Failure of Legal Reform in Delaware, 1800–1810," *JER* 3 (1983): 17–43.

28. See for instance, the role played by William Emot in Horle, *Records* 1: 522, 601; 2: 714.

29. Bucks County Quarter Sessions Dockets, March 1742, September 1764, BCHS; September 1767; Lancaster County Quarter Sessions Dockets, February 1787, May 1787, Lancaster County Historical Society, Lancaster; Northumberland County Quarter Sessions Dockets, November 1785, Northumberland County Courthouse, Sunbury; Oyer and Terminer Dockets: Courts of Oyer and Terminer, 1778–1828 (September 1778), RG-33, PMHC.

30. "Poor v. Greene," Horace Binney, ed., *Reports of Cases Adjudicated in the Supreme Court of Pennsylvania*, 6 vols., (Philadelphia, 1890–1891), 5: 554.

31. Two years previous to the passage of the Judiciary Act of 1722, a provincial court of chancery (or equity) was established. When the 1701 law was repealed the question over who was to exercise primary equity jurisdiction was reopened. Governor Evans yielded in 1708, permitting county courts to function as original courts of equity. The Judiciary Act of 1711 continued this scheme, but the Judiciary Acts of 1715 reversed this pattern and stipulated that equity jurisdiction be exercised by a supreme court. By 1720 there was enough agreement to secure the creation of the provincial court of chancery. There, the governor and six councilors oversaw equity cases. This court, modeled closely on the English High Court of Chancery, was the only separate court of equity in the early history of Pennsylvania. It lasted sixteen years before being abolished. Lawrence Henry Gipson, *The Great War for the Empire: The Victorious Years, 1758–1760* (New York: Alfred Knopf, 1949), 46–60, 144–45, 247–86; *The Great War for the Empire: The Years of Defeat, 1754–1757* (New York: Alfred Knopf, 1946), 62–95.

32. *Votes and Proceedings* (Philadelphia, 1768), 25.

33. Ibid.

34. *Votes and Proceedings . . . October 1771* (Philadelphia, 1772), 319–20, 321–22, 364; also, ibid. October–December 1773 (Philadelphia, 1773), 527.

35. *Votes and Proceedings . . . October 1771* (Philadelphia, 1772), 319–20.

36. *PCR*, 9: 386; Maclay to James Tilghman, April 2, 1773, *PA*, lst Ser. 4: 463.

37. John B. Frantz and William Pencek, eds., *Beyond Philadelphia: The American Revolution in the Pennsylvania Hinterland* (University Park: Pennsylvania State University Press, 1998), 137–43.

38. George Wilson to St. Clair, August 14, 1771, Penn Mss: Official Correspondence, 10: 268, HSP.

39. *PA* lst ser. 4: 435, 561, 603. For more on resistance to law enforcement in rural areas, 1780–1800, see Chapter 7.

40. William S. Hanna, *Benjamin Franklin and Pennsylvania Politics* (Stanford, Calif.: Stanford University Press, 1964), 45; *PA* 1st Ser. 3: 182.

41. *PA* 1st Ser. 9: 730–31; 10: 78, 142.

42. David H. Flaherty, "Crime and Social Control in Provincial Massachusetts," *Historical Journal* 24 (1981): 347.

43. *Votes and Proceedings . . . Oct., 1771* (Philadelphia, 1772), 330; *Votes and Proceedings . . . Oct., 1766* (Philadelphia, 1767), 24; *PA.* 1st Ser. 4: 142.

44. *Votes and Proceedings . . . Oct., 1763* (Philadelphia, 1764), 106; *Votes and Proceedings . . . Oct., 1768* (Philadelphia, 1769), 68; *Votes and Proceedings . . . Oct., 1769* (Philadelphia, 1770), 195; *Votes and Proceedings . . . Oct., 1770* (Philadelphia, 1771), 217; *Votes and Proceedings . . . Oct., 1771* (Philadelphia, 1772), 313, 317, 343, 356, 366–67, 380; *Votes and Proceedings . . . Oct., 1772* (Philadelphia, 1773), 463; *Votes and Proceedings . . . Oct., 1775* (Philadelphia, 1776), 225; G. S. Rowe, "The Stump Affair, 1768, and its Challenge to Legal Historians of Early Pennsylvania," *PH* 49 (1982): 275.

45. *PA,* lst Ser. 4: 42; John Penn to Thomas Penn, May 20, 1765, Penn MSS: Official Correspondence, 9: 292, HSP; John Penn to Thomas Penn, 1764, ibid. 9: 236.

46. *PCR,* 9: 393; 10: 265; Joseph J. Kelley, *Pennsylvania: The Colonial Pennsylvania, 1681–1776* (Garden City, N.Y.: Doubleday, 1980), 612.

47. John Penn to Thomas Penn, March 17, September 1, 1764, Penn Ms: Official Correspondence, 9: 218, 252–54, HSP.

48. *Votes and Proceedings . . . October 1764* (Philadelphia, 1765), 32, 50; ibid., October 1765 (Philadelphia, 1766), 52; Thomas Penn to John Penn, June 8, 1765, Thomas Penn Papers (microfilm), reel 9, HSP.

49. *Statutes,* 7: 107; also *Charter,* 304, 356–61, 407–9.

50. *An Account of the Gospel Labours and Christian Experiences of that Faithful Minister of Christ, John Churchman . . .* (Philadelphia, 1882), 209–10.

51. These events may be followed in the recent history by Fred Anderson, *Crucible of War: The Seven Years' War and the Fate of Empire in British North America, 1754–1766* (New York: Vintage, 2001), Chapters 5, 9, and 14.

52. Jane T. Merritt, *At the Crossroads: Indians and Empires on a Mid-Atlantic Frontier, 1700–1763* (Chapel Hill: University of North Carolina Press, 2003), 177–80; James H. Merrell, *Into the American Woods: Negotiators on the Pennsylvania Frontier* (New York: W.W. Norton, 1999).

53. Theodore Thayer, *Pennsylvania Politics and the Growth of Democracy, 1740–1776* (Harrisburg: PHMC, 1953), 83–85; James H. Hutson, *Pennsylvania Politics, 1746–1770: The Movement for Royal Government and Its Consequences* (Princeton, N.J.: Princeton University Press, 1972), passim.

54. [William Smith], *A Brief View of the Conduct of Pennsylvania for the Year 1755* (London, 1756), 52, 70.

55. See, for example, Sally Schwartz, *"A Mixed Multitude": The Struggle for Toleration in Colonial Pennsylvania* (New York: New York University Press, 1987), 222–25, 237–40; Melvin H. Buxbaum, *Benjamin Franklin and the Zealous Presbyterians* (University Park: Pennsylvania State University Press, 1975), 196–200.

56. Paul A. W. Wallace, *Conrad Weiser, 1696–1760, Friend of Colonist and Mohawk* (New York: Russell and Russell, 1971), 99; Randall M. Miller and Wil-

liam Pencak, *Pennsylvania: A History of the Commonwealth* (University Park: Pennsylvania State University Press, 2002), 77.

57. 1717, 1722, CCQSP; *PCR*, 3: 285–87; 4: 281–82.

58. *PG*, November 5, 1730.

59. *PCR*, 4: 675, 676, 678, 680–81, 682–85, 698, 702; *PG*, April 26, November 8, November 15, 1744; *AWM*, November 8–15, 1744; Kelley, *Pennsylvania*, 233–34. Teeters does not list this execution in his study of public executions in Pennsylvania.

60. *PCR*, 5: 543.

61. Bryan, as quoted in Thayer, *The Growth of Democracy*, 86; Theodore G. Tappert and John W. Doberstein, eds., *The Journals of Henry Melchior Muhlenberg*, 2 vols. (Philadelphia: Muhlenberg Press, 1942), 1: 709.

62. *Records of the Moravian Mission Among the Indians of North America* (Stamford, Conn.: Primary Source Microfilm) reel 6, Item 124, folder 6 contains the Renatus materials; also *PA* 8th Ser. 7: 5607; *Votes and Proceedings* (Philadelphia, 1764), 16, 19, 82.

63. He was charged on October 13, arrested on October 29, 1763.

64. See depositions of Jacob Wetterhold, Rebecca Langley, John Lisler, Margaret Elizabeth Furhrer, Peter Peterson, Conrad Reiff, and the petitions of Lewis Weiss, in *Records of the Moravian Missions*, Box 124, folder 6, reel 6. For the attempt to "appeal" the acquittal, see item 23, ibid.

65. Thayer, *The Growth of Democracy*, 85.

66. For some of the writings on the Paxton march, its causes, blame, and consequences, see George W. Franz, *Paxton: A Study of Community Structure and Mobility in the Colonial Pennsylvania Backcountry* (New York: Garland, 1989), 3, 5–7, 33–41, 71–83. James E. Crowley, "The Paxton Disturbance and Ideas of Order in Pennsylvania Politics," *PH* 37 (1970): 321–22; James Kirby Martin, "The Return of the Paxton Boys and the Historical State of the Pennsylvania Frontier," *PH* 38 (1971): 133; and Alden T. Vaughan, "The Frontier Banditti and the Indians: The Paxton Boys' Legacy, 1763–1775," *PH* 51 (1984): 2.

67. Hutson, *Pennsylvania Politics*, 84–85.

68. Thayer, *The Growth of Democracy*, 87.

69. *PG*, March 28, 1765; Deposition of Ralph Nailer, 1765; Deposition of Sergeant Leonard McGlashan, August 20, 1765; Colonel John Reid to Thomas Gage, June 4, 1765, PA 1st Ser. 4: 220, 222, 225, 234–36, 269–70.

70. Colonel John Reid to Thomas Gage, June 4, 1765; William Smith to Lieutenant Charles Grant, June 22, 1765, PCR, 9: 269–70.

71. John Penn to Thomas Gage, June 27, 1765, PCR, 9: 267–68.

72. John Ross to Benjamin Franklin, May 20, 1765, Benjamin Franklin, *Papers of Benjamin Franklin*, ed. Leonard W. Labaree et al. 37 vols. (New Haven, Conn.: Yale University Press, 1968), 12: 138–39.

73. Thomas Wharton to Benjamin Franklin, March 25, 1765, in ibid., 12: 92–95.

74. Council Minutes, January 15, 1766; Robert Callender to Bayton, Wharton and Morgan, March 2, 1766, PCR, 9: 302.

75. George Croghan to Benjamin Franklin, February 12, 1768, in Labaree, *Papers of Benjamin Franklin*, 15: 43; John Penn to Thomas Gage, December 15, 1767, *PCR*, 9: 406.

76. Thomas Gage to John Penn, December 7, 1767, PCR, 9: 403; Gage to the Earl of Shelburne, January 22, 1768, in Clarence Carter, ed., *The Correspondence of General Thomas Gage, 1763–1775*, 2 vols. (New Haven, Conn.: Yale University Press, 1931–1933), 1: 157.

77. Joseph Shippen, Jr. to James Burd, February 23, 1769, Shippen Papers, 7: 1, HSP.

78. *Votes and Proceedings. . . October, 1767* (Philadelphia, 1768), 20, 22, 23, 34–35.

79. Rowe, "Stump Affair," 259–65.

80. Deposition of William Bythe, in *PCR*, 9: 414–19; "Letter from Carlisle," *PC,* February 1–8, 1768.

81. *PCR*, 9: 412–19.

82. Patterson to Joseph Shippen, January 23, 1768, in *PCR*, 9: 453. Patterson and the men who helped him were "exposed to great Danger by the desperate Resistance made by Stump and his Friends who Sided with him."

83. These issues and machinations are explored in Rowe, "Stump Affair," 262–63.

84. John Armstrong to Penn, January 29, 1768, in *PCR*, 9: 448–49; Deposition of James Cunningham, in ibid., 449–51; *PC,* March 3, 1768.

85. *Statutes*, 6: 325–28; 7: 350–53; 8: 6–9, 120–23, 183, 366–69; Cumberland County Quarter Sessions Docket, May 1769; *PCR*, 9: 471, 673; *PG,* February 11, 1768; Wharton to Franklin, March 23, 1768, in Labaree, ed., *Papers of Benjamin Franklin,* 15: 88.

86. Rowe, "Stump Affair," 259–88.

87. Carter, *Correspondence of Thomas Gage,* 1: 152–53.

88. While dozens of cases of murder by Indians against whites, and by whites against Indians, were never adjudicated by Pennsylvania courts and, in some cases, were never brought before judicial authorities, others were resolved through diplomacy overseen by nonjudicial personnel. See Merritt, *At the Cross-roads,* 202, 243, 252–53, 299, 302, 305.

Chapter 6. Revolution

Epigraph. Benjamin Rush to John Adams, August 8, 1777, in *Letters of Benjamin Rush,* ed. Lyman H. Butterfield, 2 vols. (Princeton, N.J.: Princeton University Press, 1951), 1: 152.

1. The terms "rule at home" and "home rule" are from Carl L. Becker, *The History of Political Parties in the Province of New York, 1760–1776* (Madison: University of Wisconsin Press, 1909).

2. In some counties disenchantment with the Proprietary government had begun earlier. Typical of this phenomenon was the case of Northampton County. There, longtime land policies favoring speculators at the expense of settlers eroded respect for authorities in Philadelphia. See Francis S. Fox, *Sweet Land of Liberty: The Ordeal of the American Revolution in Northampton County, Pennsylvania* (University Park: Pennsylvania State University Press, 2000).

3. In his recent book on America's first gothic novelist, Charles Brockden Brown of Philadelphia, Peter Kafer discusses the Englightenment expectation that reason could purge from society the corruptions of the past and Brown's gothic premise that the past perdures, sometimes in dreadful ways. *Charles Brockden Brown's Revolution and the Birth of American Gothic* (Philadelphia: University of Pennsylvania Press, 2004), 124–25, 129.

4. *PCR*, 10: 469, 472–78. Also Richard A. Ryerson, *The Revolution Is Now Begun: The Radical Committees of Philadelphia, 1765–1776* (Philadelphia: University of Pennsylvania Press, 1978).

5. Fox, *Sweet Land of Liberty,* 159. The quote is by Michael Zuckerman. For

conditions in other counties see John B. Frantz and William Pencak, eds., *Beyond Philadelphia: The American Revolution in the Pennsylvania Hinterland* (University Park: Pennsylvania State University Press, 1998), 32–33, 74–75, 93–94, 126–27, 144.

6. *PCR*, 10: 486–87, 497. Petitions of sufferers can be found in Clemency Records, RG-27, Reel 36, PMHC.

7. *PP*, May 27, 1776.

8. John A. Neuenschwander, *The Middle Colonies and the Coming of the American Revolution* (Port Washington, N.Y.: Kennikat Press, 1973), 141–43; *PG*, May 22, 29, June 5, 1776; *PA* 1st Ser. 1: 94–95; William Duane, ed., *Passages of the Diary of Christopher Marshall* (Philadelphia: Hazzard and Mitchell, 1839), 85.

9. Thomas R. Meehan, "The Pennsylvania Supreme Court in the Laws and the Commonwealth, 1776–1790" (Ph.D. dissertation, University of Wisconsin, 1960), 42, 45.

10. Rowe, *McKean*, 95–96.

11. Montgomery to Wilson, April 21, 1777, Simon Gratz Collection, HSP.

12. *PCR*, 11: 217, 219, 263–64, 364; *PP*, October 22, 23, 29, 1776; November 19, 1776; J. Paul Selsam, *The Pennsylvania Constitution of 1776: A Study in Revolutionary Democracy* (Philadelphia: University of Pennsylvania Press, 1971), 205ff.

13. *PCR*, 11: 254, 270.

14. "Diary of James Allen, Esq., of Philadelphia, Counsellor-at-Law," *PMHB* 9 (1885): 282; *PG*, July 30, 1777.

15. Rowe, *McKean*, 96–120; and his *Bench*, Chapter 6.

16. Wayne L. Bockelman, "Local Politics in Pre-Revolutionary Lancaster County," *PMHB* 97 (1973): 30.

17. *PCR*, 11: 216, 244, 253.

18. Marietta, *Reformation*, 267–69; Ousterhout, passim.

19. Rowe, *McKean*, 265–66.

20. Thomas R. Meehan, "Courts, Cases, and Counselors in Revolutionary and Post-Revolutionary Pennsylvania," *PMHB* 91 (1967): 4–5, 120–21, 319–21; Louis Richards, "Jacob Rush and the Early Pennsylvania State Judiciary," Paper read by Louis Richards . . . July 2, 1914, before the Historical Society of Bucks County.

21. Ryerson, *The Revolution Is Now Begun*, esp. chapter 8.

22. See, for example, Steven Rosswurm, *Arms, Country, and Class: The Philadelphia Militia and the "Lower Sort" During the American Revolution* (New Brunswick, N. J.: Rutgers University Press, 1987).

23. Bockelman, "Local Politics," 30, 35–36. Scots-Irish Presbyterians made great gains at the expense of English Quakers.

24. *PCR*, 11: 471; Bockelman, "Local Politics," 86, 88, 194–95.

25. *FJ*, October 2, 1782; *LJ*, February 14, 1801; Meehan, "Courts, Cases, and Counselors," 11–12.

26. Rosemary S. Warden, "Chester County," in Frantz and Pencak, eds., *Beyond Philadelphia*, 5, 9, 13, 20.

27. "From 1776 to 1780 relatively few people participated in the annual elections and they usually elected Scots-Irish Presbyterians and their Reformed allies." Owen S. Ireland, *Religion, Ethnicity, and Politics: Ratifying the Constitution in Pennsylvania* (University Park: Pennsylvania State University Press, 1995), 219; Owen S. Ireland, "The Ethnic-Religious Dimension of Pennsylvania Politics, 1778–1779," *WMQ* 30 (1973): 421–48; Owen S. Ireland, "The Crux of Politics: Religion and Party in Pennsylvania, 1778–1789," *WMQ* 43 (1985): 453–75.

28. The measurement is Pearson's *r*. If jury assignments and township populations were perfectly correlated, Pearson's *r* would be 1.0. In 1775 it was 0.55, in 1785, 0.35 and in 1799, 0.48 (see Table 2.9). Of course, with respect to a different political and constitutional principle, a jury of the vicinage and of the accused's peers, this population correlation does not apply: most of the accused were not from eastern Chester County, where the population was concentrated and was predominately Quaker. Giving that the accused were rarely Quakers, juries of their peers would mean jurors selected from the less populated townships of the county. *N* of jurors (1693–1799) = 3308.

29. Pearson's *r* for 1740 is 0.76, for 1775, 0.43, and for 1785, 0.34 (see Table 2.9).

30. See Figure 2.1.

31. Figure 2.1. Jack D. Marietta, "The Distribution of Wealth in Eighteenth-Century America: Nine Chester County Tax Lists, 1693–1799," 11 *PH* 62 (1995): 540.

32. The high alternative mean percentile for the 74 was 49.5. Twelve accused women in the city could be associated with their husbands and their rank determined. It was the 28.6 percentile—obviously lower than that of the accused men in Philadelphia and much lower too than the few women accused in Chester County.

33. The new state constitution also made more explicit protections to be accorded defendants in criminal cases. "That in all prosecutions for criminal offenses," it proclaimed, "a man hath a right to be heard by himself and his council, to demand the cause and nature of his accusation, to be confronted with the witnesses, to call for evidence in his favour, and a speedy public trial, by an impartial jury . . . without the unanimous consent of which jury he cannot be found guilty; nor can he be compelled to give evidence against himself; nor can any man be justly deprived of his liberty except by the laws of the land, or the judgment of his peers." Section 9 in Poore, 1541–42.

34. *PCR*, 11: 252, 279, 288, 330–31.

35. For violations in one rural county, see Fox, *Sweet Land of Liberty*, which focuses on Northampton County, but see also Frantz and Pencak, eds., *Beyond Philadelphia*, 18, 32–33, 36–37, 52, 60–61, 63, 80–82, 93–94, 127–28.

36. Rowe, *Bench*, especially Chapter 7.

37. Quakers denied the legitimacy of the extralegal committees and protested that they could only be arrested and tried "by Civil Officers." Attorney William Lewis argued that the civil rights of Friends were being systematically trampled by committee members. Most complainants described being hastily and roughly forced before interrogators who, often reinforced by partisan and highly accusatorial crowds, pressed for answers about their conduct and beliefs, then jailed them on the most flimsy and unsubstantiated allegations. Early in 1776 Benjamin Neal railed that he had been "Confined neare three Weeks, though [sic] the spit [sic] and Malisheousness" of neighbors. He hoped that the Board of Safety would "be pleased to lett him have a hearing in Order . . . [that] your Petitioner may be released from his confinement." Joel Arpin, in January 1776, groused that he had been confined since November "without being Told what crimes were Laid to his Charges, and without having done anything which will justify his Confinement." Robert Etherington complained in July 1776 that he had been incarcerated for nine days "without any Tryal" and without anyone "Assign[ing] any Reason whatever" for his predicament. Daniel Bancroft told the Board that it should either "exhibit a charge against me" or agree to his

release. See *PCR*, 11: 288–89. All quotations are taken from Records of Pennsylvania's Revolutionary Governments, 1775–1790: Clemency Records, RG-27, roll 36, PMHC.

38. Leonard W. Levy, *Original Intent and the Framers' Constitution* (New York: Macmillan, 1988), 240.

39. "Diary of Robert Morton," *PMHB* 1 (1877): 4n; *PCR*, 2: 301–302; McKean to John Adams, September 19, 1777, McKean Papers, HSP; *An Act to Empower the Supreme Executive Council to Provide for the Security . . . thereof in special cases* (Philadelphia, 1777); *Proceedings of the General Assembly of the Commonwealth of Pennsylvania* (Philadelphia, 1777), 88–89; Rowe, *McKean*, 105–107; Rowe, *Bench*, 133–35.

40. McKean to Joseph Reed, December 12, 1780; Reed to McKean, December 13, 1780, in *PA* 1st Ser. 8: 649–50, 654–55; Rowe, *McKean*, 134–37; Rowe, *Bench*, 158–60.

41. *Statutes*, 9: 18.

42. *Votes of the Assembly*, 8: 7536; Henry J. Young, "Treason and Its Punishment in Revolutionary Pennsylvania," *PMHB* 90 (1966): 291.

43. *Statutes*, 9: 45

44. Misprision of treason was the mere knowledge and concealment of an act of treason or treasonable plot by failing to disclose it to the proper authorities.

45. *Statutes*, 9: 45.

46. Young, "Treason and its Punishment," 293.

47. For an overview, see Rowe, *Bench*, Chapter 7. Wright had burglarized a man's home and attempted to kidnap him for the British. He was charged with burglary rather than treason, and, despite pleas from his wife on behalf of their children, Wright was executed. Oyer and Terminer Dockets, 1778–1780, PMHC, Harrisburg; *PP*, December 12, 1778; Clemency Records, reel 26, PMHC.

48. Young, "Treason and Its Punishment," 287–313. Also Ousterhout, *A State Divided*.

49. *Statutes*, 10: 110–12, especially 112; Rowe, *Bench*, 148, 163.

50. *Statutes*, 9: 100,104; 10: 12–16, 189, 212, 307.

51. *Statutes*, 10: 110–12.

52. Joseph Reed to Nathaniel Greene, November 5, 1778, in William B. Reed, *Life and Correspondence of Joseph Reed*, 2 vols. (Philadelphia: Lindsay and Blakiston, 1847), 2: 38.

53. Reed to McKean, April 20, 1779, in *PA* 1st Ser. 7: 328.

54. Duane, *Passages from the Diary of Christopher Marshall*, 171.

55. The following paragraph relies heavily upon Rowe, *Bench*, Chapter 8.

56. Dallas, ed., *Reports of the Cases Ruled and Adjudged in the Courts of Pennsylvania*, 63–64; "Respublic v. Buffington," Bryan Papers, Box 1, case 63, HSP.

57. McKean to Atlee, June 5, 1778, Peter Force Collection, Library of Congress, Washington, D.C.

58. Dallas, ed., *Reports of the Cases Ruled and Adjudged in the Courts of Pennsylvania*, 1: 56–62; *PA* 1st Ser. 8: 644–46.

59. Criticism of the Pennsylvania Supreme Court and its chief justice is documented in G. S. Rowe, "Judicial Tyrant and Vox Populi: Pennsylvanians View Their State Supreme Court, 1777–1799," *PMHB* 118 (1994): 33–62.

60. Young, "The Punishment of Treason," 287–313; Rowe, *Bench*, 42–43, 64, 67–69, 88–89, 144–45, 162, 165–66.

61. Early Quaker opposition to McKean, and their subsequent reconciliation with him following his sympathetic assessment of their efforts to obtain writs of habeas corpus, are discussed in Rowe, *Bench*, Chapter 8.

62. Young, "The Treatment of Loyalists in Pennsylvania," 257.

63. "A Supplement to the Act, titled 'An Act obliging the male white inhabitants of this State to give assurances of allegiance to the same, and for other purposes therein mentioned,'" *Laws Enacted in a General Assembly of the Representatives of the Freemen of the Common-Wealth of Pennsylvania* [12 May 1777 to October 1777] . . . *Laws Enacted in the Second Sitting of the General Assembly of the Common-Wealth of Pennsylvania* (Lancaster, 1778), chap. 61; Marietta, *Reformation*, 237–39.

64. Clemency Records, RG-27, roll 38, PMHC (Hamer, Longacre).

65. August 1780, CCQSD; Records of the Supreme Court [Eastern District] RG-27; Clemency Records, roll 38, PMHC; Paul Lermack, "Peace Bonds and Criminal Justice in Colonial Pennsylvania," *PMHB* 100 (1976): 188–90; Rowe, *Bench*, Chapter 8.

66. See Chapter 7 for the reforms in the codes of 1786.

67. Ibid.

68. See, for instance, Oyer and Terminer Dockets, 1778–1786, PMHC.

69. Doan to Thomas McKean, December 27, 1786, *PMHB* 23 (1899–1900): 536.

70. Clemency File, roll 38, PMHC.

71. Penal reforms in the United States after 1776 are treated in Louis Masur, "The Revision of the Criminal Law in Post-Revolutionary America," *CJH* 8 (1987): 21–36; Kathryn Preyer, "Crime, the Criminal Law and Reform in Post-Revolutionary Virginia," *LHR* 1 (1983): 53–85; Richard Gaskins, "Changes in the Criminal Law in Eighteenth-Century Connecticut," *AJLH* 25 (1981): 309–42; Paul F. Cromwell, "Quaker Reforms in American Criminal Justice: The Penitentiary and Beyond," *CJH* 10 (1989): 77–94; Adam J. Hirsch, *The Rise of the Penitentiary: Prisons and Punishment in Early America* (New Haven, Conn.: Yale University Press, 1992). Reformist ideas regarding criminal law reform prominent before the Revolution are treated by Peter Gay, *The Enlightenment: An Interpretation*, vol. 2, *The Science of Freedom* (New York: Alfred Knopf, 1969), 423–47; and Michael Meranze, *Laboratories of Virtue: Punishment, Revolution, and Authority in Philadelphia, 1760–1835* (Chapel Hill: University of North Carolina Press, 1996). Pennsylvania leaders were acutely aware of the legal treatises of legal reformers like Montesquieu and Cesare Beccaria.

72. William Bradford, *An Enquiry How Far the Punishment of Death Is Necessary in Pennsylvania* (Philadelphia, 1793), 10–11, 62.

73. This theme is pursued in Fox, *Sweet Land of Liberty*, with details provided from Northhampton County.

74. 3-month 1734, CCQSP. Bucks County Quarter Sessions Papers, box 9; Miscellaneous Dockets, 1743–1749, Bucks County Historical Society, Doylestown; Miscellaneous Papers, 1704–1899, folder 8, RG-33, PMHC; Joseph J. Kelley, Jr., *Life and Times in Colonial Philadelphia* (Harrisburg, Pa.: Stackpole Books, 1973), 141, 146; Theodore G. Tappert and John W. Duberstein, eds., *The Journals of Henry Melchior Muhlenberg*, 3 vols. (Philadelphia: Lutheran Historical Society, 1982 reprint), 1: 111, 113, 115.

75. James H. Hutson, *Pennsylvania Politics: The Movement for Royal Government and Its Consequences* (Princeton, N.J.: Princeton University Press, 1972), 122–28.

76. Inhabitants of Cumberland County fired upon British soldiers and a British fort during their protests regarding incidents at Sideling Hill in 1765. These were, legally speaking, acts of treason against the Crown and Crown property. But these activities were not so much attacks upon British authority or imperial policy as they were actions against troops and officers they saw closing their eyes

to illegal and immoral activities on the part of Indians and merchants thought to be supplying them with weapons. See *PCR*, 9: 225, 273–75, 281, 300–304, 307; Eleanor M Webster, "Insurrection at Fort Loudoun in 1765: Rebellion or Preservation of Peace?" *WPHM* 42 (1964): 124–39; Stephen H. Cutcliffe, "Sideling Hill Affair: The Cumberland County Riots of 1765," *WPHM* 59 (1976): 39–53.

77. Hutson, *Pennsylvania Politics*, 237–40; Frantz and Pencak, eds., *Beyond Philadelphia*, xix–xxi.

78. Marietta, *Reformation*, 244–45.

79. Clemency Records, roll 39. We must keep in mind that under law, riots did not have to be large or arise from a public issue.

80. White (September 1790), Murphy (November 1790), Vagrancy Docket, 1790–1932, vol. 1.

81. For an excellent explanation of the questions raised here and of legal theory and the Revolution, see Linda K. Kerber, *Women of the Republic: Intellect and Ideology in Revolutionary America* (Chapel Hill: University of North Carolina Press, 1980), 119–55.

82. Young, "Treason and Its Punishment," 311–12; Berks County, Quarter Sessions Dockets, May, 1778, Berks County Historical Society, Reading; Oyer & Terminer Dockets, September 1778, April 1781, PMHC; Kerr, Brecht, Clemency Records, RG-27, roll 36, PMHC.

83. Longacre, Hamer, Clemency Records, RG-27, roll 38, PMHC.

84. Buller [or Bulla], Clemency Records, RG-27, roll 40; Edwards, roll 36; Cooper, roll 36, PMHC.

85. Blackstone, *Commentaries on the Laws of England*, 4 vols. (New York, 1856), 1: 28; Richard B. Morris, *Studies in the History of American Law*, 2nd ed. (New York: Octagon Books, 1974), 194.

86. This and succeeding paragraphs rely heavily upon G. S. Rowe, "Femes Covert and Criminal Prosecution in Eighteenth-Century Pennsylvania," *AJLH* 32 (1988): 138–56.

87. N. E. H. Hull, *Female Felons: Women and Serious Crime in Colonial Massachusetts* (Urbana: University of Illinois Press, 1987), 94–100.

88. Bucks County Quarter Sessions Docket (September 1752), BCHS; York County Quarter Sessions Docket (October 1764, May 1765), York County Courthouse, York.

89. Dickey to the Supreme Executive Council, June 9, 1788; Match to Supreme Executive Council, June 24, 1788, Clemency Files, RG-27, PHMC, roll 40.

90. September 1784, Philadelphia County Quarter Sessions Dockets, PMHC; April 1771,York County Quarter Sessions Dockets; March 1780, Fayette County Quarter Sessions Dockets, Fayette County Courthouse, Uniontown.

91. *Quarter Sessions . . . of Bucks County*, 57, 58, 77. BCHS.

92. Another means to investigate coverture in criminal cases is to find married women who alone committed the crime, but whose husbands were charged while wives were not. But judicial records do not contain the information to permit this enquiry.

93. Kerber, *Women of the Republic*, 154.

94. Selsam's *Pennsylvania Constitution* documents this controversy.

95. Gordon Wood, *The Creation of the American Republic, 1776–1787* (Chapel Hill: University of North Carolina Press, 1969), 114–24; Edmund S. Morgan, "The Puritan Ethic and the Coming of the American Revolution," *WMQ* 24 (1967): 3–18.

96. David Freeman Hawke, *Benjamin Rush: Revolutionary Gadfly* (New York: Bobbs-Merrill, 1971), 370–72.

97. David Freeman Hawke, *In the Midst of a Revolution* (Philadelphia: University of Pennsylvania Press, 1961), 175, 192–93.

98. Both Rush and Marshall quickly turned against the new state constitution, Marshall because he thought it fell short of his high expectations for Christian orthodoxy. Hawke, *In the Midst of a Revolution*, 192–94; Rush to Enoch Green, 1761, and Rush to Ebenezer Hazard, August 2, 1764, in Butterfield, *Letters of Benjamin Rush*, 1: 4, 7. Regarding Rush's complaint about young men's bad behavior, before 1765 accused singlemen in Chester County did not meet their percentage of the whole taxpayer population. After 1765 they always exceeded it.

99. Rush to Adams, August 8, 1777, in Butterfield, *Letters*, 1: 152.

100. For documentation of the physical conditions of the poor in Philadelphia, see Simon P. Newman, *Embodied History: The Lives of the Poor in Early Philadelphia* (Philadelphia: University of Pennsylvania Press, 2003); Alexander, *Render*.

101. Clare A. Lyons, "'Sex Among the Rabble': Gender Transitions in the Age of Revolution, Philadelphia, 1750–1830" (Ph.D. dissertation, Yale University, 1996).

102. Poore, 2: 1547–48, Section 45; Selsam, *Pennsylvania Constitution*, Chapter V; Rush to John Adams, August 8, 1777, in Butterfield, *Letters of Benjamin Rush*, 1: 152.

103. John C. Miller, *Triumph of Freedom, 1775–1783* (Boston: Little, Brown, 1948), 227.

104. Worthington Chauncy Ford, ed., *Journals of the Continental Congress, 1774–1789* (Washington: GPO, 1904–1937), 13: 1001.

105. *Statutes*, 9: 333–38; 12: 313–22; 13: 184–86; 15: 110–18.

106. The growing portions of their total offenses were in property crime (from 27.9 percent to 38.7 percent, and in assault, from 19.0 percent to 26.5 percent. Men's proportions hardly changed between the pre-Revolution and Revolution eras.

107. In New Haven Colony and County, "women came obediently before both the local magistrates and the county court to confess guilt" for bastardy. Between 1670 and 1740, Dayton found only four women pleaded not guilty. Dayton, *Women at the Bar*, 198.

108. The complements to this declined percent were that submissions in assault rose from 21.9 percent to 49.1 percent and in property crimes, from 14.1 percent to 27.0 percent.

109. These numbers include cases that resulted in verdicts of either guilty or not guilty. They do not include cases that were unresolved in the dockets, 409 for women and 424 for men. We surmise that a significantly large portion of these unresolved cases were resolved out of court by some party agreeing to take on the burden and expense of child-rearing.

110. *N* of all accused of fornication and bastardy = 2289.

111. Between 1682–1775 and 1776–1800, submissions by men dropped from 34.9 percent to 26.5. The simple conviction rate for fornication rose from 77.4 percent to 91.7 and for bastardy, from 70.0 percent to 82.5.

112. Another indication of the misleading court records of Philadelphia is the adultery prosecutions: only two of the total of 105 in Pennsylvania after 1776 were from the city—an astonishing disparity.

113. Lyons, "Sex Among the 'Rabble,'" 15–16.

114. For the growing incidence of prostitution in Philadelphia in particular, see Marcia Roberta Carlisle, "Prostitutes and Their Reformers in Nineteenth-Century Philadelphia" (Ph.D. dissertation, Rutgers University, 1982); *Constitution of the Magdalen Society of Philadelphia* (Philadelphia, 1800).

115. Mullen, May 4, 1798, Thomson, January 14, 1799, Dougherty, April 6, 1799, Prisoners for Trial Docket, 1790–1797; Wall, July 1789.

116. Carlisle, September 7, 1795, Gault, June 1790, Drain, November 30, 1790, Vagrancy Dockets, 1790–1932; Fell, December 31, 1795, Prisoners for Trial Docket, 1790–97; Kenneth and Anna Roberts, eds., *Moreau de Saint-Méry's American Journey* (Garden City, N.Y.: Doubleday, 1947), 312–13; Billy G. Smith, *The "Lower Sort": Philadelphia's Laboring People, 1750–1800* (Ithaca, N.Y.: Cornell University Press, 1990), 22–23.

117. Mary McColloch, February 3, 1790; Elizabeth Leacock, March 8, 1790, Daily Occurrence Docket, 1787–1790 (Guardians of the Poor, Alms House, City Archives, Philadelphia), vol. 1; parents of the Hyson (September 20, 1792) and Berry (October 6, 1792) children, Ann McCowan Fitzpatrick (November 28, 1795), Jane Dring (May 21, 1796), Ann Daugherty (July 10, 1797) in ibid., 1792–1797, vol. 3; Ann Spencer (May 23, 1791), Negress Sylvia (June 30, 1794), Mary French (January 27, 1795) in County Prison. Prisoners for Trial Docket, 1790–1797, vol. 1, City Archives, Philadelphia.

118. Welch, May 4, 1791, Vagrancy Dockets; also Daily Occurrence Docket (1788), 5; Hoffet, July 22, 1794, Vagrancy Docket; Connor, February 20, 1795, ibid.; Shaw, April 29, 1797, Prisoners for Trial Docket, 1790–97; Smith, *The "Lower Sorts"*, 19; Roberts and Roberts, *Moreau's American Journey*, 303, 309.

119. William E. Nelson, *Americanization of Common Law: The Impact of Legal Change on Massachusetts Society, 1760–1830* (Cambridge, Mass.: Harvard University Press, 1975), 110–11; Cornelia Hughes Dayton, *Women Before the Bar: Gender, Law, and Society in Connecticut, 1639–1789* (Chapel Hill: University of North Carolina Press, 1995), 161.

120. Daniel A. Cohen, *Pillars of Salt, Monuments of Grace: New England Crime Literature and the Origins of American Popular Culture, 1674–1860* (New York: Oxford University Press, 1993), 87, 129–130. While common in England too, the gallows statements and sermons were less common in Pennsylvania, but not rare. The social theory of crime and deviance exhibited in this literature resembles that in Quaker denominational literature and journals. Marietta, *Reformation*, 81–83.

121. One popular expression of the theory sometimes carries the epithet "broken-windows." George L. Kelling and Catherine M. Coles, *Fixing Broken Windows: Restoring Order and Reducing Crime in Our Communities* (New York: Martin Kessler Books, 1996).

122. Michael R. Gottfredson and Travis Hirschi, *A General Theory of Crime* (Stanford, Calif.: Stanford University Press, 1990), 85–94.

123. Rush published the first text in America on psychiatric medicine, *Medical Inquiries and Observations on the Diseases of the Mind* (1789), and is regarded as the honorary founder of the American Psychiatric Society.

124. The confusion of the frontier, with its competing values, is discussed in James H. Merrell, *Into the American Woods: Negotiators on the Pennsylvania Frontier* (New York: W.W. Norton, 1999); and Richard White, *The Middle Ground: Indians, Empires, and Republics in the Great Lakes Region, 1650–1815* (New York: Cambridge University Press, 1991).

125. Gregory T. Knouff, *The Soldiers' Revolution: Pennsylvanians in Arms and the*

Forging of Early American Identity (University Park: Pennsylvania State University Press, 2004), 162, 163.

126. Knouff, *Soldiers' Revolution*, 155–93; Knouff, "Soldiers and Violence on the Pennsylvania Frontier," in Frantz and Pencak, eds., *Beyond Philadelphia*, 177; Ousterhout, 229–72.

127. Knouff, "Soldiers and Violence on the Pennsylvania Frontier," 184ff; Thomas P. Abernethy, *Western Lands and the American Revolution* (New York: Russell and Russell, 1959), 267–68.

128. Nisbet to Addison, March 25, 1796, Alexander Addison Papers, Darlington Library, Pittsburgh.

129. This process can be followed in White, *Middle Ground.* See also Andrew R. L. Cayton and Fredrika J. Teute, eds., *Contact Points: American Frontiers from the Mohawk Valley to the Mississippi, 1750–1830* (Chapel Hill: University of North Carolina Press, 1998); and James H. Merrell and Peter C. Mancall, eds., *American Encounters: Natives and Newcomers from European Contact to Indian Removal, 1500–1850* (London: Routledge, 2000).

Chapter 7. Commonwealth

Epigraph: *Gale's Independent Gazetteer* (Philadelphia), January 1797.

1. Throughout the new American states there was interest in penal reforms. See Louis Masur, "The Revision of the Criminal Law in Post-Revolutionary America," *CJH* 8 (1987): 21–36; Kathryn Preyer, "Crime, the Criminal Law and Reform in Post-Revolutionary Virginia," *LHR* 1 (1983): 53–85; Richard Gaskins, "Changes in the Criminal Law in Eighteenth-Century Connecticut," *AJLH* 25 (1981): 309–42; Paul F. Cromwell, "Quaker Reforms in American Criminal Justice: The Penitentiary and Beyond," *CJH* 10 (1989): 77–94; Adam J. Hirsch, *The Rise of the Penitentiary: Prisons and Punishment in Early America* (New Haven, Conn.: Yale University Press, 1992).

2. "Considerations on the Laws of Pennsylvania," *American Museum, or Repository*, (June 1788), especially 510; William Bradford, *An Enquiry How Far the Punishment of Death is Necessary in Pennsylvania* (Philadelphia, 1793), 40. Some citizens of Chester County organized to protect themselves against gangs of thieves. See *Literary Museum* (West Chester, Pa.), May 1797, 280; Alexander, *Render*, 73–75.

3. *Statutes*, 12: 280–90; 13: 243–51, 511–28; 14: 128–39; 15, 174–81, 110–18.

4. *Statutes*, 12: 280–90.

5. See, for example, Preyer, "Crime, the Criminal Law and Reform in Post-Revolutionary Virginia," especially 77–78; Bradley Chapin, "Felony Law Reform in the Early Republic," *PMHB* 113 (1989): 163–84; Masur, "The Revision of the Criminal law in Post-Revolutionary America," 21–36.

6. See G. S. Rowe, "Infanticide, Its Judicial Resolution, and Criminal Code Revision in Early Pennsylvania," *Proceedings of the American Philosophical Society*, 95 (1991): 228–29.

7. Masur, "The Revision of the Criminal Law in Post-Revolutionary America," 21–36 and Preyer, "Crime, The Criminal Law, and Reform in Post-Revolutionary Virginia," 53–85.

8. This act was reconstituted in 1790. See *Statutes*, 13: 511–28. For background, consult Michael Meranze, "The Penitential Ideal in Late Eighteenth-Century Philadelphia," *PMHB* 108 (1984): 419–450; Harry E. Barnes, *The Evolu-*

tion of Penology in Pennsylvania (New York: Patterson, Smith, 1927); and Hirsch, *The Rise of the Penitentiary.*

9. *Statutes*, 13: 243–51; Michael Meranze, *Laboratories of Virtue: Punishment, Revolution, and Authority in Philadelphia, 1760–1835* (Chapel Hill: University of North Carolina Press, 1996), provides the background for these reforms.

10. *Statutes*, 14: 133–37.

11. *Statutes*, 14: 128–39.

12. G. S. Rowe, "Outlawry in Pennsylvania, 1782–1788 and the Achievement of an Independent State Judiciary," *AJLH* 20 (1976): 227–44.

13. Benjamin Rush's biographer, David Freeman Hawke, finds that Benjamin Rush deserves as much or more credit for the penal reforms and that Bradford initially ridiculed them. *Benjamin Rush: Revolutionary Gadfly* (New York: Bobbs-Merrill, 1971), 363.

14. *The Columbian Magazine, or Universal Asylum*, January 1793, 44–52; *American Monthly Review*, February 1795; *Philadelphia Monthly Magazine or, Universal Repository*, January 1798, 42–45; February 1798, 94–97. The quote is from Bradford's *An Enquiry*, 20.

15. *Statutes*, 15: 110–18, 174–81.

16. *Statutes*, 15: 180–81. Also see Rowe, "Infanticide," 230–31.

17. *Statutes*, 15: 110–17.

18. *PJ*, March 3, 1787; *CG*, June 13, 1787.

19. *CG*, November 19, 1788; *PP*, September 22, 1789, October 13, 1789. As Chapter 4 explains, the evidence suggests that the rape was not formally reported to authorities by the farmer who simply hurried to the market, dumped his goods, and hurried home. See also *American Museum, or Repository* (Philadelphia), May 1787, 453; "Wheelbarrow Society," *American Museum*, May 1788, 526–28.

20. Alexander, *Render*, 61.

21. *Collection of the Penal Laws of the Commonwealth of Pennsylvania* (Philadelphia, 1794), 11–12; G. S. Rowe and Billy G. Smith, "Prisoners: The Vagrancy Docket and the Prisoners for Trial Docket," in Billy G. Smith, ed., *Life in Revolutionary and Early National Philadelphia: A Documentary History* (University Park: Pennsylvania State University Press, 1995), chapter 3. Also Michael Meranze, "'Annihilated Liberty': The Penitential Ideal in Late Eighteenth-Century Philadelphia," Paper given before the Philadelphia [McNeil] Center for Early American Studies, March 1984, 22ff; and Caleb Lownes, *An Account of the Alteration and Present State of the Penal Laws of Pennsylvania* (Philadelphia, 1793).

22. *CG*, February 14, 1787; *Columbia Magazine, or Monthly Miscellanies* (Philadelphia), January 1787, 252.

23. See Rowe, "Infanticide," 230–31.

24. In 1790, Philadelphia County registered the amazing rate for all crime of 901. For the entire decade of the 1790s its rate was 558.

25. Biddle, *Extracts*, 267.

26. Kenneth Roberts and Anna Roberts, eds. *Moreau de St. Méry's American Journey, 1793–1798* (Garden City, N.Y.: Doubleday, 1947), 328, 333.

27. Bradford, *An Enquiry*, 38–39; John H. Langbein, "Shaping the Eighteenth-Century Criminal Trial: A View from the Ryder Sources," *University of Chicago Law Review* 50 (1983): 38, 45.

28. Most recently, Peter Kafer associates Brown with the James Yates episode. *Charles Brockden Brown's Revolution and the Birth of American Gothic* (Philadelphia: University of Pennsylvania Press, 2004), 113.

29. Brown, *Wieland and Memoirs of Carwin the Biloquist* (New York: Penguin, 1991), xii–xiii, 172, 179, 186–97, 264; Robert A. Ferguson, *Law and Letters in American Culture* (Cambridge, Mass.: Harvard University Press, 1984), 138–39; Cathy N. Davidson, *Revolution and the Word: The Rise of the Novel in America* (New York: Oxford University Press, 1986), 235; Elaine Forman Crane, ed., *The Diary of Elizabeth Drinker* (abridged, Boston: Northeastern University Press, 1994), 224–25; Norman S. Grabo, *The Coincidental Art of Charles Brockden Brown* (Chapel Hill: University of North Carolina Press, 1981), 67; Steven Watts, *The Romance of Real Life: Charles Brockden Brown and the Origins of American Culture* (Baltimore: Johns Hopkins University Press, 1994), 1–26, 40, 80–83.

30. Jeffrey S. Adler has explained how homicides have resulted from the burden of personal and vocational failure in "'We've Got a Right to Fight: We're Married': Ethnicity, Race, and Domestic Homicide in Chicago, 1875–1920," *Journal of Interdisciplinary History* 34 (2003): 27–48.

31. Daniel A. Cohen, "Homicidal Compulsion and the Conditions of Freedom: The Social and Psychological Origins of Familicide in America's Early Republic," *Journal of Social History* 28 (1995), esp. 725–27, 747–53; Gordon S. Wood, *The Radicalism of the American Revolution* (New York: Alfred Knopf, 1992) and his "The Significance of the Early Republic," *JER* 8 (1988): 1–20; Charles Sellers, *The Market Revolution: Jacksonian America, 1815–1846* (New York: Oxford University Press, 1992); Steven Watts, *The Republic Reborn: War and the Making of Liberal America, 1790–1820* (Baltimore: Johns Hopkins University Press, 1987); Sean Wilentz, *Society, Politics, and the Market Revolution, 1815–1848* (Washington, D.C.: American Historical Association, 1990).

32. See Linda Kealey, "Crime and Society in Massachusetts in the Second Half of the Eighteenth Century" (Ph.D. dissertation, University of Toronto, 1981) for Massachusetts burglaries.

33. *PG*, May 17, 1784; "Petition," *PP*, December 30, 1787; *PJ*, February 3, 1787.

34. Beattie, 149, 155.

35. Roger Lane writes that armed robbery was so rare in the urban East in the late nineteenth century that when one occurred in New York City in 1895, the story made the newspaper headlines in Philadelphia and continued for a week. No one was hurt in the incident. Lane, *Roots*, 103–104.

36. As Chapter 6 explained, many riots against Loyalists and other political dissenters, 1775–1783, were never prosecuted.

37. An excellent example of remedying this inattention is Terry Bouton, "A Road Closed: Rural Insurgency in Post-Independence Pennsylvania," *JAH* 87 (2000): 855–87.

38. All examples were taken from the Prisoners for Trial Docket, 1790–1797. But also see Crane, *The Diary of Elizabeth Drinker*, 150.

39. Whereas Philadelphia city had 7.3 percent of the riot accusations after 1780, its population was roughly 15 to 17 percent of the state. The southeast (Philadelphia city and Philadelphia, Bucks, and Chester Counties) had roughly between 40 and 50 percent of the state population, but 30.0 percent of riot accusations. Delaware and Montgomery Counties were excluded from both population and riot statistics used here (neither have any surviving criminal court dockets).

40. The following several paragraphs depend greatly upon the work of Bouton, "Road Closed" and E. James Ferguson, *The Power of the Purse: A History of American Public Finance, 1776–1790* (Chapel Hill: University of North Carolina Press, 1961), 221–22, 228–30, 277–80.

41. Bouton, "Road Closed," 864–67, 876–77.
42. Bouton, "Road Closed," 859–60.
43. At a rate 13.2 percent above the rate for all offenses, these two crimes were not indicted by the grand juries and not completely prosecuted by the state. The simple conviction rate for the two was 65.4 percent, 5.2 percent lower than for all offenses in the period.
44. Berks County Quarter Sessions Dockets, November 1792, Berks County Courthouse, Reading; York County Quarter Sessions Dockets, 1775, 1778, 1781, York County Courthouse, York.
45. Lance Banning, ed., *Liberty and Order: The First American Party Struggle* (Indianapolis, Ind.: Liberty Fund, 2004), 174.
46. *PA* 1st Ser. 11: 419–20; G. S. Rowe, *Bench,* chapter 12; Simon Drum case, Westmoreland County Records, 1769–1850, HSWP.
47. *CG,* May 30, 1787.
48. Huntingdon County Quarter Sessions Dockets and Papers, 1788, Huntingdon County Courthouse, Huntingdon; Milton Scot Lytle, *History of Huntingdon County, in the State of Pennsylvania* (Lancaster, Pa.: William H. Roy, 1876), 101–9. We are indebted to Terry Bouton for notice of this incident.
49. Bouton, "Road Closed," 855–56.
50. Jasper Yeates to James Read, September 8, 1786, Shippen Papers, 7: 211, HSP; Clemency Papers, reel 40.
51. Bouton, "Road Closed," 865.
52. Washington County Quarter Sessions Dockets, March 1791 and September 1792, Washington County Courthouse, Washington. Also, Bradford was a lawyer and the deputy attorney-general of Washington County. Boyd Crumrine, *The Courts of Justice, Bench and Bar of Washington County, Pennsylvania* (Washington, Pa.: R.R. Donnelley, 1902), 263.
53. Philadelphia Quarter Sessions Dockets, 1789, PMHC; Note in George Bryan Papers, Box 3, case 63, HSP; McKean to Bryan, October 11, 1788, Bryan Papers; Testimony of George Noath, December, 23, 1778, in Papers of the Continental Congress (microfilm ed.), Item 159, nos. 332–34; ibid., nos. 293–94, 296–315.
54. *CG,* September 5, 1787.
55. *Aurora* (Philadelphia), July 1, 1799; T. I. Wharton, "Memoirs of William Rawle," *Memoirs of the Historical Society of Pennsylvania* (Philadelphia, 1840), 82. A summary of these attacks is found in G. S. Rowe, "Judicial Tyrant and Vox Populi: Pennsylvanians View Their State Supreme Court, 1777–1799," *PMHB* 118 (1994): 33–62.
56. "Civis," *FG,* March 3, 1789; "A Friend," *IG,* June 14, 1787; Alexander, *Render,* 71–72.
57. Rochefoucauld, *Travels Through the United States of North America,* 2 vols. (London, 1799), 2: 347; Bradford, *An Enquiry,* 31.
58. *IG,* July 22, 1788; *PP,* August 20, 1785; *CG,* November 26, 1788; Emory Elliott, *Revolutionary Writers: Literature and Authority in the New Republic, 1725–1810* (New York: Oxford University Press, 1982), 220, 222–23.
59. Rowe, *Bench,* especially Chapters 12 and 13; Rowe, "Judicial Tyrant and Vox Populi," 51–62.
60. The Supreme Court was to "have the same powers as it hath been heretofore established," except that it was now to hold but three terms each year for two weeks' duration each. And it was now to hold courts of *nisi prius* "at such intermediate times as the justices . . . shall judge most convenient for the people." *Statutes,* 14: 110–20.

61. For the particulars of this evolution, see J. Paul Selsam, "A History of Judicial Tenure in Pennsylvania," *Dickinson Law Review* 38 (1934): 168–205, and Rowe, *Bench*, 53–55, 97–99, 202, 267–69, 290. The final adjustment in the Pennsylvania judicial arrangements before the nineteenth century came in March 1799. In that year the state replaced the courts of *nisi prius* with circuit courts. These tribunals functioned very much like the *nisi prius* courts, except that justices now were empowered to give judgment, issue decrees, and award execution on circuit as when sitting *en banc*. The right of appeal to the Supreme Court continued. The act that constituted these courts did not require it, but two justices continued to ride circuit and to sit together at trials of these courts, to the dismay of many who argued that justices sitting singly on jury trials would have been more efficient use of court personnel. William H. Loyd, *The Early Courts of Pennsylvania* (Boston: Boston Book Co., 1910), 136.

62. Hugh Henry Brackenridge, *Law Miscellanies* (Philadelphia, 1814), 283.

63. Raymond Walters, *Alexander James Dallas: Lawyer, Politician, Financier, 1759–1817* (Philadelphia: University of Pennsylvania Press, 1943); Charles A. Beard, ed., *The Journal of William Maclay* (New York: Frederick Ungar, reprint, 1965); Charles Warren, *The Supreme Court in United States History*, 2 vols. (Boston: Little, Brown, 1923), 1: 8, 10–11.

64. *CG*, September 21 and 28 and October 21, 1791. Again, our thanks to Terry Bouton for this incident.

65. Andrew Shankman, *Crucible of American Democracy: The Struggle to Fuse Egalitarianism and Capitalism in Jeffersonian Pennsylvania* (Lawrence: University of Kansas Press, 2004), 84.

66. Ibid., 14.

67. Sanford W. Higginbotham, *The Keystone of the Democratic Arch: Pennsylvania Politics, 1800–1816* (Harrisburg: Pennsylvania Historical and Museum Commission, 1952), esp. chapter 3; Rowe, *McKean*, Chapters 17–18; Rowe, *Bench*, Chapter 14; Elizabeth K. Henderson, "The Attack upon the Judiciary in Pennsylvania, 1800–1810," *PMHB* 61 (1937): 113–36; Shankman, *Crucible of Democracy*, 83–95.

68. Only 1194 recorded property crimes occurred in all of Pennsylvania before 1759.

69. Gary B. Nash and Billy G. Smith, "The Population of Eighteenth-Century Philadelphia," *PMHB* 100 (1976): 366; *Return of the Whole Number of Persons Within the Several Districts of the United States. . . .* (Washington, D.C.: Duane, 1801), 35.

70. The concentration of property crime in Philadelphia appears typical of cities. J. M. Beattie explains at length its concentration in greater London. Beattie, 184.

71. Billy G. Smith, *"The Lower Sort": Philadelphia's Laboring People, 1750–1800* (Ithaca. N.Y.: Cornell University Press, 1990), 64.

72. Thomas Doerflinger, "Farmers and Dry Goods in the Philadelphia Market Areas, 1750–1800," in Ronald Hoffman et al., eds., *The Economy of Early America: The Revolutionary Period, 1763–1790* (Charlottesville: University of Virginia Press, 1986), 175.

73. Smith, *"Lower Sort"*, 68–70, 75–76.

74. T. H. Breen, *The Marketplace of Revolution: How Consumer Politics Shaped American Independence* (New York: Oxford University Press, 2004), 60. Breen describes a very widespread and significant growth of consumption in colonial America, with Pennsylvania advancing the change as much as or more than any colony in America.

75. Smith, *"Lower Sort"*, 75, 88–89; Alexander, *Render*, 25.

76. Smith, *"Lower Sort"*, 86–86, 89, 91, 124–25, 199; Ronald Schultz, *The Republic of Labor: Philadelphia Artisans and the Politics of Class, 1720–1830* (New York: Oxford University Press, 1993), 92–93.

77. "The American Moralist," *FG*, June 13, 1789; Gale's *Independent Gazetteer*, January 1789, quoted in Alexander, *Render*, 78–79. Also *American Monthly Review* (September 1795), 291–95, 395–96. Simon P. Newman extensively depicts the desperate lives of the Philadelphia poor in *Embodied History: The Lives of the Poor in Early Philadelphia* (Philadelphia: University of Pennsylvania Press, 2003).

78. See Elliott, *Revolutionary Writers*, 224–25, 229, 232–33. In Brown's *Wieland* the poverty and rootlessness of the protagonist, Carwin, created not only a ruthless and unprincipled demeanor, but a deep desire to indulge in criminal acts for the mere thrill of it.

79. Ibid; Ferguson, *Law and Letters in American Culture*, 138–39.

80. Latrobe to Philip Mazzei, December 19, 1806, in Philip Mazzei, Margherita Marchione *Selected Writings and Correspondence* (Prato, Italy: Cassa di Risparmi e Depositi, 1983), 439.

81. Matthew Carey, *A Short Account of the Malignant Fever* (Philadelphia, 1793); Grabo, *The Coincidental Art of Charles Brockden Brown*, 104.

82. Newman, *Embodied History*, names and describes scores of humble or transient men and women who would fit the category of those missing from tax lists, but would possibly end up prosecuted as criminals.

83. Smith, *"Lower Sort"*, 59–61; Alexander, *Render*, 79, 181.

84. Beattie, 251–52, 262–63; J. A. Sharpe and Peter Linebaugh agree with Beattie. Sharpe, *Crime in Early Modern England, 1550–1750* (London: Longman, 1984); Linebaugh, *The London Hanged: Crime and Civil Society in the Eighteenth Century* (Cambridge: Cambridge University Press, 1991), 107–11.

85. *An Account of the Robberies Committed by John Morrison . . .* (Philadelphia, 1750–51); *The Lamentations and Confessions of the Poor Condem'd Criminals in the Dungeon . . . signed on February 11, 1750–51* (Philadelphia, 1750–51).

86. *PP*, December 30, 1785; *IG*, November 17, 1785.

87. Compared with contemporary criminal-justice populations, that percentage for women ranks at or near the top. In adjacent New York, whose society resembled Pennsylvania's more closely than any other in America, women comprised 9.9 percent of the accused. In Massachusetts in the second half of the eighteenth century, women comprised 7.5 percent of the total. In North Carolina, they were 9.4 percent. England alone, it seems, exceeded Pennsylvania by a large margin. There, in the county of Surrey, women comprised 21.1 percent of the total. The New York data are odd because they include no distinctly sexual crimes. If they did, women's portion would certainly be higher. Douglas Greenberg, *Law Enforcement in the Colony of New York* (Ithaca, N.Y.: Cornell University Press, 1976), 51; Kealey, "Crime and Society in Massachusetts in the Second Half of the Eighteenth Century"; Donna J. Spindel and Stuart W. Thomas, Jr., "Crime and Society in North Carolina, 1663–1740," *JSH*, 49 (1983), 223–24; Donna J. Spindel, *Crime and Society in North Carolina, 1663–1776* (Baton Rouge: Louisiana State University Press, 1989), 73; J. M. Beattie, "The Criminality of Women in Eighteenth-Century England," *JSH* 8 (1975): 80–116. Hugh Rankin gives no statistics, but he makes clear that women constituted a very small portion of Virginia's colonial defendants. Hugh F. Rankin, *Criminal Trial Proceedings in the General Court of Colonial Virginia* (Charlottesville: University Press of Virginia, 1965). However, in seventeenth-century Maryland, where women were comparatively few, their crimes comprised 22.1 percent of the total. Mary Beth

Norton, "Gender, Crime, and Community in Seventeenth-Century Maryland," in James A. Henretta, Michael Kammen, and Stanley N. Katz, eds., *The Transformation of Early American History* (New York: Alfred Knopf, 1991), 135, 141.

88. Greenberg puts women's property crime in New York at the comparatively highest figure of 36.1 percent, but the New York total includes no sexual and morals crimes and 36.1 cannot be useful for comparison. If illicit sex were prosecuted and recorded in New York, it would greatly lower the shares of the total of other crimes. Greenberg, *Law Enforcement in New York*, 50; Spindel, *Crime in North Carolina*, 83; Norton, "Gender, Crime, and Community in Maryland," 135. Linda Kealey's study of Massachusetts concentrates on major crimes, not morals and sexual offenses.

89. Beattie, 241–43.

90. The data for the preceding generalizations are: Women taxpayers in Chester County, 1682–1800, were 955 of 34,448 taxpayers; women in Philadelphia are from the 1780 tax list and number 419 of 6,065 taxpayers. In Chester women's mean tax was 97.5 percent of men's; in Philadelphia, women's mean property assessment was 113.9 percent of men's. Karin Wulf found that in 1756 in Philadelphia County, women were about 2.0 percent of the taxpayers, and in Philadelphia city at the same time, they were 4.5 to 5.7 percent. The consistency of these figures with ours supports the reliability of both. Wulf, *Not All Wives: Women of Colonial Philadelphia* (Ithaca, N.Y.: Cornell University Press; reprint Philadelphia: University of Pennsylvania, 2000), 91.

91. Wulf, *Not All Wives*, 99–102.

92. Figure 7.3 illustrates charges or accusations against women and the total population of Pennsylvania, not just women's.

93. Clemency Records, rolls 41, 38, 37; William Moore Docket, 1772–1776, 2, CCHS.

94. Ann Winter, May 1, 1795, Negress Ellen, August 23, 1795, Prisoners for Trial Dockets, 1790–1797; Clemency Files, roll 36; Mary Carlisle, April 18, 1796, Prisoners for Trial Dockets, 1790–97.

95. *AWM*, January 15, 1734.

96. G. S. Rowe, "Women's Crime and Criminal Administration in Pennsylvania, 1763–1790," *PMHB* 109 (1985): 335–36; Prisoners for Trial Docket, 1790–97.

97. *An Account of the Robberies Committed by John Morrison . . .* (Philadelphia, 1750–51), 5–11. Also Breen, *The Marketplace of Revolution*, 107–109.

98. *PCR*, 4: 209, 224; 5: 506. For a discussion of serious crimes allegedly committed by females in Massachusetts, see N. E. H. Hull, *Female Felons: Women and Serious Crime in Colonial Massachusetts* (Urbana: University of Illinois Press, 1987).

99. Negley K. Teeters, "Public Executions in Pennsylvania, 1682–1834," in Eric H. Monkkonen, ed., *Crime and Justice in American History: The Colonies and Early Republic*, 2 vols. (Westport, Conn.: Meckler, 1991), 2: 827. Hall's petition November 16, 1781, Clemency Files, roll 37.

100. Teeter, "Public Executions," in Monkkonen, *PCR*, 3: 110. *AWM*, October 20, November 17, 1720. In the cases of Mary Hall and Huson their crimes were reported as both "robbery" and "burglary."

101. McGriggor petitions, November 9, 1782, April 7, 1783, Clemency Files, roll 38; *CG*, February 14, 1787; *An Account of the Robberies Committed by John Morrison*, 10–11.

102. T. H. Breen, "An Empire of Goods: The Anglicization of Colonial America, 1690–1776," in Stanley N. Katz, John M. Murrin, and Douglas Greenberg, eds., *Colonial America: Essays in Politics and Social Development*, 4th ed. (New York: McGraw Hill, 1993), 367–98, esp. 376–85; Thomas Doerflinger, "Farmers

and Dry Goods in the Philadelphia Market Area, 1750–1800," in Ronald Hoffman et. al, *The Economy of Early America: The Revolutionary Period, 1763–1790* (Charlottesville: University of Virginia Press, 1986), 166–95.

103. For a discussion of the symbolic value of consumer items like china, tea, and porcelain, see Nathan G. Goodman, ed., *A Benjamin Franklin Reader* (New York: Thomas Y. Crowell, reprint, 1971), 117; Stephanie Grauman Wolf, *As Various as Their Land* (New York: HarperCollins, 1993), 80–81.

104. Breen, *Marketplace of Revolution*, 109.

105. McKenzie, McKeever, Clemency Files, roll 39; Eddleton, February 21, 1798, Prisoners for Trial, 1798–1802 (vol. 2).

106. Clark and Buchanan, May 2, 1797, Prisoners for Trial Docket, 1790–97; Mary Dickey, Phoebe Duglis, and Catherine Ingram, Clemency Files, roll 40; Petition of John Baker, October 9, 1780, Clemency Files, roll 37. For Sarah Craig, Clemency Files 41 (November 4, 1785, September 24, 1790)

107. Lane, *Roots*, 28.

108. For treatments of free blacks prior to 1865, see Jane H. Pease and William H. Pease, *They Who Would Be Free: Blacks' Search Freedom, 1830–1861* (New York: Atheneum, 1974); Leon F. Litwack, *North of Slavery: The Negro in the Free States, 1790–1860* (Chicago: University of Chicago Press, 1961); Ira Berlin, *Slaves Without Masters: The Free Negro in the Antebellum South* (New York: Oxford University Press, 1974).

109. John Chester Miller, *The Wolf by the Ears: Thomas Jefferson and Slavery* (New York: The Free Press, 1977), 61–64. Ironically, Virginia had been created in part to help relieve Elizabethan and Stuart England of criminals and vagrants, "masterless men," who plagued it and troubled the minds of most Englishmen. But Virginia only reproduced the problem of the criminal class by successfully transporting white indentured servants to the Chesapeake. The threat of a criminal class or fear of one is woven into much of American history.

110. Edmund S. Morgan, *American Slavery, American Freedom: The Ordeal of Colonial Virginia* (New York: W.W. Norton, 1975), 387.

111. *PJ*, January 31, February 5, 21, 1781.

112. Higginbotham, *In the Matter of Color*, Statutes, 2: 233–36.

113. Horle, *Records*, 1: 691.

114. *PCR*, 2: 11, 18, 112, 160, 211, 222–23.

115. *PCR*, 2: 405; 4, 243–44.

116. See, for instance, "Phileleutheros," *PG*, February 2, 1780 or "A Letter on Slavery," *PP*, February 21, 1781.

117. *PCR*, 1: 380; 4: 243.

118. *AWM*, April 18, 1723.

119. See, for instance, Billy G. Smith and Richard Wojtowicz, *Blacks Who Stole Themselves: Advertisements for Runaways in the Pennsylvania Gazette, 1728–1790* (Philadelphia: University of Pennsylvania Press, 1989).

120. *PCR*, 2: 405.

121. *AWM*, July 6, 12, 1721; July 24, 1735; July 29–August 5, 1736; August 18–25, 1737; March 12–19, 1741.

122. G. S. Rowe, "Black Offenders, Criminal Courts, and Philadelphia Society in the Late Eighteenth Century," *JSH* 22 (1989): 687.

123. Rowe, "Black Offenders," 687.

124. *Statutes*, 10: 70.

125. The figures for 1780 and 1800 are obtained by equating the census category "other free persons" with African Americans and adding the enumerated slaves.

126. "A Letter on Slavery," *PP*, March 25, 1780, January 31, February 5 and 21, 1781; "Phileleutheros," *PG*, February 2, 1780; Robert L. Brunhouse, *The Counter-Revolution in Pennsylvania, 1776–1790* (New York: Octagon Books, 1971), 102.

127. Nash, *Forging*, 106–8.

128. Nash was partly correct when he wrote that "in the 1790s, free blacks avoided crime to a greater extent than white immigrants and other Philadelphians of the same economic position." That was not the case after 1794, when poor blacks were accused of theft more often than anyone else. More clearly, he was incorrect in stating that "the black crime rate began to soar in the early nineteenth century"—but he was off by only five or six years. Nash, *Forging*, 157.

129. That is a maximum figure, since some prosecutions in the county may have been against persons not in the Philadelphia suburbs.

130. Rowe, "Black Offenders," 692; Jerome H. Wood, Jr., "The Negro in Pennsylvania: The Lancaster Experience, 1730–1790," in Elinor Miller and Eugene Genovese, eds., *Plantation, Town, and County: Essays on the Local History of American Slave Society* (Urbana: University of Illinois Press, 1974), 447.

131. The population data are from Nash, *Forging*, 72, 137, 143.

132. Nash, *Forging*, 136–42; Nash, "Reverberations of Haiti in the American North: Black Saint Dominguans in Philadelphia," *Explorations in Early American Culture: Pennsylvania History* 65 (1998), 45–47, 50–51.

133. From a sample of records in the first decade of the nineteenth century, Nash found that blacks sentenced to prison were very largely found guilty of stealing clothing, food, and small articles for resale. *Forging*, 158.

134. Alexander, *Render*, 78–79.

135. *PP*, September 3, 1785; June 11, December, 30, 1787; *IG*, November 17, 1785; *FG*, June 13, 1789; *Philadelphia Monthly Magazine*, February, March 1798, 2: 92–97, 178.

136. Nash, "Reverberations of Haiti," 58.

137. In Table 7.11 the annual figures for the black population of Philadelphia were linear interpolations from the 1790 to the 1800 census. This is a less than satisfactory way of calculating the population, since its growth was due to abrupt influxes of immigrants and not the steadier growth by reproduction. And since the numbers were small the black rates are extrapolations to 100,000.

138. Nash, *Forging*, 73–74.

139. Rowe, "Black Offenders," 694–95.

140. Negro Peter, September 1782, Clemency Files, reel 37; *The Trial of Alice Clifton* (Philadelphia, 1787).

141. For an elaboration of this point, see Jack D. Marietta and G. S. Rowe, "Rape, Law, Courts and Custom in Pennsylvania, 1682–1800," in Merril D. Smith, ed., *Sex Without Consent* (New York: New York University Press, 2001), 81–102.

142. Susan Brownmiller, *Against Our Will: Men, Women, and Rape* (New York: Simon and Schuster, 1975), 15, 133–38, 211, 248–54, 308, 391. Eldridge Cleaver in his *Soul on Ice* (New York: McGraw-Hill, 1968), 13–14 and others have maintained that rape frequently is a "political crime," but observe Brownmiller's perceptive disclaimer (211, 248–53). She does concede that revenge often motivates rapists (254).

143. The most sustained argument that blacks actively "rebelled" has come from Gary B. Nash. See his *Forging*, 38–65.

144. Bradford, *An Enquiry*, 31; *PCR*, 3: 244; Donald A. Shelley, ed., *Lewis*

Miller: Sketches and Chronicles (York, Pa.: York County Historical Society, 1966), 35.

145. Nash, "Reverberations of Haiti," 62.

146. See jurors' petition for Martin, May 2, 1787, Clemency Files, roll 40; for Sukey, ibid., roll 37. Negress Patty was also accused of burning her master's barn, hay, and grain in 1781, but those accusations were eventually thrown out by the court. *FJ*, December 12, 1781.

147. Smith, *Blacks Who Stole Themselves*; Henry Melchior Muhlenberg, *The Journals of Henry Melchior Muhlenberg*, Theodore G. Tappert and John W. Duberstein, ed. 3 vols. (Philadelphia: Muhlenberg Press, 1942–53), 3: 78; Nash, *Forging*, chapter 2; Gary B. Nash and Jean R. Soderlund, *Freedom by Degrees: Emancipation in Pennsylvania and Its Aftermath* (New York: Oxford University Press, 1991), Chapter 3.

148. Nash, *Forging*, 220.

149. Biddle, *Autobiography*, 314–15.

150. Vagrancy Dockets, 1790–1932, vol. 1, City Archives, Philadelphia.

151. Nash, "Reverberations of Haiti," 56.

152. For a situation, see Lane, *Roots*, 106–8, 122–33.

153. Martin, May 2, 5, 1787, Negress Sarah, November 4, 1785, Clemency Files, rolls 40, 39. *Universal Asylum and Columbian Magazine* (August 1790), 74; *The Trial of Alice Clifton*.

154. In terms of the effectiveness of prosecution of criminal charges, the city and county of Philadelphia were in general the most effective locality in Pennsylvania.

155. This was quite different from the "color blind justice" that Roger Lane found that African Americans enjoyed in nineteenth-century Philadelphia. Lane, *Roots*, 87.

156. Nash and Soderlund, *Freedom by Degrees*, 138.

157. Phillip P. Moulton, ed., *The Journal and Major Essays of John Woolman* (New York: Oxford University Press, 1971), 221, 226.

158. Nash, *Forging*, 172–73.

159. Nash, *Forging*, 217, 251–53.

160. Lane, *Roots*, 140–41, 163–64; Lane, *Murder*, 187–88; Lane, *Violent Death*, 133–34.

161. Lane, *Roots*, 42; Lane, *Murder*, 187.

162. Lane, *Roots*, 95–132.

Epilogue

Epigraph: William Penn, *The Excellent Privilege of Liberty and Property Being the Birth-Right of the Free-Born Subjects of England* (1687), quoted in James W. Ely, Jr., *The Guardian of Every Other Right: A Constitutional History of Property Rights* (New York: Oxford University Press, 1998), 13.

1. Some of the ways are treated recently in Christopher Tomlins and Bruce Mann, eds., *The Many Legalities of Early America* (Chapel Hill: University of North Carolina Press, 2001).

2. To offer one example of such a liberal, and a very appropriate one for Pennsylvania: Thomas Paine. Christopher Lasch, *The True and Only Heaven: Progress and Its Critics* (New York: W.W. Norton, 1991), 177–78; Eric Foner, *Tom Paine and Revolutionary America* (New York: Oxford University Press, 1976), 152–60.

3. See the Introduction.

4. For a recent opinion on violence and human nature by a psychologist, see Steven Pinker, *The Blank Slate: the Modern Denial of Human Nature* (New York: Viking, 2002), 306–36.

5. Peter H. Lindert, *Growing Public: Social Spending and Economic Growth Since the Eighteenth Century* (Cambridge: Cambridge University Press, 2004), 4, 7.

6. In this respect, they resemble the accused criminals in the next century. Roger Lane discovered that at least 47 percent of persons accused of homicide in antebellum Philadelphia were transients or newcomers to the city. Similarly for antebellum New York City, Eric Monkkonen found that 39 percent of murder victims and 31 percent of murderers were foreign-born. Lane, *Murder,* 125; Monkkonen, "Diverging Homicide Rates: England and the United States, 1850–1875," in Ted Robert Gurr, ed., *The History of Crime: Violence in America,* 2 vols. (Newbury Park, Calif.: Sage, 1989), 1: 90.

7. Charles L. Griswold, Jr., *Adam Smith and the Virtues of Enlightenment* (New York: Cambridge University Press, 1999), 278–80, 289; Adam Smith, *An Inquiry into the Nature and Causes of the Wealth of Nations,* ed. R. H. Campbell, A. S. Skinner, and W. B. Todd (Oxford: Oxford University Press, 1976), 793.

8. Steven F. Messner and Richard Rosenfeld, *Crime and the American Dream,* 2nd ed. (Belmont, Calif.: Wadsworth, 1994), 78. A helpful work on the dynamics of exit and membership is Albert P. Hirschman, *Exit, Voice, and Loyalty: Responses to Decline in Firms, Organizations, and States* (Cambridge, Mass.: Harvard University Press, 1970), 16–17, 106–8. Some modern, classically liberal economists like Milton Friedman espouse "exit" over exercising "voice" in an organization as the most expeditious, efficient way of having effect. The strategy is generalized from economic markets to social, religious, and political aspects of life in America.

9. Charles E. Lindblom, *The Market System: What It Is, How It Works, and What To Make of It* (New Haven, Conn.: Yale University Press, 2001), 200.

10. Jerry Z. Muller, *Adam Smith in His Time and Ours* (Princeton, N.J.: Princeton University Press, 1993), 57–60.

11. Lindblom, *Market System,* 43–44, 125–28; Allen Buchanan, *Ethics, Efficiency, and the Market* (Totowa, N.J.: Rowman and Littlefield, 1985), 78–80.

12. Christopher J. Berry, "Adam Smith and the Virtues of Commerce," in John W. Chapman and William A. Galston, eds., *Virtue* (New York: New York University Press, 1992), 80–82, 296–98. Smith's discussion of impartiality and empathy, which he called sympathy, is found in his *The Theory of Moral Sentiments,* ed., D. D. Raphael and A. L. Macfie (Oxford: Oxford University Press, 1976). Modern research on the application of empathy faults Smith's expectation of it spreading broadly. Martin L. Hoffman, "The Contribution of Empathy to Justice and Moral judgment" in Nancy Eisenberg and Janet Strayer, eds., *Empathy and its Development* (Cambridge: Cambridge University Press, 1987), 67–69. Smith's faith in the civilizing effect of commerce circulated in Pennsylvania too, where Philadelphians asserted that when transportation (canals) reached the west and trade opened, Scots-Irishmen would quit their violent ways. *PC,* January 8, 1770, cited in J. E. Crowley, *This Sheba, Self: The Conceptualization of Economic Life in Eighteenth-Century America* (Baltimore: Johns Hopkins University Press, 1974), 114.

13. Smith, *Lectures on Jurisprudence,* 333; Griswold, *Adam Smith,* 298–300.

14. Allen E. Buchanan, *Marx and Justice: The Radical Critique of Liberalism* (Totowa, N.J.: Rowman and Littlefield, 1982), 13, 39.

15. Lindblom, *Market System,* 206, 191. The unwelcome effects of the market

economy on personal character are found in Smith himself, Hegel, Feuerbach, and of course, Marx. Griswold writes that Smith understood "the paradoxical prospect that the very system that is meant to improve us undermines us." Griswold, *Adam Smith*, 128. Many of the faults of market can be assembled under the rubric of "alienation." See also Buchanan, *Ethics, Efficiency, and the Market*, 95–97, and Buchanan, *Marx*, 42–43, 79.

16. Alan Wolfe, *Whose Keeper? Social Science and Moral Obligation* (Berkeley: University of California Press, 1989), 30.

17. Lindblom, *Market System*, 207, 208. Smith's successors fault him for not being aggressive enough about the universal application of the market ethic. Contemporary economists like Gary Becker and Gordon Tullock urge that market behavior be extended to intimate realms like marriage and family. Buchanan, *Ethics, Efficiency*, 101, 103; Gary S. Becker, *The Economic Approach to Human Behavior* (Chicago: University of Chicago Press, 1976); Richard B. McKenzie and Gordon Tullock, *Modern Political Economy* (New York: McGraw-Hill, 1978).

18. J. Hector St. Jean de Crèvecoeur, *Letters from an American Farmer* (New York: Fox, Duffield, 1904), 63–64.

19. Richard Jackson to Benjamin Franklin, June 17, 1755 in Benjamin Franklin, *The Papers of Benjamin Franklin*, ed. Leonard W. Labaree et al., 34 vols. (New Haven, Conn.: Yale University Press, 1959–1999), 6: 76, 81–82. For more such observations by Dr. Alexander Hamilton and Andrew Burnaby, see Crowley, *This Sheba Self*, 99.

20. Lane, *Murder*, 348.

21. Kerby A. Miller, *Emigrants and Exiles: Ireland and the Irish Exodus to North America* (New York: Oxford University Press, 1985), 193, 291, 320. Lane, *Murder*, 104–8, 125, 183; Eric H. Monkkonen, *Murder in New York City* (Berkeley: University of California Press), 138–39; Paul A. Gilje, *Rioting in America* (Bloomington: Indiana University Press, 1996), 60–75.

22. Miller, *Emigrants and Exiles*, 315, 317–18. Eric Monkkonen has discovered that the proportion of foreign immigrants among named killers in ante-bellum New York City is as high as 80 percent. Lane, *Murder*, 135.

23. An Irish traveler in the United States wrote in 1852, "Some twenty years ago there was an opening for industry in America; but its sea-board—nay, three or four hundred miles inside it, is now satiated with labor." Miller, *Emigrants and Exiles*, 319, 321; Lane, *Murder*, 108–9.

24. Lane, *Murder*, 108–9; Eric Foner, *Free Soil, Free Labor, Free Men: The Ideology of the Republican Party Before the Civil War* (New York: Oxford University Press, 1970), xxi, xxvi, 15–18, 20, 23–24.

25. George Fitzhugh, *Sociology for the South or the Failure of Free Society*, 36. Electronic Edition: Documenting the American South.

26. U.S. Department of Commerce, Bureau of the Census, A Statistical Abstract Supplement, Historical Statistics of the U.S., Colonial Times to 1957, pp. 56–57.

27. Lane, *Murder*, 164.

28. Luciano J. Iorizzo, "The Padrone and Immigrant Distribution," in Silvio M. Tomasi and Madeline H. Engel, eds., *The Italian Experience in the United States* (Staten Island, N.Y.: Center for Migration Studies, 1970), 43.

29. Lane, *Roots*, 164.

30. Lane, *Roots*, 164; Iorizzo, "Padrone," 43; Wolfe, *Whose Keeper?* 215. The plight of historical people involved in crime confirms the wisdom of the require-

ment by philosopher of liberalism, John Rawls, that the public must redress conditions that limit an individual's choices when the individual is not responsible for these limits. Contrary-minded philosopher Robert Nozick's insistence upon no interference with markets rights and no redistributions of wealth appears unwise. Rawls, *A Theory of Justice* (Cambridge, Mass.: Harvard University Press, 1971), 136–41, 251–57; Nozick, *Anarchy, State, and Utopia* (New York: Basic Books, 1974).

31. Lane, *Murder*, 106; Lane, *Roots*, 37–42.

32. For the origins and timing of social spending, see Lindert, *Growing Public*, 39–48.

33. For an explanation that the United States has basically hewed to "conservative" (i.e., classical liberal) values and behavior, see John Micklethwait and Adrian Wooldridge, *The Right Nation: Conservative Power in America* (New York: Penguin Press, 2004).

34. Griswold, *Adam Smith and the Virtues of Enlightenment*, 3. Lawrence Friedman writes, "[crime] is a part of us, our evil twin, our shadow . . . [it] is a high price to pay for our liberty. It is a cost that is badly and unfairly distributed. But for now, at least, there may be nothing to do but grit our teeth and pay the price." *Crime and Punishment in American History* (New York: Basic Books, 1993), 464–65.

Index

Bullock, William, 111
Bunting, William, 122
Burglary, 10, 11, 19, 20, 30, 38, 49, 66, 75,
    77, 78, 93, 211, 213, 215, 218–20, 231,
    234–36, 242, 243, 247, 255
Burke, James, 111
Burns, Joseph, 192
Bushel's Case, 55
Butts, Alexander, 150

Calahan, Charles, 78
Calvert, Charles, 11
Calvert County (Maryland), 92
Calvert Family, 67–68
Calvinism, 49
Cane, Phillip, 122, 124
Cannon, James, 242
Capital offenses, 3, 10, 12, 14, 19, 22, 24,
    33, 35, 75, 77, 88, 90, 97, 144, 159, 168,
    175, 189, 212–15, 227. *See also* individual
    offenses
Card playing, 3
Carey, Matthew, 234
Carlisle (Pennsylvania), 116, 175, 176, 224,
    225, 237
Carlisle, Abraham, 188, 190
Carlisle Gazette, 138, 141, 226
Carlisle, Mary, 205, 241
Carnahan, John, 166
Carr, Catherine, 147
Carter, Landon, 245
Casey, James, 149
Cash, Martha, 78, 243
Castration, 17, 18, 88
Catholics, 70
Chance Medley. *See* Murder
Chandler, George, 42
Charles, Ann Barbara, 148
Charles II, 7
Charter of Pennsylvania (1682), 7, 10, 23,
    32, 56
Charter of Pennsylvania (1701), 53, 160
Charter of Privileges, 52
Chesapeake, 62
Chester Borough, 11, 13, 24, 53, 60, 91, 92,
    185, 237
Chester County, 1, 16, 31, 38, 40, 44, 48, 50,
    67, 68, 109, 119, 125, 126, 159, 164, 168,
    181, 214; accused, 90, 93, 97–101;
    assaults, 149–52; constables, justices,
    sheriffs, 130–33, 184–85; homicide rate,

74; jurors, 55–61, 184–85; property
    crimes, 38, 231; riots, 38, 220; sentences,
    45, 85–87, 192, 203; resolutions of pros-
    ecutions, 47; Scots-Irish, 70–74; victims,
    102–3, 135–36, 145, 185–86
Chester Assembly of 1682, 11–12, 21, 24
Chester courts, 44, 45, 52
Chew, Benjamin, 167, 182
Chief Justice. *See* Pennsylvania Chief Justice
Child molestation, 137
Children, 12, 51, 75, 85, 110, 118, 119, 135,
    137, 145–47, 212, 268
Christian (an Indian), 45
Christy, John, 70
Church of England. *See* Anglicans
Churchman, John, 39, 69–70, 168, 169
Circuit. *See* Judicial circuit
Civil cases, 25
Clark, Mary, 139
Clark, William, 139
Clarke, Letitia, 244
Clarke, Thomas, 160
Claypool, James, 15, 51
Claypool, Norton, 161
Clayton, Patience, 145
Clayton, William, 51
Clemens, Paul, 91
Clerks, 158, 163
Clifton, Alice, 117, 143, 255, 259
Clines, Wilhelm, 92, 94, 95
Clotz, Lewis, 166
Cloud, William, 111
Cock, Bridget, 15, 139
Cock, Peter, 15, 139
Cockburn, J. S., 57
Cockley, Timothy, 141
Cohan, William, 148
Cohen, Daniel A., 218
Collett, Wildham, 42
Colley, Mary, 197
Collins, Ann, 147
Conductor Generalis, or the Office, Duty, . . . ,
    159
Conestoga Manor, 173
Congregationalists, 39
Connecticut, 14, 40, 205
Connally, John, 92
Connolly, Elizabeth, 149
Connor, Catherine, 242
Connor, Elinor, 94
Connor, Mary, 205

Acknowledgments

First, we the coauthors wish to acknowledge each other. This shared adventure, so brief in its conception, so lengthy in its completion, has tested the ties that bound its authors and deepened our appreciation of the trials of collaborative work. The undertaking brought forth friends, met and unmet, whose contributions helped in the writing of this book. We incurred numerous debts from the individuals, institutions, and organizations we name below. As for the larger group of persons we never met, we hope the notes and bibliography convey the extent of our debt to the labor of those historians and scholars.

Randy Roth and an anonymous reader for the University of Pennsylvania read the entire manuscript and gave us many pages of thoughtful comments that produced a reshaped and improved work. We thank them especially. Thomas A. Green also commented on the entire manuscript in an earlier, longer version. From the University of Northern Colorado, friends and colleagues John Loftis, Charles Meyer, and Barry Rothaus either criticized portions of the manuscript, listened to and discussed its ideas, or provided moral support. Over many years two groups of colleagues have evaluated our work and encouraged us. One is the Front Range Early American Consortium (FREAC), including Jack Main (deceased) and Gloria Main, Billy G. Smith, Ron Hatzenbuehler, Mick Nichols, Fred and Virginia Anderson, Ken Lockridge, Harry Fritz, Dick Burg, Clifford Egan, Don Hickey, and Jenny Pulsipher. An equally significant group is the Criminal Justice/Legal History network of the Social Sciences History Association, including Roger Lane, Eric Monkkonen (deceased), Jeff Adler, Lee Beier, Doug Eckberg, and Mary Beth Emmerichs. Our friendship with Roger Lane, which dates to 1973, deserves singular attention. His example and seminal writings on crime in the United States has inspired us and deeply informed this book.

Terry Bouton shared with us unpublished research about the 1780s and '90s. Professor Howard Ohline and Joe Foster of Temple University helped to secure materials at a crucial time. Diana Suhr, John W. Fox, and Susan Klepp instructed us in and otherwise helped in computer programming and statistical methods. Leigh Pruneau conscientiously coded data for us. Lucas Guthrie assisted with the many figures and tables. Lucille Schweers of the University of Northern Colorado's Interlibrary Loan Service responded to numerous requests for books and microfilm with alacrity and unfailing good humor.

As any reader of this work will recognize, it could not have been written without the resources of the Chester County Archives and the Chester County Historical Society. Therefore, we are very indebted to Laurie Rofini, archivist at the County Archives, and to assistant archivist Barbara Weir. Year in and year out, they welcomed us and brought to our attention every resource that might help us. Chester County has perhaps the finest county archives in America and we acknowledge people unknown to us who made it so.

We enjoyed the friendship and guidance especially of Lucy Simler (deceased), who unriddled for us the tax lists and other records of Chester County. Lucy's published work as well eased our attempt to understand Chester and Pennsylvania society. We profoundly regret that we delayed too long the day when we could have sent Lucy an inscribed copy of the work. At the Historical Society of Pennsylvania Linda Stanley and Peter J. Parker deserve special attention. The same is true of Ward J. Childs and his staff at the Philadelphia City Archives, and Roland Baumann then and others now at the Pennsylvania Historical and Museum Commission, Harrisburg. We visited twenty-five county depositories including twenty-one courthouses in the course of our research, from Wayne County in the northeast to Greene County in the southwest. We thank every clerk of criminal courts who welcomed us and opened courthouse basements to us. A few were indifferent and unhelpful, and if they told us there were no extant records, we can only report to readers that such a void in the public records presumably exists.

Without a grant from the National Science Foundation there would hardly be a sentence of economic analysis in this book. It was the largest single source of fiscal support for our work. Generous grants from the National Endowment for the Humanities and the McNeil Center for Early American Studies in Philadelphia provided us access to record collections, as did a half-dozen grants from the Research and Publications Board of the University of Northern Colorado. The University of Arizona helped with the subvention of the book.

Beginning in the 1990s the McNeil Center for Early American Studies has provided inestimable support. Richard Dunn, founding director of the center, and Bill Pencak, former editor of publications, encouraged the presentation and publication of our preliminary work. Currently, Dan Richter, successor to Richard Dunn, has been our mainstay and has critiqued the entire manuscript. At the University of Pennsylvania Press,

Robert Lockhart and Alison Anderson shepherded the manuscript from CDs to paper and ink.

We apologize to anyone whose name we omitted—as well as to anyone who would have preferred we not link them with this work.

For your immense patience for twenty years, thank you Kay and Mary.